D0823201

ABORIGINAL PEOPLE

a selected bibliography

concerning Canada's first people

by

Don Whiteside (sin a paw) Ph. D.

NATIONAL INDIAN BROTHERHOOD

Ottawa

NATIONAL INDIAN BROTHERHOOD
130 ALBERT STREET SUITE 1610
OTTAWA, ONTARIO CANADA

Printed by Mail-O-Matic Printing, Ottawa, Canada

INTRODUCTION

Volume I

In Canada there are five major problems with the usual "professional bibliography" about Aboriginal People. First, in Canada a large number of studies and reports are mimeographed and thus tend to have both a very limited circulation and, in time become "lost". The second problem is that while a large amount of analytical material about Aboriginal relations in Canada is found in newspaper articles they are usually omitted from "professional" bibliographies, as are references which specifically relate to the philosophy and acts of resistance by Aboriginal People. A fourth problem, and in many ways the most important, is that the thoughts of aboriginal people are not widely disseminated because their speeches at conferences, and their reports, tend to be mimeographed, and as was previously noted, these have a very limited distribution. The fifth major problem is that material about Aboriginal People in other countries is usually omitted from consideration.

This bibliography, while it contains a fair sampling of the major published works, emphasizes unpublished speeches, reports, and proceedings of various conferences as well as salient newspaper articles. This bibliography also emphasizes the works of Aboriginal People (see *in the Author Index) and includes a section on the philosophy of Indian resistance as well as a section on Aboriginals in other than North American countries.

It must be noted that because of the special emphasis this bibliography is limited to the extent that references could be located for inclusion. A few words of additional caution are in order.

Foremost among these is that references are classified under a topic heading on the basis of personal interest and evaluation. In many instances a reference could be listed under a number of topic headings. However, in order to increase the utility of the bibliography it was decided to list each reference only once. Thus, the classification of each reference must be considered as being subjective. More importantly, the user must assume that additional references related to any topic can be found under more than a single topic heading. In order to minimize the effects of this weakness, in addition to the usual Subject Index, an Author Index is included which contains a brief summary title of each reference.

The Research and Documentation Library, Department of Secretary of State, Ottawa; the Indian Claims Commission Library, Ottawa; and the library of the Canadian Association in Support of Native People (formerly the Indian-Eskimo of Canada) were invaluable sources of information. Appreciation is also extended to Ms. Pat Russo, Librarian, National Indian Brotherhood who prepared the Subject Index.

For a nominal reproduction fee most of the unpublished material listed in this bibliography can be obtained from the National Indian Brotherhood Library, Ottawa.

It is anticipated that additional volumes will be published periodically.

TABLE OF CONTENTS

PART 1

GENERAL

Allan, Iris, White Sioux: Major Walsh of the Mounted Police, Sidney, B.C., Gary's Publishing Co. 1969, 209 pp

Allen, Victor, "The Eskimo and the Indian today," Proceedings: Fourth National Northern Development Conference, Edmonton, 1967, pp. 41-45.

Andras, Robert K., "Address, Third Annual National Citizenship Seminar of the Canadian Council of Christians and Jews," Halifax, August 30, 1968, 14 pp.

Andrews, J. Eldon, Toward a better understanding of the Canadian Indian, (a series of articles which appears in "Glad Tidings," 1953, The Presbyterian Church in Canada), Toronto, 1957, 12 pp.

Armillas, Pedro, Program of the history of American Indians, Washington, D.C., Studies and Monographs, IV, Pan American Union, 1962, 142 pp.

Baetz, Reuben, "We must avoid mere tokenism," Canadian Welfare (Ottawa), July-August, 1969, 45:5.

Baillie, Pierre, Etude générale de la situation juridique et sociale des Indiens et des Esquimaux au Canada, Ottawa, Etude inédite, Université d'Ottawa, février 1967.

Baird, Irene, "The Eskimos in Canada," Canada One Hundred 1867-1967 , Ottawa, Dominion Bureau of Statistics, 1967, pp. 56-63.

Baraca, Bishop, "Lecture on the Customs and Manners of the Indians, Sunday, August 23, 1863, in St. Martin's Church, in Cincinnati, by the Right Reverend Bishop of Sault Ste. Marie," Acts et Dicta, (translated by Msgr. J.L. Zaploknik) Wartheitsfreund, Volume 5, pp. 102-110.

Berry, Brewton, Almost White, New York, MacMillan Co., 1963.

Berry, John W., "Psychological research in the north," Anthropologica, 1971, n.s. 13:141-157.

Boyd, Eric E., "The Indian people and the next one hundred years," Address, Teach-in on the Canadian Indian at St. Francis Xavier University, Antigonish, N.S.

Brennan, L.A., No stone unturned -- an almanac of North American prehistory, Random House, 1959, 370 pp.

Bright David, "Canada remiss in duty to these Indians," Saturday Night, (Toronto), June 29, 1946, p. 19.

Burnford, Sheila, Without Reserve, Toronto, McClelland and Stewart Ltd., 1969, 242 pp.

1

Cahn, Edgar S., ed., Our brother's keeper: the Indian in white America, A New Community Press Book, 1969, 197 pp.

Catlin, George, North American Indians, Volume 1, Edinburgh, Scotland, John Grant, 1926, 286 pp.

Cohen, Warren H. and Philip J. Mause, "The Indian: the forgotten American," Harvard Law Review, June 1968, 81:1819-1858.

Collier, John, Indians of the Americas: the long hope, New York, W.W. Morton, 1947, 191 pp. (also available in Mentor Pocketbook).

Cooke, Katherine B., "Notes on Volume 2: Survey of Contemporary Indians of Canada," Ottawa, unpublished memorandum, March 6, 1968, 12 pp.

Cooper, John M., "Land tenure among the Indians of eastern and northern North America," The Pennsylvania Archaelogist, July, 1938, 55-59.

Crerar, Hon. Thomas Alexander, The rehabilitation of our Indian wards, Ottawa, February 13, 1939.

Crerar, Hon. Thomas Alexander, "The Indians of Canada," Ottawa: unpublished C.B.C. Radio Talk, 1939.

Cruikshank, Julie M., "The potential of traditional societies, and of anthropology, their predator," Anthropologica, 1971, n.s. 13:129-142.

Curtis, Edward S., The North American Indian, Vol. IX, Cambridge: At the University Press, 1913.

Curtis, Edward S., Portraits from North American Indian life, a collection of photographs, Toronto, New Press, 1972.

Curtis, N., The Indian Book, New York, 1923, 582 pp.

Daly D., Report on the affairs of the Indians in Canada, June 24, 1947.

Davis, Arthur Kent, et. al., eds., A northern dilemma: reference papers, Bellingham, Washington, Western Washington State College, Volume I, April, 1967, 585 pp.

Davis, Arthur Kent, Cecil French, William D. Knill, and Henry Zentner, eds., A northern dilemma: reference papers, Bellingham, Washington, Western Washington State College, Volume II, August 1966.

Davis, Arthur Kent "Toward mainstream," The Western Canadian Journal of Anthropology, 1969, 1:97-111.

Davis, Arthur Kent, ed., Canadian Confrontations, (selected speeches and papers presented to the Western Association of Sociology and Anthropology, Annual Conference, Banff, December, 1969), Edmonton, University of Alberta, 1970.

Delisle, Andrew Tanahokate, "The Canadian Indian -- 1968," Address, National Citizenship Seminar, Mt. St. Vincent University, Halifax, August 28, 1968, 6 pp.

Dennison, Wally (reporter), "White man listen; an interview with Dave Courchene, President of the Manitoba Indian Brotherhood," Canadian Welfare, (Ottawa), March-April, 1971, 47:10, 11, 13.

Dodge, R.I., Our Wild Indians, Hartford, Connecticut, A.D. Worthington and Co., 1890, 653 pp.

Dorian, E.M. and W.N. Wilson, Hokahey: American Indians then and now, New York, McGraw-Hill, (c. 1957) 112 pp.

Driver, Harold Edson, Indians of North America, The University of Chicago Press, 1961, 668 pp.

Dunstun, William, "Canadian Indians Today," Canadian Geographical Journal, December, 1963, 67:182-193.

Earle, Frazer George, "You are an Indian," Winnipeg, unpublished manuscript, 1955.

Eggan, Fred, ed., Social anthropology of North American tribes, enlarged edition, University of Chicago Press, 1955.

Eiseley, Loren C., "Review: land tenure in the northeast: a note on the history of a concept," American Anthropologist, 1947, 49:680-681.

Elliot, Jean Leonard, ed., Minority Canadians: Native Peoples, Toronto, Prentice-Hall, 1971.

Embree, Edwin R., Indians of the Americas, New York, MacMillan, 1939, (reprinted 1970, 270 pp.)

Ericson, Robert and D. Rebecca Snow, "The Indian battle for self-determination, Comment," California Law Review, 1970, 58:445-498.

Erskine, J.S., "The Indian dilemma," Dalhousie Review, Spring, 1970, pp. 34-39.

Farb, Peter, Man's rise to civilization as shown by the Indians of North America from primeval times to the coming of the industrial state, New York, Avon Books, 1969, 400 pp.

Fenton, William N., American Indian and white relations to 1830, needs and opportunities for study, Chapel Hill, University of North Carolina, 1957.

Fey, Harold Edward, and D'Arcy McNickle, Indians and other Americans: two ways of life meet, rev. ed., Harper Row (Perennial Library), 1970, 274 pp.

Flucke, A.F., "Whither the Eskimo?" North, January-February, 1963, (reprinted in Richard Laskin ed. Social Profiles: a Canadian profile, McGraw-Hill, 1964, pp. 109-111, 116-128).

Foreman, Grant, *Indians and Pioneers*, Norman, University of Oklahoma Press, 1930.

Forsyth, Thomas, "The French, British and Spanish methods of treating Indians," *Ethnohistory*, Spring, 1957, 4:210-216.

Fowler, W.S., *Ten thousand years in America*, New York, Vintage, 1957, 160 pp.

Glynn-Ward, H., "Canada's Indian problem," *Dalhousie Review*, April, 1945, 25:46-49.

Gooderham, Kent ed., *Nestum Asa*, (The way it was in the beginning) Toronto, Griffin House, 1970, 48 pp.

Gray, James H., (reporter), "The unhappy state of Indian life," *The Montreal Star*, November 11, 1967.

Green, Leslie C., "Book Reviews: *Native Rights in Canada* (1970) and *Citizens Plus* (1970)," *Canadian Bar Review*, December 1970, 48:783-787.

Hagan, William T., *American Indians*, University of Chicago Press, 1961, 190 pp.

Hallowell, Alfred Irving, "The impact of the American Indian on American culture," *American Anthropologist*, April, 1957, 59:201-217.

Hamilton, C. Everett, *Cry of the thunderbird -- the American Indian's own story*, New York, MacMillan, 1950, 283 pp.

Hawthorn, Harry Bertram, "Research on the Indians of Canada," Research Papers presented at the National Seminar, Sponsored by the Indian Eskimo Association of Canada, Toronto, 1960, 17 p.

Hawthorn, Harry Bertram, "Research on the Indian," Vancouver, unpublished manuscript, University of British Columbia, 1966.

Hawthorn, Harry Bertram, ed., *A Survey of the contemporary Indians of Canada, a report of economic, political, educational needs and policies* (in two volumes) Ottawa, Department of Indian Affairs and Northern Development, Volume I, October 1966, Volume II, October, 1967, 660 pp.

Henderson, Norman B., "Cross-cultural action research: some limitations, advantages and problems," *Journal of Social Psychology*, 1967, 73:61-70.

Hewitt, J.N.B., *A constitutional league of peace in stone age of America*, Washington, D.C., 1918.

Hibben, F.C., *Treasure in the dust -- exploring ancient North America*, 1951, 311 pp.

Hibben, F.C., *L'homme primitif americain des origines préhistoriques à l'arrivée de l'homme blanc*, Payot, Paris, 1953, 315 pp.

4

Hlady, Walter M., "The sociology of Native Canadians," Address, First Interprovincial Conference on Schools in the Forest for Professional Educators, Edmonton, January, 1963, 7 pp.

Hodge, Fred Webb, Handbook of Indians of Canada, Ottawa, C.G. Parmelee, 1913, (reprinted Toronto, Coles Publishing Co., 1971, 632 pp).

Hornaday, William T., "The extermination of the American bison, with a sketch of its discovery and life history," Annual Report for 1887, Smithsonian Institution, Washington D.C., 1889, Part II, pp. 367-548.

Howard, Frank, "We made the Indian poor and irresponsible," Saturday Night, (Toronto), January 23, 1960.

Howard, James H., "True partnership here in our land," Address, Eleventh Indian-Metis Conference, Winnipeg, February 7, 1965, 7 p.

Hrdlicka, Ales, "The genesis of the American Indian," Proceedings of the XIXth International Congress of Americanists, Washington, D.C., 1915, pp. 559-568.

Hynam, Charles A.S., "Whither the Indian? Some areas of agreement," Edmonton, unpublished manuscript, Department of Sociology, University of Alberta, ca 1968, 5 pp.

Innes, Harold Adams, The fur trade in Canada: an introduction to Canadian economic history, (rev.ed.), University of Toronto Press, 1970, 463 pp.

Innes, Harold Adams, "Expansion of white settlements in Canada," in Charles T. Loram and Thomas F. McIlwraith, eds., The North American Indian Today, University of Toronto Press, 1943, pp. 43-48.

Jacobs, Paul and Saul Landau, To serve the devil: a documentary analysis of America's racial history and why it has been kept hidden, Vintage Press, 1971, Vol. I.

Jacobs, Wilbur R., Dispossessing the American Indian: Indians and Whites on the colonial frontier, New York, Charles Scribners' Sons, 1972.

James, Thomas, Three years among the Indians and Mexicans, J.B. Lippincott Company, 1962, 173 pp.

Jenness, Diamond, The Indian background of Canadian history, Ottawa, National Museum of Canada, (Bulletin No. 86, Anthropological Series No. 21), 1937, 46 pp.

Jenness, Diamond, "Canada's Indian problems," Annual Report for 1940 Smithsonian Institution, Washington, D.C., 1942, pp. 367-380.

Jenness, Diamond, "Canada's Indians yesterday -- what of today?" *Canadian Journal of Economic and Political Science*, February 1954, 20:

Jenness, Diamond, "Canada's debt to the Indians," *Canadian Geographical Journal*, October 1962, 65:

Jenness, Diamond, *The Indians of Canada*, 6th ed., Ottawa, National Museum of Canada, (Bulletin 65 Anthropological series no. 15) 1963, 452 pp.

Johnson, Peter A., (reporter), "The Canadian Indian and the Just Society," *The Gazette* (Montreal) August 7, 1968.

Josephy, Alvin M. Jr., *The Indian Heritage of America*, Alfred A. Knopf, 1968, 384 pp.

Kieran, Sheila H., "Indians," *Canadian Citizenship Council Journal*, May, 1965, 1:

Kopit, Arthur, *Indians*, New York, Hill and Wang, Inc., 1969, 114 pp.

Kurtness, Jacques, "From nomadism to sedentarisme," *recherches amerindiennes au Quebec*, November 1972, 2:43-48.

Lafarge, Oliver, *Pictorial history of the American Indian*, New York, Brown Publishers, 1957 (3rd printing), 272 pp.

Lafarge, Oliver, *Laughing Boy*, New York, Houghton Mifflin, 1929 (reprint Mentor Books, 1971).

Lagasse, Jean-Henry, "The people of Indian ancestry in Canada," unpublished address, Mexico, March, 1966.

Lagasse, Jean-Henry, "Indians of Canada," *America Indigena*, October, 1966, 26:387-394.

Lavander, David, *The American Heritage history of the great west*, New York, American Heritage Publishing Co., 1965, 416 pp.

Leboeuf, Robert, "Les Indiens, le plus grave probleme social au Canada," *Le Nouvelliste* (Trois-Rivieres) fevrier 10, 1969.

Leechman, John Douglas, *Native Tribes of Canada*, Toronto, Gage, 1956, 357 pp.

Lefebvre, Madeleine, "Quand un recit m'etait livre," in *Interpretation*, (Montreal), 1969, 3:53-66.

Levine, Stuart and Nancy Oestreich Lurie, eds., *The American Indian today*, Baltimore, Md. Penguin Books, 1968, 352 pp.

L'Heureux, Camille, (reporter), "Le cas des Indiens," *Le Droit* (Ottawa), April 1, 1963.

Lindquist, G.E.E., "The history of white expansion in the United States," in Charles T. Loram and Thomas F. McIlwraith eds. *The*

<u>North American Indian Today</u>, University of Toronto Press, 1943, pp. 49-58.

Lloyd, Antony John, "Indians of Canada," <u>American Indigena</u>, January 1960, 20:15-23.

Locke, Jeannine (reporter), "The Canadian Indians," <u>Canadian Weekly</u>, September, 1964.

Locke, Jeannine (reporter), "What our Indians really want and need," (Part 4), <u>Canadian Weekly</u>, October 1, 1964.

Lockwood, Thomas J., "A history of Royal Commissions," <u>Osgood Hall Law Journal</u>, 1967, 5:172-209.

Long, J., <u>Voyages and travels of an Indian interpreter and trader</u>, London, 1791 (reprinted Toronto, Coles Publishing Co., 1971, 295 pp.)

Loram, Charles T. "The fundamentals of Indian-White contact in the United States and Canada," in Charles T. Loram and Thomas F. McIlwraith eds. <u>The North American Indian Today</u>, University of Toronto Press, 1943, pp. 3-18.

Loram, Charles T. and Thomas F. McIlwraith, eds. <u>The North American Indian Today: University of Toronto -- Yale University Seminar Conference</u>, September 4-16, 1939, University of Toronto Press, 1943, 361 pp.

Lurie, Nancy Oestreich, "Historical background," in Stuart Levine and Nancy Oestreich Lurie eds. <u>The American Indian Today</u>, Baltimore, Md., Penguin Books, 1970, pp. 49-81.

MacLean, John, <u>Canadian savage folk: the native tribes of Canada</u>, Toronto, 1896 (reprinted Coles Publishing Co., Toronto, 1971).

MacLean, Robinson (reporter), "Rivers still run, grass still grows but Indians go hungry under treaty: Queen Victoria's word has been broken they say, as laws keep their pots empty," <u>Toronto Telegram</u>, July 19, 1939.

Manuel, Chief George, "Justice in the world as it applies to the Indians of Canada, unpublished letter to Patrick Kerans, Co-director, Canadian Catholic Conference, September 10, 1971.

Manuel, Chief George, "The Indians of Canada are not against the idea of integration in North American society," <u>Le Soleil</u> (Quebec City), March 24, 1972.

Marriott, Alice Lee, <u>Greener fields -- experiences among the American Indians</u>, Toronto, Doubleday Canada Ltd., 1962, 232 pp.

Marshall, John (reporter), "Let Indians tell the story -- even if it is embarrassing," <u>Toronto Telegram</u>, March 27, 1969.

Martin, P.S., <u>Indians before Columbus</u>, University of Chicago Press, 1948, 582 pp.

McIlwraith, Thomas F., "Basic cultures of the Indians in Canada," in Charles T. Loram and Thomas F. McIlwraith, eds., The North American Indian Today, University of Toronto Press, 1943, pp. 30-40.

McIlwraith, Thomas F., "The Indians of Canada," The Annals of the American Academy of Political and Social Science, September 1947, 253:164-168.

McLuhan, Teri C., Touch the earth, Toronto, New Press, 1971, 185 pp.

McNab, Frances (reporter), "The forgotten Canadians," Chatelaine, (Toronto), June 1962, pp. 34-35, 104-109.

McNickle, D'Arcy, "Indian and European: Indian-White relations from discovery to 1887," The Annals of the American Academy of Political and Social Science, May, 1957, 311:1-11.

McNickle, D'Arcy, The Indian tribes of the United States: ethnic and cultural survival, New York, Oxford University Press, 1962.

McNutt, C.S., "Life on an Indian reservation," United Church Observer, (Toronto), September 24, 1960, pp. 12-13.

Melling, John, Right to a future: the Native Peoples of Canada, The Anglican Church and the United Church of Canada, 1967.

Morey, S., "Can the Red Man help the White Man?," Gilbert Church, n.d.

Morris, William J., "The plight of the Indian in Canada," Canadian Commentator, June 1959, July 1959, August 1959 (reprinted in Richard Laskin, ed. Social Problems: a Canadian profile, Toronto, McGraw-Hill, 1964).

Mortimore, George E., "The Indians of Canada," Series of 52 articles in Victoria Colonist, 1958.

Morton, W.L., "The West and Confederation 1857-1871," Canadian Historical Booklet #9, Ottawa, 1968.

Mulvihill, James P., "Tell us about Indians," in Seven articles on Indian Affairs, (reprinted in The Dilemma, 1963).

Mulvihill, James P., "What is wrong with reserves? as seen through the eyes of the white man," in Seven articles on Indian Affairs, (reprinted in The Dilemma, 1963).

Mulvihill, James P., "How can we help them?," Seven articles on Indian Affairs, (reprinted in The Dilemma, 1963).

Mulvihill, James P., The dilemma for our Indian people, Ottawa, Indian and Eskimo Welfare Commission, 1963, 44 p.

Nablo, Ron, "Detailed review of the recommendations on the Hawthorne study on the contemporary Indians of Canada," Ottawa,

8

unpublished manuscript, Department of Indian Affairs and Northern Development, ca 1968, 53 p.

Nader, Ralph, "American Indians: people without a future," Harvard Law Record, April, 1956, 22:

Nagler, Mark, ed., Perspectives on the North American Indians, Toronto, McClelland and Stewart, 1972, 302 pp.

Naroll, Raoul, "What have we learned from cross-cultural surveys?, "American Anthropologist," December 1970, 72:1227-1288.

Nash, Philleo, "Programmes of action in areas other than Kenora," Address, Resolving Conflicts -- a cross-cultural approach, April 24, 1967, Kenora, Ontario, pp. 134-144.

O'Connell, Martin P., "Citizen Indians," Address, Annual Meeting of the Canadian Save the Children Fund, Indian-Eskimo Association of Canada, Toronto, May, 1966.

O'Connell, Martin P., "Re address at a Workshop on Indian Affairs to be held in North Vancouver," unpublished letter, January 25, 1969.

Okpik, Abraham, "What does it mean to be an Eskimo," North, (Ottawa), March-April, 1962.

Osborne, Ralph, ed., Who is the chairman of this meeting? a collection of essays, Toronto, Neewin Publishing Co., 1972, 100 pp.

Owen, Roger C., James J.F. Deer, and Anthony Dwight Fisher, eds., The North American Indian: a source book, New York, MacMillan, 1967, 752 pp.

Parsons, Elsie Clews ed., American Indian Life, B.W. Huebsch 1922 (reprinted University of Nebraska Press, 1967, 419 pp).

Patterson, E. Palmer III, The Canadian Indian: a history since 1500, Toronto, Collier MacMillan, 1972, 210 pp.

Patterson, Palmer and Nancy-Lou Patterson, "The changing people: a history of the Canadian Indians, Toronto, Collier-Macmillan, 1971, 58 pp.

Pelletier, Wilfred, "The plight of Canadian Indians," Information, December, 1964.

Phillips, Robert A.J., "Slum dwellers of the wide-open spaces: while civilization swept across the map of Canada the Eskimo was forgotten. Now the tragic effect of white man's thoughtlessness can no longer be ignored," Weekend Magazine, (Montreal) November 15, 1959.

Platiel, Rudy, "1970 in retrospect," Indian-Eskimo Association of Canada Bulletin, December 1970, 11:

Pohorecky, Zenon, <u>Saskatchewan</u> Indian <u>heritage</u>: <u>the first two</u> <u>hundred centuries</u>, Saskatoon, Extension Division, University of Saskatchewan, 1970, 172 pp.

Poole, D.G., "A discussion of Indian objectives and some practical considerations toward the realization of these," Grantham's Landing, B.C., January 10, 1965, 26 pp.

Powell, John Wesley, <u>French policy toward the Indians</u>, Washington, D.C., Eighteenth Annual Report of the Bureau of American Ethnology, 1899.

Powell, John Wesley, <u>English policy toward the Indians</u>, Washington, D.C., Eighteenth Annual Report of the Bureau of American Ethnology, 1899.

Radin, Paul, <u>The story of the American Indian</u>, rev. ed., Liveright Publishing Corporation, 1934.

Radin, Paul, <u>The road of life and death, a ritual drama of the</u> <u>American Indian</u>, New York, Pantheon, 1945, 345 pp.

Reading, R.S., <u>Indian Civilizations</u>, San Antonio, Texas; Naylor, 1961.

Regeher, Theodore D., "Land ownership in Upper Canada, 1783-1796: a background to the First Table of Fees," <u>Ontario History</u> <u>Quarterly</u>, 1963, 55:35-48.

Renaud, André, "Les Canadiens de descendance Indienne," <u>Anthropologica</u>, 1957, 4:139-158.

Renaud, André, "The Twentieth Century Indian at home, on the reserve," <u>Bien-etre social canadien</u>, (Ottawa), January-February 1958, 7 pp.

Renaud, André, "The Indian Canadians," <u>Bien-etre social canadien</u> (Ottawa), March-April, 1958, 7 pp.

Renaud, André, "From oldest to newest: our Indian citizen," <u>Food</u> <u>for Thought</u>, 1959.

Renaud, André, "The Indians of Canada as an ethnic minority," Ottawa: Indian and Eskimo Welfare Association, 1960.

Renaud, André, "Indian and Metis and possible development as ethnic groups," Address, Third Annual Short Course on Northern Community Development at the Centre for Community Studies, University of Saskatchewan, Saskatoon, April 14, 1961.

Renaud, André, "The possible development as ethnic groups of Indian and Metis," Address to <u>Resolving Conflicts -- a cross-</u><u>cultural approach</u>, April 17, 1967, Kenora, Ontario, pp. 118-113.

Richardson, Boyce (reporter), "The emergent Indian, six articles from <u>The Montreal Star</u>, December, 1968," 1969, 26 p.

Richardson, Boyce (reporter), "Indian lives could make good novels," The Montreal Star, December 20, 1968.

Rivers, W.H.R., Social Organization, edited by W.J. Perry, New York: Alfred A. Knopf, 1924.

Rogin, Michael, "And then there were none," (Book reviews), The New York Times Book Review, December 24, 1972.

Rousseau, Jacques, "Les première canadiens," Cahiers des Dix, 1960, 25:9-64.

Rowley, Graham W., "What are Eskimos?," The Arctic Circular, 2-510.

Sahlins, D. Marshall, Tribesmen: Englewood Cliffs, New Jersey, Prentice Hall, 1968, 115 pp.

Sauer, C.O., Man in nature -- American before the days of the white man, New York, Scribner's 1939, 273 pp.

Sharpe, Fred, (reporter), "Our Canadian Indian: who cares?," Town and Country, (Ottawa), 4 parts, June 23 -- July 21, 1971.

Sheffe, Norman, ed., Issues for the Seventies: Canada's Indians, McGraw-Hill and Co., 1970, 87 pp.

Shepard, Harvey L., "The new doctors of the Indian frontier," (First of 3 parts), United Church Observer, (Toronto), March 1, 1967.

Shulsinger, Stephanie Cooper, "Great Indian speeches," Real West Magazine, March, 1971, 17-21, 68.

Shumiatcher, Morris C., Welfare: hidden backlash, a hard look at the welfare issue in Canada, what it has done to the Indian, what it could do to the rest of Canada, Toronto, McClelland and Stewart, 1971, 215 pp.

Silver, A.I., "French Canada and the prairie frontier," Canadian Historical Review, 1969, 1:

Silverman, Peter G. and Karl E. Francis, "Dealing with the government of Canada: a strategy for political action," Toronto, unpublished manuscript, September 1972, 9 pp.

Slight, Benjamin, Indian researches of facts concerning the North American Indian, Montreal, J.E.L. Miller, 1844, 17pp.

Smythe, Marion and Morris Isaac, Indian Summer, Ottawa, Department of Indian Affairs and Northern Development, 1969, 28 pp.

Spindler, George Dearborn and Louise Schauber Spindler, "American Indian personality types and their sociocultural roots," The Annals of the American Academy of Political and Social Science, May, 1957, 311:147-157.

Stanley, George F.G., "The Indian background of Canadian history," The Canadian Historical Association (Report of the Annual

Meeting held at Quebec, June 4-6, 1952, With Historical Papers), pp. 14-21.

Stewart, Julian H., "Limitation of applied anthropology: the case of the Indian New Deal," Journal of the Steward Anthropological Society, 1969.

Stirling, M.W., et al, Indians of the Americas, Washington, D.C., National Geographic Society, 1955, 432 pp.

Surtess, Robert J., The Original Peoples, Toronto, Holt, Rinehart and Winston, 1971, 101 p.

Symington, Fraser, The Canadian Indian, the illustrated history of the great tribes of Canada, Toronto, McClelland and Stewart, 1969, 272 pp.

Symons, R.D., Still the wind blows; a historical novel of the Canadian Northwest 1869-1916, Saskatoon, Prairie Books, 1971, 283 pp.

Tail, Francis, "The role of cultural minorities in a bilingual society," Address, Calgary Indian Friendship Centre, 1968, 3 pp.

Tax, Sol, ed., Heritage of conquest, Glencoe, Illinois, Free Press, 1952, 312 pp.

Tax, Sol, "The importance of preserving Indian culture," Indian Voices, (Chicago), April, 1965.

Taylor, Walter, "The relevance of the Indian heritage to the survival of man," Exploration, November 1969, 10:25-30.

Terrell, John Upton, American Indian Almanac, New York, The World Publishing Co., 1971, 494 pp.

Thompson, P., "The reserve tomorrow," The Northern, 1965, 2:11-15.

Trigger, Bruce Graham, "Champlain judged by his Indian policy: a different view of early Canadian history," Anthropologica, 1971, n.s. 13:85-114.

Underhill, Ruth Murray, "Some basic cultures of the Indians of the United States," in Charles T. Loram and Thomas F. McIlwraith, eds. The North American Indian Today, University of Toronto Press, 1943, pp. 23-29.

Underhill, Ruth Murray, Redman's America -- history of the Indians in United States, University of Chicago Press, 1953, 410 pp.

Vallee, Frank G., Indians and Eskimos of Canada, an overview of studies of relevance to the Royal Commission on Bilingualism and Biculturalism, Ottawa, September 1966, 2 vols 308 pp.

Van Steen, Marcus, "Canadian Indians or just Canadians?," Saturday Night, (Toronto), April 11, 1959.

12

Van Steensel, Maja, ed., <u>People</u> <u>of</u> <u>light</u> <u>and</u> <u>dark</u>, (essays, originally written as radio talks, broadcast over the Northern Service of the Canadian Broadcasting Corporation under the title "The Changing North"), Ottawa, Department of Indian Affairs and Northern Development, 1966, 156 pp.

Verrill, A. Hyatt, <u>The</u> <u>real</u> <u>Americans</u>, New York, G.P. Putnam's Sons, 1954.

Vestal, Stanley, <u>New</u> <u>sources</u> <u>of</u> <u>Indian</u> <u>history 1850-1891</u>, Norman, University of Oklahoma Press, 1934.

Wallace, Dillon, <u>The</u> <u>Indians</u> <u>of</u> <u>Canada</u>, Ottawa, National Museum of Canada, 1939.

Washburn, Wilcomb E., "A moral history of Indian-White relations, needs and opportunities for study," <u>Ethnohistory</u>, Winter 1957, 4:50-51.

Waugageshig, (Harvey McCue), ed, <u>The</u> <u>only</u> <u>good</u> <u>Indian</u>: <u>essays</u> <u>by</u> <u>Canadian</u> <u>Indians</u>, New Press, Toronto, 1970.

Wilson Edmund and J. Mitchell, <u>Apologies</u> <u>to</u> <u>the</u> <u>Iroquois</u>, New York, Vintage Books, 1966, 310 pages.

Wissler, Clark, <u>An</u> <u>American</u> <u>Indian</u>: <u>introduction</u> <u>to</u> <u>the</u> <u>anthropology</u> <u>of</u> <u>the</u> <u>new</u> <u>world</u>, New York, D.C. McMurtrie, 1917.

Wissler, Clark, <u>The</u> <u>American</u> <u>Indian</u>, New York, Oxford University Press, 1922, 474 pp.

Wolf, E., <u>Sons</u> <u>of</u> <u>the</u> <u>Shaking</u> <u>Earth</u>, University of Chicago Press, 1959.

Wolfe, Louis, <u>Indians</u> <u>Courageous</u>, Dood, 1956.

Wuttunee, William Ivan Clark, "Renaissance of the Indians," <u>The</u> <u>Beaver</u>, Summer, 1962, 291:46-47.

Wuttunee, William Ivan Clark, <u>Ruffled</u> <u>feathers</u>: <u>Indians</u> <u>in</u> <u>Canadian</u> <u>society</u>, Calgary, Alberta, Bell Books, 1971, 174 pp.

Zakoji, Miles, <u>The</u> <u>Indian</u> <u>research</u> <u>study</u>, Section I and II, Albuquerque, University of New Mexico, USOE Co-operative Research Project. n.d.

Miscellaneous Reports

by date of publication

<u>Facts</u> <u>relative</u> <u>to</u> <u>the</u> <u>Canadian</u> <u>Indians</u>, London, The Aborigines' Committee, the Meeting for Sufferings, Harvey and Darton and Co., 1839, 24 pp.

"A captive white girl: captured in an Indian raid: the Canadians at the fort think she is the daughter of an American officer -- she has a pale face and golden hair, while a full-blooded Indian claims he is her father, and is thus able to claim an additional pension -- great interest in 'The World' readers in the little girl's fate," Sunday World, January 5, 1890.

Indians and the Land, Contributions by the Delegation of the United States, First Inter-American Conference on Indian Life, Patzcuaro, Mexico, 1940.

"Human problems in the Canadian north," article prepared for inclusion in the 1954-55 Annual Report of the Department of Northern Affairs and National Resources, n.d., 18 pp.

No vanishing race: the Canadian Indian today, Toronto, Ryerson Press (United Church of Canada) 1955, 68 pp.

"American Indians and American life," The Annals of the American Academy of Political and Social Science, May 1957, volume 311.

The Canadian Indian: a reference paper, Ottawa, Indian Affairs Branch, Department of Citizenship and Immigration, 1959, 18 pp.

"Let us try, then what love can do ... : glimpses of the Indian Canadian situation as seen through the eyes of individual Canadian Friends," 2nd ed., Canadian Friends Service Committee, Toronto, 1959, 23 pp.

Research and the Indians of Canada, report of a national seminar, Toronto, Indian-Eskimo Association of Canada, 1960, 29 pp.

The Indian today, Ottawa, Indian Affairs Branch, Department of Citizenship and Immigration, 1962.

The Way of the Indian, Ottawa, Thirteen Documentary Programs Broadcast on C.B.C. Radio, 1961, Canadian Broadcasting Company, 1963, 61 pp.

"Presentation by the I.O.D.E. to The Honourable R.A. Bell, Re: A Proposal for a Research Programme to Assist Canadian Citizens of Indian Origin," January 1963, 5 pp.

"Submission to the Honourable John P. Roberts, Q.C., M.P.P., Prime Minister of Ontario from the Indian-Eskimo Association of Canada," Toronto, January 1963, 2 pp.

"Citizenship projects among Indians: a collection of articles from Citizen," Ottawa, Canadian Citizenship Branch, Department of Citizenship and Immigration, 1965, 37 pp.

"A Brief to the Commission on Bilingualism and Biculturalism," Indian-Eskimo Association of Canada, Toronto, May, 1965, 9 pp.

Introduction to our native peoples, Volume I, British Columbia Heritage Series, Series I, Victoria, B.C., 1966, 41 pp.

"Canada's Native People," Royal Bank of Canada, <u>Monthly</u> <u>Letter</u>, February, 1966.

"The Indian People of Canada," <u>Notes</u> <u>on</u> <u>the</u> <u>Canadian</u> <u>Tree</u>, Ottawa, Citizenship Branch, Department of the Secretary of State, 1967, pp. 167-175, 229-235.

<u>Pavilion</u> <u>tells</u> <u>Indians'</u> <u>story</u>, (Indian Pavilion at EXPO 67, Montreal), Ottawa, Department of Indian Affairs and Northern Development, 1967, 8 pp.

"The emerging Indian crisis," <u>Canadian</u> <u>Welfare</u>, (Ottawa), July-August 1967, 43:10-32.

"Come join us, and be lonely," <u>Cavalier</u>, ca 1968, pp 28, 90-94.

"Report on Northern Area Studies, Lakehead University," unpublished manuscript, prepared for Department of Indian Affairs and Northern Development, November 1968, 8 pp.

Three Maps of Indian Country: (1) Probable Location of Indian Tribes North of Mexico About 155 A.D.; (2) Culture Areas and Approximate Location of American Indian Tribes Today; (3) Indian Reservations Under Federal Jurisdiction, (Except Alaska), Bureau of Indian Affairs, United States Department of the Interior, ca 1969.

"The divine right to be human," <u>The</u> <u>Labour</u> <u>Gazette</u>, 1969, 69:66-71.

"The Indian in the history of America," <u>Exploration</u>, November 1969, 10:20-24.

<u>Indian</u> <u>voices</u>; <u>the</u> <u>first</u> <u>convocation</u> <u>of</u> <u>American</u> <u>Indian</u> <u>scholars</u>, San Francisco, Indian Historian Press, 1970, 390 pp.

<u>The</u> <u>Indians</u> <u>of</u> <u>Canada</u>: <u>a</u> <u>survey</u>, Toronto, Royal Ontario Museum, 1970, 20 pp.

"First Americans last again?" <u>The</u> <u>Economist</u> (Great Britain), July 18, 1970, pp. 41-42.

"Canada's native people," from the summarized federal program of the New Democratic Party, published at Ottawa in 1972, based on positions of the federal convention in Ottawa, 1971, 1 p.

"Native Peoples," Ottawa, Progressive Conservative National Headquarters, 1972, 1 p.

PART II

HISTORY OF NATIVE PEOPLE --
SPECIFIC CULTURAL AND LINGUISTICS GROUPS

Aginsky, Burt W. "Culture element distributions. XXIV. Central Sierra," University of California Anthropological Records (Berkeley), 1943 8:393-486.

Bailey, Alfred Goldsworthy. The conflict of european and eastern Algonkian cultures, 1504-1700: a study in Canadian civilization. Second Edition, University of Toronto Press, 1970. 218 pp.

Barbeau, Charles Marius, "Iroquoian clans and phratries," American Anthropology. July-September 1917, n.s. 19:392-402.

Barnett, Homer G., "Culture element distributions. VII. Oregon Coast," University of California Anthropological Records (Berkeley), 1937 1:155-204.

Barnett, Homer G., "The Coast Salish of Canada," American Anthropologist, 1938, 40:118-141.

Barnett, Homer G., "Culture element distributions. IX. Gulf of Georgia Salish," University of California Anthropological Records (Berkeley), 1939 1:221-295.

Basso, Keith H., "Ice and travel among the Fort Norman Slave: folk taxonomies and cultural rules," Language in Society, c 1970, 1:31-49.

Basso, Keith H., The Cibecue Apache, Holt, Rinehart and Winston, 1970, 101 pp.

Bauman, Gwelda, et. al., "Metis of Saskatchewan," unpublished term paper, May 1958, 70 pp.

Bilby, Julian W., Among unknown Eskimos: an account of twelve years intimate relations with the primitive Eskimos of ice-bound Baffin Land with a description of their ways of living, hunting, customs and beliefs, Philadelphia, Lippincott, 1923.

Birkett-Smith, Kaj, and Frederica DeLaguna, The Eyak Indians of the Copper River Delta, Alaska. Copenhagen, Levin and Munksgaard, 1938.

Birkett-Smith, Kaj, The Eskimos, 2nd ed., London, Metheun, 1959.

Birkett-Smith, Kaj, "Present status of the Eskimo problem," in Sol Tax, ed., Indian Tribes of Aboriginal America: Selected Papers of the 29th International Congress of Americanists, New York, Cooper Square Publ. 1967, pp. 8-18.

Bissett, Don, "Historical antecedents: Kutchin Indians," in The Lower Mackenzie Region: an area economic survey. Ottawa

Department of Indian Affairs and Northern Development, Part I, October, 1967, pp. 28-49.

Boas, Franz. "Second General Report on the Indians of British Columbia," Report of the 60th Meeting of the British Association for the Advancement of Science, 1890, London, 1891. pp. 562-715.

Boas, Franz. "Third General Report on the Indians of British Columbia," Report of the 61st Meeting of the British Association for the Advancement of Science, 1891, London, 1892, pp. 408-447.

Boaz, Franz. "The half-blood Indian," The Popular Science Monthly, October 1894, pp. 761-770.

Boaz, Franz. "An Eskimo winter," in Elsie Clews Parsons, ed., American Indian Life, 1922, (University of Nebraska Press, 1967, pp. 363-378).

Bock, Phillip K., The Micmac Indians of Restigouche: history and contemporary description, Ottawa, National Museum of Canada, (Bulletin 213, Anthropological Series No. 77) 1966. 95 pp.

Brant, Charles Sanford. The life of a Kiowa Apache Indian, Dover Publications, 1969, 143 pp.

Brownie, P.W. Where the fishers go: the story of Labrador-Montagnais Indians. New York, Cochrane Publishing Co., 1901.

Bruemmer, Fred. "The Delewares of Moraviantown," The Canadian Geographical Journal, 1964, 68:94-97.

Bruemmer, Fred. "The outmost bound of the habitable world," Weekend Magazine (Montreal) January 15, 1972.

Burch, Ernest S. Jr., "A study of 'The Structure of Two Eskimo Societies'," Winnipeg, Department of Anthropology, University of Manitoba, February 10, 1969, 23 pp.

Burgesse, J.A. "Les Indiens du Saguenay," Bulletin de la Société historique du Saguenay, 1946, No. 2, pp. 2-11.

Chance, Norman A., The Eskimo of North Alaska, Holt, Rinehart and Winston, 1966. 102 pp.

Clarke, George Frederick. Someone before us: our Maritime Indians, Fredericton, N.B., Unipress, 1968, 240 pp.

Clifton, James A. and Barry Isaac, "The Kansas Prairie Potawatomi: on the nature of a contemporary Indian community," Transactions, Kansas Academy of Science, Spring, 1964, 67:1-24.

Codere, Helen, "The Harrison Lake Physical Type." In Marian W. Smith, ed., Indians of the urban Northwest, New York, Columbia University Press, 1949, pp. 175-184.

Corkran, David H., The Cherokee frontier: conflict and survival 1740-1762, Norman, University of Oklahoma, Press, 1962.

Corkran, David H., The Creek frontier, 1540-1783, Norman, University of Oklahoma Press, 1967, 343 pp.

Debo, Angie Elbertha, The rise and fall of the Choctaw Republic, Norman, University of Oklahoma Press, 1934.

Dempsey, Hugh A., A Blackfoot winter count, Calgary, Glenbow Foundation, 1965, 20 pp.

Dobbin, L.L., A History of Cote, Keeseekoose and Key Reserves compiled and edited from annual reports of the Department of Indian Affairs and Missionaries of the Presbyterian and United Churches, 1873-1958, Regina, ca 1960.

Dockstader, John, The Forgotten People, Ottawa, Native Council of Canada, March, 1972.

Driver, Harold Edson, "Culture element distributions, V. Southern California," University of California Anthropological Records (Berkeley), 1937 1-52.

Duff, Wilson, ed., Histories, territories, and laws of the Kitwancool, Victoria, B.C., Anthropology in British Columbia Memoir No. 4, British Columbia Provincial Museum, Department of Education, 1959, 45 pp.

Dumond, D.E., "Toward a prehistory of the Na-Dene, with a general comment on population movements among Nomadic hunters," American Anthropologist, October 1969, 71:857-863.

Essene, Frank. "Culture element distributions. XXI. Round Valley," University of California Anthropological Records (Berkeley), 1942 8:1-98.

Evans, Enos, "The Cree Indians," Ottawa, unpublished term paper, Carleton University, 1969, 12 pp.

Ewers, John Canfield, The Blackfeet, raiders on the northwestern plains, Norman, University of Oklahoma Press, 1958, 348 p.

Feit, Harvey and José Mailhot, "Part A, James Bay Region (Quebec): ethnological bibliography," recherches amérindiennes au quebec, Juin 1972, 2:5-42.

Fenton, William N. "No. 1, Introduction: the concept of locality and the program of Iroquois research," in William N. Fenton, ed., Symposium on local diversity in Iroquois culture, Washington, D.C., Smithsonian Institute, Bureau of American Ethnology, Bulletin 149, 1951, pp. 3-12.

Fenton, William N. "No. 3, Locality as a basic factor in the development of Iroquois social structure," in William N. Fenton, ed., Symposium on local diversity in Iroquois culture, Washington, D.C., Smithsonian Institute, Bureau of American Ethnology, Bulletin 149, 1951, pp. 39-54.

Fischer, Ann, "History and current status of the Yuma Indians," in Stuart Levine and Nancy O. Lurie, eds., The American Indian Today, Baltimore, Md., Penguin Books, 1970, pp. 212-235.

Fisher, Anthony Dwight. "The Algonquin Plains?" Anthropologica, 1968, n.s. 10:219-234.

Fisher, Anthony Dwight. "The Cree of Canada, some ecological and evolutionary considerations," The Western Canadian Journal of Anthropology, 1969, 1:7-19.

Flannery, Regina. An analysis of coastal Algonquin culture. Washington, D.C., ("Catholic University of America Anthropological Series," No. 7), 1939.

Foreman, Grant. The Five Civilized Tribes, Norman, University of Oklahoma Press, 1934.

Forer, Mort. The Humback. McClelland and Stewart.

Fraser, William Bernard, The Alberta Indian: his past, his future, Calgary, Friends of the Indian Society, 1959. 27 pp.

Freeborn, Elizabeth D. "The Kutenai," Ottawa, unpublished term paper, Department of Anthropology, Carleton University, 1969, 18 pp.

Freilich, Morris, "Scientific possibilities in Iroquoian studies: an example of Mohawks past and present," Anthropologica, 1963, 5:171-186

Gerin, D. "The Hurons of Lorette," Transactions of the Ottawa Literary and Scientific Society, June 1900.

Giddings, James Louis, Ancient men of the Arctic, New York, Alfred A. Knopf, 1967, 391 pp.

Gifford, E.W. "Culture element distributions. XII. Apache-Pueblo," University of California Anthropological Records (Berkeley), 1940 4:1-208.

Giraud, Marcel. Le metis canadien: son role dans l'histoire des provinces de l'Ouest. Paris, Travauz et Memoires de l'Institute d'Ethnologie, No. 44, 1945. (part reprinted) "Metis settlement in the Northwest Territories" Saskatchewan History, 1956, 9: and "The Western Metis after the insurrection," Saskatchewan History, 1956, 9:)

Goddard, Pliny Earle, "Has Tlingit a genetic relation to Athapascan?" International Journal of American Linguistics, 1917-1920, 1:266-279.

Hall, E.T. Early stockade settlements in the Governador, New Mexico: a marginal anasazi development from basket maker III to Pueblo I Times. New York, Columbia University Press, 1944.

Hall, Robert L., Indians of Wisconsin, Madison, State Historical Society of Wisconsin, n.d. 16 p.

Hallowell, Alfred Irving, "Ojibway ontology, behavior, and world view," in S. Diamond, ed., Culture in history, essays in honor of Paul Radin, New York, Columbia University Press, 1960, pp. 19-52.

Hanks, Lucien Mason Jr., and Jane Richardson Hanks, Tribe under trust: a study of the Blackfoot Reserve of Alberta, University of Toronto Press, 1950, 206 pp.

Harrington, John P. "Culture element distributions. XIX. Central California Coast," University of California Anthropological Records (Berkeley), 1942 7:1-46.

Harris, Marianne. "The Bella Coola Indians of the North Pacific Coast," Ottawa, unpublished term paper. Department of Anthropology, Carleton University, 1969, 14 pp.

Hatt, Fred Kenneth. "Social science and the Metis: recent perspectives," Address, 12th Annual Meeting, Western Association of Sociology and Anthropology, Calgary, December, 1971. 32 pp.

Hickerson, Harold, "Algonkians of the Upper Great Lakes," American Anthropologist, February, 1960, 62:81-102.

Hodge, Fred Webb. "The narrative of Alvar Nunez Cabeca de Vaca". Spanish explorers in the southern United States, New York, Charles Scribner's Sons, 1907. p. 1-126.

Hoebel, Adamson E., The Cheyennes: Indians of the Great Plains, case studies in cultural anthropology, Holt, Rinehart and Winston, 1960, 103 pp.

Honigmann, John Joseph, and Irma Honigmann, Eskimo Townsmen, Ottawa, University of Ottawa Research Centre, 1965.

Honigmann, John Joseph. "Formation of Mackenzie Delta frontier culture," Anthropologica, 1971, n.s. 13:185-192.

Horwood, Harold (reporter), "The people who were murdered for fun: Newfoundland's proud and peaceful Beothuck Indians are extinct today because, for more than two centuries, a favorite sport of the island's whites was the hunting the native like big game," Maclean's Magazine, (Toronto), October 10, 1959.

Howard, James H., "The Plains Ojibway or Bungi: hunters and warriors of the northern prairies with special reference to the Turtle Mountain Band," South Dakota Museum, Anthropological Papers, No. 1 Vermillion, S.D., University of South Dakota, 1965.

Howley, James Patrick. The Beothuks or Red Indians, the aboriginal inhabitants of Newfoundland, Cambridge University Press, 1915.

Hyde, George E., Red Cloud's folk: a history of the Oglala Sioux, Norman, University of Oklahoma Press, 1937.

Hyde, George E., _Indians of the high plains_, Norman, University of Oklahoma Press, 1959, 231 pp.

Hyde, George E., _Indians of the woodlands_, Norman, University of Oklahoma Press, 1962, 279 pp.

Johnson, Greg, "Indians in the Maritimes," Address, National Citizenship Seminar, Mount St. Vincent University, Halifax, N.S. August 28, 1968, 2 pp.

Jones, Dorothy V. "John Dougherty and the Pawnee rite of human sacrifice: April, 1827," _Missouri Historical Review_, April, 1969, 63:293-316.

Jones, Peter. _History of the Ojibway Indians_, London, 1861.

Kehoe, Alice B. "The Dakotas in Saskatchewan," in Ethel Nurse, ed., _The modern Sioux, social systems and reservation culture_, Lincoln, University of Nebraska Press, 1970, pp. 148-172.

Kluckhohn, Clyde, and Dorothea Leighton, _The Navaho_, Anchor Books, 1962, 355 pp.

Knirck, Carola, "The Assiniboine Indians of Canada," Ottawa, unpublished term paper, Carleton University, 1968, 23 pp.

Knirck, Carola, "The Beothuks of Newfoundland," Ottawa, unpublished term paper, Carleton University, March 1969, 17 pp.

Kroeber, Alfred Louis. _Cultural and natural areas of native North America_. Berkeley, University of California Press, 1947, 242 pp.

Kupferer, Harriet J., "The isolated eastern Cherokee," in Stuart Levine and Nancy O. Lurie, eds., _The American Indian Today_, Baltimore, Md., Penguin Books, 1970, pp. 143-159.

Lagasse, Jean-Henry _The people of Indian ancestry in Manitoba: a social and economic study; main report_, Winnipeg, Department of Agriculture and Immigration, Volume I, 1959, 179 pp.

Lagasse, Jean-Henry , Walter E. Boek, and Jean K. Boek, _The people of Indian ancestry in Manitoba, a social and economic study; Appendix I: The people of Indian ancestry in greater Winnipeg_, Winnipeg, Department of Agriculture and Immigration, 1959, Volume II, 132 pp.

Lagasse, Jean-Henry , Wlater M. Hlady and B. Ralph Poston, _The people of Indian ancestry in Manitoba: a social and economic study; Appendix II, The people of Indian ancestry in rural Manitoba_, Winnipeg, Department of Agriculture and Immigration, Volume III, 1959, 134 pp.

Larsen, Helge, "The Ipiutak culture: its origin and relationship," in Sol Tax, ed., _Indian tribes of aboriginal America: selected papers of the 29th International Congress of Americanists_, New York, Cooper Square Pub., 1967, pp. 22-30.

LaViolette, G., The Sioux Indians of Canada, Regina, The Marian Press, 1944, 130 pp.

Le Clerco, Father Chrestien, New relation of Gaspesia: with the customs and religion of the Gaspesian Indians, trans. by William Ganong (reprinted Toronto, The Champlain Society, 1910).

Leechman, John Douglas. Vanta Kutchin, Ottawa, Bulletin No. 130, Anthropological Series No. 33, Department of Northern Affairs and National Resources, 1954, 35 pp.

Linderman, Frank Bird, A brief historical sketch of the Blackfoot Indian Tribe, St. Paul, Minn., The Great Northern Railway Co., 1947, 12 pp.

Lotz, James R., "The future of the Eskimo," Futureres, 1968, pp. 54-65.

Lowie, Robert H., The Crow Indians, New York, Farrar and Rinehart, 1935, 350 pp.

Lowie, Robert H., Indians of the Plains, New York, McGraw-Hill, 1954, 222 pp.

Magoon, M.A., Ojibway Drums, New York, Longmans, 1955.

Malan, Vernon D., "The social system of the Dakota Indians," Extension Circular 606, Extension Service, South Dakota State College, 18 pp.

Mandelbaum, David G., "The Plains Cree," American Museum of National History, Anthropological Papers, 1940, volume 37, Part 2. pp. 163-316.

Mandelbaum, David G., "Anthropology and people: the world of the Plains Cree," University of Saskatchewan Lecture, Number 12, 1967, 14 pp.

Markoosie, Harpoon of the hunter, Montreal, McGill-Queen's University Press, 1970, 81 p.

Marshall, John (reporter). "Northern Ontario's Indians -- tough people in a rough land," Toronto Telegram, March 26, 1969.

Mason, John Alden, "The Indians of the Great Slave Lake area," Yale University Publications in Anthropology Number 34.

Milloy, John S., The Plains Cree: a preliminary trade and military chronology 1670-1870, Ottawa, Master's Thesis, Carlton University, September 1972, 356 pp.

Monture, Gilbert C., "The Indians of the north," Dans Queen's Quarterly, Winter, 1960, 66:556-563.

Morgan, Lewis Henry, League of the Ho-De-No-Sau-Nee, or Iroquois, 1851, (reprinted, New York, Corinth Books, 1962, 477 pp.)

Mowat, Farley G., *The desperate people*, Boston, Little Brown, 1959.

Murdock, George P., "The Polar Eskimos," in *Our Primitive Contemporaries*, New York, MacMillan Co., 1935, Chapter 8.

Murdock, George P., "The Haidas of British Columbia," in *Our Primitive Contemporaries*, New York, MacMillan Co., 1935, Chapter 9.

Murdock, George P., "The Crows of the western plains," in *Our Primitive Contemporaries*, New York, MacMillan Co., 1935, Chapter 11.

Murdock, George P., "The Iroquois of Northern New York," in *Our Primitive Contemporaries*, New York, MacMillan Co., 1935, Chapter 11.

Murdock, George P., "The Hopi of Arizona," in *Our Primitive Contemporaries*, New York, MacMillan Co., 1935, Chapter 12.

Oliver, Symmes C., "Ecology and cultural continuity as contributing factors in the social organization of the Plains Indians," *University of California Publications in American Anthropology and Ethnology*, (Berkeley) 1962, 48:

Olson, R.L. "The Quinault Indians," *University of Washington Publications in Anthropology* (Seattle) 1936, 6:1-190.

Opler, Morris Edward, "The Creek 'Town' and the problems of Creek Indian political reorganization," in Edward H. Spicer, ed., *Human problems in technological change*, New York, Russel Sage Foundation, 1952, pp. 165-180.

Oschinsky, L. *The most ancient Eskimos: a serious attempt at determining the racial affinities of the people who created the Dorset Culture in the Canadian Arctic*, Ottawa, Canadian Research Centre for Anthropology, St. Paul University, 1964, 112 pp.

Paget, Amelia M. (edited by Duncan C. Scott), *The people of the plains*, Toronto, William Briggs, 1909.

Parker, Seymour, "The Kwakiutl Indians: 'amiable' and 'atrocious'," *Anthropologica*, 1964, 6:131-158.

Peithmann, Irvin M., *Indians of Southern Illinois*, Toronto, The Ryerson Press, 1964, 125 pp.

Peithmann, Irvin M., *Red Men of Fire: a history of the Cherokee Indians*, Carbondale, Southern Illinois University Press, 1964, 165 pp.

Pinart, Alphonse L., "A few words on the Alaska Dene: in answer to Father Morice, accompanied by a short vocabulary of the A'tana or Copper River Indian Language," *Anthropos*, 1906, 907-913.

Pritchett, John P., "Historical aspects of the Canadian Metis," in *Acculturation in the Americas*, (selected papers of the 29th International Congress of Americanists), University of Chicago Press.

Quimby, George I., *Indian life in the upper Great Lakes, 11,000 B.C. to 1800 A.D.*, University of Chicago Press, 1960, 182 pp.

Quimby, George I., "A year with a Chippewa family, 1763-64," *Ethnohistory*, Summer, 1962, 9:217-239.

Rachlin, Carol K., "Tight Shoe Night: Oklahoma Indians Today," in Stuart Levine and Nancy O. Lurie, eds. *The American Indian Today*, Baltimore, Md., Penguin Books, 1970, pp. 160-183.

Radin, Paul, "Culture element distributions. XXII. Plateau," *University of California Anthropological Records* (Berkeley) 1942, 8:99-262.

Reaman, G. Elmore, *The trail of the Iroquois Indians*, Toronto, Peter Martin Associates, 1967, 138 pp.

Rogers, Edward S. and Jean H. Rogers, *The individual in Mistassini society from birth to death*, Ottawa, National Museum of Canada Bulletin No. 1990, Department of Northern Affairs and National Resources, 1960, 22 pp.

Rogers, Edward, S., *Indians of the North Pacific Coast*, Toronto, Royal Ontario Museum, 1970, 18 pp.

Rogers, Edward S., *Algonkians of the Eastern Woodlands*, Toronto, Royal Ontario Museum, 1970, 15 pp.

Rogers, Edward S., *Indians of the Plains*, Toronto, Royal Ontario Museum, 1970, 16 pp.

Rogers, Edward S., *Indians of the Subarctic*, Toronto, Royal Ontario Museum, 1970, 17 pp.

Rohner, P. Ronald and C. Evelyn Rohner, *The Kwakiutl, Indians of British Columbia*, New York, Holt, Rinehart and Winston, 1970, 110 pp.

Ruddell, Rosemary, "The Kwakiutl," Ottawa, unpublished term paper, Department of Anthropology, Carleton University, 1968, 47 pp.

Schumiatcher, Morris C., "The Plains Indians," *Saturday Night*, (Toronto), June, 1967.

Smitheram, Henry (Butch) Arthur, "Native Indians of British Columbia," Vancouver, unpublished manuscript, 1971, 10 pp.

Speck, Frank Gouldsmith, "In Montagnais Country," in Elsie Clews Parsons, ed., *American Indian Life*, 1922, (University of Nebraska Press, 1967, pp. 87-97).

Speck, Frank Gouldsmith, *Beothuk and Micmac*, Museum of the American Indian, Heye Foundation, 1922, 187 pp.

Speck, Frank Gouldsmith, Naskapi: the savage hunters of the Labrador Peninsula, Norman, University of Oklahoma Press, 1935.

Sprenger, G. Herman, "The rise of the Metis Nation: a study in ecological adaptation," Winnipeg, unpublished thesis proposal, December 1969. 62 pp.

Standing Arrow (Frank Thomas), "History of the Iroquois as told to Mike Sykes," The Ottawa Journal, April 19, 1969.

Swanton, John Reed, Early history of the Creek Indian and their neighbors, Washington D.C., Bureau of Ethnology, Bulletin 73, 1922.

Taylor, Christopher James, "Brief outline of Metis and Non-Status Indian history of the prairies and British Columbia," Ottawa, unpublished manuscript, Native Council of Canada, January 1973, 17 pp.

Taylor, J. Garth, The Canadian Eskimo, Toronto, Royal Ontario Museum, 1971. 15 pp.

Thomas, Joseph Doan, "Indians of the Southwest," Prologue, (Washington, D.C.) Summer, 1972, 4:71-76.

Thomas, Robert K., "The present 'problem' of the eastern Cherokees," June 1958, 20 pp.

Torok, Charles Hamori, "The Tyendinaga Mohawks: the village as a basic factor in Mohawk social structure," Ontario History Quarterly, 1965, 57:69-77.

Trigger, Bruce Graham, "The French presence in Huronia: the struggle of Franco-Huron relations in the first half of the seventeenth century," The Canadian Historical Review, June 1968, 49:107-141.

Trigger, Bruce Graham, The Huron: farmers of the north, Holt, Rinehart and Winston, 1969, 126 pp.

Trigger, Bruce Graham, "Order and freedom in Huron society," Anthropologica, 1963, 5:151-169 (reprinted in Mark Nagler ed. Perspectives on the North American Indian, Toronto, McClelland and Stewart, 1972, pp. 43-56).

Unant, Ewen, "Before the coming of the white man, the Passamaquoddy roamed what is now called northeastern United States and southeastern New Brunswick, today they live on 200 acres in the State of Reservation," 1969, pp. 12-14.

Underhill, Ruth Murray, The Navahos, Norman, University of Oklahoma Press, 1956.

Valentine, Victor Fortune, and R.G. Young, "The situation of the Metis of northern Saskatchewan in relation to his physical and social environment," The Canadian Geographer, 1954, 4:49-56.

Valentine, Victor Fortune, "Some problems of the Metis of northern Saskatchewan," The Canadian Journal of Economics and Political Science, February, 1954, 20:89-95. (reprinted in W.E. Mann, ed., Canada: a sociological profile, Toronto, Copp Clark, 1968, pp. 207-212).

Valentine, Victor Fortune, "The Forgotten People," in Maja van Steensel, ed., People of light and dark, Ottawa, Department of Indian Affairs and Northern Development, 1966, pp. 110-114.

Valentine, Victor Fortune, and Frank G. Vallee, Eskimos of the Canadian Arctic, 1968.

Vyvyan, C.C. Arctic Adventure, London, P. Owen, 1961.

VanStone, James W., The Snowdrift Chipewyan, Ottawa, Department of Northern Affairs and National Resources, 1963, 115 pp.

Villiers, Desme, "A preliminary review of the literature on Metis people," Ottawa, unpublished manuscript, Citizenship Branch, Department of the Secretary of State, July 30, 1971. 28 pp.

Voegelin, Erminie W., "Culture element distributions. XX. Northeast California," University of California Anthropological Records (Berkeley), 1942. 7:47-252.

Voget, Fred, "Kinship changes at Caughnawaga," American Anthropologist, August 1953, 55:385-394.

Wallis, Wilson Dallam, and Ruth Sawtell Wallis, The Micmac Indians of Eastern Canada, Minneapolis, University of Minnesota Press, 1955, 535 pp.

Warren, W.W., History of the Ojibway Nation, Ross and Haines, 1957, 535 pp.

Welfish, Gene, The Lost Universe, Ballantine Books.

Whitaker, Jody, "The Cowichan Indian Tribe of Vancouver Island," Exploration, November, 1969, 10:36-39.

Wilmott, Jill A., Indians of British Columbia: a study discussion text, Vancouver, University of British Columbia Press, 1963, 290 pp.

Wilson, Edward F., The Ojibway language: a manual for missionaries and others employed among the Ojibway Indians, Toronto, Rowsell and Hutchison, undated (reprinted by Department of Indian Affairs and Northern Development, Ottawa, n.d. 412 pp.)

Wilson, H., "An inquiry into the nature of plains Indian cultural development," American Anthropology, April, 1963, 55:355-369.

Winterberg, W.J., Distinguishing characteristics of Algonkian and Iroquoian cultures, Ottawa, National Museum of Canada, Bulletin No. 67, 1929, pp. 65-126.

Wissler, Clark, "Material culture of the Blackfoot Indians," American Museum of Natural History and Anthropological Papers, 1910.

Wissler, Clark, "The social life of the Blackfoot Indians," American Museum of Natural History and Anthropological Papers, 1911.

Wissler, Clark, North American Indian of the plains, American Museum of Natural History, 1941, 172 pp.

Wylie, Elizabeth A., "The Malecite Indians of New Brunswick," Ottawa, unpublished term paper, Carleton University, November 1968, 13 pp.

Miscellaneous Reports
by date of Publication

Indians of Canada, Introductory Leaflet, Guide to the Anthropological Exhibits, National Museum of Canada, 1939, 5 pp.

The Algonkians, Leaflet No. 1, Guide to the Anthropological Exhibits, National Museum of Canada, 1938, 8 pp.

The Iroquoians, Leaflet No. 2, Guide to the Anthropological Exhibits, National Museum of Canada, 1937, 12 pp.

Mackenzie River Tribes, Leaflet No. 3, Guide to the Anthropological Exhibits, National Museum of Canada, 1938, 6 pp.

Plains Indians, Leaflet No. 4, Guide to the Anthropological Exhibits, National Museum of Canada, 1938, 10 pp.

The Eskimo, Leaflet No. 5, Guide to the Anthropological Exhibits, National Museum of Canada, 1939, 12 pp.

Pacific Coast Tribes, Leaflet No. 6, Guide to the Anthropological Exhibits, National Museum of Canada, 1939, 17 pp.

The Cordillera Indians, Leaflet No. 7, Guide to the Anthropological Exhibits, National Museum of Canada, 1939, 11 pp.

Kootenay, British Columbia Heritage Series, Series 1, Our Native Peoples, Volume 8, Victoria, B.C., 1952, 51 pp.

Dene, British Columbia Heritage Series, Series 1, Our Native People, Volume 9, Victoria, B.C., 1953, 59 pp.

Queen Charlotte Island, British Columbia Heritage Series, Series 11, Our Pioneers, Volume 1, Victoria, B.C., 1953, 68 pp.

The Metis in Manitoba, Canadian Association of Social Workers, Manitoba Branch, 1954.

"Background Information of Metis and Indians of Manitoba," Indian and Metis Conference, Winnipeg, Manitoba, February, 1959, 9 pp.

Bella Coola, British Columbia Heritage Series, Series 1, Our Native Peoples, Volume 10, 1964, 77 pp.

American Indians in California, San Francisco, Department of Industrial Relations, November, 1965, 41 pp.

Tsimshian, British Columbia Heritage Series, Series 1, Our Native Peoples, Volume 6, Victoria, B.C., 1966, 61 pp.

Interior Salish, British Columbia Heritage Series, Series 1, Our Native Peoples, Volume 3, Victoria, B.C., 1966, 53 pp.

Indians in Rural and Reservation Areas, Sacramento, California State Advisory Commission on Indian Affairs, 1966, 53 pp.

Indians of Ontario, (an historical review), Ottawa, Department of Indian Affairs and Northern Development, 1966, 40 pp.

Indians of Quebec and the Maritime Provinces, (an historical review), Ottawa, Department of Indian Affairs and Northern Develpment, 1966, 36 pp.

"A history of the lands of the Mohawks of Akwesasne, an internationally located community of North American Indians situated in Ontario, Quebec and New York State, commonly known as the St. Regis Reserve." Ottawa, 1966, 16 pp.

Indians of British Columbia, (an historical review), Ottawa, Department of Indian Affairs and Northern Development, 1967, 16 pp.

Indians of Yukon and Northwest Territories, Ottawa, Department of Indian Affairs and Northern Development, 1967, 20 pp.

"The Indians of Prince Edward Island," Ottawa, unpublished manuscript, Department of Indian Affairs and Northern Development, January 30, 1968, 11 pp.

"Metis People in Alberta," Report of the First Alberta Native Women's Conference, Edmonton, March, 1968, pp. 33-35.

Indians of the Prairie Provinces, (an historical review), Ottawa, Department of Indian Affairs and Northern Development, revised 1969, 25 pp.

PART III

POPULATION DISTRIBUTION
(see also Health and Welfare)

Berlin, Heinrich, "El Indigena frente al estado," America Indigena, October, 1944, 4:

Bermejo, Vladimiro, "La Ley y el Indio en el Peru," America Indigena, 1944, 4:

Berry, Brewton, "The myth of the vanishing Indian," Phylon, Spring, 1960, pp. 53-57.

Biro de Stern, Ana, "The re-evaluation of the American aborigine," American Indigena, July, 1958, 18:

Botelho de Magalhaes, Amilcar A., "Indios Do Brazil," America Indigena, April, 1947, 7:

Brand, Donald D., "The present Indian population of the Americas," New Mexico Anthropologist, 1943, 6-7:

Caso, Alfonso, "Definicion del Indio y lo Indio," America Indigena, October 1948, 8:244-246.

Chafe, Wallace L., "Estimates regarding the present speakers of North American Indian Languages," International Journal of American Linguistics, July, 1962, 28:162-171.

Chafe, Wallace L., "Corrected estimates regarding speakers of Indian languages," International Journal of American Linguistics, October, 1965, 31:345-346.

Dobyns, Henry F., H.P. Thompson, et al., "Estimating aboriginal American population," Current Anthropology, 1966, pp. 345-449.

Dodsell, Philip, "The vanishing Stoney Indians," Canadian Geographical Journal, October, 1934, pp. 179-188.

Drapeau, Claude and Victor Piche, "Internal migration among the Indian population of the James Bay area," Ottawa, unpublished seminar paper, University of Ottawa, April, 1970, 28 pp.

Freeman, Milton M.R., "A social and ecologic analysis of systematic female infanticide among the Netsilik Eskimo," American Anthropologist, October 1971, 73:1011-1018.

Hackenberg, Robert A., A Navajo population register, preliminary considerations, Report prepared in connection with the University of Arizona Navajo Population Register Project, June, 1964.

Hadley, J. Nixon, "The demography of the American Indians," The Annals of the American Academy of Political and Social Science, May, 1957, 311:23-30.

Hlady, Walter M., "Indian migration in Manitoba and the West," Historical and Scientific Society of Manitoba, Series III, 1960-1961, (7).

Kelly, William H., Methods and resources for the construction and maintenance of a Navajo population register, Report prepared for the National Cancer Institute by the Bureau of Ethnic Research Department of Anthropology, University of Arizona, 1964.

Knirck, Carola, "Some remarks on the Indian and Metis Population in Canada," Ottawa, unpublished manuscript, Research and Documentation, Citizenship Branch, Secretary of State, December 1971, 9 pp.

Long Lance, Chief Buffalo Child, "When the Crees moved West," Ontario Sessional Papers, Toronto 1924.

Mooney, James, The aboriginal population of America north of Mexico, Washington, D.C., Smithsonian Miscellaneous Collections, 1928, Volume 80, 40 pp.

Owl, Frell, M., "Who and what is an American Indian?," Ethnohistory, Spring, 1962, 9:265-284.

Rosenthal, Jack (reporter), "1970 Census finds Indian no longer the vanishing American," The New York Times, October 20, 1971.

Tax, Sol. et al., "The North American Indians: 1950 distributions of descendants of the aboriginal population of Alaska, Canada and the United States in 'Letter to Indians'," University of Chicago, December 27, 1960.

Wahrhaftig, Albert L., "The tribal Cherokee population of eastern Oklahoma," Current Anthropology, December 1968, 9:510-518.

Whiteside, Don, "Registered Indian population, Canada 1865-1972," Ottawa National Indian Brotherhood, April 1973.

Miscellaneous Reports
by date of Publication

"Census of Manitoba, North-West Territories and Keewatin," House of Commons Debates, 1886, p. 43.

Schedule of Indian Reserves in the Dominion of Canada, Revised and Corrected to 31st March, 1928, Part I, Ottawa, Department of Indian Affairs, 1929, 77 pp.

Census of Indians in Canada, Ottawa, Department of Citizenship and Immigration, 1961, 45 pp.

"Indians in the hemisphere today: guide to the Indian population,"
Indianist Yearbook (Inter-American Indian Institute, Mexico),
1962, 22:142 pp.

Schedule of Indian Reserves and Settlements, Part I, (Prince
Edward Island, Nova Scotia, New Brunswick, Quebec, Ontario,
Manitoba, Saskatchewan, Alberta, Yukon and Northwest
Territories), Ottawa, Indian Affairs Branch, Department of
Citizenship and Immigration, Revised January 31, 1964.

Schedule of Indian Reserves and Settlements, Part II, Province of
British Columbia, Revised to April 30, 1966, Ottawa, Department
of Indian Affairs, and Northern Development, 1967.

Saskatchewan Region, Indian labour force survey, Ottawa,
unpublished report, Indian Affairs Branch, Department of Indian
Affairs and Northern Development, July 1967.

Indian Affairs facts and figures, Ottawa, Department of Indian
Affairs and Northern Development, September, 1967, (annual).

Linguistic and cultural affiliations of Canadian Indian Bands,
Ottawa, Department of Indian Affairs and Northern Development,
ca 1968.

"Map of Manitoba showing areas populated by Indians and Metis,"
Winnipeg, The Community Welfare Planning Council, 1968.

"Registered Indian membership by band and residence: distributed
by Agency or District within regions," Ottawa, Department of
Indian Affairs and Northern Development, December, 1968, 1969,
1970, 1971.

"Residential distribution of Indians by Province, 1959-69,"
(Annual) Ottawa Central Statistics Division, Department of
Indian Affairs and Northern Development, April 9, 1969, 4 pp.

Alberta Region Statistical Report 1968-1969, Edmonton, Indian
Affairs and Northern Development Alberta Region, 1970.

Atlas of Indian Reserves and Settlements of Canada, Ottawa,
Department of Indian Affairs and Northern Development, 1971.

"Eskimo population of Canada, 1941-1970," Ottawa, Statistics
Division, Department of Indian Affairs and Northern
Development, December 1971, 5 pp.

Schedule of Indian Reserves and Settlements of Canada, Ottawa,
Department of Indian Affairs and Northern Development, 1972,
358 pp.

PART IV

VALUES, TRADITIONS, TALES AND CRAFTS, BIOGRAPHIES

A -- Values and Traditions
B -- Tales
C -- Crafts and Designs
D -- Biographies

A -- Values and Traditions

Baldwin, Gordon C., _Games of the American Indian_, New York, W.W. Norton, 1969, 150 pp.

Balikci, Asen, "Bad friends," _Human Organization_, 1968, 27: (reprinted in Nagler, Mark, ed. _Perspectives on the North American Indian_, Toronto, McClelland and Stewart, 1972, pp. 72-87).

Buthee, Julia M., _The rythm of the redman in song, dance and decoration_, New York, A.S. Barnes, 1930.

Carpenter, E.S., "The timeless present in the mythology of the Akvalik Eskimos," in Victor Fortune Valentine and Frank G. Vallee, eds., _Eskimo of the Canadian Arctic_, Toronto, McClelland Stewart, 1968, pp. 39-42.

Clutesi, George, _Potlach_, Sidney, B.C., Gray Publishing Co., 1969, 188 p.

Currie, Walter, "Too impatient? Too unconcerned?," _The Labour Gazette_, 1969, 69:646-650.

Driver, Harold Edson and William C. Massey, "Comparative studies of North American Indians," _Transactions of the American Philosophical Society_, Philadelphia, 1957, n.s. 47 (prt. 2):165-456.

Easton, Robert, "Humour of the American Indian," _Mankind_, 2:37-41, 72-73.

Frazer, Robin, "Indian culture," _Performing Arts in Canada_, (Ottawa) Summer 1972, 9:7-13.

French, Cecil L., "Social class and motivation among Metis, Indians, and Whites in Alberta," in Arthur Kent Davis, et. al. _A northern dilemma: reference papers_, Bellingham, Washington, Western Washington State College, volume 1, April 1967, pp. 124-169.

Gagne, Raymond C., "Special concepts in the Eskimo language," in Victor Fortune Valentine and Frank G. Valle, eds., _Eskimo of the Canadian Arctic_, Toronto, McClelland Stewart, 1968, pp. 30-38.

Harkins, Arthur M., _Attitudes_ _and_ _characteristics_ _of_ _selected_ _Wisconsin_ _Indians_, Minneapolis, University of Minnesota, 1969, 86 pp.

Hill, Willard Williams, "Navajo trading and trading ritual," _Southwestern_ _Journal_ _of_ _Anthropology_, 1948, pp. 371-396.

Howard, James H., "Indian cultures: their history and contributions," Address to _Resolving_ _conflicts_ -- _a_ _cross-_ _cultural_ _approach_, February 27, 1967, Kenora, Ontario, pp. 16-30.

Hryniuk, Morris D., ed., "The stories of Wesakachak, as written by the Grade Fives at the Onion Lake (Saskatchewan) Catholic School," _Involvement_, (Newmarket, Ontario), Fall, 1971, 4:27-29.

Hungry Wolf. Adolf, _Good_ _medicine_, _traditional_ _dress_, Golden, B.C. Good Medicine Books, 1971.

Hungry Wolf. Adolf, _Good_ _Medicine_, _companion_ _issue_, Golden, B.C. Good Medicine Books, 1971.

Hungry Wolf. Adolf, _Good_ _Medicine_ _in_ _Glacier_ _National_ _Park_, Golden, B.C., Good Medicine Books, 1971.

Johnson, E. Pauline (Tekahionwake), _Flint_ _and_ _feather_: _the_ _complete_ _poems_ _of_ _Pauline_ _E._ _Johnson_, Toronto, General Publishing Co., 1972, 164 pp.

Kitpou, Shaman, "Tribal laws of the children of light," _Ts'igonde_ (Talking Tree), (Yellowknife, N.W.T.), December 1972.

Motyl, John, ed., "Insights into cultural differences," A compilation of study material from a seminar on cultural differences for the instruction of people working with ethnic groups in the Edmonton area, June 13-15, 1963.

Ondrack, Jack W., "The 'Sasquatch' phenomenon in Alberta," Address, 11th Annual Meeting of the Western Association of Sociology and Anthropology, Banff, Alberta, December 28-29, 1969.

Pelletier, Wilfred, _Two_ _articles_, Neewin Publishing Co., 1969, 30 pp.

Pelletier, Wilfred, "Childhood in an Indian village," _This_ _magazine_ _is_ _about_ _schools_, Spring 1969, (reprinted in _Northian_ - Journal of the Society for Indian and Northern Education - , Spring, 1970, 7:20-23).

Pelletier, Wilfred, "Time," in Ralph Osborne, ed., _Who_ _is_ _chairman_ _of_ _this_ _meeting_? _a_ _collection_ _of_ _essays_, Toronto, Neewin Publishing Co., 1972, pp. 53-66.

Poole, Ted, "A modern legend," in Ralph Osborne, ed., _Who_ _is_ _chairman_ _of_ _this_ _meeting_? _a_ collection _of_ _essays_, Toronto, Neewin Publishing Co., 1972, 67-78.

Redbird, Duke, "Living and learning the Indian way," Involvement (Newmarket, Ontario), November-December, 1972, 5:18-21.

Reynolds, E.E., ed., A book of Grey Owl: pages from the writings of Wa-Sha-Quon-Asin, Toronto, 1938 (reprinted, Macmillan of Canada, 1971, 272 pp.).

Rogers, Edward S., "Notes on lodge plans in the Lake Indictor area of south-central Quebec," Arctic, December 1963, 16(4):219-227.

Rogers, Edward S., "Ojibwa culture: the traditional culture history," Address to Resolving Conflicts -- a cross-cultural approach, March 6, 1967, Kenora, Ontario, pp. 32-44.

Roheim, Geza, "Culture hero and trickster in North American mythology," in Sol Tax, ed., Indian tribes of aboriginal America: selected papers of the 29th International Congress of Americanists, New York, Cooper Square Pub. 1967, 190-194.

Saulnier, Joseph Maurice, "Teamwork at Red Earth," Ottawa, unpublished manuscript, 1956, 9 pp.

Shimpo, Mitsuru, "Social structure and value system of fringe Saultaux," Saskatoon, Centre for Community Studies, July, 1964, 19 p.

Sprague, Chester L., "American Indian communities: toward a unity of life and environment," Technology Review, July/August, 1972, pp. 14-25.

Steinbring, Jack, "Ojibwa culture: the modern situation and problems," Address to Resolving conflicts -- a cross-cultural approach, March 13, 1967, Kenora, Ontario, pp. 46-71.

Tompkins, William, Universal Indian sign language of the Plains Indians of North America author, San Diego, California, 1931 (reprinted as Indian sign language, Dover Publications, 1969, 108 pp.).

Willmott, W.E., "The flexibility of Eskimo social organization," Anthropologica, 1960, 2:48-59 (reprinted in Mark Nagler, ed., Perspectives on the North American Indian, Toronto, McClelland and Stewart, 1972).

Yellowbird, Lydia, "You are an Indian," Indians of all tribes (California), 1971 (reprinted in Involvement (Newmarket, Ontario) Fall, 1971, 4:52.)

Zentner, Henry, "The pre-machine ethic of the Athabascan-speaking Indians: avenue or barrier to assimilation?," in Arthur Kent Davis, et. al. eds., A northern dilemma: reference papers, Bellingham, Western Washington State College, volume 1, April 1967, pp. 69-89.

Zentner, Henry, "Reservation social structure and anomie: a case study," in Arthur Kent Davis, et. al., eds, A northern dilemma: reference papers, Bellingham, Western Washington State College, volume 1, April 1967, pp. 112-123.

B -- Tales

Alexander, Hartley Burr, The world's rim: great mysteries of the
    North American Indians, Lincoln, University of Nebraska Press,
    1957, 259 pp.

Austin, Mary, One Smoke stories, New York, Houghton Mifflin Co.,
    1934.

Bierhorst, John, ed., In the trail of the wind: American Indian
    poems and ritual orations, Canada, Doubleday, 1971, 201 pp.

Catlin, George, Letters and notes on the manners, customs and
    conditions of the North American Indians, New York, Wiley and
    Putnam, 1842.

Clark, Ella Elizabeth, Indian legends of Canada, Toronto,
    McClelland and Stewart, 1960, 177 pp.

Desbarats, P., ed., What they used to tell about Indian legends
    from Labrador, Toronto, McClelland and Stewart Ltd., 1969.

Dewdney, S., ed., Legends of my people the Great Ojibway,
    Illustrated and told by Norval Morrisseau, Toronto, Ryerson
    Press, 1965, 130 pp.

Dundes, Alan, "Washington Irving's version of the Seminole origin
    of races," Ethnohistory, Spring, 1962, 9:257-264.

Gooderham, Kent, ed., I am an Indian, Toronto, J.M. Dent and Sons,
    1969, 196 pp.

Hazeltine, A.I., Red man white man: legends, tales and true
    accounts of the American Indian, New York, Lethrop, c. 1957,
    309 pp.

Hook, H.M., Thunder in the mountain: legends of Canada, Oxford
    University Press, 1947, 233 pp.

Jenness, Diamond, The Corn Goddess and other tales from Indian
    Canada, Ottawa, National Museum of Canada, Bulletin 141, 1956,
    11 pp.

Lewis, Richard, I breath a new song: poems by the Eskimo, New
    York, Simon and Schuster, 1971, 128 pp.

Lowie, Robert H., "Windigo, a Chipeyan story," in Elsie Clews
    Parsons ed., American Indian Life, 1922, (University of
    Nebraska Press, 1967, pp. 225-235).

McKay, Fortescue, "An Indian tale of brich bark musk-rat tails and
    rabbits ears," North, (Ottawa), November-December, 1966.

Morrisseau, Norval, Legends of my people, Toronto, Ryerson Press,
    1965, 130 pp.

Ressler, T.W., _Treasury of American Indian tales_, New York, Association Press, 1957, 310 pp.

Sanderson, James F., "Indian Tales of the Canadian Prairies," _Alberta Historical Review_, Summer, 1965, 13:7-21.

Savard, Reme, "L'Hote Maladroit, essai d'analyse d'un conte montagnais," in _Interpretation_, (Montreal), 1969, 3:5-52.

Schwartz, H.T., _Windigo and other tales of the Ojibways_, illustrated by Norval Morrisseau, McClelland and Stewart, 1969, 40 pp.

Spence, Lewis, _Myths and Legends of the North American Indians_, Toronto, McClelland and Goodchild, (reprinted).

Stevens, James and Carl Ray, _Sacred Legends of the Sandy Lake Cree_, Toronto, McClelland and Stewart, 1971.

Stump, Sarain, _There is my people sleeping_, Sidney, British Columbia, Grey's Publishing Ltd., 1970.

Vandersteen, Roger, "Some Woodland Cree Traditions and Legends," _The Western Canadian Journal of Anthropology_, 1969, 1:40-65.

Weatherby, H., _Tales the Totems Tell_.

C -- Crafts -- Designs

Barbeau, Charles Marius, _Totem Poles_, 2 volumes, Bulletin No. 119, Anthropological Series No. 30, Ottawa, Department of Resources and Development, Development Services Branch, National Museum of Canada, 1950.

Bruce, Louis, R., Jr., "The development of Indian craftsmanship," in Charles T. Loram and Thomas F. McIlwraith eds., _The North American Indian Today_, University of Toronto Press, 1943, pp. 323-330.

Covarrubias, M., _The Eagle, The Jaguar, and The Serpent: Indian Art of the Americas_, New York: Alfred A. Knopf, 1954.

Culin, Stewart, "Zuni Pictures," in Elsie Clews Parsons, ed., _American Indian Life_, 1922, (University of Nebraska Press, 1967, pp. 175-178).

D'Harnoncourt, Rene, "Function and production of Indian art," in Charles T. Loram and Thomas F. McIlwraith, eds., _The North American Indian Today_, University of Toronto Press, 1943, pp. 318-322.

Denman, Murrie, _Art in the life of the Indian of South Dakota_, Master of Arts Thesis, University of South Dakota, 1953.

Ewers, John Canfield, _Plains Indian Painting_, London, Oxford University Press, 1939, 84 pp.

Ewers, John Canfield, "Folk art in the fur trade of the Upper Missouri," _Prologue_, (Washington, D.C.), Summer, 1972, 4:99-108.

Houston, James A. "Eskimo Carvings," Ottawa, Department of Indian Affairs and Northern Development, n.d.

Kuh, Katherine, "The first Americans as artists," _Saturday Review_, September 4, 1971.

Lapierre-Assiniwi, Bernard, _Talent Among Canadian Indians_, Ottawa Department of Indian Affairs and Northern Development, May, 1968.

Lyford, Carrie A., _Iroquois crafts_, (ed. by Willard W. Beatty) Washington, D.C., Bureau of Indian Affairs, Branch of Education, Department of the Interior, 1945, 97 pp.

Monahan, Gene Ritchie, "Report on the experiment in art exposure among the Indians of the isolated communities of Northwestern Ontario at Sandy Lake Reserve," Youth and Recreation Branch, Ontario Department of Education, Dryden, Ontario, 1968, 17 pp.

Spinden, Herbert J., "Power animals in American Indian Art," in Sol Tax, ed., _Indian Tribes of Aboriginal America: Selected papers of the 29th International Congress of Americanists_, New York, Cooper Square Pub. 1967, 195-199.

Tozzer, Alfred M., "The Toltec architect of Chichen Itza," in Elsie Clews Parsons ed., _American Indian Life_, 1922, (University of Nebraska Press, 1967, pp. 265-272).

Weltfish, Gene, "The study of American Indian crafts and its implications for art theory," in Sol Tax, ed., _Indian Tribes of Aboriginal America: Selected papers of the 29th International Congress of Americanists_, New York, Cooper Square Pub. 1967, pp. 200-209.

Miscellaneous Reports
by date of Publication

The Salish Basket Makers of Mount Currie, B.C., Ottawa, Indian Affairs Branch, Department of Citizenship & Immigration, 1964.

"Before the White Man: a gallery of paintings by Lewis Parker," _Canadian Magazine_, (Toronto), May 15, 1971.

Ksan, Breath of our grandfathers, Ottawa, National Museums of Canada, 1972, 107 p.

D -- Biographies (see also Resistance)

      1 -- General
      2 -- Contemporary Canadian Indians

1 -- General

Barrett, S.M., ed., <u>Geronimo</u>: <u>his</u> <u>own</u> <u>story</u>, New York, Ballantine Books, 1970.

Dempsey, Hugh A., <u>Crowfoot</u> <u>Chief</u> <u>of</u> <u>the</u> <u>Blackfeet</u>, Edmonton, Hurtig Publishers, 1972, 226 pp.

Dyk, Walter, <u>Son</u> <u>of</u> <u>Old</u> <u>Man</u> <u>Hat</u>, Author, 1966, 378 pp.

Foreman, Grant, <u>Sequoyah</u>, Norman, University of Oklahoma, 1938.

Goddard, P.E., "Slender-Maiden of the Apache," in Elsie Clews Parsons ed. <u>American</u> <u>Indian</u> <u>Life</u>, 1922, (University of Nebraska Press, 1967, pp. 147-159).

Goldenweiser, Alexander A., "Hanging-Flower, The Iroquois," in Elsie Clews Parsons ed., <u>American</u> <u>Indian</u> <u>Life</u>, 1922, (University of Nebraska Press, 1967, pp. 99-106).

Harrington, M.R., "The Thunder Power of Rumbling - Wings," in Elsie Clews Parsons ed., <u>American</u> <u>Indian</u> <u>Life</u>, 1922 (University of Nebraska Press, 1967, pp. 107-125).

Josephy, Alvin M. Jr., <u>The</u> <u>Patriot</u> <u>Chiefs</u> -- <u>a</u> <u>chronicle</u> <u>of</u> <u>American</u> <u>Leadership</u>, Viking Press, 1961, 364 pp.

Kroeber, Alfred Louis, "Earth-Tongue, A Mohave," in Elsie Clews Parsons ed. <u>American</u> <u>Indian</u> <u>Life</u>, 1922, (University of Nebraska Press, 1967, pp. 189-202.

Lowie, Robert, H., "A Crow Woman's tale," in Elsie Clews Parsons ed., <u>American</u> <u>Indian</u> <u>Life</u>, 1922, (University of Nebraska Press, 1967, pp. 35-40).

Lowie, Robert H., "Takes -- The -- Pipe, a Crow warrior," in Elsie Clews Parsons ed., <u>American</u> <u>Indian</u> <u>Life</u>, 1922, (University of Nebraska Press, 1967, pp. 17-33).

McKee, Sandra Lynn, ed., <u>Gabriel</u> <u>Dumont</u>: <u>Indian</u> <u>fighter</u>, Calgary, Frontier Publishing Co., 1968, 49 pp.

Miller, George William, "The Handsome Lake Movement: a millenarian interpretation," Montreal, unpublished term paper, (Anthropology) McGill University, April 1971, 59 pp.

Minor, Nono, "The American Indian: Famous Indian Women in Early American," <u>Real</u> <u>West</u> <u>Magazine</u>, March, 1971, 35, 78.

Monture, Ethel Brant, <u>Brant</u>, <u>Crowfoot</u>, <u>Oronhyatehka</u> <u>Famous</u> <u>Indians</u>, Toronto, Clarke, Irwin, 1960, 160 pp.60 pp.

Parsons, Elsie Clews, "Waiyatitsa of Zuni, New Mexico," in Elsie Clews Parsons ed. American Indian Life, 1922 (University of Nebraska Press, 1967, pp. 157-173).

Radin, Paul, "Thunder-Cloud, A Winnebago Shaman, Relates and Prays," in Elsie Clews Parsons ed. American Indian Life, 1922 (University of Nebraska Press, 1967, pp. 75-80).

Reed, T.B. and Elsie Clews Parsons, "Cries-For-Salmon, A Ten'a Woman," in Elsie Clews Parsons ed. American Indian Life, 1922 (University of Nebraska Press, 1967, pp. 337-361).

Sapir, Edward, "Sayach'apies, A Nootka Trader," in Elsie Clews Parsons ed. American Indian Life, 1922, (University of Nebraska Press, 1967, pp. 297-323).

Schultz, J.W., My life as an Indian, Greenwich, Connecticut, Fawcett Publications, 1935, 204 pp.

Sister of Crashing Thunder, Mountain Wolf Women -- the autobiography of a Winnebago Indian, University of Michigan Press, 1966, 142 pp.

Sluman, Norma, Poundmaker, Toronto, Ryerson Press, 1967, 301 pp.

Swanton, John Reed, "Tokulki of Tulsa," in Elsie Clews Parsons, ed. American Indian Life, 1922, (University of Nebraska Press, 1967, pp. 127-145).

Tucker, Glenn, Tecumseh, Vision of Glory, Indiannapolis: The Bobbs Merrill Co., 1956.

Van Dusen, Conrad, Indian Chief; an account of the labors, losses, sufferings and oppression of Ke-Zig-Ko-e-ne-ne, (Ojibway Chief), London, Ontario: William Nichols, 1867, 204 pp.)

2 -- Contemporary Canadian Indians

Bell, Dennis (reporter), "William Wuttunee: friend or foe of the Indians," The Vancouver Sun, September 17, 1970.

Bell, Dennis (reporter), Wild radical or new messiah," (Harold Cardinal) The Vancouver Sun, September 17, 1970.

Campbell, Maria, Halfbreed, McClelland and Stewart, 1973, 157 pp.

Campbell, Marjorie Freeman (reporter), "The lyric voice of Canada's Indians: this year Canada celebrates the centenary of the birth of Mohawk poet Pauline Johnson," The Globe and Mail, (Toronto) February 25, 1961.

Dunn, Marty, Red on White: the biography of Duke Redbird, Toronto, New Press, 1971, 120 pp.

Fotheringham, Allan, "Dan George's last stand," <u>MacLeans</u> <u>Magazine</u>, (Toronto), July, 1971, 28-30, 50-51.

Gzowski, Peter (reporter), "Portrait of a Beautiful Segregationist," (Kahn-Tineta Horn) <u>MacLean's</u> <u>Magazine</u>, (Toronto), May 2, 1964.

Gzowski, Peter (reporter), "How Kahn-Tineta Horn Became an Indian," <u>MacLean's</u> <u>Magazine</u>, (Toronto), May 16, 1964.

Hodge, Frederick Webb, ed., <u>Handbook</u> <u>of</u> <u>the</u> <u>American</u> <u>Indians</u> <u>North</u> <u>of</u> <u>Mexico</u>, (Bulletin of the United States Bureau of American Ethnology, No. 30), Washington, D.C., 1910.

Isaac, Morris, "Funny -- I'm still looking for that place," <u>Anthropologica</u>, 1971, n.s. 13:23-36.

Klyn, Doyle (reporter), "Girl with the best of two worlds, Kahn-Tineta is a Mohawk Indian and a big-city fashion model," <u>Weekend</u> <u>Magazine</u>, (Montreal), May 4, 1963, pp. 6-9.

Louttit, Neil (reporter), "David Courchene, Tough, Fair, and Never on Tiptoe," <u>Weekend</u> <u>Magazine</u>, (Montreal), November 21, 1970.

Patterson, E. Palmer, <u>Andrew</u> <u>Paull</u> <u>and</u> <u>the</u> <u>Canadian</u> <u>Indian</u> <u>Resurgence</u>, Ph D. dissertation, University of Washington, 1964.

Pennier, Henry, <u>Chiefly</u> <u>Indian</u>, Graydonald, c 1972, 130 pp.

Purdie, James (reporter), "Rythms and contours of Prairie hills flow through designs of Metis architect," (Douglas Cardinal), <u>The</u> <u>Globe</u> <u>and</u> <u>Mail</u>, (Toronto), August 18, 1972.

Ruddy, Jon (reporter), "Portrait of the artist as a young half-breed," Willie Dunn: writer of songs, maker of films (and trouble), and -- in 1970 -- his own man," <u>MacLean's</u> <u>Magazine</u>, (Toronto), June, 1970.

Sayres, William C., <u>Sammy</u> <u>Louis</u>: <u>the</u> <u>life</u> <u>of</u> <u>a</u> <u>young</u> <u>Micmac</u>, New Haven, The Compass Publishing Co., 1956.

Tetso, John, <u>Trapping</u> <u>is</u> <u>my</u> <u>life</u>, new and enlarged ed., Toronto, P. Martin and Association, 1970, 115 pp.

Wapiti, Marisa, "Ashes of fire, manuscript of just a little halfbreed," Smithers, B.C., Tanglewood Press, January 1972, 102 pp.

Wapiti, Marisa, "Ropes of sand, manuscript of just a little halfbreed," Smithers, B.C., Tanglewood Press, February 1972, 226 pp.

Wuttunee, William Ivan Clark, "Under Attack," television interview, ca 1971, 24 pp.

Miscellaneous Reports
by date of Publications

"Dr. Gilbert C. Monture," Canadian Indians of Today, (Indian-Eskimo Association of Canada), February Bulletin, 1965.

"Miss Ann Padlo," Canadian Indians and Eskimos of Today, (Indian-Eskimo Association of Canada), April Bulletin, 1966, No. 3.

"Miss Annee Meekitjik," Canadian Indians and Eskimos of Today, (Indian-Eskimo Association of Canada), May Bulletin, 1966, No. 4.

"Appointment of the Commissioner General of the Indians of Canada Pavilion at Expo '67," (Andrew Delisle) Ottawa, Department of Northern Affairs and National Resources, March 23, 1966.

"Profile of the Week," (Wally Firth), News of the North, (Yellowknife, N.W.T.), March 13, 1969.

"Co-editor Appointed" (Morris Isaac), The Indian News, (Ottawa), May 1969.

Indian, Metis and Eskimo Leaders in Contemporary Canada, (Allen Sapp; Dr. Gilbert Monture: Simonie Michael; Andrew Delisle; Kahn-Tineta Horn; Annee Meekituk; Harold Cardinal; Sen. James Gladstone; Frank Calder; Dan George; David Courchene; Dr. Howard Adams; Jim Neilson; Len Marchand; Mary Cousins). Saskatoon, Curriculum Resources Centre, University of Saskatchewan, 1971,

"Bill Thomas, Treaty Indian Gets Important Post in Education," Kainai News, (Cardston, Alberta), May 15, 1971.

"I have two names, one is Rarihokwats from the Mohawk Nation, Bear Clan, and other is Jerry Gambill," The First Citizen, (Vancouver), Edition 13, p. 6.

"An interview with Buckley Petawabano," The First Citizen (Vancouver), Edition 14.

"Personality Profile: Adrian Hope," The Native People, (Edmonton) May 12, 1972 5(6)

"Profile: N. Doucette Heads Unique Union," The Forgotten People, (Ottawa) October 1972.

"Profile: Tony Belcourt," The Forgotten People, (Ottawa) Christmas 1972.

"Stan Daniels, President, Metis Association of Alberta," The Forgotten People (Ottawa) January 1973.

"Kermot Moore, President, Laurential Alliance of Metis and Non-Status Indians," The Forgotten People (Ottawa) January 1973.

PART V

RELIGIOUS BELIEFS -- EXPERIENCES, AND CEREMONIES

A   --   Religious Beliefs
B   --   Ceremonies
C   --   Other

A -- Religious Beliefs

Aberle, David F., The Peyote Religion Among the Navaho. New York.
Viking Fund Publications in Anthropology. 1966.

Barbeau, Charles Marius, Huron-Wyandot Mythology, Ottawa,
("Memoirs of the Ottawa Department of Mines," No. 80), 1915.

Barbeau, Charles Marius, "The Hydra Reborn in the New World," Art
Quarterly, (Detroit), 1949 12:156-64.

Barbeau, Charles Marius, Medicine-Men on the North Pacific Coast,
Ottawa, National Museum of Canada, Bulletin No. 152,
Anthropological Series No. 42, Department of Northern Affairs
and National Resources, 1958, 95 pp.

Benedict, Ruth Fulton, "The Concept of the Guardian Spirit in
North America," Memoirs of the American Anthropological
Association, (Lancaster, Pa.), 1923.

Boas, Franz, "The Doctrine of Souls and of Disease among the
Chinook Indians," Journal of American Folklore (New York),
1893, 6:39-43.

Boas, Franz, Indianische Sagen von der nore-pacifischen Kueste
Amerikas, Berlin, A. Asher and Co., 1895.

Boswell, Marion Joan, State and church and the Canadian Indian,
1867-1930, Ph D dissertation, University of Ottawa, (in
process).

Brown, Jennifer, "The cure and feeding of Windigos: a critique,"
American Anthropologist, February 1971, 73:20-22.

Brown, Joseph Epes, The Spiritual Legacy of the American Indian,
Lebanon, Pa., Pendle Hill Pamphlet No. 135, May, 1964, 32 pp.

Castaneda, Carlo, The Teachings of Don Juan: a Yaqui Way of
Knowledge, New York, Ballantine Books, 1970, 276 pp.

Castaneda, Carlo, "Further Conversations with Don Juan," Esquire,
March, 1971.

Castaneda, Carlo, A Separate Reality: Further Conversations With
Don Juan, Simon and Schuster Touchstone Paperback, 1971, 317
pp.

Codere, Helen, "The Swaixwe Myth of the Middle Fraser River,"
Journal of American Folklore (New York), 1948, 41:1-18.

Collier, Donald, "Conjuring among the Kiowa," *Primitive Man* (Washington, D.C.), 1944, 17:45-49.

Cooper, J.M., "The Shaking Tent Rite among Plains and Forest Algonquins," *Primitive Man* (Washington, D.C.), 1944, 17:60-84.

Dempsey, Hugh A., *The Blackfoot Ghost Dance*, Calgary, Glenbow Institute, 1968, 19 pp.

Dorsey, George Amos, "The Dwamish Indian Spirit Boat and its use," *Bulletin of the University of Pennsylvania Free Museum of Science and Art*, (Philadelphia) 1902, 3:227-238.

DuBois, Cora, "The 1970 Ghost Dance," *University of California Anthropological Records*, 1939.

Duesenberry, Verne, *The Montana Cree: a Study in Religious Persistence*, Almquist and Wikesell, 1962.

Garner, Bea Medicine, "The Use of Magic Among the Stoney Indians," Bozeman, unpublished manuscript, Department of Anthropology, University of Montana. c 1968 18 pp.

Garthson, Robert J.W., *The imperial process of attempted de-Indianization in British Upper-Canada to the year 1860: Protestant missionary-government co-operation in the destruction of the material bases of Indian culture and Indian response*, London, Ontario Ph M. dissertation, University of Waterloo, 1970.

Hale, H., *The Iroquois Book of Rites*, University of Toronto Press, 1963, 215 pp.

Hay, Thomas H. "The Windigo psychosis: psychodynamic, cultural and social factors in aberrant behaviour," *American Anthropologist*, February 1971, 73:1-19.

Hickerson, Harold, "Notes on the Post Contact Origin of the Midwiwin," *Ethnohistory*, 1962, 9:402-432.

Hill, Willard Williams, "The Navaho Indians and the Ghost Dance of 1890," *American Anthropologist*, 1944, 46:523-527.

Hodge, William H., "Navaho Pentecostalism," *Anthropological Quarterly*, 1964, 37:73-93.

Huel, Raymond, "Adrien-Gabriel Morice, O.M.I., brief sojourn in Saskatchewan," *Revue de l'Université d'Ottawa*, April-June 1971, 41:82-293.

Hungry Wolf, Adolt, *Good Medicine: Life in Harmony with Nature*, Golden, British Columbia, Good Medicine Books, 1970.

Hurt, Wesley R. Jr., "The Yankton Dakota Church: a Nationalistic Movement of Northern Plains Indians," in G.L. Dole and R.L. Carneiro, eds., *Essays in the Science of Culture in Honour of Leslie A. White*, New York, Thomas Y. Crowell, 1960, pp 269-287.

Johnston, Alexander, "The use of Native Plants by the Blackfoot Indians," _Alberta Historical Review_, 1960, 8:8-13.

Kehoe, Alice B., _Saskatchewan Indian Religious Beliefs_, Regina, Popular Series Number 7, Saskatchewan Museum of Natural History, March, 1963, 15 pp.

Keirstead, Charles Wesley, _The Church History of the Canadian North-West_, New Haven, Connecticut, Ph D. dissertation, Yale University, 1936, 550 pp.

LaBarre, Weston, _The Peyote Cult_, New Haven, Connecticut, Yale University Press, 1938 (reissued Shoe String Press, Hamden, Conn., 1964, 260 pp.)

LaBarre, Weston, et. al., "Statement on Peyote," _Science_, 1951, pp 582-583.

LaBarre, Weston, "Twenty Years of Peyote Studies," _Current Anthropology_, 1960, pp 45-60.

LaBarre, Weston, _The Ghost Dance: Origins of Religion_, Dell Publishing Co., (Delta Book), 1970.

Lesser, Alexander, "Cultural Significance of the Ghost Dance," _American Anthropologist_, 1933, pp 108-115.

Lowie, Robert H., "A trial of Shamans," in Elsie Clews Parsons, ed. _American Indian Life_, 1922, (University of Nebraska Press, 1967, pp 41-43).

Mead, Margaret, "The Mountain Arapesh, II. Supernaturalism," _Anthropological Papers of the American Museum of Natural History_, 1940, Volume 37, Part III, pp 317-451.

McKern, Sharon S. and W. Thomas, "The Peace Messiah," _Mankind_, Vol. 2, (Number 9), pp 59-69.

Mooney, James, "Sacred Formulas of the Cherokee," Washington, D.C., _7th Annual Report, Bureau of American Ethnology_, 1891.

Mooney, James, "The Ghost Dance Religion and the Sioux Outbreak of 1890," _14th Annual Report, Bureau of American Ethnology_ 1896 (reprinted University of Chicago Press, 1965).

Neihardt, John G., _Black Elk Speaks_, New York, 1932 (reprinted University of Nebraska Press, 1961).

O'Brodovich, Lloyd, and Steven Julius, "Plains Cree Sun Dance -- 1968," _The Western Canadian Journal of Anthropology_, 1969, 1:71-87.

Park, W.Z., _Shamanism in Western North America_, Evanston, Ill., Northwestern University Press, 1928, 166 pp.

Parker, Seymour, "Motives in Eskimo and Ojibwa Mythology," _Ethnology_, 1962, 1:516-523.

Prufer, O.H., "The Hopewell Cult," Scientific American, December, 1964, pp 90-102.

Rapoport, Robert N., "Changing Navajo Religious Values -- a Study of Christian Missions to the Rimrock Navajos," Papers of the Peabody Museum of American Archology and Ethnology, (reports of the Rimrock Project Values Series No. 2) Harvard University, Vol. 41, 1954, 152 pp.

Ridington, Robin, "The Anthropology of Experience," Paper presented at the Annual Meeting of the American Anthropological Association, 1969, 30 pp.

Ridington, Robin, "The Medicine Fight: An Instrument of Political Process Among the Beaver Indians," unpublished manuscript, Department of Anthropology, University of British Columbia, n.d. 18 pp.

Rohrl, Vivian J. "A nutritional factor in Windigo psychosis," American Anthropologist, February 1970, 72:97-101.

Savard, Reme, "A differenciation des activités secuelles et alimentaires (représentations mythiques esquimaudes et indiennes)," Anthropologica, 1965, n.s. 7:39-58.

Seton, Ernest Thompson and Julia M. Seton, The Gospel of the Redman:an Indian Bible, London, Mehuen and Co., 1937 (reprinted Seton Village Press, Seton Village, Sante Fe, New Mexico 1966).

Seton, Ernest Thompson and Julia M. Seton, The Gospel of the Redman: a Way of Life, New York, Thomas Gaus Sons Ltd., 1963.

Silverman, J., "Shamans and Acute Schizophrenia," American Anthropologist, 1967, pp 21-31.

Skinner, Alanson, "Little Wolf Joins the Medicine Lodge," in Elsie Clews Parsons, ed., American Indian Life, 1922 (University of Nebraska Press, 1967, pp 63-73).

Slobodin, Richard, "The Kutchin Indian Concept of Reincarnation," Paper presented at the Annual Meeting of the Canadian Sociology and Anthropological Association, York University, June 1969, 15 pp.

Slotin, J.S., The Peyote Religion, Glencoe, Ill., Free Press, 1956.

Spier, Leslie, "The Ghost Dance of 1870 Among the Klamath of Oregon," University of Washington Publications in Anthropology, 1927.

Spier, Leslie, The Prophet Dance of the Northwest and Its Derivatives: The Source of the Ghost Dance, ("General Series in Anthropology," No. 1.) Menasha, Wis., 1935.

Spindler, Louise Schauber, "Witchcraft in Menomini Acculturation," American Anthropologist, 1952, 54:593-602.

Stephen, A.M., "When John the Jeweler was Sick," in Elsie Clews Parsons, ed., American Indian Life, 1922 (University of Nebraska Press, 1967, pp 153-156).

Thomas, Robert M., The Mission Indians: A Study of Leadership and Cultural Change -- Ed. D. Thesis, University of California, Los Angeles, Calif., 1964.

Underhill, Ruth Murray, "Religion Among American Indians," The Annals of the American Academy of Political and Social Science, May, 1957, 311:127-136.

Underhill, Ruth Murray, Red Man's Religion: Beliefs and Practices of the Indians North of Mexico, University of Chicago Press, 1965.

Vogel, Virgil J., American Indian Medicine, Norman, University of Oklahoma Press, 1970, 583 pp.

Wallace, Anthony F.C., "Dreams and Wishes of the Soul: a Type of Psychoanalytic Theory Among the Seventeenth Century Iroquois," American Anthropologist, 1958, 60:234-248.

Wallace, Anthony F.C., The Death and Rebirth of the Seneca, New York, Alfred A. Knopf, 1970, 384 pp.

Wallace, Paul A.W., The White Roots of Peace, Port Washington, Long Island, New York, Ira J. Friedman, 1946, (Reissued 1968), 57 pp.

Waters, Frank, Book of the Hopi, Ballantine Books.

Wike, Joyce, "The Role of the Dead in North-West Coast Culture," in Sol Tax, ed., Indians Tribes of Aboriginal America: Selected Papers of the 29th International Congress of Americanists, New York, Cooper Square Pub., 1967, pp 97-103.

Wissler, Clark, "Smoking Star, A Blackfoot Shaman," in Elsie Clews Parsons, ed., American Indian Life, 1922 (University of Nebraska Press, 1967, pp 45-62).

Wood, Kerry, The Medicine Man, Red Deer, Alberta, n.d. 90 pp.

B -- Ceremonies

Barbeau, Charles Marius, Indian Days on the Western Prairie, Bulletin No. 163, Anthropological Series No. 46, National Museum of Canada, 1954 (reprinted, 1960, 112 pp.).

Corrigan, Samuel W., "The Plains Indian Pow-wows, Cultural Integration in Manitoba and Saskatchewan," Arctic, 1971.

Fenton, William N., "Masked Medicine Societies of the Iroquois," Washington, D.C., Smithsonian Report, 1940, pp. 397-430.

Fenton, William N., "Museum and Field Studies of Iroquois Masks and Ritualism," Smithsonian Report, 1940.

Fenton, William N., "Towanda Longhouse Ceremonies," Smithsonian Institution Bulletin, 1941.

Fenton, William N., "The Iroquois Eagle Dance," Bureau of American Ethnology Bulletin, 1953.

Hickerson, Harold, "The Socio-historical Significance of Two Chippewa Ceremonies," American Anthropologist, 1963, 65:67-85.

Houle, Robert, "False Face Society," Tawow (Ottawa) Autumn/Winter, 1970, 1:2-9.

Keller, H. Phyllis, Indian Dance Interpretations, Detroit, Mich. author. n.d. 21 pp.

Kurath, Gertrude Prokosch, Dance and Song Rituals of Six Nations Reserve, Ontario, Bulletin No. 220, Folklore Series No. 4, National Museum of Canada, 1969, 205 pp.

Nelson, N.C., "Wixi of the Shellmound People," in Elsie Clews Parsons, ed., American Indian Life 1922, (University of Nebraska Press, 1967, pp 273-288).

Parsons, Elsie Clews, and R.L. Beals, "The Sacred Clowns of the Pueblo and Mayo Yaaniqui Indians," American Anthropologist, 1939, pp 491-517.

Ridington, Robin, "Beaver Indian Dreaming and Singing," Anthropologica, 1971 n.s. 13:115-128.

Speck, Frank Gouldsmith, Midwinter Rites of the Cayuga Longhouse, Philadelphia, University of Pennyslvania Press, 1944.

Spier, Leslie, "Havasupia Days," in Elsie Clews Parsons, ed., American Indian Life, 1922, (University of Nebraska Press, 1967, pp 179-187).

Stewart, Julien H., "The Ceremonial Buffons of the American Indian," Michigan Academy of Sciences, 1930, pp 187-207.

Underhill, Ruth Murray, "Ceremonial Patterns in Greater Southwest," American Ethnological Society Memoir, 1948.

C -- Other

Angule, Jaime De., "The Background of the Religious Feeling in a Primitive Tribe," American Anthropologist, 1926, 28:352-60.

Barber, Bernard, "Acculturation and Messianic Movements," American Sociological Review, 1941, 6:663-68 (also in S.N. Eisenstadt, ed., Comparative Perspectives on Social Change, Little Brown, 1968).

Berkhofer, Robert F., _Salvation and the Savage: An Analysis of Protestant Missions and American Indian Response, 1787-1862_, Lexington, University of Kentucky Press, 1963.

Berkhofer, Robert F., "Protestants, Pagans and Sequences Among the North American Indians 1760-1860," _Ethnohistory_, Summer 1963, 10:201-232.

Dawber, Mark A., "Protestant Missions to the Indians in The United States," in Charles T. Loram and Thomas F. McIlwraith, eds., _The North American Indian Today_, University of Toronto Press, 1943, pp 98-109.

Hendry, Charles E., "Traplines and Beyond, Does the Church Really Care?: Towards an Assessment of the Work of the Anglican Church of Canada With Canada's Native People," Toronto, unpublished 1st draft, January, 1969, 42 pp.

Lanternari, Vittorio, _The Religions of the Oppressed_, New York, A Mentor Book Published by The New American Library, 1965, 254 pp.

Lavaque, Yvone, O.M.I., "Your brother is an Indian," _Indian Record_ (Winnipeg), July-August, 1972, 35:

Memorian, Brother, "Roman Catholic Missions in Canada," in Charles T. Loram and Thomas F. McIlwraith, eds., _The North American Indian Today_, University of Toronto Press, 1943, pp 90-97.

Pressly, Thomas J., "Freedom of Religion for the American Indian in the Twentieth Century," in Ralph W. Johnson, ed., _Studies in American Indian Law_, Georgetown University, June 1970, pp 285-325.

Savoie, Donat, ed., _Les Amerindiens du Nord-Ouest Canadien au 19e siècle, selon Emile Petitot, Volume I: Les Esquimaux Tchiglit_, Ottawa, Department of Indian Affairs and Northern Development, June 1970, 230 pp.

Savoie, Donat, ed., _Les Amerindiens du Nord-Ouest Canadien au 19e siècle, selon Emile Petitot, Volume II: Les Indiens Loucheux_, Ottawa, Department of Indian Affairs and Northern Development, 1970, 214 pp.

Tennelly, Rev. J.B., "Catholic Indian Missions in the United States," in Charles T. Loram and Thomas F. McIlwraith, eds., _The North American Indian Today_, University of Toronto Press, 1943, pp 81-89.

Wallace, Anthony, F.C., "Revitalization Movements," _American Anthropologist_, pp 264-280.

Wallis, Wilson Dallam, _Messiahs: their Role in Civilization_, Washington, D.C., American Council on Public Affairs, 1943.

Westgate, Rev. T.B.R., "The History, Policy and Problems of Protestant Missions to the Indians in Canada," in Charles T. Loram and Thomas F. McIlwraith, eds., _The North American Indian Today_, University of Toronto Press, 1943, pp 110-122.

Witt, Shirley Hill, "Nationalistic Trends Among American Indians in Stuart Levine and Nancy O. Lurie eds., <u>The American Indian Today</u>, Baltimore Md., Penguin Books, 1970, pp 93-127.

PART VI

ABORIGINAL RIGHTS AND TREATIES

A   --   Treaties, Canada
B   --   Discussion of Treaty Rights, Canada
          1.   Specific Legal Cases
C   --   Congressional action and dicussion, United States

A -- Treaties, Canada

Treaty of St. Germain, (New France, Acadia, Canada), March 29, 1632.

Treaty of Breda, (Acadia), 1667.

Treaty of Ryswick, 1697.

The submission and agreement of the eastern Indians at Fort William Henry in Pemmaguid, the 11th day of August, in fifth year of the reign of our Sovereign Lord and Lady, William and Mary, by the grace of God, of England, Scotland, France, and Ireland, King and Queen, Defenders of the Faith, etc., 1693.

Treaty of Utrecht, (Bay and Straits of Hudson, Nova Scotia, Acadia, Newfoundland, etc.), 1713.

"Treaty of 1713," at Portsmouth, in her Majesty's Province of New Hampshire, in New England, the thirteenth day of July, in the twelfth year of the reign of our Sovereign Lady Anne, by the Grace of God, of Great Britain, France, and Ireland, Queen, Defender of the Faith, etc.

"Treaty of 1717," Georgetown, on Arrowsick Island, in his Majesty's Province of the Massachussetts Bay in New England, the 12th day of August, 1717.

"Treaty No. 239, Articles of submission and agreement made at Boston, in New England," by Sanguaaram alias Loron Arexus, Francois Xavier and Meganumbe, delegates from Penobscott, Naridgwack, St. Johns, Cape Sables and other tribes inhabiting within his Majesty's territories of Nova Scotia or New England, December 15, 1725.

"Treaty, Micmac Indians of the Miramichi," June 17, 1749.

"Treaty at St. Johns, Chibucto Harbour," August 15, 1749.

"Articles of Peace, Chibucto, St. Johns," September 4, 1749.

"Treaty of Articles of Peace and Friendship Renewed, Mick Mack Indians," November 22, 1752.

"Treaty or articles of Peace and Friendship renewed December 6, 1752," (Annapolis, Halifax and St. Johns River).

"Treaty of Peace and Friendship concluded with the Delegates of the St. John and Passamaquody Tribe of Indians at Halifax," February, 1760.

"Micmac Treaty," March 10, 1760.

"Articles of Capitulation Between their Excellencies Major General Amherst, Commander in Chief of his Britannic Majesty's troops and forces in North-America, on the one part, and the Marquis de Vaudreuil, & Governor and Lieutenant-General for the King in Canada on the other," 1760.

"A Proclamation," Halifax, Nova Scotia, May 1762.

"The definitive Treaty of Peace and Friendship between his Britannic Majesty, the Most Christian King, and the King of Spain," 1763.

"Royal Proclamation of 7th October, 1763," Government of England.

"Gulf of St. Lawrence Treaty," Windsor, Nova Scotia, September 22, 1779.

"Treaty of Paris," (Great Britain and the United States), 1783.

"The Constitutional Act of 1791," in Adam Shortt, and Arthur G. Doughty, eds., Canadian Archives Constitutional Documents (1759-1791), Session Paper No. 18, J. de L. Tachi, 1918, pp. 1031-1051.

"Treaty of Amity Commerce and Navigation (Jay Treaty), 1794."

"Identure Between the Chippeway or Saulteaux Nations and of the Killistine or Cree Nations and The Honorable Thomas Earl of Selkirk," (1817), Government of England.

Robinson Treaty Made in the Year 1850 with the Ojibewa Indians of Lake Superior Conveying certain lands to the Crown (reprinted 1964, Ottawa).

"Vancouver Island Treaties," 1854.

Treaties 1 and 2 between Her Majesty The Queen and the Chippewa and Cree Indians of Manitoba and Country adjacent with adhesions (1871), (reprinted 1957, Ottawa).

Treaty No. 3 between Her Majesty The Queen and the Saulteaux Tribe of the Ojibeway Indians at the Northwest Angle on the Lake of the Woods with Adhesions, (1873), (reprinted 1957, Ottawa).

Treaty No. 4 between Her Majesty The Queen and the Cree and Saulteaux tribes of Indians at Qu'appelle and Fort Ellece (1874), (reprinted 1966, Ottawa).

Treaty No. 5 between Her Majesty The Queen and the Saulteaux and Swampy Cree Tribes of Indians at Beren's River and Norway House with Adhesions (1875), (reprinted 1969, Ottawa).

Treaty No. 6 between Her Majesty The Queen and the Plain and Wood Cree Indians and other tribes of Indians at Fort Carlton, Fort Pitt and Battle River with Adhesions (1876), (reprinted 1964, Ottawa).

Treaty and Supplementary Treaty No. 7 between Her Majesty The Queen and the Blackfeet and Other Indian Tribes (1877), (reprinted 1966, Ottawa).

Treaty No. 8 Made June 21, 1899, and Adhesions, Reports, etc., (1899), (reprinted 1969, Ottawa).

The James Bay Treaty -- Treaty No. 9 made in 1905 and 1906 and Adhesions Made in 1929 and 1930, (reprinted 1931, Ottawa).

Treaty No. 10 and Reports of Commissioners (1906), (reprinted 1966, Ottawa).

Treaty No. 11 (June 27, 1921) and Adhesion (July 17, 1922) with reports, etc. (1926), (reprinted 1967, Ottawa).

Treaty made October 31, 1923 between His Majesty the King and the Chippewa Indians of Christian Island, Georgina Island, and Rama, (reprinted 1967, Ottawa).

Treaty made November 15, 1923, between His Majesty the King and the Mississauga Indians of Rice Lake; Mud Lake; Scugog Lake and Alderville, (reprinted 1957, Ottawa).

The Treaties Between Her Majesty Queen Victoria and the Indians of British North America, The Provincial Committee on Minority Groups, and The Federation of Saskatchewan Indians, March 1961, 44 pp.

Deloria, Vine Jr., ed., Of Utmost Good Faith: The Case of the American Indian Against the Federal Government of the United States as Documented in Treaties, Speeches, Judical Rulings, Congressional Bills and Hearings from 1830 to the Present, Straight Arrow Books, 1971, (New York, Bantam Books, 1972, 402 pp.).

Morris, Alexander, The Treaties of Canada with the Indians of Manitoba and the Northwest Territories including the negotiations on which they were based and other information relating thereto. Toronto, Belford, Clarke and Co., 1880 (reprinted Toronto, Coles Publishing Co. 1971).

B -- Discussion of Aboriginal and Treaty Rights, Canada

Aalborg, Gordon (reporter), "Metis get 4,150 acres in aboriginal claims," The Edmonton Journal, July 20, 1972.

Alvord, Clarence Walworth, "The Genesis of The Proclamation of 1763," Michigan Pioneer and Historical Society, (Lansing), 1908, 36:20-52.

Angers, Jean-Claude, "Indians-Federal and Provincial Statutes-Treaty Rights -Hunting and Fishing," University of New Brunswick Law Journal, 1966, 15:66-69.

Avali-Oliver, Philip B., "A Statement on the Rights of Minorities Within Canada and a Plea for Constitutional Protection of the Rights of the Native People of Canada to the Special Joint Committee of the Senate and the House of Commons on the Constitution of Canada," Trois-Rivieres, March 16, 1971, pp. 78-83.

Battle, Robert F., "Address to the Manitoba and North Dakota International Symposium on the Legal Rights of Indians, Grand Forks, North Dakota," Ottawa, Department of Indian Affairs and Northern Development, March 7, 1969, 20 pp.

Beattie, Jessie Louis, The Split in the Sky, Chronicle of the Six Nations of the Iroquois Confederation, Toronto, Ryerson Press, 1960, 246 pp.

Benedict, Ernest, "Brief Presented on Behalf of the Union of Ontario Indians to the Special Joint Committee of the Senate and of the House of Commons on the Constitution of Canada," Toronto, December 7, 1970, pp. 52-60.

Braddock, John, "Indian reserves; how long will they last?, The Maliseet dilemma," The Atlantic Advocate, (Fredericton, N.B.), December 1965, 56(4):50-54.

Brun, Henri, "The Indian title to Quebec territory," Les cahiers de droit, 1969, 10:417-474.

Cail, Robert Edgar, Disposal of Crown Lands in British Columbia 1871-1913, Master's Thesis, (Department of History) University of British Columbia, September, 1956, 526 pp.

Cameron, E.R., "A Review of the Cases Dealing with Indian Lands in Canada Based Upon the St. Catherines Milling and Lumber Company v. The Queen, 13 S.C.R. 577, 14 App. Css. 46," Canada Supreme Court Reports.

Chretien, Hon. Jean, "Brief Presented to the Special Joint Committee of the Senate and of the House of Commons on the Constitution of Canada," December 3, 1970, pp. 4-37.

Conn, Hugh R., "Brief on Indian Treaties as Related to Wildlife and Fishery Resources," Joint Committee of the Senate and the House of Commons on Indian Affairs, Minutes of Proceedings and Evidence, No. 11, May 11, 1961.

Conn, Hugh R., "Indian treaties and the Game and Fishery Laws: a summary," unpublished manuscript, n.d. 9 pp.

Conn, Hugh R., "A paper identifying the inconsistencies and discrepancies in the application of the principles of the Royal Proclamation of 1763 to the question of hunting and fishing rights for the Indians of Canada," unpublished manuscript, n.d. 14 pp.

Conn, Hugh R., "Integrity of the Territory of the Province of Quebec," Ottawa, unpublished manuscript, n.d. 11 pp.

Cork, Ella, The worst of the bargain: concerning the dilemmas inherited from their forefathers along with their lands by the Iroquois Nation of the Canadian Grand River reserve, San Jacinto, California, Foundation for Social Research 1962, 196 pp.

Courchene, Dave, "Address," Treaty Centennial Commorations, Lower Fort Garry, Winnipeg, August 2, 1971, 11 pp.

Courchene, Dave, "Address," St. James Collegiate, Winnipeg, January 12, 1971, 14 pp.

Cumming, Peter A., "Why Eskimos Fear Rights Not Protected by Ottawa," The Globe and Mail, (Toronto), August 1, 1970.

Cumming, Peter A., "Indian Rights -- A Century of Oppression," (in substance a reprint of an article in The Globe and Mail, (Toronto), February 24, 1969), Indian-Eskimo Association of Canada, May 1969, 10 pp.

Cumming, Peter A., "Native Rights -- Contemporary Issues," Report of Discussions: Legal Status of Indians in the Maritimes, Halifax, October 16, 1970, 24-29.

Cumming, Peter A., "Brief Presented on Behalf of the Indian-Eskimo Association of Canada to the Special Joint Committee of the Senate and the House of Commons on the Constitution of Canada," Ottawa, May 13, 1971, pp. 4-28.

Dallaire, Jacques, "It is time to safeguard the Indians' rights," (discussion of hunting and fishing rights brief presented by the Association of Quebec Indians) n.d.

Delisle, Andrew Tanahokate, Michael McKenzie and Max 'one-onti' Gros-Louis, "Brief on Indians of Quebec territorial rights," Montreal, submitted to the Commission d'étude sur l'integrité du Territoire du Québec (reprinted in recherches amerindiennes au quebec, November 1972, 2:13-27).

De Mestral, A.L.C., "Michael Sikyea v. Her Majesty The Queen," McGill Law Journal, 1965, 11:168-173.

De Puy, Henry Farr, Bibliography of the English Colonial Treaties with the American Indians, New York, Printed for Lennox Club, 1917, 109 pp.

Doirne, Chief Peter R., "Letter; Six Nations Iroquois Confederacy to Honourable James Chuter, Home Secretary, London, England," unpublished, February 1952.

Doucette, Noel, "Brief presented on Behalf of the Union of Nova Scotia Indians to the Special Joint Committee of the Senate and of the House of Commons on the Constitution of Canada," Sydney, N.S., October 21, 1970, pp. 3-14.

Duran, James A., Jr., "Canisius Professor Contends St. Regis Indians Are Right, Jay Treaty Never Abrogated," unpublished manuscript, ca 1969, 3 pp.

Duran, James A. Jr., Walter Currie, Walter P. Deiter, Douglas Sanders, Nancy O. Lurie and William Fox, "Panel Discussion on Canadian Indian Treaty and Aboriginal Rights," Ottawa, Carleton University, May 7, 1970, 34 pp.

Ewing, A.F., J.M. Douglas and E.G. Braithwait, "Commission Into the Conditions of the Half-breed Population in the Province of Alberta," Edmonton, Province of Alberta, 1936, 15 pp.

Finnie, Richard (reporter), "Treaty Time at Fort Rae," The Beaver, May, 1940, 10-13.

Francis, Anthony, "Submissions by the Union of New Brunswick Indians to the Special Joint Committee of the Senate and the House of Commons on the Constitution of Canada," Ottawa, June 15, 1971, pp. 68-74.

Gambill, Jerry T., "Controversy: Hunting and Fishing Rights of Indians of Ontario, How Our Political Considerations Deny Justice," Cornwall, unpublished manuscript, May, 1968, 11 pp.

Ghobashy, Omar Z., The Caughnawaga Indians and the St. Lawrence Seaway, New York, Devin-Adair Company, 1961, 137 pp.

Goodleaf, Chief Frank, "Letter: to Members of Parliament," unpublished, August 30, 1950, 4 pp.

Gorman, Mrs. John C., "The Legal Status of the Canadian Indian," Paper presented at the Annual Meeting of The Canadian Bar Association, Ottawa, 1955, 17 pp.

Graham, W.R., "Indian treaties and the settlement of the Northwest," Saskatchewan History, 1949, 19:

Hall, Hon Mr. Justice, "Frank Calder, et al, v Attorney-General of British Columbia and The Committee for the Original People's Entitlements," Ottawa, The Supreme Court of Canada, January 31, 1973, 70 pp.

Harper, Allan G., "Canada's Indian Administration: The Treaty System," America Indigena, April, 1947, 7:129-148.

Hodges, Percy G. and F.D. Noonan, Saskatchewan Metis, brief on investigation into the legal equitable and moral claims of the Metis people of Saskatchewan in relation to the extinguishment of the Indian title, July 1943, 136 pp.

Hooper, Anthony, "Aboriginal Title -- Has it Been Extinguished in the Northwest Territories?" Quebec, unpublished manuscript, Laval University, 1969, 116 pp.

Hunt, Richard P., "The whiporwill cries, the fox whimpers, and misfortune follows, says a Seneca tradition. These days, threatened by a dam, the Seneca Nations fears the worst -- the loss of its land and of its soul," New York Times Magazine, June 10, 1962, pp. 14-15, 59-60.

Hutchins, Peter W., "Draft report on the status of the Oka Indians and their lands," Ottawa, unpublished manuscript, September 1972, 17 pp.

Inglis, Gordon Bahan, The Canadian Indian Reserve: community, population, and social system, Ph.D. dissertation, University of British Columbia, 1970.

Johnston, Charles M., "Joseph Brant, The Grand River Lands and the Northwest Crisis," Ontario History Quarterly, 1963, 55:267-282.

Johnston, Charles M., ed., The valley of the Six Nations. A collection of documents on the Indian lands of the Grand River, University of Toronto Press, (Ontario series of the Champlain Society, vol. 7), 1964, 344 pp.

Judson, Hon. Mr. Justice, "Frank Calder, et. al., v Attorney-General of British Columbia and The Committee for the Original People's Entitlement," Ottawa, The Supreme Court of Canada, January 31, 1973, 28 pp.

Keeper, Cyril George, "A survey of commissions of Inquiry and investigation relating to land claims of people of Native ancestry in Canada," Ottawa, unpublished manuscript, July 1969, 18 pp.

Lacoste, Sir Alexander, The Seminary of Montreal: Their Rights and Title, St. Hyacinthe, Courrier de St. Hyacinthe Power Presses, 1880, 248 pp.

Laird, Hon. David, "North-West Indian Treaties," in Our Indian Treaties, Historical and Scientific Society of Manitoba, Transaction No. 66, The Manitoba Free Press, 1905, pp. 3-11.

Larner, Jack and James O'Reilly, Aboriginal People of Canada and Their Environment, Brief submitted to the United Nations Conference on the Environment, Stockholm Sweden, National Indian Brotherhood, June, 1972.

Lysyk, Ken, "Report on the British Columbia Land Question in Relation to Proposed Indian Claims Legislation," Ottawa, Department of Indian Affairs and Northern Development, September, 1967, 107 pp.

Lysyk, Ken, "The unique constitutional position of the Canadian Indian," Canadian Bar Review, September, 1967, 45:513-553.

MacKenzie, N.A.M., "Indians and Treaties in Law," The Canadian Bar Review, October, 1929, 8:561-568.

McInnes, R.W., "Indians Treaties and Related Disputes," Faculty of Law Review, (University of Toronto), c 1969, pp. 52-71.

McInnes, T.R.E., Report on the Indian Title in Canada With Special Reference to British Columbia, House of Commons, Sessional Paper No. 47, Ottawa, 1914, 107 pp.

McNelly, Peter (reporter), "He Paid as Little as Possible for Land: Douglas Chiselled Indians with Legal Treaties," Victoria, Daily Times, September 21, 1971.

Manuel, Chief George, "Brief Presented on Behalf of the National Indian Brotherhood to the Special Joint Committee of the Senate and the House of Commons on the Constitution of Canada," Ottawa, June 15, 1971, pp 3-15, 56-67.

Manuel, Chief George, "Original rights and the Native people," recherches amerindiennes au quebec, November 1972, 2:29-31.

Mickenberg, Neil H., "Aboriginal Rights in Canada and the United States," Osgoode Hall Law Journal, August, 1971, 9:119-156.

Montgomery, Malcolm, "The Legal Status of the Six Nations Indians in Canada," Ontario History Quarterly, 1963, 55:93-105.

Montgomery, Malcolm, "Historiography of the Iroquois Indians, 1925-1963," Ontario History Quarterly, 1963, 55:247-257.

Montgomery, Malcolm, "The Six Nations Indians and the MacDonald Franchise," Ontario History Quarterly, 1965, 57:13-25.

Morris, James Lewis, Indians of Ontario, Ontario, Department of Lands and Forests, 1943, 75 pp.

Nelson, John C., Descriptions and Plans of Certain Indian Reserves in the Province of Manitoba and the North-West Territories, Regina, Department of Indian Affairs, May, 1887, 113 pp.

Palmer, C.A.G., "Annotation: The Unilateral Abrogation of Indian and Eskimo Treaty Rights," Criminal Reports, 1966, 47:395-400.

Pigeon, Louis-Philippe, "The Bill of Rights and the B.N.A. Act," Canadian Bar Review, 1959, 37:

Pigeon, Hon. Mr. Justice Louis-Philippe, "Frank Calder, et. al., v Attorney-General of British Columbia and The Committee for the Original People's Entitlement," Ottawa, The Supreme Court of Canada, January 31, 1973, 6 pp.

Raby, Stewart, "Indian Treaty No. 5 and The Pas Agency, Saskatchewan, N.W.T.," Saskatchewan History, August 1972, 25:92-114.

Raby, Stewart, "Indian land surrenders in southern Saskatchewan," Ottawa, unpublished manuscript, November 1972, 39 pp.

Robertson, Heather, "One hundred years after the treaties: should the conquered celebrate," Canadian Dimension, June-July, 1970.

Rubin, Abraham, "Brief Presented on Behalf of the Committee for the Original Peoples Entitlement, The Northwest Territories, to the Special Joint Committee of the Senate and of the House of Commons on the Constitution of Canada, Inuvik, N.W.T.," June 10, 1971, pp 23-48.

Sampat-Metha, Ramdeo, The Jay Treaty as it affects North American Indians (The International Boundary between the U.S.A. and Canada), Ottawa, Beauregard Press, 1972, 20 pp.

Sanders, Douglas Edmond, et. al., Native Rights in Canada: Report on Research Project on Treaty and Aboriginal Rights of Canadian Indians and Eskimos, Toronto, Indian-Eskimo Association of Canada, 1969, 205 pp.

Sanders, Douglas Esmond, "The new Indian policy and Native Claims," Address to the Progressive Conservative Policy Conference, Niagara Falls, Ontario, October 1969.

Sanders, Douglas Esmond, "Native Rights," Report of Discussions: Legal Status of Indians in the Maritimes, Halifax, October 16, 1970, 3-23.

Sanders, Douglas Esmond, "Indian Law Center," Windsor, unpublished brief Presented to Carleton University, 1970, 23 pp.

Sanders, Douglas Esmond, "Native Hunting and Fishing Rights," Ottawa unpublished manuscript, May, 1972, 39 pp.

Sanders, Douglas Esmond, "Group rights -- the constitutional position of the Canadian Indian," Address to the Committee of Constitutional Law Teachers, March 1972.

Sanders, Douglas Esmond and P. Taylor, "Annotated bibliography of Canadian Indian case law, 1867-1972," Ottawa, unpublished manuscript, June 1972.

Sanders, Douglas Esmond, "The foundations of Canadian Indian Law after 1867," Ottawa, unpublished manuscript, October 1972.

Scott, Rev. William, "Letters to the Editor of the Daily Witness: The Oka Indian Question," April 17, 1883.

Scott, Rev. William, Report Relating to the Affairs of the Oka Indians Made to the Superintendent General of Indian Affairs, Ottawa, MacLean, Rogers and Co., 1883, 74 pp.

Shipley, Nan, "Twilight of the Treaties," Queen's Quarterly, n.d.

Snow, Alpheus Henty, The Question of Aborigines in the Law and Practice of Nations, New York, G.P. Putman's Sons, 1921.

Snyderman, George S., "No 2, Concepts of land ownership among the Iroquois and their neighbours," in William N. Fenton, ed., Symposium on local diversity in Iroquois culture, Washington, D.C., Smithsonian Institution, Bureau of American Ethnology, Bulletin 149, 1951, pp. 15-34.

Staats, Howard E., "Some Aspects of the Legal Status of Canadian Indians," Osgoode Hall Law Journal, April, 1964, 3:36-51 (reprinted by Indian-Eskimo Association of Canada, Toronto, 1971, 22 pp.)

Stanley, George F.G., "The Indian Problem: The Treaties," in The Birth of Western Canada: a History of the Riel Rebellions, University of Toronto Press, 1936, Chapter 10, pp. 194-215.

Stanley, George F.G., "The Indian Problem: The Reserves," in The Birth of Western Canada: a History of the Riel Rebellions, University of Toronto Press, 1936, Chapter 11, pp 216-242.

Stanley, George F.G., "The First Indian 'Reserves' in Canada," Revue d'Histoire de l'Amérique française, September 1950, 4:178-210.

Steen, Marcus Van, "Indians insist: 'We are not Canadians'," Canada Month, (Montreal), July 1963.

Surtees, Robert J., "The Development of an Indian Reserve Policy in Canada," Quarterly Journal of the Ontario Historical Society, June 1969, pp. 87-98.

Thompson, Andrew T., "Report by Col. Andrew T. Thompson, Commissioner, to investigate and enquire into the affairs of the Six Nations Indians, 1923," Ottawa, Department of Indian Affairs, 1924, 26 pp.

Tyndall, Donna, "Brief Presented on Behalf of the Union of British Columbia Indian Chiefs to the Special Joint Committee of the Senate and of the House of Commons on the Constitution of Canada," Vancouver, January 8, 1971, pp. 77-92.

White, James, Boundary Disputes and Treaties, Toronto, Glasgow, Brook and Co., 1914, 917 pp.

Whiteside, Don, "Material in Sessional Papers 1867-1925 Relating to Non-Status Indians and Half-Breeds," Ottawa, unpublished manuscript, November 24, 1972, 7 pp.

Whiteside, Don, "Brief bibliography of articles in the press, etc., on the Cornwall (Akwesasne) Bridge blockade," Ottawa, National Indian Brotherhood, February 22, 1973. 6 pp.

Williams, A.S., R.V. Sinclair and U. McFadden, Report of Commissioners (Re-Chippewa Indians and Mississauga Indians) to the Superintendent General of Indians Affairs, Ottawa, Ottawa, December 1, 1923, 17 pp.

Woods, Doris, "Indian Claims Act Commission," unpublished memorandum, Department of Secretary of State, September 24, 1969, 1 p.

Miscellaneous Reports
by Date of Publication

"Correspondence between the Secretary of State for the Colonies and Governor Douglas," (enclosure from The Aborigines Protection Society) 1858-1861, 15 pp.

"An Act to provide for the extinction of feudal and seignourial
rights and surthens on land held a Titre de Fief and a Titre de
Cens, in the Province of Lower Canada; and for the gradual
conversion of those tensures into the tenure of free and common
soccage; and for other purposed relating to the said Province,"
Statutes United Kingdom Revised, 5 George 4 Cap 59, June 22,
1825.

Papers Connected with the Indian Land Question, 1850-1875,
Victoria, British Columbia, Richard Wolfenden, 1875, 186 pp.

"Indians Under the Robinson Treaty," House of Commons Debates,
March 8, 1886, pp. 62-65.

"Memorandum re: Gun Shot Treaty for 1787, to Deputy Superintendent
General," Ottawa, unpublished, Department of Indian Affairs,
November 25, 1904, 1 pp.

"Report of the Committee of the Privy Council, approved by the
Governor General on the 20th July, 1906," (land in
Saskatchewan, and Alberta).

"Report of the Committee of the Privy Council, approved by the
Governor General on the 26th November, 1907," (land in
Saskatchewan, and Alberta).

Indian Treaties and Surrenders from 1680 to 1890, Ottawa, King's
Printer, vols. 1 and 2, 1905, vol. 3, 1912.

Report of the Royal Commission on Indian Affairs for the Province
of British Columbia, (Under Order-in-Council dated 10th day of
June, 1913) British Columbia, 1916, 29 pp.

"Certified copy of a Report of the Committee of the Privy Council,
approved by His Excellency the Governor General on the 14th
March, 1921".

House of Commons, Special Committee of the Senate and the House of
Commons, meeting in Joint Session to Inquire into the Claims of
the Allied Indian Tribes of British Columbia, as set forth in
their petition submitted to Parliament in June 1926, Ottawa,
King's Printer, 1927.

"Report of the Royal Commission Appointed to Investigate the
Unfulfilled Provisions of Treaties 8 and 11 as They Apply to
the Indians of the Mackenzie District," 1959, 10 pp.

Minutes of Proceedings and Evidence, Joint Committee of the Senate
and the House of Commons on Indian Affairs, May 11, 1961.

"Summary of Submissions on the Indian Claims Bill C-130,"
Department of Indian Affairs and Northern Development, 1964-
1965.

Application of the Mohawk Nation of the Grand River Against
Canada, as Successor of Great Britain, The Government of the
Mohawk Nation of the Grand River, December 1966, 40 pp.

"Mémoire sur le droit de chasse et de pêche des Indiens de la province de Québec," unpublished manuscript, Indian Association of Quebec, 1967, 19 pp.

"The legalities of being Indian: an examination of the Indian Act, Indian Treaties, Claims, Rights, Provincial Laws and on-legislative policies which affect Indians in Canada," Ottawa, Company of Young Canadians, 1967.

"Indian hunting rights and the Migratory Birds Convention Act," Brief to the Government of Canada, Toronto, Indian-Eskimo Association of Canada, July 1967, 15 pp.

"This is one wrong to Indians Canada can, and should, right," (bridge blockade) editorial, Standard-Freeholder (Cornwall), December 10, 1968.

"The Jay Treaty," Ottawa, Department of Indian Affairs and Northern Development, ca 1968, 2 pp.

"Notes from discussions with Mr. Hugh Conn," Ottawa, unpublished manuscript, National Indian Brotherhood's National Committee on Indian Rights and Treaties, 1969, 7 pp.

"Terms of the Indian Claims Commission," Minutes of a meeting of the Committee of the Privy Council, approved by His Excellency the Governor General December 19, 1969.

"The Indian Claims Commission," Selections from speeches by Ministers of Indian Affairs and senior Departmental officials, Department of Indian Affairs and Northern Development, 1969, 1 p.

"Reasons for Judgment of the Honourable Mr. Justice MacLean, Court of Appeal, Between the Corporation of the District of Surrey, and the Local Board of Health of the Municipality of Surrey, (Respondents) and Peace Arch Enterprises Ltd. and Surfside Recreations Ltd. (Appellants), Vancouver, British Columbia, April 22, 1970, 10 pp.

"No aboriginal rights for Canadian Indian," (Prime Minister) The Globe and Mail, (Toronto), August 11, 1969.

"Jurisprudence as it Affects Indian Treaties and Claims," unpublished manuscript, 1970, 4 pp.

"National Committee on Indian Rights and Treaties," Resolutions passed by the Assembly of the National Indian Brotherhood, March 27, 1970, 6 pp.

"Indian Affairs -- Claims Commission Inclusion of Aboriginal and Treaty Rights in Terms of Reference," House of Commons Debates, October 6, 1970, 8853-8854.

"The Metis people and the land question in Alberta," Brief to the Government of Alberta, Edmonton, Metis Association of Alberta, 1971 19 pp.

"Tax Liability of Caughnawaga Band and Members-Situs of Income," Brief presented to the Hon. Herbert E. Gray, Minister of National Revenue, by Martineau, Walker, Allison, Beaulieu, Phelan and MacKell, Advocates, Montreal, January 15, 1971.

"A brief on the Migratory Birds Convention Act," Toronto, The Union of Ontario Indians, February 5, 1971.

"National Committee on Indian Rights and Treaties, Report on Activities for the Period from February 1970 through April 15, 1971," Ottawa, National Indian Brotherhood, 1971.

"The New Treaty Map," Ottawa, National Indian Brotherhood, July 13, 1971, 2 pp.

Treaty Days (excerpt from Wahbung), Winnipeg, Manitoba Indian Brotherhood, August 1971, 58 pp.

"Summary of Minutes of Meeting to discuss and define Aboriginal Title," Ottawa, National Indian Brotherhood, August 1971.

"Aboriginal Title," Ottawa, National Indian Brotherhood, September 18, 1971 (revised) 13 pp.

Claim Based on Native Title, Submission to the Prime Minister and Government of Canada by the Union of British Columbia Indian Chiefs, Vancouver, B.C., December 1971, (presented July 6, 1972) 62 pp.

"Indian Affairs: Conviction of Indian under game laws of Alberta -- request for Aid in appeal to Supreme Court," House of Commons Debates, December 10, 1971, 115:10354.

"Indian Affairs -- Request for Statement on Action to Protect Rights, in Relation to James Bay Hydroelectric Project," House of Commons Debates, May 4, 1972, 116:1926-1927.

"Indian Affairs -- Northwest Territories -- Inquiry as to cash offer to Settle Aboriginal Rights," House of Commons Debates, May 18, 1972, 116:2384.

"Indian Affairs -- James Bay Hydroelectric Project -- Rights of Natives," House of Commons Debates, May 18, 1972, 116:2384-2385.

"Minister told 'Return land or else'," Ontario Native Examiner, (Toronto), May-June, 1972, 1(4):1.

"Afton Band Fights Fishing Rights," MicMac News (Sidney, N.S.), June 1972, 2(6):7.

"A Proposal to the Government of Canada Regarding Metis and Non-Status Indian Land Claims," Brief submitted to the Hon. Gerard Pelletier, P.C., M.P., Department of the Secretary of State, Native Council of Canada, June 27, 1972, 6 pp.

"A summary of the nature, basis and extent of the claim based on Indian title as developed for the Union of British Columbia

Indian Chiefs," Vancouver, unpublished manuscript, July 6, 1972.

"2 Indian nations claim their border rights violated," Toronto Star, August 24, 1972.

"Metis and non-status Indian land claims a suggested approach for development of a research program design," Ottawa, unpublished manuscript, Native Council of Canada, November 1972.

"The Dorion Report and its implications for the Eskimos of New Quebec," Ottawa, unpublished manuscript, North Science Research Centre, Department of Indian Affairs and Northern Development, November 1972, 12 pp.

A proposal for progress, position paper, Brief submitted to Hon. Peter Lougheed Premier of Alberta, Metis Associations of Alberta, January 2, 1973, 55 pp.

"Indians have more land rights than he thought, Trudeau says," The Globe and Mail, (Toronto), February 2, 1973.

Together today for our children tomorrow: a statement of grievances and an approach to settlement by the Yukon Native Brotherhood, Whitehorse, Yukon Native Brotherhood, January 1973.

"Cash, land settlement and royalties: P.M. agrees to negotiate claims of Yukon Indians," The Globe and Mail, (Toronto), February 15, 1973.

Specific Legal Cases

Campbell v. Hall, Judicial Committee of the Privy Council, November 1774, pp. 1-8. (Duty upon sugar imported from Grenada.)

The St. Catherine's Milling and Lumber Company and The Queen, Supreme Court of Canada, June 20, 1887, pp. 577-611.

St. Catherine's Milling and Lumber Company v. The Queen, appeal Judicial Committee of the Privy Council, December 12, 1888, pp. 14-35. (Land claim, Ontario v. the Crown.)

Angus Corinthe and Others (Plaintiffs) and Ecclesiastics of the Seminary of St. Sulpice of Montreal (Defendants) on Appeal, July 15, 1921, pp. House of Lords and Privy Council, pp. 872-879. (Oka land claim.)

Sero v. Gault, Ontario Supreme Court, March 20, 1921, pp. 327-333. (Fishing on reserve.)

Rex v. Syliboy Appeal, Inverness County Court, Nova Scotia, September 10, 1928, p. 307-315. (Hunting and trapping.)

Rex v. Wesley, Alberta Supreme Court, June 6, 1932, pp. 775-791. (Game Act.)

"Point v. Dibble Construction Co. Ltd., et. al.," Ontario Reports, January 30, 1934, (Road Construction St. Regis Reserve).

"Factum Presented to the Supreme Court of Canada by The Attorney-General of Canada: Miller v. The King, 1950," (Flooding of lands).

Regina v. Strongquill, Saskatchewan Court of Appeal, March 13, 1953, pp 248-272. (Game Act.)

Skiyea v. The Queen, Appeal, Supreme Court of Canada, October 6, 1964, pp 80-84. (Duck hunting out of season.)

Regina v. White and Bob, British Columbia Court of Appeal, December 15, 1964, pp. 614-66 (Game Act).

Regina v. George, Appeal, Supreme Court of Canada, January 25, 1968, pp 387-98. (Migratory Bird Regulations.)

Regina v. Johnston, Saskatchewan Court of Appeal, March 17, 1966, pp. 749-754. (Failure to pay hospital tax.)

Daniel v. The Queen, Appeal, Supreme Court of Canada, April 29, 1968, pp. 1-25. (Migratory Bird Convention Act.)

C. Congressional Action and Discussion, United States

Ames, David W. and Burton R. Fisher, "The Menominee Termination Crisis: Barriers in the Way of a Rapid Cultural Transition," Human Organization, 1959, 18:110-111.

Barney, Ralph A., "Some Legal Problems Under the Indian Claims Commission Act," The Federal Bar Journal, 1960, 20:235-239.

Block, William E. Jr., "Alaskan Native Claims," Natural Resources Lawyer, April, 1971, 4:223-250.

C   , W.F. Jr., "The Constitutional Rights of the American Tribal Indian," Virginia Law Review, 1965, 51:121-142.

Cohen, Felix S., et. al., Handbook of Federal Indian Law, Washington, D.C., U.S. Government Printing Office, 1942.

DuMars, Charles T., "Indictment Under the 'Major Crimes Act' -- An Exercise in Unfairness and Unconstitutionality," Arizona Law Review, Winter 1968, 10:691-705.

Edgerton, R.B., "Menominee Termination: Observations on the End of a Tribe," Human Organization, 1962, 21:10-16.

Forbes, Jack D., "The Constitutional Powers of the U.S. Government in Indian Affairs: a Preliminary Sketch," The Warpath, (San Francisco), 1970, 2:4-5.

Haas, Theodore H., The Indian and the law, -1, Washington, D.C., Tribal relations pamphlets, 2, United States Indian Service, 1949, 34 pp.

Haas, Theodore H., The Indians and the law, -2, Washington, D.C., Tribal relations pamphlets, 3, United States Indian Service, 1949, 35 pp.

Holland, N. Huntley, "The Last Days -- An Inquiry Into the Proposed Colville Termination," in Ralph W. Johnson, ed., Studies in American Indian Law, Volume 2, University of Washington, Seattle, 1971, 316-402.

LaClair, Leo, "Muckleshoot Fishing Rights Question," in Ralph W. Johnson, ed., Studies in American Indian Law, Volume 2, University of Washington, Seattle, 1971, pp. 256-315.

LaFarge, Oliver, "Termination of Federal Supervision: Disintegration of the American Indians," The Annals of the American Academy of Political and Social Science, May, 1957, 311:41-46.

Lurie, Nancy Oestreich, "The Indian Claims Commission Act," The Annals of the American Academy of Political and Social Science, 1963, :56-70.

Lurie, Nancy Oestreich, "Anthropologists in the U.S. and the Indian Claims Commission," Paper presented at the AES-WHAS Meetings, Ottawa, May 1970, 13 pp.

McGimpsey, Earl R., "Indian Tribal Sovereignty," in Ralph W. Johnson, ed., Studies in American Indian Law, VOlume 2, University of Washington, Seattle, 1971, pp. 1-75.

McLoone, John J., "Indian Hunting and Fishing Rights," Arizona Law Review, Winter 1968, 10:725-739.

Morton, Rogers B., "Letter to the President: Draft Bill to Provide for the settlement of certain land claims of Alaska natives, and for other purposes," Washington, D.C., United States Department of the Interior, Office of the Secretary, April 5, 1971.

O'Brien, John and Donna Gill (reporters), "Termination Brings Instant Poverty," Chicago Tribune, August 26, 1971 (reprinted in Akwesasne Notes, Early Autumn, 1971, 3:18).

Olguin, John Phillip, "Where Does the 'Justified' Resentment Begin?; An Indian Viewpoint on the Land controversy," New Mexico Business, J. 1967, 20:11-16.

Peterson, Rod, "The History, Meaning, and Effect of Termination of Federal Supervision over Indian Reservations," in Ralph W. Johnson, ed., Studies in American Indian Law, Georgetown University, June 1970, pp. 1-47.

Reiblich, G. Kenneth, "Indian Rights Under the Civil Rights Act of 1968," Arizona Law Review, Winter 1968, 10:617-648.

Royce, Charles, ed., Indian Land Sessions in the United States, Washington, D.C., Eighteenth Annual Report of the Bureau of American Ethnology, 1896-97, Part 2, 1899, pp. 527-643.

Sloan, Marilyn, "The Indian Bill of Rights," in Ralph W. Johnson, ed., Studies in American Indian Law, Georgetown University, June, 1970, pp. 88-149.

Trimble, Charles E., "Pyramid Lake: a Symbol of Indian Water Rights," The Sentinel, (U.S.), Winter, 1971, pp. 4-6.

Vogel, Bart, "Who is an Indian in Federal Indian Law," In Ralph W. Johnson, ed., Studies in American Indian Law, Georgetown Unviersity, June 1970, pp. 48-87.

Wagner, Ruth Ellen, "Indian Rights Secured by Treaties: a Survey of Remedies," in Ralph W. Johnson, ed., Studies in American Indian Law, Volume 2, University of Washington, Seattle, 1971, pp. 200-255.

Wallen, Woodrow, "Indian Hunting and Fishing Rights: Northwest Developments," in Ralph W. Johnson, ed., Studies in American Indian Law, Georgetown University, June 1970, pp. 375-422.

Watkins, Arthur V., "Termination of Federal Supervision: The Removal of Restrictions Over Indian Property and Person," The Annals of the American Academy of Political and Social Science, May, 1957, 311:47-55.

Williams, Ethel J., "The Indian Heirship Land Problems," in Ralph W. Johnson, ed., Studies in American Indian Law, Georgetown University, June 1970, pp. 150-231.

Zakoji, Hiroto, Termination and the Klamath Indian education program 1955-1961, Salem, Oregon, State Department of Education, 1961.

Miscellaneous Reports
by date of Publication

"Indians, The American: A.D. 1893-1899 -- Negotiations and agreements with the Five Civilized Tribes," Recent History (1894-1895 to 1901) Vol. 6, History for Ready Reference and Topical Reading, pp. 263-267.

"Tribal Property Interests in Executive-Order Reservations: a Compensable Indian Right," The Yale Law Journal, 67:627-642.

"An Act to provide for the allotment of lands in severalty to Indians in various reservations, and to extend the protection of the laws of the United States and the Territories over the Indians, and for other purposes," (Dawes Act, Allotment Act of

66

February 8, 1887) 24 Stat. 388. Forty-Ninth Congress, Chapter 119.

"An Act to amend and further extend the benefits of the act approved February eighth, eighteen hundred and eighty-seven..." Fifty-First Congress, Chapter 383, February 28, 1891, 26 Stat. 794.

Winters v. the United States, In The Supreme Court of the United States, October Term 1907, 207 U.S. 564.

"An Act to provide for determining the heirs of deceased Indians, for the disposition and sale of allotments of deceased Indians, for the leasing of allotments, and for other purposes," Sixty-First Congress, Chapter 431, June 25, 1910, 36 Stat. 855.

Public Law 68-233 -- Citizenship Act -- June 2, 1924, 43 Stat. 253 (Certificates of Citizenship to Indians).

Prospectus: Revision of the Indian Reorganization Act of 1934, Institute of Indian Studies, University of South Dakota.

"An Act authorizing the Secretary of the Interior to arrange with States or Territories for the education, medical attention, relief of distress, and social welfare of Indians, and for other purposes," Public Law - No. 167, 73d Congress, April 16, 1934, (Johnson -- O'Malley Act) 48 Stat. 596.

Con. Res. 108, 83d Congress, in the Senate of the United States, Concurrent Resolution, August 1, 1953 (Termination).

Public Law 88-352, 88th Congress, H.R. 7152, July 2, 1964 (Civil Rights Act of 1964).

Tlingit and Haida Indians of Alaska, Hearings Before the Subcommittee on Interior and Insular Affairs, House of Representatives, Eighty-Ninth Congress, Washington, March, April, 1965, 121 pp.

"The Indians Claims Commission Act, As Amended," Public Law 726, 79th Congress, Chapter 959, 2d Session, May, 1967, 12 pp.

Public Law 90-284, 90th Congress, H.R. 2516, April 11, 1968, (Civil Rights Act 1968), "Indian Bill of Rights," 82 Stat. 73.

"Alaska Native Claims," Washington, D.C., unpublished manuscript, The Canadian Embassy, May 17, 1971, 3 pp.

"Report to the American Indian Law Students Association," Indian Civil Rights Task Force, Office of the Solicitor, United States Department of the Interior, March 1972, 6 pp.

PART VII

THE INDIAN ACTS

A -- The Indian Acts -- Canada (by date of Assent)

Acts Relating to Indian Matters in the Province of Canada; (1839-
    1850) Toronto, Derbishire and G. Desbarats, 1858.

"An Act for the better protection of the lands and property of the
    Indians in Lower Canada," Statutes of Canada, 1850.

"An Act to repeal in part and to amend an Act, in titled, 'An Act
    for the better protection of the lands and property of the
    Indians in Lower Canada," Statutes of Canada, 1851.

"An Act to encourage the gradual civilization of the Indian Tribes
    in the Province, and to amend the laws respecting Indians,"
    Statutes of Canada, 1857.

"An Act respecting civilization and enfranchisement of certain
    Indians, Consolidated Statutes of Canada, 1859.

"An Act to prevent trespasses to public and Indian Lands,"
    Consolidated Statutes of Upper Canada, 1859.

"An Act respecting Indians and Indian Lands," Consolidated
    Statutes of Lower Canada, 1860.

"An Act for the gradual enfranchisement of Indians, the better
    management of Indian Affairs, and to extend the provisions of
    the Act 31, Victoria, Chapter 42," Assented to June 22, 1869,
    32-33 Victoria, Chapter 6.

"An Act to amend and consolidate the laws respecting Indians,"
    Assented to April 12, 1876, 39 Victoria, Chapter 18.

"An Act to amend the 'Indian Act 1876'," Assented to May 15, 1879,
    42 Victoria, Chapter 34 (withdrawal of half-breeds from treaty,
    etc.).

"An Act to amend and consolidate the laws respecting Indians,"
    Assented to May 7, 1880, 43 Victoria, Chapter 28.

"An Act to amend 'The Indian Act 1880'," Assented to March 21,
    1881, 44 Victoria, Chapter 17 (sale of Indian products,
    squatters, appointment and role of Indian Commissioners, etc.).

"An Act to further amend 'The Indian Act of 1880'," Assented to
    May 17, 1882, 45 Victoria, Chapter 30 (administration of
    justice).

"An Act to amend ... and to amend the Indian Act of 1880," Assented to May 25, 1883, 46 Victoria, Chapter 6.

"An Act to further amend 'The Indian Act, 1880'," Assented April 19, 1884, 47 Victoria, Chapter 27 (gifts of ammunition, Indian festivals, enfranchisement, etc.).

"An Act for conferring certain privileges on the more advanced Bands of Indians of Canada, with the view of training them for the exercise of municipal powers; 'The Advancement Act'," Assented April 19, 1884, 47 Victoria, Chapter 28 (election procedures).

"The Indian Advancement Act," 1886, Chapter 44.

"The Indian Act," Revised Statutes of Canada, 1886.

"An Act to amend 'The Indian Act'," Assented to June 23, 1887, 50-51 Victoria, Chapter 33.

"Revised Statutes of Canada," 1887, Chapter 43.

"An Act to further amend 'The Indian Act', Chapter forty-three of the Revised Statutes," Assented to May 22, 1888, 51 Victoria, Chapter 22.

"An Act to further amend 'The Indian Act', Chapter forty-three of the Revised Statutes," Assented to May 16, 1890, 53 Victoria, Chapter 29.

"An Act to amend 'The Indian Advancement Act', Chapter forty-four of the Revised Statutes," Assented to May 16, 1890, 53 Victoria, Chapter 30.

"An Act further to amend the 'Indian Act'," Assented to August 28, 1891, 54-55 Victoria, Chapter 30.

"An Act further to amend 'The Indian Act'," Assented to July 23, 1894, 57-58 Victoria, Chapter 32.

"An Act to further amend the Indian Act," Assented to July 22, 1895, 58-59 Victoria, Chapter 35.

"An Act further to amend the Indian Act," Assented to June 13, 1898, 61 Victoria, Chapter 34.

"An Act to amend the Indian Act," Assented to July 13, 1906, 6 Edward VII, Chapter 20.

"Revised Statutes of Canada," 1906, Chapter 81.

"An Act to amend the Indian Act," Assented to May 4, 1910, 9-10 Edward VII, Chapter 28 (contracts with Indians, etc.).

"An Act to amend the Indian Act," Assented to May 19, 1911, 1-2 George V, Chapter 14 (compensation for land taken for railways, removal of Indians from reserves, etc.).

"An Act to amend the Indian Act," Assented to June 12, 1914, 4-5 George V, Chapter 35.

"An Act to amend the Indian Act," Assented to May 24, 1918, 8-9 George V, Chapter 26 (legal wills, lease of land, illegal celebrations, etc.).

"An Act to amend the Indian Act," Assented to July 7, 1919, 9-10 George V, Chapter 56 (lease of land surface rights, application of soldier settlement act, etc.).

"An Act to amend the Indian Act," Assented to July 1, 1920, 10-11 George V, Chapter 50 (power of council, enfranchisement, schools and school attendance, etc.).

"An Act to amend the Indian Act," Assented to June 28, 1922, 12-13 George V, Chapter 26 (enfranchisement, land for Indian soldier settlers).

"An Act to amend the Indian Act," Assented to July 19, 1924, 14-15 George V, Chapter 47 (responsibility for Eskimos, Indian estates, loans, enfranchisement, trespassing, etc.).

"An Act to amend the Indian Act," Assented to March 31, 1927, 17 George V, Chapter 32 (payment for prosecution of claims, poolrooms, totem poles, etc.).

"Revised Statutes of Canada," 1927, Chapter 98.

"Reference to Provisions of Present Indian Act Cap. 98, R.S.C. 1927, as Amended and Not Included in Reprint of Bill 267," Department of Indian Affairs, 3 pp.

"An Act to amend the Indian Act," Assented to April 10, 1930, 20-21 George V, Chapter 25 (Eskimo affairs, liens on Indian property, etc.).

"An Act to amend the Indian Act," Assented to May 23, 1933, 23-24 George V, Chapter 42 (enfranchisement, truant officers, Indian dances, etc.).

"An Act respecting the Caughnawaga Indian Reserve and to amend the Indian Act," Assented to June 28, 1934, 24-25 George V, Chapter 29 (voiding Order-in-Council re division of reserve).

"An Act to amend the 'Indian Act'," Assented to June 2, 1936, I Edward VII, Chapter 20.

"An Act to amend the Indian Act," Assented to June 24, 1938, 2 George VI, Chapter 31.

"An Act to amend the 'Indian Act'," Assented to June 14, 1941, 4-5 George VI, Chapter 19.

"The Indian Act: Consolidated for Office Purposes Only," Ottawa, 1947.

"An Act respecting Indians," Assented to June 20, 1951, 15 George VI, Chapter 29.

"Revised Statutes of Canada," 1952, Chapter 149.

"An Act to amend the Indian Act 1951," Assented to May 14, 1953
    1-2 Elizabeth II, Chapter 41.

Indian Act, R.S.C. 1952, c 149 as amended 1952-1953, c 41, and
    1956 c 40, Administrative Codification, 1957.

"An Act to amend the Indian Act," Assented to August 14, 1958, 4-
    5 Elizabeth II, Chapter 40.

"An Act to amend the Indian Act," Assented to August 14, 1958, 7
    Elizabeth II, Chapter 19.

"An Act to amend the Indian Act," Assented to March 31, 1960, 8-9
    Elizabeth II, Chapter 8 (section 86).

"An Act to amend the Indian Act," Assented to March 9, 1961, 9-10
    Elizabeth II, Chapter 9.

Indian Act, R.S.C. 1952, c 149 as amended by 1952-53, c 41, 1956,
    c 40, 1958, c 19, 1960, c 8, 1960-61, c 9, 1969.

"Revised Statutes of Canada," 1970, Chapters 1-6.

B -- Miscellaneous Acts -- Canada by Date of Assent or Date of Introduction

"The Charter Incorporating the Hudson's Bay Company, Granted by
    His Majesty, King Charles The Second, in the 22nd Year of his
    Reign, A.D. 1670."

"A Proclamation by the Hon. Jonathan Belcher, Province of Nova
    Scotia, Acadia, Respecting Indians," May 4, 1762.

"An Act for the regulations of the Indian Trade," Province of Nova
    Scotia, July 20, 1762.

"The Quebec Act: An Act for making more effectual Provision for
    the Government of the Province of Quebec in North America,"
    Imperial Act, 14 George 3, Chapter 83, 1774.

"Order in Council Dividing the Province of Quebec into the
    Provinces of Upper and Lower Canada," Court of St. James,
    August 24, 1791.

"An Act to repeal certain parts of 'An Act for making more
    effectual provisions for the Government of the Province of
    Quebec in North America," 3 George, Chapter 31, 1792.

"Agreement between New Brunswick and the Micmac Indians of the
    River St. John, July 27, 1807."

"An Act for regulating the Fur Trade ... ," Assented to July 2,
    1821, Imperial Statutes 1 and 2, George 4, Cap. 66.

"An Act to provide for the extinction of feudal and seigneurial rights and burthens on lands held a Titre de Fief and a Titre de Cens, in the Province of Lower Canada; and for the gradual Conversion of those tenures into the tenure of free and common soccage; and for other purposes relating to the said province," Statutes of the United Kingdom, 3 George 4, to 1-2 William 4, Chapter 59. 1824-1831.

"An Act to amend and make permanent an Act passed in the fifth year of His Late Majesty Reign, intitulated An Act to Prevent the sale of Spirituous Liquors to Indians," Province of Upper Canada, Passed February 10, 1840.

"An Act to re-unite the Provinces of Upper and Lower Canada, and for the Government of Canada," Assented to July 23, 1840.

"An Act to provide for the Instruction and permanent Settlement of Indians," Nova Scotia 1842.

"An Act to regulate the management and disposal of the Indian Reserves in this Province," New Brunswick, assented to September 3, 1844 (repealed by first federal Indian legislation in 1868).

"Act to explain and amend an Act of Parliament of the Late Province of Upper-Canada, passed in the second year of Her Majesty's Reign, entitled 'An Act for the Protection of the Lands of the Crown in This Province from Trespass and Injury', and to make further provisions for that purpose," Assented to April 25, 1849, 12 Victoria, Chapter 9.

"Return to an Address of the Legislative Assembly Dated 24th July, 1850 ... regarding the setting apart of a Tract of Land in the Valley of the River Gatineau for the use of certain Indians, ... ".

"An Act for the Protection of the Indians in Upper Canada from imposition, and the property occupied or enjoyed by them from trespass and injury," Statutes of Canada, 1850.

"An Act to Authorize the setting Apart of Lands for the Use of Certain Indian Tribes in Lower Canada," 14th and 15th Victoria Chapter 56, Assented to August 30, 1851, Statutes of Canada, 1851.

"An Act respecting the Assessment of Property in Upper Canada," 16 Victoria, Chapter 182, s 93, 1853.

"An Act respecting the Territorial Division of Upper Canada," Title 2, Chapter 3, Revised Statutes 1859.

"An Act concerning Indian Reserves," Nova Scotia Laws, 22 Victoria, Chapter 14, 1859.

"An Act Respecting the Management of Indian Lands and Property," 23 Victoria, Chapter 151, Statutes of the Province of Canada, Quebec, 1860.

"The British North America Act, 1867," (Canadian Constitution), Section 91 (24).

"An Act providing for the organization of the Department of the Secretary of State of Canada, and for the management of Indian and Ordnance Lands," Assented to May 22, 1868, 31 Victoria, Chapter 42.

"The Manitoba Act, 1870," Statutes of Canada, 1870.

"An Act to amend and continue the Act 32, and 33 Victoria, Chapter 3: and to establish and provide for the Government of the Province of Manitoba," Assented to May 12, 1870, 33 Victoria, Chapter 3.

"Instrument of acceptance of the surrender by the Hudsons Bay Company of certain Land privileges and rights within the Territory of Rupert's Land," Public Archives of Canada, C.O. 380, volume 2, June 2, 1870.

"Order of Her Majesty in Council, Admitting Rupert's Land and the North-Western Territory into The Union, At the Court at Windsor, 23rd day of June, 1870."

"The Rupert's Land Act," Assented to July 31, 1868, Statutes of Canada, 35 Victoria, 1872.

"An Act respecting the Northwest Territories and to create a separate territory out of part thereof: Act Creating the District of Keewatin," 39 Victoria, Chapter 21, 1876.

"Dominion Lands Act, 1879," Statutes of Canada, 1879.

"Order of Her Majesty in Council admitting all British Territories and possessions in North America and all islands adjacent thereto into the Union," Isle of Wright, July 31, 1880.

"An Act for the settlement of certain questions between the Government of Canada and Ontario respecting Indian Lands," Assented to May 4, 1891, 54 Victoria, Chapter 3, Statutes of Ontario.

"An Act for the settlement of certain questions between the Governments of Canada and Ontario respecting Indian Lands," Chapter 5, 54-55 Victoria, July, 1891.

"An Act respecting the administration of justice in the district of Quebec," Statutes of Quebec, 1898, pp. 26-28.

"An Act respecting the north-western, northern and north-eastern boundaries of the province of Quebec," Statutes of Quebec, 1898, pp 49-50.

"An Act to extend the Boundaries of the Province of Quebec," Assented to April 1, 1912.

"An Act for the settlement of certain questions between the Governments of Canada and Ontario respecting Indian Reserve

Lands," Assented April 17, 1924, 14 George V, Chapter 15, Statutes of Ontario.

"An Act to exempt American Indians born in Canada from the operation of the Immigration Act of 1924," Approved April 2, 1928 (U.S. Congress).

"The Manitoba Natural Resources Act," Assented to May 30, 1930, 20-21 George 5, Chapter 29.

"The Saskatchewan Natural Resources Act," Assented to May 30, 1930, 20-21 George 5, Chapter 41.

"The Alberta Natural Resources Act: An Act respecting the transfer of the Natural Resources of Alberta," Assented to May 30, 1930, 20-21 George 5, Chapter 3.

"The Railway Belt, and Peace River Block Act: An Act respecting the transfer of the Railway Belt and the Peace River Belt," Assented to May 30, 1930, 20-21 George 5, Chapter 37.

"The Saskatchewan Natural Resources Act No. 2," Assented to August 3, 1931, 21-22 George 5, Chapter 51.

"The Alberta Natural Resources Act, No. 2: An Act to amend the Alberta Natural Resources Act," Assented to August 3, 1931, 21-22 George 5, Chapter 15.

"An Act respecting the Department of Mines and Resources," Assented to June 23, 1936, 1 Edward VIII, Chapter 33.

"The Natural Resources Transfer (Amendment) Act, 1938: An Act to amend the Manitoba Natural Resources Act, the Alberta Natural Resources Acts, and the Saskatchewan Natural Resources Acts," Assented to June 24, 1938, 2 George 6, Chapter 36.

"The Metis Population Betterment Act," Edmonton, Government of Alberta, 1940.

"The Natural Resources Transfer (Amendment) Act, 1941: An Act to amend the Alberta Natural Resources Act," Assented to June 14, 1941, 4-5 George 6, Chapter 22.

"The British Columbia Indian Reserve Mineral Resources Act," Assented to July 24, 1943, George 6, Chapter 19.

"The Alberta Natural Resources Transfer (Amendment) Act, 1945: An Act to amend the Alberta Natural Resources Act," Assented to December 18, 1945, 9-10 George 6, Chapter 10.

"The Manitoba Natural Resource Transfer (Amendment) Act, 1948," 11-12 George 6, Chapter 60.

"The Saskatchewan Natural Resources Act, No. 4," Assented to June 30, 1948, 11-12 George 6, Chapter 69.

"The Manitoba Natural Resource Transfer (Amendment) Act, 1951," Assented to June 30, 1951, 15 George 6, Chapter 53.

"The Saskatchewan Natural Resources Transfer (Amendment) Act, 1951," Assented to June 30, 1951, 15 George 6, Chapter 60.

"The Alberta Natural Resources Transfer (Amendment) Act, 1951: An Act to vary the Alberta Natural Resources Agreement," Assented to June 30, 1951, 15 George 6, Chapter 37.

"An Act to amend the Canadian Citizenship Act," Assented to June 7, 1956, 4-5 Elizabeth II, Chapter 6 (2), (declaration that Indians and Eskimos are Canadian citizens).

"Indian Reserves of New Brunswick: Memorandum of Agreement made between the Government of Canada and the Government of the Province of New Brunswick," 7-8 Elizabeth II, Chapter 17, March 25, 1958.

"An Act respecting an Agreement between the Government of Canada and the Government of Nova Scotia for the settlement of Questions respecting Indian Reserve Lands," Assented to March 26, 1959, Chapter 2-3, 8 Elizabeth II.

"An Act to confirm an agreement between the Government of Canada and the Government of the Province of Nova Scotia respecting Indian Reserves," Assented to July 18, 1959, 7-8 Elizabeth II, Chapter 50.

"An Act to Amend the Canada Elections Act," Assented to March 31, 1960, Statutes 24, Parliament, 3 Session (Dominion franchise).

"The Metis Betterment Act Regulations Governing the Allotment of Land: The Constitution of Settlement Associations; Administration of Funds; Taxation of settlers; etc.," Alberta Regulation 110/60, Department of Public Welfare, Government of Alberta, April, 1960.

"The Natural Resources Transfer (School Lands) Amendment Act 1961," Assented to September 29, 1961, 9-10 Elizabeth 2, 1960-61, Chapter 62.

"Bill C-130, An Act to Provide for the Disposition of Indian Claims," First Reading, December 4, 1963, House of Commons, Twenty-six Parliament, First Session.

"For the Betterment of the Metis Population of Alberta," Edmonton Metis Rehabilitation Branch, Department of Public Welfare, Government of Alberta, 1960.

"Bill C-123: An Act to Provide for the Disposition of Indian Claims," First Reading, June 21, 1965, The House of Commons Twenty-sixth Parliament, Third Session.

"Bill II-C-120 An Act to Amend the Indian Act (Rights Guaranteed by Treaties)," 1st Reading, May 29, 1967, House of Commons, Twenty-seventh Parliament, Second Session.

"Bill C-7, An Act to Repeal the British Columbia Indian Reserves Mineral Resources Act," House of Commons, September 20, 1968.

"Bill C-84, An Act to Amend the Indian Act (rights of Indian women upon marriage)," 1st Reading, October 30, 1969, House of Commons, Twenty-eight Parliament, Second Session.

"Bill C-124: An Act respecting the Hunting and Fishing Rights of Indian Canadians," House of Commons, Twenty-eight Parliament, Second Session.

"Bill No. 30 of 1969, An Act to Establish the Saskatchewan Indian and Metis Department," Government of Saskatchewan.

"Canadian Bill of Rights," Revised Statutes of Canada, 1970.

"Bill C-108: An Act respecting the Hunting and Fishing Rights of Indian Canadians," 1st Reading, October 20, 1970, House of Commons, Twenty-eight Parliament, Third Session.

"Bill C-77, An Act to Amend the Indian Act (rights of Indian women upon marriage)," 1st Reading October 20, 1970, House of Commons, Twenty-eight Parliament, Third Session.

"Bill 2, Cultural Property Act," Assented to July 8, 1972, Third Session, Twenty-ninth Legislature, National Assembly of Quebec, 1972, 14 p.

C -- Discussion of the Indian Acts

Bethune, W.C., "Brief on Land Sales, Leases, Allotment of Land, Oil and Gas, Mining, Timber, Transfer of Control to and Reserves in General, Joint Committee of the Senate and House of Commons on Indian Affairs, Minutes of Proceedings and Evidence," No. 12, May 16, 1961.

Bowker, W.F., "The Canadian Bill of Rights -- S. 94(b) Indian Act -- Irreconsilible Conflict -- Equality Before the Law," Alberta Law Review, 1970, 8:409-418.

Bucknall, Brian, "Indians," Osgoode Hall Law Journal, 1967, 5:113-123.

Chapman, Harold H., "Band Membership," Ottawa, unpublished memorandum, Department of Indian Affairs and Northern Development, December 2, 1970.

Chapman, Laura A., "Women's rights and special status for Indians -- Some social implications of the Lavell Case," Ottawa, unpublished honours paper (Sociology), Carleton University, June 1972, 77 pp.

Dennison, Wally (reporter), "Non-status Indian challenge Courchene," Winnipeg Free Press, December 19, 1972.

Dore, Mrs. Cecilia Phillips, "Brief Presented on Behalf of the Equal Rights for Indian Women to the Special Joint Committee of the Senate and the House of Commons on the Constitution of Canada," Montreal, April 26, 1971.

Early, Mary Two Axe, et. al. "Injustices to Indian Women Married to Non-Indian Men as outlined in The Indian Act," Brief to the Royal Commission on the Status of Women, March 20, 1968, 3 pp.

Gorman, Mrs. John C., "Report of Committee on legal status and civil rights of the Canadian Indian," Civil Liberties Section, The Canadian Bar Association, August 30, 1956, 5 pp.

Harper, Allan G., "Canada's Indian Administration: The 'Indian Act'," America Indigena, October 1946, 6:297-314.

Holmes, Alvin, The Social Welfare Aspects and Implications of the Indian Act, Vancouver, Master Social Work Thesis, University of British Columbia, 1961.

Horn, Kahn-Tineta, "Letter to the Editor: Indian Status for Metis?," The Globe and Mail (Toronto) April 6, 1972.

Horn, Kahn-Tineta, "The Canadian Bill of Rights," News Bulletin, (Indian Legal Defence Committee, Caughnawaga), January 1973.

Jack, M.R., "Civil Rights and Liberties of Indians in Canada," Report to the Director, Civil Liberties Committee, Canadian Bar Association, May 23, 1955, 23 pp.

Laing, Hon. Arthur, "The Indian People and The Indian Act," Address, Ryerson Men's Club, Vancouver, B.C.

Leigh, L.H. "The Indian Act, The Supremacy of Parliament, and the Equal Protection of the Laws," McGill Law Journal, 1970, 16:389-398.

Leslie, A.G., "Remarks on Reserve Trusts," Special Joint Committee of the Senate and the House of Commons Appointed to Examine and Consider the Indian Act, Minutes of Proceedings and Evidence, No. 10, July 4, 1946; and No. 11, July 9, 1946.

MacDonald, John A., "The Canadian Bill of Rights: Canadian Indians and the Courts," The Criminal Law Quarterly, May, 1968, 10:305-319.

O'Reilly, James A., "Judgement of the Federal Court of Appeal in the case of Jeannette Corbiere-Lavell," Montreal, unpublished letter to the National Committee on Indian Rights and Treaties, December 9, 1971, 10 pp.

Randle, M.C., "New (Canadian) Indian Act," The Canadian Forum, (Toronto), March 1952, pp. 272-274.

Sanders, Douglas Esmond, "The Bill of Rights and Indian Status," University of British Columbia Law Review, 1972, 7:81-105.

Sanders, Douglas Esmond, "The implications of the Lavell case," Ottawa, unpublished manuscript, National Indian Brotherhood, October 1972, 13 pp.

Schrader, Alvin, The Background of the Indian Act of 1877, Ottawa, Master of Arts Thesis, Carleton University, 1966.

Sinclair, J. Grant, "The Queen v. Drybones: The Supreme Court of Canada and the Canadian Bill of Rights," Osgoode Hall Law Journal, 1970, 8:599-619.

Weaver, Sally Mae, "Report on Archival Research Regarding Indian Women's Status, 1868-1869," unpublished manuscript for Waterous, Holden, Kellock and Kent, Barristers and Solicitors, Brantford, Ontario, November 9, 1971, 20 pp.

Western, Maurice (reporter), "Recognition of Rights Denied," Winnipeg Free Press, (reprinted in Indian Record, (Winnipeg), September-October, 1970).

Whiteside, Don (sin a paw) "The Lavell Case: another Indian tragedy or an opportunity for the possible return to the traditional judical authority of the tribal and band councils?," The Indian Voice (Vancouver), March 1973, reprinted in part in The Forgotten People (Ottawa) January 1973.

Whiteside Don, "Brief bibliography of articles in the press, etc., regarding the Indian Act and the Canadian Bill of Rights, particularly the Lavell-Bedard cases," Ottawa, National Indian Brotherhood, March 7, 1973, 14 pp.

Whiteside, Don (sin a paw), "Viewpoint," (possible consequences of the Lavell case) The Forgotten People, (Ottawa), March, 1973.

Miscellaneous Reports by Date of Publication

Special Committee to whom was referred Bill No. 14, An Act to amend the Indian Act ... , Journal of the House of Commons, volume 58, 1920.

Special Joint Committee of the Senate and the House of Commons, appointed to examine and consider the Indian Act, Ottawa, Minutes of Proceedings and Evidence, 1946, 877 pp.

Special Joint Committee of the Senate and the House of Commons appointed to continue and complete the examination and consideration of the Indian Act, Ottawa, Minutes and Proceedings and Evidence, Vols. I and II, 1947, 1008 pp.

Special Joint Committee of the Senate and the House of Commons appointed to continue and complete the examination of the Indian Act, Ottawa, Minutes of Proceedings and Evidence, 1948, 223 pp.

"A Brief Concerning an Act to replace The Indian Act," Submitted to the Prime Minister and The Cabinet and particularly to The

Minister of Citizenship and Immigration," Canadian Civil
Liberties Union, Vancouver Branch, 1948, 43 pp.

"Memorandum to the Deputy Minister re Bishop Ragg, of Calgary on
the Provisions of the Indian Bill," Ottawa, unpublished
memorandum, Department of Indian Affairs, October 23, 1950.

Special Committee appointed to consider Bill 79, An Act respecting
Indians, Ottawa, Minutes and Proceedings and Evidence, 1951,
300 pp.

"Provisions of the 1951 Indian Act relating to lands," Ottawa,
unpublished manuscript.

"The Indians -- Three Points of View: (1) John Collier on Indian
Equality: (2) Dan Kennedy Discusses Bill 79: (3) John Laurie,
Western Indians and The New Act," Saskatchewan Community, (A
Bulletin published by the Adult Education Division, Department
of Education and the Saskatchewan Arts Board), May 21, 1952,
3:1-8.

"Shame on Canada," Editorial, The Albertan (Calgary) April 20,
1954, (Half-breed script takers and descendants of such persons
being removed from Hobbema Reserve.)

Joint Committee of the Senate and the House of Commons on Indian
Affairs, Ottawa, Minutes and Proceedings and Evidence, 1959,
252 pp.

"Brief to the Parliamentary Committee on Indian Affairs," Toronto,
The Indian Eskimo Association of Canada, March 1960, 28 pp.

"Brief, Anglican Church of Canada," Joint Committee of the Senate
and the House of Commons on Indian Affairs, Minutes of
Proceedings and Evidence, June 2, 1960, pp. 794-809.

"The Status of the Six Nations in Canada," Joint Committee of the
Senate and House of Commons on Indian Affairs, Minutes of
Proceedings and Evidence, No. 13, June 22, 1960, Appendix "M1",
pp. 1198-1306.

"Brief from the Oka Band, Oka, Quebec," Joint Committee of the
Senate and the House of Commons on Indian Affairs, Minutes of
Proceedings and Evidence, No. 1., March 1, 1961, March 14,
1961.

Joint Committee of the Senate and the House of Commons on Indian
Affairs, Ottawa, Minutes and Proceedings and Evidence, 1960,
1417 pp.

Choosing a Path: a Discussion Handbook for Indian People, Ottawa,
Department of Indian Affairs and Northern Development, 1968.

Discussion Notes on The Indian Act, Ottawa, Department of Indian
Affairs and Northern Development, c 1968, 31 pp.

"The Indian Act and The Government's Role," Selections from
speeches by Ministers of Indian Affairs and senior Departmental

officials, Department of Indian Affairs and Northern Development, 1968, 6 pp.

Report of the Indian Act Consultation Meeting, Ottawa, Department of Indian Affairs and Northern Development:
1)   Yellowknife, N.W.T., July 1968, 33 pp.
2)   Moncton, N.B. July, 1968, 100 pp.
3)   Toronto, Ontario, August 1968, 51 pp.
4)   Fort William, Ont., August 1968, 74 pp.
5)   Sudbury, Ont., August 1968, 75 pp.
6)   Regina, Sask., September 1968, 111 pp.
7)   Quebec City, Que., September, October 1968, 94 pp.
8)   La Maison Montmorency, Courville, Que., October 1968, 72 pp.
9)   Prince George, B.C., October 1968, 113 pp.
10) Whitehorse, Yukon Terr., October 1968, 53 pp.
11) Terrace, B.C. October 1968, 72 pp.
12) Nanaimo, B.C., October, November 1968, 77 pp.
13) Kelowna, B.C., November 1968, 115 pp.
14) Chilliwack, B.C., November 1968, 142 pp.
15) Edmonton, Alberta, December 1968, 95 pp.
16) Winnipeg, Manitoba, December 1968, 52 pp.
17) Toronto, Ontario, January 1969, 88 pp.
18) Terrace, B.C., January 1969, 57 pp.

Rapporteur's Account of National Conference on Indian Act, Ottawa, Department of Indian Affairs and Northern Development, 1969, 115 pp.

Summary of Discussions and Recommendations of The Regional Indian Advisory Councils on the Indian Act, Ottawa, Department of Indian Affairs and Northern Development, 1969, 47 pp.

"Resume of Reports of the Indian Act Consultation Meetings," Ottawa, Department of Indian Affairs and Northern Development, March 1969, 26 pp.

Verbatim Report of National Conference on Indian Act, April 28--May 2, 1969, Ottawa, Department of Indian Affairs and Northern Development, 1969, 384 pp.

Standing Committee on Indian Affairs and Northern Development, House of Commons, Twenty-eight Parliament, Second Session, 1969-1970, Index of Proceedings, Issues Nos. 1 to 29.

"Caughnawaga notifies whites to give up land," The Globe and Mail, (Toronto), September 4, 1971.

"Indian Affairs: Reference to Supreme Court of Rights of Indian Women Married to Non-Indians -- Costs of Legal Counsel," House of Commons Debates, December 1, 1971, 115:10066.

"Indian Affairs: Rights of Indian Women Married to Non-Indians -- Request for Consideration of Retroactive Aspects of Court Decision," House of Commons Debates, December 1, 1971, 115:10066.

"Supreme Court to rule whether anti-women bias in Indian Act," Toronto Daily Star, December 2, 1971.

"Won fight to remain on reserve, women will fix home, may baby-sit," The Globe and Mail, (Toronto), December 17, 1971, (Mrs. Yvonne Bedard).

Minutes of Proceedings and Evidence of the Standing Committee on Indian Affairs and Northern Development respecting Estimates 1972-1973, (Department of Indian Affairs and Northern Development) Twenty-eight Parliament 1972, March 16, 1972, 35 pp.

"Proposal for a National Committee on Indian Rights for Indian Women," Edmonton, unpublished proposal submitted to the Department of Secretary of State, April, 1972.

"Guarantees violated: Judge rules Indian Act conflicts with Bill of Rights," Toronto Star, August 10, 1972.

"Native women consider loss of treaty rights just," (Vicki Crowchild), by Cheryle Hawkes (reporter), The Leader-Post (Regina), December 1972.

Indian Status in Canada, Edmonton, Indian Chiefs of Alberta, February 1973, 14 pp.

1. Specific Legal Cases

"Warman, v. Francis, et. al.," (New Brunswick, 1958), May 1958, pp 197-216 (timber cutting on reserves).

"Logan v. Styres," Ontario High Court, September 3, 1959, pp. 416-424, challenge by hereditary chiefs to land sale by elected chief), lost.

"Her Majesty The Queen v Joseph Drybones," Ottawa, Supreme Court of Canada, November 20, 1969.

"Reasons for Judgement in the matter of the Indian Act, R.S.C. 1952, c 149 as amended between Jeannette Vivian Corbiere Lavell and The Attorney-General of Canada," County Court, District of York, June 21, 1971, 13 pp.

"Notice of Motion in the matter of an application for the issuance of a writ of Certiorari and in the matter of The Indian Act, R.S.C. 1970, c. 149, S.(4), as amended between Jeannette Vivian Corbiere Lavell and the Attorney-General of Canada," Federal Court of Canada, June 30, 1971, 6 pp.

"Jeannette Vivian Corbiere Lavell vs The Attorney-General of Canada," Federal Court of Appeal, October 8, 1971, 8 pp.

"Factum of The Attorney-General of Canada in The Supreme Court of Canada between the Attorney-General of Canada and Jeannette Vivian Corbiere Lavell," September 18, 1972.

"Respondent's Factum in The Supreme Court of Canada between The Attorney-General of Canada and Jeannette Vivian Corbiere Lavell," 1972.

"Appeal Case in The Supreme Court of Canada between the Attorney-General of Canada and Jeannette Vivian Corbiere Lavell," 1972.

"Factum of the intervenants, The Supreme Court of Canada, between the Attorney-General of Canada and Jeannette Vivian Corbiere Lavell and between Richard Issac, et. al., and Yvonne Bedard," Indian Association of Alberta, et. al., January 1973, 30 pp.

"Factum of The Native Council of Canada (Intervenant) in The Supreme Court of Canada, The Attorney-General of Canada and Jeannette Vivian Corbiere Lavell," Ottawa, February 1973, 42 pp.

"The treaty women of Canada speak in opposition to the Lavell case," Submission to the Supreme Court of Canada, The Treaty Voice of Alberta, The Saskatchewan Native Womens Movement, February 1973, 1 p.

"Factum of the intervenant, Anishnawbekwek of Ontario, Inc., in the Supreme Court of Canada an appeal from the Federal Court of Appeal between: The Attorney-General of Canada and Jeannette Vivian Corbiere Lavell," February 1973, 19 pp.

"Factum of the intervenant, The Treaty Voice of Alberta Association, in the Supreme Court of. Canada between The Attorney-General of Canada and Jeannette Vivian Corbiere Lavell," February 1973, 9 pp.

"Factum of the intervenants, The Alberta Committee on Indian Women's Club of Toronto, The University Women Graduates, Viola Shannacappo, Rose Wilhelm, The North Toronto Business and Professional Women's Club, Monica Agnes Turner in the Supreme Court of Canada, Jeannette Vivian Corbiere Lavell and the Attorney-General of Canada," February 1973, 20 pp.

PART VIII

DISCUSSION OF INDIAN ADMINISTRATION
(See also Resistence)

A   --   Canada
B   --   United States

A -- Canada

Abbott, Frederick H., The Administration of Indian Affairs in
   Canada; Report of an investigation made in 1914 under the
   Direction of the Board of Indian Commissioners, Washington,
   D.C., 1915, 148 pp.

Bailey, Alfred Goldsworthy, "(The) Indian Problem in Early
   Canada," American Indigena, 1942, 2:35-39.

Baptie, Sue, "Edgar Dewdney," Alberta Historical Review, 1968,
   16:1-10.

Battle, Robert F., "An Historical Review of Indian Affairs
   Policies and New Directions for the Future," Address, Trinity
   College Conference on the Canadian Indian, Toronto, January 22,
   1966

Bell, G.E., "Notes on Presentation of Red Paper (Citizens Plus) to
   the Prime Minister and Cabinet," Ottawa, unpublished
   manuscript, Government of Canada, June 4, 1970.

Bennett, Peter H., "Acceptable and unacceptable words and phrases
   in the Indian Context," Ottawa, unpublished letter, Department
   of Indian Affairs and Northern Development, November 8, 1971,
   3 pp.

Bergeron, Léandre, The History of Quebec: a Patriote's Handbook,
   Toronto, New Canada Press, 1971, 243 pp.

Best, R. Alfred, "Comments re: Native Rights in Canada," Toronto,
   unpublished letter to Professor Douglas Sanders, October 23,
   1969, 3 pp.

Cameron, Mr. (Member of Parliament), "Indian Administration in the
   North-West," Debates of the House of Commons, Fourth Session,
   April 15, 1886, pp. 718-746.

Cameron, Rossi (reporter), "Violence and despair are ways of life:
   Priest on Alberta Janvia Reserve says, 'sometimes only 2 or 3
   here aren't drunk'," The Globe and Mail (Toronto), August 19,
   1972.

Cameron, Rossi (reporter), "The apathetic silence of a defeated
   reserve," The Globe and Mail (Toronto), August 23, 1972.

Chance, Norman A., "The Changing Role of Government Among The
   North Alaskan Eskimo," Arctic Anthropology, 1964, 2:

Chrétien, Hon. Jean, Indian Policy, Statement of the Government of Canada, Ottawa, 1969, 13 pp.

Chrétien, Hon. Jean, "Why an Old Indian Pattern was broken," The Globe and Mail (Toronto), July 8, 1969.

Chrétien, Hon. Jean, "Statement of the Government of Canada on Indian Policy in the House of Commons," Ottawa, Department of Indian Affairs and Northern Development, June 25, 1969, 5 pp.

Chrétien, Hon. Jean, "Statement by The Honourable Jean Chrétien, Minister of Indian Affairs and Northern Development," Based on a Speech Delivered in Regina, October 2, 1969.

Chrétien, Hon. Jean, "Indian Policy -- Where does it stand?" Address, Empire Club, Toronto, October 16, 1969. 13 pp.

Chrétien, Hon. Jean, "From the Minister of Indian Affairs," Canadian Welfare, (Ottawa), January-February, 1970, 46:2, 26-28.

Chrétien, Hon. Jean, "Address," Canadian Institute of Forestry, Vancouver Island Section, Duncan, B.C., February 27, 1970.

Chrétien, Hon. Jean, "Address," Native Women's Society of British Columbia, in North Vancouver, B.C.," February 28, 1970.

Chrétien, Hon. Jean, "Opening Statement to The Standing Committee on Indian Affairs and Northern Development," Ottawa, March 19, 1970.

Con, Ronald J., "Canadian Immigrants, Indians and Government Policy," Address, Conference of Official Human Rights Agencies, Portland, Oregon, July, 1968.

Conn, Hugh R., "Integrity of the territory of the Province of Quebec," Ottawa, unpublished manuscript, Department of Indian Affairs and Northern Development, ca 1969, 11 pp.

Courchene, Dave, "Remarks at the presentation of 'Citizens Plus' by the Indian Chiefs of Alberta to the Prime Minister of Canada and Cabinet," Ottawa, unpublished manuscript, June 4, 1969, 5 pp.

Cummings, Peter A. and Neil H. Mickenberg, Native Rights in Canada, 2nd ed., Toronto, Indian-Eskimo Association of Canada in association with General Publishing Co., 1972, 352 pp.

Dennis, Ken, "Indians split on election issue," The Indian Voice (Vancouver), February, 1973.

Dodgetts, J.E., "Indian Affairs: The White Man's Albatross," Pioneer Public Service: an Administrative History of the United Canadians 1841-1867, University of Toronto Press, 1955, Chapter 13, pp. 205-225.

Dunning, Robert William, "Some Aspects of Governmental Indian Policy and Administration," Anthropologica, 1962, 4:209-231.é

Duran, James A. Jr., "Indian Policy: A Reply to the Minister," Letters to the Editor, The Canadian Forum, (Toronto), June, 1970, pp. 142-143.

Dyck, Noel Evan, The Administration of Indian Aid in the North-West Territories, 1879-1885, Master's Thesis, University of Saskatchewan, September, 1970, 103 pp.

Edmonson, Munro S., Status terminology and the social structure of North American Indians, Seattle, University of Washington Press, 1958, 84 pp.

Fairclough, Hon. Ellen L., "The Minister reports: a review of Indian Affairs," The Indian News (Ottawa), April, 1961.

Favreau, Hon. Guy, "Notes for an Address, Third Annual Conference of the National Indian Council," Winnipeg, August 15, 1963.

Forget, A.E., Letter, office of the Commissioner of Indian Affairs, Regina, January 14, 1895, Red Group, 10, Circular Volume 1135 (re marriage of girls at residential schools).

Fulton, E. David, "Federal government white paper policy on Indian Affairs; the questions of an Indian Claims Commission, and aboriginal claims of Indian people," Vancouver, unpublished letter to Union of B.C. Chiefs', December 17, 1969, 18 pp.

Gambill, Jerry T., "Sitting Bull: Canada's Indian hero," Ottawa, unpublished manuscript, May 26, 1968, 24 pp.

Godsell, Philip H., "Indians and Indian Affairs in Canada," Canadian Magazine, (Toronto), 1920, 56:384-386.

Godsell, Philip H., Red Hunters of the snows, Toronto, Ryerson Press, 1938.

Green, Leslie C., Canadian's Indians: Federal Policy, International and Constitutional Law, Edmonton, Government of Alberta, 1969, 35 pp.

Haas, Theodore H., "The Legal Aspects of Indian Affairs from 1887 to 1957," The Annals of The American Academy of Political and Social Science, May, 1957, 311:12-22.

Harper, Allan G., "Canada's Indian Administration: Basic Concepts and Objectives," America Indigena, April, 1945, 2:119-132.

Herron, Shawn, "Time to bury the hatchet," The Vancouver Sun, September 26, 1972.

Howe, Josephy (Commissioner), "Report on Indian Affairs to His Excellency, the Lieutenant-Governor," Nova Scotia, 1844.

Hussey, James H. (reporter), "slipping backward: Province's only Indian settlement to receive special government attention," St. John's Daily News (Newfoundland), April 4, 1972.

Hutchins, Peter W., "The Legal Status of the Canadian Eskimo," unpublished manuscript, 95 pp.

Hutton, Elizabeth Ann, "Indian Affairs in Nova Scotia, 1960-1834," Collections of the Nova Scotia Historical Society, 1963, 34:33-54.

Jefferson, Robert, "Fifty Years on the Saskatchewan," Canadian North-West Historical Society Publications, (Battleford, Saskatchewan), 1929, 1(5), 162 pp.

Jenness, Diamond, Eskimo Administration: I, Alaska, Montreal, Arctic Institute of North America, Technical Paper, No. 10, 1962, 68 pp.

Jenness, Diamond, Eskimo Administration: II Canada, Montreal, Arctic Institute of North America, Technical Paper No. 14, May, 1964, 186 pp.

Jenness, Diamond, Eskimo Administration: III, Labrador, Montreal, Arctic Institute of North America, Technical Paper No. 16, May, 1965, 94 pp.

Jenness, Diamond, Eskimo Administration: IV, Greenland, Montreal, Arctic Institute of North America, Technical Report, No. 19, ca 1968.

Jenness, Diamond, Eskimo Administration: V, Analysis and Reflections, Montreal, Arctic Institute of North America, Technical Paper No. 21, March, 1968, 72 pp.

Kassirer, Eve, Programs of Interest to Indians and Metis, Ottawa, Department of Regional Economic Expansion, June, 1970. 31 pp.

Kemp, Herbert Douglas, The Department of the Interior in the West 1873-1883, an Examination of Some Hitherto Neglected Aspects of the Work of the Outside Service, Master of Arts Thesis, University of Manitoba, April 1950, 159 pp.

Kerwin, Patrick, "The Plight of Canadian Indians," The Black i, (Ottawa), March, 1972, 1:11-13.

King, Wain (reporter), "The Mounties -- their first 100 years: the red enforcers and the red men," Ottawa Journal, January 9, 1973.

La Forest, Gerard V., "Property in Indian Lands," in Natural Resources and Public Property Under the Canadian Constitution, University of Toronto Press, 1969.

Lagassé, Jean-Henry, "Notes for an Address to the Trinity College Conference on the Canadian Indian," Toronto, January 21-23, 1966.

Lagassé, Jean-Henry, "A few comments on social factors affecting native development in Canada," Address, Inter-American Indian Institute, Mexico, ca 1972, 21 pp.

Laing, Hon. Arthur, "Cultural identity of the Indian and Eskimo People," Speeches by Ministers of Indian Affairs and Senior Departmental Officials, Ottawa, Department of Indian Affairs and Northern Development, 1967.

Laing, Hon. Arthur, "The tripod: the Indian people, the Government, and the Canadian community," Address, University of Western Ontario, February 16, 1968.

Langevin, Hector L., "Re appointment of Samuel P. Fairbanks, as Indian Agent," Ottawa, Government of Canada unpublished letter, September 28, 1888.

LeBlanc, Dudley J., "Acts of Unbelievable Cruelty to Acadians and Indians by the English," Acadian Miracle, Lafayette, La. Evangeline Press, 1966, Chapter 25, pp. 269-280.

Levaque, Rev. Yvon, "Eskimos should manage their own affairs: an open letter to Jean Chrétien on the independence of Eskimos," Indian Record, (Winnipeg), September-October, 1970, 33:14.

MacInnes, T.R.L., "History of Indian Administration in Canada," Annual Report of the Smithsonian Institute, 1942.

MacInnes, T.R.L., "The History and Policies of Indian Administration in Canada," in Charles T. Loram and Thomas F. McIlwraith, eds., The North American Indian Today, University of Toronto Press, 1943, pp. 152-163.

MacInnes, T.R.L., "History of Indian Administration in Canada," Paper presented at the Annual Meeting of the Canadian Political Science Association, Toronto, May 24, 1946, (The Canadian Journal of Economics and Political Science, August, 1946, pp. 387-394).

Manuel, Chief George, "Daily press serve as agents of Indian Affairs," Ottawa, Press release, National Indian Brotherhood.

Manuel, Chief George, "Address," British Columbia Association of Non-status Indians, November 17, 1971, 5 pp.

Manuel, Chief George, "Address," Progressive Conservative Youth Federation Annual Meeting, December 4, 1971, 14 pp.

Marshall, Brian David, Some Problems in Indian Affairs Field Administration, Master of Arts Thesis (Political Science), Carleton University, 1962.

Matheson, G.M., "Historical sketch of administrators of Indian Affairs," Ottawa, unpublished manuscript, Department of Indian Affairs, March 31, 1934, 11 pp.

Matheson, G.M., Historical directory of Indian agents and agencies in Canada, Ottawa, Department of Indian Affairs and Northern Affairs, c1935, (revised periodically, 297 pp.).

McEwen, Ernest Roy, "Reflections upon the needs for a comprehensive government policy embracing all of Canada's Native People," Ottawa, unpublished manuscript, January 1972, 10 pp.

McGill, Dr. H.W., "Policies and Problems in Canada," in Charles T. Loram and Thomas F. McIlwraith, eds., The North American Indian Today, University of Toronto Press, 1943, pp. 132-139.

McGilp, John G., "The relations of Canadian Indians and Canadian government," Canadian Public Administration, September, 1963, 6:299-308.

Melling, John, "Recent Indian Affairs in Canada," Continuous Learning, 1962, 1:

Melling, John, "Recent Development in Official Policy Towards Canadian Indians and Eskimos," Race, April, 1966, 7:379-399.

Morin, Francoise and Jacques Mousseau, "La Paix Blanche: a Conversation with French Anthropologist Robert Jauline," Psychology Today, September 1971 (reprinted in Akwesasne Notes, Late Autumn 1971).

Morris, William, "Let's liberate Canada's Indians from paternalism: an anthropologist proposes radical changes in policy and administration, designed to lead the Indian toward mature self-determination," Weekend Magazine, December 3, 1960.

Mussell, William Julius, "To Richard F. Salisbury, President, Canadian Sociology and Anthropology Association," Ottawa, Unpublished letter, Department of Indian Affairs and Northern Development, October 5, 1970.

Nablo, Ron, "Working Paper for the Memorandum to The Cabinet," Ottawa, unpublished manuscript, Department of Indian Affairs and Northern Development, September 1968.

Nablo, Ron, "Report of a Meeting Held with Representatives of the National Indian Brotherhood, October 15, 1970," Ottawa, unpublished memorandum, Social and Human Analysis Branch, Department of Regional Economic Expansion, October 10, 1970. 5 pp.

Presant, Joan Elizabeth, The Indian Affairs Branch of Canada: an Aspect of Acculturation, Ithica, New York, Master's Thesis, Cornell University, 1954, 102 pp.

Rosset, H.M., Governmental policy with respect to Canadian Indians, Ph.D. dissertation, University of Toronto, 1969.

Russell, Frances and Donald Newman (reporters), "10 Indian officials quit; legislature in uproar," The Globe and Mail (Toronto), May 17, 1969.

Salisbury, Richard F., "To the Hon. Jean Chrétien," unpublished letter, September 18, 1970.

Scott, Duncan Campbell, The Administration of Indian Affairs in Canada, Ottawa, Canadian Institute of International Relations, 1961.

Shackleton, Doris, "Editorial," Canadian Welfare, (Ottawa), September-October, 1969, 45:3, 30.

Shankel, George Edgar, The Development of Indian Policy in British Columbia, Seattle, Ph.D. dissertation, University of Washington, 1945, 340 pp.

Sheppard, Douglas (reporter), "The Winds of Change Rise at Indian Affairs: Ottawa still spends more on foreign aid than on direct aid to Indians and Eskimos. But the gap is narrowing ... slowly," The Toronto Telegram, November 24, 1970.

Sinclair, R.V., Canadian Indians: Letters, Articles and Editorials in the Ottawa Evening Journal, Ottawa, Fothingham and Popham, 1911, 31 pp.

Swankey, Ben, National Identity or Cultural Genocide?, Toronto, Progress Books, ca. 1970, 38 pp.

Tierney, Ben (reporter), "Indian Affairs Minister Chrétien Answers Some Questions: Are the 'Red' and White Papers So Far Apart?," The Calgary Herald, July 10, 1970.

Tierney, Ben (reporter), "Three years of futile effort: Trudeau gets nowhere with Indians," Ottawa Citizen, November 5, 1971.

Trudeau, Hon. Pierre Elliott, "Statement by the Prime Minister at a meeting with the Indian Association of Alberta and the National Indian Brotherhood," Ottawa, June 4, 1970, 7 pp.

Vallee, Brian (reporter), "Native Peoples angry, frustrated over policies," Windsor Star, (Ontario), March 8, 1972.

Whiteside, Don (sin a paw), "A Good Blanket Has Four Corners: Comparison of Aboriginal Administration in Canada and the United States," in Christopher Beattie and Stewart Crysdale, eds. Canadians: a sociological reader, 1973 (forthcoming).

Whiteside, Don (sin a paw), "Patterns of racial discrimination aboriginal administration in Canada and the United States," Address, Annual Meeting, of the American Sociological Association, New York, 1973, 14 pp.

Wilson, R.N., Our Betrayed Wards: a Story of 'Chicanery, Infidelity and the Prostitution of Trust', Ottawa, 1921, 40 pp.

Wrinch, Leonard A., Land Policy of the Colony of Vancouver Island, 1849-1866, Master of Arts Thesis (History), University of British Columbia, October 1932, 279 pp.

Wuttunee, William Ivan Clark, "Conflicts Between Indian Values and Western Society as Expressed in the New Indian Policy," Paper presented to The Humanities Society of Calgary, January 5, 1970, 15 pp.

Zeleny, Carolyn, Governmental treatment of the Indian problem in Canada, New Haven, Master of Arts Thesis, Yale University, 1939, 233 pp.

"Instructions to Governors, 1761, instruction for the governors of Nova Scotia, New Hampshire, New York, Virginia, North Carolina, South Carolina, and Georgia forbidding them to grant lands or make settlements which may interfere with the Indians bordering on those Colonies."

"Instruction to Governor Murray," Given at our Court at St. Jame's, December 7th, 1763.

Report on the Indians of Upper-Canada: the sub-committee appointed to make a comprehensive inquire into the state of Aborigines of British North America, present thereupon the first part of their general report, 1839 (reprinted by Canadian House, Toronto, 1968, 52 pp.

Annual Reports -- 1864-1972, Ottawa, Department of Indian Affairs.

Report of the Indian Branch of the Department of the Secretary of State for the Provinces, Ottawa, 1872, 35 pp.

"Select Committee appointed to inquire into the conditions and affairs of the Six Nation Indians on the counties of Brant and Halimand, of the Province of Ontario ... " Journals of the House of Commons, Volume 8, 1874.

"Index: Report of the Deputy Superintendent-General Indian Affairs," 1879-1940.

"Supply-Indian Administration in the North-West," House of Commons Debates, April 15, 1886, pp. 718.

The Facts Respecting Indian Administration in the North-West, Ottawa, Department of Indian Affairs, ca 1886.

Regulations of the Six Nations Indians on the Grand River, confirmed by His Excellency in Council on the 6th November, 1906, 3 pp.

By-Laws, Rules and Regulations of the Mississaugas of the Credit, confirmed December 5, 1908, 16 pp.

"Kispiox Indians are taught a lesson: Armed special constables from Hazelton invade village at daybreak and arrest breeders of trouble there," Victoria Times, November 8, 1909.

"Auditor General's Report, 1921-1922, Part I, Indian Affairs Department: Details of Expenditure and Revenue and Trust Fund," Sessional Paper No. 1, 1923.

McKenna McBride Report, Evidence, Royal Commission on Indian Affairs for the Province of British Columbia, volume 12, ca 1925.

"'Not a word of truth' in Nazi charge Indians ill-treated, Crerar asserts," Regina Leader-Post, November 22, 1938.

"Appendix XI, A preliminary statement showing the position of Newfoundland's Indians and Eskimos in the event of union," Ottawa, Meetings between delegates from the National Convention of Newfoundland and representatives of the Government of Canada, 1949.

"A Guide for Area Supervisors," Edmonton, Metis Rehabilitation Branch, Department of Public Welfare, Government of Alberta, ca 1960. 4 pp.

"A Submission from the Government of Saskatchewan on the Administration of Indian Affairs to the Government of Canada," October, 1964.

"Location of Offices and Agencies," Ottawa, Indian Affairs Branch, Department of Citizenship and Immigration, 1964.

The Northwest Territories Today, A Reference Paper for the Advisory Commission on the Development of Government in the Northwest Territories, 1965. 136 pp.

"The Canadian Indian: A Reference Paper," Ottawa, Department of Indian Affairs and Northern Development, 1966, 13 pp.

"Indian Leaders Attack Government Over New Indian Policy," Toronto, Indian-Eskimo Association of Canada Bulletin, July, 1967.

Minutes of Fifth Meeting, National Indian Advisory Board, Ottawa, Department of Indian Affairs, August 2-4, 1967.

The work of the Northern Administrative Branch of -- Indian Affairs and ... Canadian Eskimos, Ottawa, Department of Indian Affairs and Northern Development, November, 1967.

A handbook for Indian band chiefs and councillors, Ottawa, Department of Indian Affairs and Northern Development, 1968, 24 pp.

"Cultural Identity of the Indian and Eskimo People," Selections from Speeches by Ministers of Indian Affairs and Senior Departmental Officials, Department of Indian Affairs and Northern Development, Ottawa, c 1968, 3 pp.

"A List of Federal Royal Commissions in Canada to Study Matters Pertaining to Indians and Metis," unpublished manuscript, Research and Documentation, Department of the Secretary of State, Ottawa, May, 1968, 3 pp.

"Reference List of Shared Cost Agreements and Major Service Contracts with the Provinces and Voluntary Agencies," Ottawa, Department of Indian Affairs and Northern Development, November, 1968. 3 pp.

"A presentation on future relations between the Government of Canada and the Indian people," Brief presented to the Hon. Jean Chrétien, Manitoba Indian Brotherhood, December 5, 1968, 8 pp.

Government Activities in the North 1968 Report and 1969 Plans,
    Advisory Committee on Northern Development, 299 pp.

"A review of activities, 1948-1968," Ottawa, unpublished
    manuscript, Department of Indian Affairs and Northern
    Development, ca 1969, 76 pp.

The Indian in Transition, The Indian Today, Ottawa, Department of
    Indian Affairs and Northern Development, 1969, 26 pp.

Annual report of the Commissioner of the Northwest Territories,
    1969, 64 pp.

"History of Government: Indian Policy," Ottawa, Department of
    Indian Affairs and Northern Development, ca 1969, 3 pp.

"Excerpts from the House of Commons debates, March 1969 and July
    11, 1969," Ottawa, Department of Indian Affairs and Northern
    Development.

"The Real Plight of our Indian Reserves," The Telegram (Toronto),
    May 8, 1969.

"Social and Cultural Programs," Ottawa, Department of the
    Secretary of State, unpublished manuscript, September 9, 1969.

"Financial Assistance Available to Indian Associations from
    Federal Departments, Ottawa, Department of Indian Affairs and
    Northern Development, 1970.

Citizens Plus, A Presentation by the Indian Chiefs of Alberta to
    the Right Honourable P.E. Trudeau, Prime Minister and the
    Government of Canada, June 1970, 100 pp.

"Indian Affairs -- Quebec-Transfer of Administration to the
    Province," House of Commons Debates, October 7, 1970.

A Declaration of Indian Rights: the B.C. Indian Position Paper,
    The Union of British Columbia Indian Chiefs, November, 1970, 39
    pp.

"Slaves Charge Misuse of Band Funds," The Native People
    (Edmonton), February 1970, 2:1-2.

"Proposed Preamble to Alternative Policy to Government of Canada,"
    Toronto, unpublished manuscript (draft) Union of Ontario
    Indians, 1971, 35 pp.

"Brief to the Honourable Robert Stanbury, P.C., M.P., Secretary of
    State, Re: funding of Metis and Non-Status Indian
    Organizations," Ottawa, Native Council of Canada, 1971, 5 pp.

Programs for Persons of Native Ancestry in Canada: a Task Force
    Report, Ottawa, Department of Regional Economic Expansion,
    January, 1971, Part 1, 41 pp.

Programs for Persons of Native Ancestry in Canada: a Task Force
    Report, rev. ed., Ottawa, Department of Regional Economic
    Expansion, June 1971, Part 2, Reference Papers, 282 pp.

"Minutes of Regional Directors' Meeting, June 22-23, 1971,"
Ottawa, unpublished report, Department of Indian Affairs and
Northern Development, July, 1971.

"The threat to the Indian in the North-West Territories,"
unpublished brief presented to the National Indian Brotherhood
at Regina, by the President of the Indian Brotherhood of the
N.W.T., July 1971, 10 pp.

"Indian Treaty Maps Redrawn by Ottawa, Brotherhood Charges," The
Globe and Mail (Toronto), July 19, 1971.

Wahbung: Our Tomorrows, The Indian Tribes of Manitoba, October,
1971, 196 pp.

The Association of Iroquois and Allied Indians Position Paper,
November 27, 1971, 66 pp.

"Brief Presented to the Honourable Gérard Pelletier, Secretary of
State, by the Native Council of Canada and its Member
Associations," Ottawa, June 6, 1972, 14 pp.

B -- United States

Angle, Jerry, "Federal, State and Tribal Jurisdiction on Indian
Reservations in Arizona," Bureau of Ethnic Research, University
of Arizona, American Indian Series No. 2, 1959, 46 pp.

Axtell, James, "The White Indians of Colonial America," Address,
87th Annual Meeting of the American Historical Association, New
Orleans, December 28-30, 1972, 25 pp.

Bayard, Charles Judah, The Development of the public land policy,
1783-1820, with special reference to Indians, Ph.D.
dissertation, University of Indiana, 1956, 319 pp.

Beaty, Robert E., "A Study of B.I.A. Timber Management on the
Quinault Indian Reservation, 1950-1970," in Ralph W. Johnson,
ed., Studies in American Indian Law, Volume 2, Unviersity of
Washington, Seattle, 1971, pp. 403-451.

Berkhofer, Robert F. Jr., "Comments on papers delivered at the
National Archives Conference on Indian-White Relations,"
Washington, D.C., June 1972, 13 pp.

Blair, William M. (reporter), "U.S. suit clouds Indian problem:
Reservation residency held not needed for broad aid," The New
York Times, November 19, 1972.

Bowker, Mabel Edna, The Indian Policy of the United States from
1789 to 1841, Ph.D. dissertation, Boston University, 1926, 344
pp.

Brohough, Gustav O., <u>Sioux</u> <u>and</u> <u>Chippewa</u> <u>half-breed</u> <u>script</u> <u>and</u> <u>its</u> <u>application</u> <u>to</u> <u>the</u> <u>Minnesota</u> <u>Pine</u> <u>Lands</u>, Madison, Master of Arts Thesis, University of Wisconsin, 1906, 69 pp.

Brophy, William A., et al., "Policies Which Impede Indian Assimilation," in <u>The</u> <u>Indian:</u> <u>America's</u> <u>Unfinished</u> <u>Business</u>, <u>Report</u> <u>of</u> <u>the</u> <u>Commission</u> <u>on</u> <u>the</u> <u>Rights,</u> <u>Liberties,</u> <u>and</u> <u>Responsibilities</u> <u>of the American Indian</u>, Norman, University of Oklahoma Press, 1966, pp. 179-213.

Bruce, Louis R., "Remarks," National Archives Conference on Research in the History of Indian-White Relations, Washington, D.C., June 16, 1972, 16 pp.

Burnette, Robert, <u>The</u> <u>Tortured</u> <u>Americans</u>, Englewood Cliffs, N.J., Prentice-Hall, 1971, 160 pp.

Burney, Dudley Haskell, <u>The</u> <u>Indian</u> <u>Policy</u> <u>of</u> <u>the</u> <u>United</u> <u>States</u> <u>Government</u> <u>from</u> <u>1870</u> <u>to</u> <u>1906</u> <u>with</u> <u>particular</u> <u>reference</u> <u>to</u> <u>land</u> <u>tenure</u>, Ph.D. dissertation (history), Stanford University, January 1936, 287 pp.

Burns, Melton James, <u>Administration</u> <u>of</u> <u>Indian</u> <u>Affairs</u> <u>in</u> <u>the</u> <u>allotment</u> <u>and</u> <u>citizenship</u> <u>period,</u> <u>1887</u> <u>to</u> <u>date</u>, Master of Science Thesis, University of Idaho, 1954, 119 pp.

Callahan, Rosalie A., <u>Changing</u> <u>Governmental</u> <u>policy</u> <u>toward</u> <u>the</u> <u>Indians</u>, 1928-1955, New York, Master of Arts Thesis, Hunter College, 1955.

Cambria, Claudia E., <u>The</u> <u>Indian</u> <u>reform</u> <u>movement</u> <u>in</u> <u>the</u> <u>United</u> <u>States</u> <u>from</u> <u>1865</u> <u>to</u> <u>1887</u>, Master of Arts Thesis, Columbia University, 1946, 76 pp.

Canby, William C. Jr., "Book Reviews: The Indian -- America's Unfinished Business, by William A. Brophy and Sophia D. Aberle, eds., <u>Arizona</u> <u>Law</u> <u>Review</u>, Winter 1968, 10:741-746.

Cohen, Felix S., "Indian Rights and the Federal Courts," <u>Minnesota</u> <u>Law</u> <u>Review</u>, 1940, 24:

Cohen, Felix S., "The Spanish Origin of Indian Rights in the Law of the United States," <u>Georgetown</u> <u>Law</u> <u>Review</u>, November, 1942, 31:1-21.

Cohen, Felix S., "Indians are Citizens, "<u>The</u> <u>American</u> <u>Indian</u>, Summer, 1944, 1:

Cohen, Felix S., "Indian Claims," <u>The</u> <u>American</u> <u>Indian</u>, Spring, 1945, 2:3-11.

Cohen, Felix S., "Original Indian Title," <u>Minnesota</u> <u>Law</u> <u>Review</u>, 1948, 32:28-59.

Cohen, Felix S., "Erosion of Indian Rights, 1950-1953: A Case Study in Bureaucracy," <u>Yale</u> <u>Law</u> <u>Review</u>, February, 1953, 62:

Collier, John, "Policies and Problems in The United States," in Charles T. Loram and Thomas F. McIlwraith, eds., <u>The</u> <u>North</u>

American _Indian_ _Today_, University of Toronto Press, 1943, pp. 140-151.

Collier, John, "The Indian Bureau and Self-Government: 1949, a Reply," _Human_ _Organization_, 1949, 8:22-25.

Collier, John, "Divergent views on 'Pluralism and the American Indian'" in Roger Owen, et al. ed., _The_ _North_ _American_ _Indian_: _a_ _sourcebook_, Toronto, MacMillan, 1967, Chapter 52, pp. 682-692.

Coulter, Robert T., "Federal law and Indian tribal law: The rights to civil counsel and the 1968 Indian Bill of Rights," _Columbia_ _Survey_ _of_ _Human_ _Rights_ _Law_, January 1971, 3:49-93.

Dozier, Edward P., "Key-note Address" American Indian Chicago Conference, June 13-20, 1961.

Ducheneaux, Franklyn, "Indian Legislation 1971: Retrospect and Prospect," _The Sentinel_, (Washington, D.C.), Winter, 1971, pp. 17-19.

Dunning, Robert William, "Indian Affairs: review of The Indian: _America's_ _Unfinished_ _Business_," _The_ _Canadian_ _Forum_ (Toronto), March, 1967, pp. 274-275.

Embree, John F., "The Indian Bureau and Self-Government," _Human_ _Organization_, Spring 1949, 8:

Embree, John F., "Rejoiner to Dr. Collier's Remarks," _Human_ _Organization_, Spring, 1949, 8:25-26.

Fairholm, Cy I., "United State termination policy, reports and documents," Ottawa, unpublished manuscript,, Department of Indian Affairs and Northern Development, September 22, 1969.

Flickinger, Samuel J., "The American Indian," _The_ _Federal_ _Bar_ _Journal_, ca. 1959, pp. 212-216.

Freeman, John Leiper, Jr., _New_ _Deal_ _for_ _Indians:_ _a_ _study_ _in_ _Bureau-Committee_ _relations_ _in_ _American_ _Government_, Ph.D. dissertation, Princeton University, 1952, 45 pp.

Gallaher, Ruth A., "The Indian agent in the United States before 1850," _The_ _Iowa_ _Journal_ _of_ _History_ _and_ _Politics_, 1916, 14:

Gossett, Thomas Frank, _The_ _idea_ _of_ _Anglo-Saxon_ _superiority_ _in_ _American_ _thought_, _1865-1915_, Ph.D. dissertation, University of Minnesota, 1953, 416 pp.

Gross, Harold M., "The Nixon Administration: The Thunder and Rain, a Critical Review of the Administration, Decisions and Promises," _The_ _Sentinel_, (Washington, D.C.) Winter, 1971, pp. 12-16, 31, 33.

Hagen, William T., "Indian Policy After the Civil War: The Reservation Experience," _Lectures_, _1970-1971_, Indianapolis Indiana Historical Society, 1971.

Henry, Hill, _From Where the Sun Now Stands_, New York, Random House, 1960.

Hilliard, Sam B., "Indian Land Cessions", Map Supplement Number 16, _Annals of the Association of American Geographers_, June 1972, Vol. 62.

Jacobs, W.R., _Diplomacy and Indian Gifts_, Stanford, California, Stanford University Press, 1950, 208 pp.

Johnson, President Lyndon Baines, "The American Indian: a Message from the President of the United States Transmitting a Message Relating to the Problems of the American Indians, To The Congress of the United States," March 6, 1968.

Josephy, Alvin M., Jr., "The American Indian and the Bureau of Indian Affairs -- 1969: a Study with Recommendations," Washington, D.C., February 24, 1969, 94 pp.

Kappler, Charles J., _Indian Affairs: Laws and Treaties_, 4 vols., Senate Document 452, 57th Congress 1st session, serial 4253, 4254; Senate Document 419, Congress 2nd Session, serial 6164; Senate Document 53, 70th Congress, 1st Session, serial 8849.

Keeler, W.W. et al., "The Secretary's Task Force on Indian Affairs," Washington, D.C., Bureau of Indian Affairs, 77 pp.

Kelly, William H., "Indian Adjustment and the History of Indian Affairs," _Arizona Law Review_, Winter 1968, 10:559-578.

Kennedy, President John Fitzgerald, "To All American Indians: Text of President John F. Kennedy's Speech Upon Presentation of the Declaration of Indian Purpose," American Indian Congress, Chicago, December 1, 1962.

LaCourse, Richard, "Who Runs Indian Affairs? Hidden Powers in the 'Indian Business', _The Sentinel_, (Washington, D.C.), Winter, 1971, pp. 9-11, 30, 31.

Manners, Robert A., "Pluralism and the American Indian," _American Indigena_, 1962, 22:25-38, (reprinted in Roger Owen et al. eds., _The North American Indian: a sourcebook_, Toronto, MacMillan, 1967, pp. 669-682).

Meriam, Lewis, et al., _The Problem of Indian Administration_, Baltimore, Md., The John Hopkins Press, 1928, 850 pp.

Morning Runner, "New Directions in Native Affairs: A Position Paper from the Malibu Meeting," Denver, Colorado, January 1971.

Morris, Lillian, and Philip Procter, "The Trail of Tears," _Mankind_, 1970, 2:11-18.

Nader, Ralph, "Lo, the Poor Indian," _The New Republic_, March 30, 1968.

Nammack, Georgiana, _Fraud Politics and the Dispossession of the Indians_, Norman, University of Oklahoma Press, 1969, 128 pp.

Newman, Nicholas C., "Jurisdiction over Indians and Indian Lands in Washington," in Ralph W. Johnson, ed. Studies in American Indian Law, Georgetown University, June 1970, pp. 232-284.

Nixon, President Richard Milhouse, "To The Congress of the United States: Indian Affairs," Address, July 8, 1970, 14 pp.

Peithmann, Irvin M., Broken Peace Pipes, Toronto, The Ryerson Press, 1964, 298 pp.

Shames, Deborah ed., Freedom with Reservation; the Menominee struggle to save their land and people, Madison, Wisc. National Committee to Save the Menominee People and Forest, 1972, 116 pp.

Sherman, Paschal, The Indian policy of the United States, Washington, D.C., Master's thesis (Arts), Catholic University of America, 1917, 43 pp.

Smith, Michael, "Tribal sovereignty and the 1968 Indian Bill of Rights," Civil Rights Digest, Summer 1970, 3:9-15.

Swanton, John Reed, "An Indian Social Experiment and Some of its Lessons," Scientific Monthly, 1930, 31:368-376.

Sykes, Merlyn C., A history of the attempts of the United States Government to re-establish self-government among the Indian Tribes, 1934-1949, Master of Arts Thesis, Bowling Green State College, (Kentucky), 1950, 169 pp.

Udall, Stewart L., "The State of the Indian Nation -- An Introduction," Arizona Law Review, Winter 1968, 10:553-557.

Vance, John, "Indian claims, the U.S. experience," Address, Symposium on the Indian and the Law, Saskatoon, March 18, 1973, 14 pp.

Washburn, Wilcomb E., Red Man's Land -- White Man's Law: a Study of the Past and Present Status of The American Indian, Charles Scribner, 1970.

White, Jay V., "Taxing Those They Found Here," in Ralph W. Johnson, ed., Studies in American Indian Law, Volume 2, University of Washington, Seattle, 1971, pp. 76-199.

Zimmerman, William Jr., "The Role of the Bureau of Indian Affairs Since 1933," The Annals of the American Academy of Political and Social Science, May, 1957, 311:31-40.

Miscellaneous Reports by Date of Publication

"Report on Indian Legislation," Washington D.C., Friends Committee on National Legislation, periodic.

Executive Orders Relating to Indian Reservations, 2 vols.,
Washington, D.C., Government Printing Office, 1912, 1922.

Constitution and bylaws of the Rosebud Sioux Tribe, South Dakota,
Washington, D.C., Approved December 20, 1935, United States
Department of the Interior Office of Indian Affairs, 1936, 10
pp.

Corporate Charter of the Metlakatla Indian Community, Washington,
D.C., ratified December 19, 1944, United States Department of
the Interior, Office of Indian Affairs, 1946, 2 pp.

Constitution and bylaws of the Metlankatla Indian Community,
Annette Island Reserve, Alaska, Washington, D.C., United States
Department of the Interior, Office of Indian Affairs, 1946, 11
pp.

Constitution and bylaws of the Confederated Tribes of the Warm
Springs Reservation of Oregon, Washington, D.C., approved
February 14, 1938, United States Department of the Interior,
Bureau of Indian Affairs, 1957, 12 pp.

Corporate Charter of the Tulalip Tribes of the Tulalip
Reservation, Washington, Washington, D.C., ratified October 3,
1936, United States Department of the Interior, Bureau of
Indian Affairs, 1957, 6 pp.

"Federal Indian Policies: A Summary of Major Developments from the
Pre-Revolutionary Period to the 1960's, "Washington, D.C.,
United States Department of the Interior, Bureau of Indian
Affairs, 25 pp.

"The United States Indian Service: A Sketch of the Development of
the Bureau of Indian Affairs and of Indian Policy, Department
of the Interior, Bureau of Indian Affairs," Washington, D.C.,
November 1961, (adapted from Cohen, Felix S., Handbook of
Federal Indian Law, Government Printing Office, Washington,
D.C., 1945, pp. 575-596).

Answers to Questions About The American Indian and Suggested
Reading Lists, Washington, D.C., United States Department of
the Interior, Bureau of Indian Affairs, 1964. 38 pp.

Report of Annual Conference on Indian Affairs, Pierre Boarding
School, Pierre, South Dakota, October 29-30, 1969, 86 pp.

"Tribal Official's Guide to Federal Assistance for Indians,"
National Council on Indian Opportunity, Washington, D.C.,
Spring, 1970. 22 pp.

Transcript of Regional Hearings on President's Indian Message,
July 8, 1970 and on Attendant Legislative Package, No. II,
Hollywood, Florida, Alburquerque, Oklahoma City, Fairbanks,
Alaska, Washington, D.C., National Council of Indian
Opportunity, 75 pp.

"A New Deal Coming for American Indians?," U.S. News and World
Report, September 14, 1970, pp. 68-70.

"Senate to Act on Alaska Land," <u>Indian</u> <u>Affairs</u>, (New York), March 1971.

<u>American</u> <u>Indian</u> <u>civil</u> <u>rights</u> handbook, <u>a</u> <u>guide</u> <u>to</u> <u>rights</u> <u>and</u> <u>liberties</u>, <u>under</u> <u>Federal</u> <u>Law</u>, <u>of</u> <u>Native</u> <u>Americans</u> <u>living</u> <u>on</u> <u>and</u> <u>off</u> <u>reservations</u>, Washington, D.C., United States Commission on Civil Rights, March 1972, 96 pp.

"Position paper: Brazilian Government's Indian Policy," unpublished manuscript, U.S. Delegation to the Seventh Inter-American Indian Institute, held in Brazilia, August 7-12, 1972, 2 pp.

"Position paper: Agrarian reform," unpublished manuscript, U.S. Delegation to the Seventh Inter-American Indian Institute held in Brazilia, August 7-12, 1972, 6 pp.

"United States National Report: recent progress for Indian Affairs in the United States," A paper presented by the United States Delegation to the VII Congress of Inter-American Indian Institute held in Brazilia, August 7-12, 1972, 10 pp.

PART IX

PREJUDICE AND DISCRIMINATION

Adams, Ian, "The Indians: an Abandoned and Dispossessed People, Rejected and Discriminated Against. They Look upon White Society with Hate and Hostility," Weekend Magazine, (Montreal), November 31, 1965.

Aginsky, Burt W., "The Interaction of Ethnic Groups: A Case Study of Indians and Whites," American Sociological Review, April, 1949, 14:288-302.

Anderson, Francis Garfield, Personal Contact Affecting City Children's Knowledge of and Attitudes Toward Alberta Indians, Master's Thesis (Education), University of Calgary, 1969, 113 pp.

Arnold, A.J., "Human Rights and Social Welfare Experience in Western Canada," Winnipeg, unpublished manuscript, Department of Health and Social Development, 1968, 24 pp.

Bedford, C.M., "The Rights of the Indian People," Charlottetown, Home and School and Parent-Teachers' Association, July 13, 1964.

Belcourt, A. (Tony) E., "Address," Canadian Conference on Social Welfare, Laval University, Quebec City, P.Q., June 21, 1972, 8 p.

Binding, Frederick Richard, A sociometric study of racial cleavage in Indian-White groups, Master's Thesis, University of Manitoba, 1963, 148 pp.

Bishop, William L., "Blacks and America's Tribal Indians: a Comparison of Civil Rights," Ralph W. Johnson, ed., Studies in American Indian Law, Volume 2, University of Washington, Seattle, 1971, pp. 452-551.

Boag, Thomas J., "The White Man in the Arctic: a preliminary study of Problems of Adjustment," American Journal of Psychiatry, 1952, vol. 109.

Boon, T.C.B. (reporter), "The Indian Speaks -- 'Let us Listen'," Winnipeg Free Press, April 8, 1967.

Bowsfield, Hartwell, ed., Louis Riel: Rebel of the Western Frontier or Victim of Politics and Prejudice, Toronto, Copp-Clarke Publishing Co., 1969, 227 pp.

Braroe, Niels Winther, "Reciprocal Exploitation in an Indian White Community," Southwestern Journal of Anthropology, 1965, 21:166-178.

Brookbank, C. Roy, "The Search for Justice," Address, National Citizenship Seminar, Mount St. Vincent University, Halifax, August 25, 1968, 6 pp.

Bruyere, Gail, "Essay on Discrimination," The Calumet, (Toronto), November 30, 1968, (reprinted in N. Sheffe, ed. Issues in the Seventies: Canada's Indians, Toronto, McGraw-Hill, 1970, pp. 45-46).

Bucksar, Richard G., "Moosonee and the Squatters," Canadian Welfare, (Ottawa), 1968, 44:15-16.

Caibaiosai, Lloyd Roland, "As you are ... Towards a New Orientation," Address to Members of the Ninth Annual Meeting of the Indian-Eskimo Association of Canada, Toronto, September, 1968, 6 pp.

Card, Brigham Young, "Ethnic Minorities in Slow Growing Regions," Edmonton unpublished manuscript, Department of Education, University of Alberta, 1968, 31 pp.

Cardinal, Harold, "Address," Indian-Eskimo Association of Canada and the Native Council of Canada, Toronto, December 14, 1971, 21 pp.

Chapin, Miriam, "Our Changing Indians," Queen's Quarterly, Autumn, 1955.

Cheechoo, Margaret, "White Squaw," John Bull, (England), March 24, 1951, March 31, April 7, 1951.

Childerhose, R.J. and Peter Ferguson (reporters), "For the First Canadians, Second-Class Citizenship," The Telegram, (Toronto), March 14, 1967.

Cohen, Joan (reporter), "A Casebook of Confusion: Why Our Indians are Frustrated," Ottawa Citizen, December 22, 1971.

Collins, Douglas (reporter), "A Win for the Indians," The Globe and Mail (Toronto), March 14, 1964.

Costo, Rupert ed., Textbooks and the American Indian, San Francisco, California, The Indian Historian Press, 1970, 269 pp.

Coté, François (reporter), "Les Griefs des Indiens de la Région de Sept-Iles," Le Nouveau-Québec, Juillet 1er, 1964.

Creswell, Dean (reporter), "Frustration: trial in a foreign language," Star-Phoenix (Saskatoon), March 17, 1973.

Currie, Walter, "Legislated Discrimination," Address, Nineteenth Annual Conference of Commissions for Human Rights, Royal York Hotel, Toronto, July 7, 1967, 16 pp. (reprinted in Human Relations, (Toronto), March 1968).

Currie, Walter, "Progress Toward Equal Opportunity," Address Seventh Annual Meeting of Members, Vancouver, (Indian-Eskimo Association), December 2, 1966, 5 pp.

Dagg, M.H., The Indian in Canadian literature, Fredericton, Ph.D. dissertation, University of New Brunswick, (in progress).

Dallyn, Frederick John Gallinger and Frazer George Earle, "A Study of Attitudes Towards Indians and People of Indian Descent, Selkirk, Manitoba," Winnipeg, Canadian Council of Christians and Jews, October 1957, 25 pp.

Dallyn Frederick, John Gallinger and Frazer George Earle, "A Study of Attitudes Towards Indians and People of Indian Descent, Portage La Prairie, Manitoba," Winnipeg, Canadian Council of Christians and Jews, March 1959, 30 p.

Dallyn, Frederick, John Gallinger and Frazer George Earle, "A Study of Attitudes Towards Indians and People of Indian Descent, The Pas, Manitoba," Winnipeg, Canadian Council of Christians and Jews, July 1965, 33 pp.

Davis, E.N. (reporter), "Neglect Charged on Indian Reserve," The Globe and Mail (Toronto), January 4, 1964.

Delisle, Chief Andrew Tanahokate, "Human Rights and the Indian," Address Fredericton, N.B., March 26, 1968.

Dennett, Chris (reporter), "Manitoba town's Indians seethe over treatment by RCMP," (Grand Rapids, Man.) Toronto Star, March 29, 1973.

Densmore, Hattie (reporter), "Indians Want to Stay on Reserves, but Move Freely in White Community," The Chronicle-Herald (Halifax), January 16, 1969.

De Weerdt, Mark M., "Indians, Eskimos: The Administration of Justice in the N.W. Territories," Toronto, unpublished manuscript, Legal Committee, Indian-Eskimo Association of Canada, circa. 1967, 7 pp.

Diagle, Alban, "Keynote Address," Human Rights and the Indian: A Report, Proceedings of a Conference, Centre of Continuing Education, Elliot Lake, Ontario, October, 1967, pp. 1-11.

Donoghue, Tom (reporter), "M.I.B. withdraws from Toal Commission Hearing," Brandon Sun (Manitoba), February 22, 1972.

Dunning, Robert William, "Ethnic Relations and the Marginal Man in Canada," Human Organization, Fall, 1959, 18:117-122.

Edmonds, J.K. (reporter), "Our Fast-Growing Indian Problem," The Financial Post (Toronto), February 9, 1963.

Elkin, Frederick, The Employment of Visible Minority Groups in Mass Media Advertising, A Report Submitted to the Ontario Human Rights Commission, August, 1971 79 pp.

Fairfield, Roy P., "Indignation Keeps Us Warm," Humanist, September-December, 1967.

Ferguson, John, "Exploitation and Discrimination in the Alberta Beet Fields," The Native People (Edmonton), November 1969, 2.

Fisher, Douglas (reporter), "Indian Integration: Prospects are Poor," The Telegram (Toronto), June 15, 1965.

Fisher, Douglas and Harry Crowe (reporters), "The Indian Dilemma," The Telegram (Toronto), December 16, 1968.

Frum, Barbara and Helene Pilotte, "Nos Indiens dépossédés," Chatelaine, (Montreal), November 1968, vol. 9.

Gambill, Jerry T., "On the Art of Stealing Human Rights," Address, New Brunswick Conference on Human Rights, Tobique Reserve, August 1968, (extracts reprinted in Native Youth News, (Native Youth Association, Ottawa), June, 1972).

Gambill, Jerry T., "How Students Meet the North American Indians: An Analysis of High School Textbooks," Cornwall, Ontario, unpublished manuscript, April, 1968, 9 pp.

Gazan, Albert, "Social Conflict and Problems of Acculturation of the Canadian Indian," unpublished term paper, of University of Saskatchewan, December, 1963, 12 pp.

George, Chief Dan, "Thoughts by Chief Dan George: Brotherhood and Understanding," Address, Brotherhood Banquet, Sudbury, Ontario, February 22, 1972, 2 pp.

Getty, Harry Thomas, Interethnic Relationships in the Community of Tuscon, Ph.D. Dissertation, University of Arizona, 1950.

Godsell, Philip H., "Relief in the Sub-Arctic. The Tragic Economic Story of the Northern Indians: a Thirty-year Decline from the Freedom of their Ancient Hunting Grounds to a Place in the Breadline," Natural History, 1936, 38:

Goodfellow, W.A. (chairman), Civil Liberties and Rights of Indians in Ontario, Toronto, Select Committee on Indian Affairs of the Legislative Assembly of Ontario, 1954, 23 pp.

Goodwill, Jean Ida, "An Indian looks at the Branch," Canadian Welfare, (Ottawa), July-August, 1967, 43:

Goodwill, Jean Ida, "Squaw is a Dirty Word," The Indian News, (Ottawa), (also in N. Sheffe (ed) Issues for the Seventies: Canada's Indians, McGraw-Hill, 1970, pp. 50-52).

Gradburn, Nelson H.H., "Eskimo Law in Light of Self-and-Group Interest," Law and Society Review, e:45-60.

Greenwood, Martin H., "The Structure and Functions of Social Segregation: The Indian in Town," unpublished research project outline, Lakehead University, January 1968, 13 pp.

Gunn, Herbert, "A Letter to The Attorney-General," The Saskatchewan Indian (Saskatoon), June 1972, 3(6):4.

Gzowski, Peter, "This is our Alabama: not yet as bloody or bitterly committed to open warfare as the American South, nonetheless west-central Saskatchewan is the arena where white Canadians are beginning a struggle to hold off the encroachments of 'second-class' race ... ," MacLean's Magazine, (Toronto), July 6, 1963.

Harding, James, "Canada's Indians: A Powerless Minority," Regina, The Student Union for Peace Action, January 1965.

Hawthorne, Harry Bertram, "Relations between whites and Indians," in W.E. Mann, ed., Canadian Society: sociological perspectives, Toronto, MacMillan, 1961, pp. 544-555.

Hirabayashi, Gordon K., "Social Distance and the Modernizing Metis," in Brigham, Y. Card, et. al., eds., The Metis in Alberta Society, Edmonton, 1963, Chapter 12, pp. 355-373.

Hlady, Walter M., "Power Structure in a Metis Community," Center for Community Studies, University of Saskatchewan, April, 1960, 6 pp.

Hughes, Barry Conn, "Town on a powder keg," (Kenora, Ont.), Canadian Magazine, (Toronto), March 30, 1968, p. 2-6.

Hutchinson, Bonnie (reporter), "What Indians Want is Dignity," Ottawa Citizen, February 19, 1971.

Hycock, Ronald G., The Image of the Indian, Waterloo Lutheran University Press, 1971.

Johnson, William D., An Exploratory Study of Ethnic Relations at Great Whale River, Ottawa, Northern Coordination and Research Centre, Department of Northern Affairs and Natural Resources, 1962, 21 pp.

Johnston, Basil, "An Address on the General Meaning of Human Rights and Some Applied Aspects to the Indians in Canada," Human Rights and the Indian: A Report, Proceedings of a conference, Centre for Continuing Education, Elliot Lake, Ontario, October 1967, pp. 35-43.

Kawakami, K.J., "Canada as a White Man's Country," Current History, February 1924, 19:

Keiser, Albert, The Indian in American literature, 1933, (reprinted New York, Octagon Books, 1970, 312 pp.).

Lacroix, Marc, "Integration or Disintegration?", The Beaver, Spring, 1959, 289:37-40.

Lemay, Guy (reporter), "Les Indiens sont bien décidés à faire respecter leur autonomie," La Patrie, (Montreal), June 4, 1953.

Leon, Robert L., "Maladaptive Interaction Between Bureau of Indian Affairs Staff and Indian Clients," American Journal of Orthopsychiatry, 1964, 35:723-728.

Lieberson, S., Ethnic Patterns in American Cities, New York, Free Press of Glencoe, 1963, 230 pp.

Linklater, Clive, "Improving Indian-White Relationship," Address, Friends of the Indians Society, Indian Night, Calgary, March 7, 1964, 4 pp.

List, Wilfred (reporter), "The Social Worker Who's Become Ombudsman to Indians," (Pat Kerwin) The Globe and Mail, (Toronto) February 1, 1969.

Locke, Jeannine (reporter), "Outcasts in Their Own Land," (Part 2), Canadian Weekly, September 1964.

Lotz, James R., "Human Rights of Indians and Eskimos," Canadian Labour, (Ottawa), December, 1967, pp. 12-13.

Loutitt, Neil (reporter), "For the Metis, Discrimination is an Everyday Occurrence, and Accepted Fact of Life," The Globe and Mail (Toronto), March 29, 1972.

Luebben, Ralph A., "Prejudice and Discrimination Against Navahos in a Mining Community," The Kiva (Journal of the Arizona Archaelogical and Historical Society), October 1964, 30:1-17.

Lurie, Nancy Oestreich, "The Voice of the American Indian: Report on the American Indian Chicago Conference," Current Anthropology, December, 1961, 2:478-500.

Lurie, Nancy Oestreich, "The Enduring Indian," Natural History, 1966, 75:10-22.

Lysyk, Ken, "Human Rights and Canada's Native People," Address, Ninth Annual Conference of the Indian-Eskimo Association of Canada, Toronto, September 27, 1958, 15 pp. (reprinted in Human Relations, (Toronto), April, May, 1969, 9:13-15).

Marshall, John (reporter), "The plight of James Bay Crees: Ottawa's impractical rules," Toronto Telegram, March 24, 1969.

McCloud, Mrs. Janet, "The Continuing 'Last Indian War'," Humanist, September-December, 1967.

McDiarmid, Garnet L. and David Pratt, Teaching Prejudice: a Content Analysis of Social Studies Textbooks Authorized for Use in Ontario, Toronto, Curriculum Series 12, The Ontario Institute for Studies in Education, 1971, 131 pp.

McDowell, Stanley (reporter), "Alberta Indians admit defeat, will drop federal programs: Chrétien denies blackmail used to break school strike," The Globe and Mail, (Toronto), November 24, 1971.

McEwen, Ernest Roy, "The Voluntary Sponsorship of Self-Help Among Indians and Eskimos: An Account of the Work of the Indian-Eskimo Association of Canada," Address, Second Institution of the National Committee of Canadian Schools of Social Work, Toronto, 1965.

McEwen, Ernest Roy, "Rights of Canada's First Citizens, the Indian and the Eskimo," Resource paper prepared for World Council of Churches Consultation on Racism, London, England, by the Indian-Eskimo Association of Canada, May, 1969, 13 pp.

McKay, Sandy, et. al., "The attitudes of Toronto students toward the Canadian Indians," Toronto, unpublished manuscript, Glendon College, ca 1969, 28 pp.

McKernin, Harold J., "Indian Integration -- The Perth, N.B., Situation," unpublished manuscript, July, 1965, 5 pp.

McNeil, Garry (reporter), "Humble Indian maid becomes a Saint," Ottawa Citizen, January 25, 1961.

McNeil, J.D., "Changes in Ethnic Reaction Tendencies During High School," Journal of Educational Research, 1960, 53:199-200.

Means, John E., "Human Rights and Canadian Federalism," Phylon, 1969, 30:398-412.

Metcalfe, Robert (reporter), "No miracles, just faith, hope and dignity restored: Dorothy Betz knows the pain of being an Indian ... ," Weekend Magazine, (Montreal), November 13, 1971.

Merzwinski, Alexandre, et al., The Administration of Justice beyond the 50th parallel, Montreal, Government of Quebec, December 1972, 135 pp.

Morris, William (reporter), "His choice: is it integration or cultural suicide?," The Toronto Daily Star, February 12, 1963.

Morrow, Honourable Justice William George, Inquiry re Administration of Justice in the Hay River of the Northwest Territories: Report, Yellowknife, NWT, February, 1968, 111 pp.

Morrow, Hon. Justice William George, "Administration of justice and native people," Address, Symposium of the Law and Native People, Saskatoon, March 17, 1973, 13 pp.

Mortimer, George E., "The Indians were here FIRST, treat them as 'Citizens Plus'," Human Relations, (Toronto), June, 1967, 7(15):4-6.

Nash, Philleo, "An Introduction to the Problem of Race Tension," in Charles T. Loram and Thomas F. McIlwraith, eds., The North American Indian Today, University of Toronto Press, 1943, pp. 331-338.

Nicholson, Patrick, "Look at Canada's Indian Ghettos," Chronicle-Telegram, (Quebec City), August 3, 1968.

O'Reilly, James A., "Whiter the Indian," Paper prepared for the Civil Liberties Section of the Canadian Bar Association, Annual Meeting, 1969, 54 pp.

Parsons, George F., Arctic Suburb: a Look at the North's Newcomers, Ottawa, Northern Sciences Research Group, Department of Indian Affairs and Northern Development, February, 1970, 94 pp.

Paudash, Anne Rosemary, "I married an Indian," MacLean's Magazine, (Toronto), December 1, 1951.

Pelletier, Victor F., "Fair Employment Practices Branch, Department of Labour," Ottawa, Ontario Metis and Non-Status Association Orientation Workshop, November 1972.

Pelletier, Wilfred, et al., eds. For Every North American Indian Who Begins to Disappear, I Also Begin to Disappear, Toronto Neewin, 1971, 162 pp.

Peters, Omer, "Human Rights and the Indian," Human Rights and the Indian: A Report, Proceedings of a Conference, Centre for Continuing Education, Elliot Lake, Ontario, October 1967, 12-19.

Peters, Omer, "Human Rights for Indian and Eskimos," Address, Thinkers Conference on Cultural Rights, Toronto, December 13-15, 1968 (reprinted in N. Sheffe (ed.) Issues for the Seventies: Canada's Indians, McGraw-Hill, 1970, pp. 7-11).

Platiel, Rudy (reporter), "Will White backlash against Indians spread from Yellowknife?," The Globe and Mail, (Toronto), April 14, 1971.

Platiel, Rudy (reporter), "Has Ottawa imposed reverse discrimination in favour of the Indians in NWT?," The Globe and Mail, (Toronto), April 15, 1971.

Podolinsky, Alika, "The bitter plight of Labrador's Indians," Canada Month, (Montreal), January, 1962, 2:27-29.

Poole, D.G., "Integration," Thunderbird (Toronto), June 1965, and September 1965, (reprinted in The Ignorant Society: White? or Indian?, Proceedings of a Seminar held at Paradise Lake Camp, St. Clement's, Ontario, October, 1967, and in Wilfrid Pelletier, et. al. For Every North American Indian Who Begins to Disappear I also Begin to Disappear, Toronto, Neewin Publication Co., 1971, pp. 25-51).

Richardson, Boyce (reporter), "Indians, non-Indians Live in 'Two Separate Worlds'," The Montreal Star, December 19, 1968.

Richardson, Boyce (reporter), "White structure unhappy: 'Native Power' becoming fact in Territories," The Montreal Star, December 16, 1970.

Rogers, Edward S., "Thatown," Toronto, unpublished manuscript, 1966, 9 pp.

Savard, Remi, "Et les autres Québecois ... ," Interprétation, (Montreal) 1970, 4:117-131.

Savoie, Donat, "Discriminatory situation at The Pas and means to cope with it," Ottawa, unpublished memorandum, Social and Human Analysis Branch, Department of Regional Economic Expansion, January 8, 1971.

Schmeiser, Douglas A., Civil Liberties in Canada, Oxford University Press, 964, 300 pp.

Simmons, Ellen (reporter), "It's a White Man's Canada," Winnipeg Free Press, December 10, 1964.

Simmons, Ellen (reporter) "The Indian's problems in microcosm: The lessons of Kenora," Winnipeg Free Press, December 2, 1965.

Sluman, Mrs. Norma, "Survey of Canadian History Textbooks now in use in Manitoba Schools in order to determine to what extent they tend to promote a patronizing and degrading attitude on the part of the white people towards Indians, are harmful to the Indian child's sense of racial dignity and deal inaccurately with Indian life," Indian and Metis Conference Committee of the Community Welfare Planning Council, Winnipeg, Manitoba, November, 1964, 19 pp.

Sophia, Elmer, Q.C., "Human Rights and the Law," Human Rights and the Indian: A Report, Proceedings of a Conference, Centre for Continuing Education, Elliot Lake, Ontario, October, 1967, pp. 26-34.

Stearns, Mary Lee, "Mechanisms of role definition in an intercultural situation," (B.C.), unpublished manuscript, n.d. 19 pp.

Stockand, Dave (reporter), "Indians tell of Fred's (Quilt) death," Vancouver Sun, December 21, 1971.

Thatcher, W. Ross, "Address," Conference Between the Province of Saskatchewan and the People of Indian Ancestry, Saskatoon, September 22-24, 1964, 9 pp.

Tierney, Ben (reporter), "Saskatchewan Metis rewriting history books to help selves," Ottawa Citizen, August 22, 1970.

Tierney, Ben, (reporter), "Indians want own schools," Ottawa Citizen, December 30, 1971.

Toombs, Farrell C., "The Indian in Canada: a query on dependance," Ottawa, 1965, (reprinted in the Ignorant Society -- White? or Indian?, Proceedings of a Seminar held at Lake Camp, St. Clement's, Ontario, October, 1967).

Trant, W., "Treatment of the Canadian Indians," Westminster Review, November 1895, pp. 506-527.

Troyer, Warner, "The Only Good Indian is a Quiet Indian," Quest, October, 1967, 5:13-14, 38.

Tyre, Robert (reporter), "The day integration came to Kenora: many adults were worried and some were angry when both white and Ojibway children began attending the same school in an area which isn't noted for friendliness toward Indians," The Star Weekly Magazine, February 18, 1961.

Vanderburgh, Mrs. "The Canadian Indian in Ontario's School Texts; A Study of Social Studies Textbooks, Grades 1 through 8, Report," University of Women's Club of Port Credit (Ontario), 1968, 41 pp.

Van Rijn, Nick (reporter), "Brandon petition on Indians described as discriminatory," Winnipeg Tribune, July 21, 1971.

Wabegijig, Carol, "The Canadian Indian in International Year for Human Rights," Toronto: Young Women's Christian Association of Canada, March, 1968.

Wax, Rosalie H. and Robert K. Thomas, "American Indians and White People," Phylon, Winter, 1961, 22:305-317.

West, Bruce (reporter), "Indian Issue," The Globe and Mail (Toronto), January 26, 1966.

Western, Maurice (reporter), "Bad way to win Indians' confidence," The Vancouver Sun, October 17, 1964.

Whiteside, Don, et. al., "A Study into the Attitudes of Edmonton Landlords toward Native Tenants," Edmonton, unpublished manuscript, Alberta Human Rights Association, September 19, 1969, 15 pp.

Whiteside, Don, "Human Rights Conventions," Ottawa, unpublished manuscript, Citizenship Branch, Department of Secretary of State, November 1971, 9 pp.

Whiteside, Don, "Brief bibliography of articles in the Press, etc. on the death of Fred Quilt of William's Lake, B.C. (1971)," Ottawa, National Indian Brotherhood, May 31, 1973, 15 pp.

Wilkinson, Douglas, "A vanishing Canadian," The Beaver, Spring, 1959, 289:25-28.

Wolfleg, Rose, "Indian students suffer from discrimination in Saskatoon," Involvement (Newmarket, Ontario), Fall 1971, 4:34-38.

Worsley, Peter M., "Democracy from on top: the problem of the White man," Address, Third Annual Short Course, University of Saskatchewan, Saskatoon, April, 1961, 13 pp.

Wray, Robert, "Yellowknife," Yellowknife, N.W.T., unpublished manuscript, October 1968, 18 pp.

Miscellaneous Reports by Date of Publications

Wisconsin Indians, Madison, Governor's Commission on Human Rights, 1952, 80 pp.

"Memorandum Relating to the Menominee Indian Tribe," Madison, unpublished memorandum, Governor's Commission on Human Rights, March 5, 1954, 6 pp.

"Protecting Our Birthright: Disallowance of Bill of Rights," Winnipeg Free Press, May, 1954.

"Segregation Manitoba Style," Editorial, The Emerson Journal (Emerson, Manitoba), October 24, 1958.

"The integration story at Gleichen," Calgary Herald (reprinted in Indian News (Ottawa), June 1961, 5:5)

"Proposed Declaration of the Human Rights of the Indians of Canada," Annual Meeting of the Canadian Home and School and Parent-Teacher Federation, Charlottetown, P.E.I., July 13, 1964, 8 pp.

"Social Justice for Canada's Indians," Human Relations, (Toronto) December, 1964, 5:

"Submissions to Kenora Town Council, re: Indian-Non-Indian Relations," Kenora, Ontario, unpublished manuscript, Seven Indian Bands, November 22, 1966, 6 pp.

"Chief says no bias against $15,000 a year Indians, Winnipeg Free Press, November 30, 1965.

"Aid Kenora Indians' Brief," Canadian Labour, (Ottawa), January 1966, p. 38.

Human Rights and the Indian; a Report, Conference at the Centre for Continuing Education, Elliot Lake, Ontario, October 27-29, 1967.

"Panel Discussion: Human Rights and Education," Human Rights and the Indian: a Report, Conference, Centre for Continuing Education, Elliott Lake, Ontario, October 1967, pp. 20-25.

"Indian, Eskimos and the Administration of Justice in the North-west Territories," Brief to the Commission of Enquiry into the Administration of Justice in the NWT, NWT Division of the Indian-Eskimo Association of Canada, Yellowknife, NWT, November, 1967, 11 pp.

"Minority Group Research in Ontario: selected Bibliography of Graduate Research Carried out at the University of Toronto in the Area of Human Rights and Minority Groups in Ontario," Toronto Research Division of the Ontario Human Rights Commission, 1968, 8 pp.

"The Right to an Identity," Ottawa, The Canadian Baha'i Community, 1968.

"Canadian Conference on Human Rights, Participating Organizations," Ottawa, The Canadian Baha'i Community, 1968.

Human Rights and the Indian, Ottawa, Catholic Charities Council of Canada, January, 1968.

"Submission of the Manitoba Indian Brotherhood to the Brandon Conference on Human Rights," February 28, 1969, 8 pp.

"Pub Fight that Could Lead Indians to More Protection in the Courts," The Globe and Mail, (Toronto), March 14, 1969.

"Report of an Independent Committee of Inquiry Established to Examine the Conditions of Migrant Workers in the Sugar Beet Industry in Alberta," Edmonton, Alberta, Human Rights Association, Alberta Metis Association, Canadian Labour Congress, and the Indian Association of Alberta, 1970, 20 pp.

"Case for Human Rights," The Native People (Edmonton), May, 1970, 3(1):2.

"Indians-Metis Demand C.F.I. Employment Rights," The Pas, Herald(Manitoba), September 30, 1970.

"Illegal Sentencing," The Indian News, (Ottawa), November 1970, 13(8):7.

"Death Indicates Need for Sharing Facilities," The Ottawa Citizen, December 2, 1970.

"Buffalo and Welfare," Metis News (Metis Association of Alberta) February 12, 1971, No. 42, p. 1.

"Whites in N.W.T. imitating racist attitudes of whites in Rhodesia," The Native People (Edmonton), August 1971, 4(1):2.

"Chief is shot, badly wounded by Mountie," (Ed. Bird), The Globe and Mail, (Toronto), August 10, 1971.

"Man may lose leg: school Watchman charged in Indian shooting," The Globe and Mail, (Toronto), August 25, 1971.

"Conference on Human Rights," Manitoba Metis Federation, Winnipeg, Manitoba, September 12, 1971, 16 pp.

"Indian's Misery Stuns Official -- 'I can't stand any more'," Toronto Daily Star, October 2, 1971.

"1,087 Students join Indians' boycott," Edmonton Journal, October 16, 1971.

"Cold Lake, Alberta," Casserole, (a Supplement of The Gateway Edmonton, University of Alberta), October 29, 1971.

"Judge is Critical of Indian Attitudes: points Out Trials Cost $3,000 Daily," Sudbury Star, (Ontario), November 17, 1971.

"Northeastern Alberta -- Action by Minister to Solve School Dispute -- Discussion of Long-Range Educational Program," House of Commons Debates, November 26, 1971, 115:9922-9923.

"Just What Was Said, The Easy Way to Beat Indians," (excerpts from an editorial in the Canadian-Jewish News), The Globe and Mail, (Toronto), December 9, 1971.

"Royal Canadian Mounted Police: Death of Indian at Williams Lake Attributed to Beating by Officer," House of Commons Debates, December 17, 1971, 115:10570-10571.

"Brief to the Hon, John Turner, P.C., M.P., Minister of Justice and Attorney-General of Canada, and the Honourable J.P. Goyer,

P.C., M.P., Solicitor-General of Canada," Ottawa, Native Council of Canada, December 17, 1971, 15 pp.

"Tear gas halts B.C. pen revolt: Indian's death angers inmates," Nanaimo Daily Free Press, (B.C.) August 8, 1970.

"Judge says CRTC Powerless to Prevent 'Racist' TV Programs," Toronto Daily Star, December 23, 1971.

"Report on Five Human Rights Seminars Held 1971 in British Columbia, Alberta, Saskatchewan, Manitoba and Ontario," Native Council of Canada and Indian-Eskimo Association of Canada, 1972.

"Kenora Project Killed by Racism, Mayor says," Toronto Daily Star, January 14, 1972.

"Survey reveals prejudice exists," Sidney Cape Breton Post (Nova Scotia), February 19, 1972.

"South African Tells Conference Here False Love Still Killing Canadian Indians," Calgary Herald, February 28, 1972.

"Like Rhodesia's blacks' Canada's Indians Claim," Toronto Daily Star, March 10, 1972.

"Press Release: re: Judge Collins of Sudbury, Ontario," Ottawa, Native Council of Canada, April 21, 1972, 1 p.

"Discrimination Against Indians in Saskatchewan Textbooks," Brief on Education, Presented by the Saskatchewan Association on Human Rights, Spring, 1972, 30 pp.

"Papago Youth's Death Angers Many," Akwesasne Notes, (Rooseveltown, N.Y.), Summer, 1972, pp. 4-5.

"The Government has Ordered Canada's 13,000 Eskimos to Adopt New Names, Toronto Daily Star, May 6, 1972.

"Judge will Conduct Second Quilt Inquest," The Globe and Mail, (Toronto), May 9, 1972.

"Exodus: Whites Leave Jobs, Troubled Reserve," The Ottawa Citizen, July 29, 1972.

"Inquest Verdict Open on RCMP-Quilt Conflict," The Ottawa Citizen, August 4, 1972.

"Indian, Metis to Press Prejudice Claims," Saskatoon Star Phoenix, August 8, 1972.

"Charge Attorney-General fails to act on reports: Manitoba Indians plan to publicize discrimination," The Globe and Mail, (Toronto), August 29, 1972.

"Anti-loitering bylaw in Saskatchewan is called racist: directed against Indians association charges," The Globe and Mail, (Toronto), October 11, 1972.

112

"Manitoba Indian raps human rights laws," The Leader-Post (Regina) October 17, 1972.

"Racial bias denied after Indian youths are beaten in jail," The Globe and Mail, (Toronto), October 22, 1972.

"Citizens and the law north of '60," in Douglas H. Pimlott, Kitson M. Vincent and Christine E. McKnight, eds., Arctic Alternatives, a national workshop, Ottawa, Canadian Arctic Resources Committee, 1973, pp 361-388.

"Saskatchewan natives, Metis say situations tense: RCMP harassing Indians, committing sexual acts against women, head of group charges," (Jim Sinclar) The Globe and Mail, (Toronto) January 13, 1973.

"Policeman 'allowed beatings'," Ottawa Citizen, February 6, 1973.

"The hypocrisy that is Canada," Edmonton Journal, February 7, 1973.

"Fined for attack, policeman 'learned lesson'," The Montreal Star, February 7, 1973.

"Nothing will be left undone, Human Rights letter draws word from A-G," (William's Lake, B.C.), The New Nation (Winnipeg), February, 1973.

"Acquittal of whites is called an outrage," (indecent assault at William's Lake, B.C.), The Globe and Mail, (Toronto), March 3, 1973.

"23 Metis students get four-day ban," Winnipeg Free Press, March 17, 1973.

"And even the Cleveland Indians are in trouble," Edmonton Journal, March 30, 1973

"RCMP Disciplines 'very aggressive' members," Edmonton Journal April 18, 1973

"Injustice towards Indians disclosed," (C.C.L.A. report), The Leader-Post, (Regina), May 1, 1973.

"Brief presented to the participants to the Consultation on the 25th Anniversary of the Adoption of the Universal Declaration of Human Rights and the Decade to Combat Racism and Racial Discrimination," Department of Secretary of State, Ottawa, National Indian Brotherhood, May 3, 1973, 4 pp.

PART X

NATIVE ASSOCIATIONS (FORMAL), AND
CONFERENCES NOT LISTED ELSEWHERE

A -- General
B -- National Associations and Conferences (See also General)
C -- Provincial Associations and Conferences (See also General)
D -- Non-Native (Indian-Eskimo) Associations
E -- Directories

A -- General

Drucker, Philip, The Native brotherhoods: modern intertribal organizations on the Northwest coast, Washington, Smithsonian Institute, Bureau of American Ethnology, Bulletin 168, 1968, 194 pp.

Hodgson, Stuart M., "Letter to Honourable Jean Chrétien, re native organizations," Yellowknife, N.W.T., unpublished, October 8, 1971.

Kerri, James N., "Utilization of a Native Peoples' voluntary association as a channel of communication: The case of C.O.P.E. in Inuvik, N.W.T." A Report submitted to the Prairie Region Department of Manpower and Immigration, Winnipeg, Manitoba, October 1970, 84 pp.

Luchaire, Andre (reporter), "Ottawa--many promises, seldom kept," La Presse (Montreal), June 12, 1967.

Lueger, Rick, "An introduction to Canadian Indian political organizations: a preliminary report," Ottawa, unpublished manuscript, National Indian Brotherhood, August 1972, 100 pp.

McNickle, D'Arcy, "Private intervention," Human Organization, 1961, 20:208-215.

Smith, Maurice G., "Political organization of the plains Indians," University of Nebraska Publications, 1925, Volume 24 (1 and 2).

Smitheram, Henry (Butch) Arthur, "Modern Indian organizations and their ideology," Vancouver, B.C., unpublished manuscript, 1971, 7 pp.

Miscellaneous Reports by date of publication

Indian-Eskimo Association, Learned Societies Meeting, Queen's University, Kingston, Ontario, June 1960.

Trinity College Conference on the Canadian Indian, Toronto, January, 1966.

"U.S. Indians less reliant on whites," Edmonton Journal, November 18, 1966.

Thinkers' Conference on Cultural Rights, King Edward Sheraton Hotel, Toronto, December 13-15, 1968.

"Minutes: Winnipeg Native Club," unpublished, Winnipeg, September 22, 1972.

"Brief in respect to the formation of an Indian political base," Winnipeg, Manitoba, unpublished manuscript, The National Indian Movement, October 27, 1972, 4 p.

B -- National Associations (by date of publication)

"Indian League of Nations," (League of Indians of Canada), editorial, Journal (Edmonton), December, 1918.

"Redskins organize: seek return of rights lost with spread of white civilization," (The United League of Indians), Saskatoon Star, January 3, 1938.

"Proceedings of the Indian convention," (formation of North American Indian Brotherhood), June 5-7, 1944, Ottawa.

The second session of the North American national government, Detroit, Michigan, September 15-17, 1947, (printed in Canada), 12 pp.

"Minutes of the Second Annual Conference," National Indian Council, Toronto, August 30 -- September 1, 1962.

"Third Annual Conference of the National Indian Council," Winnipeg, Manitoba, August 1963.

"National Indian Brotherhood Conference," Winnipeg, July 1969.

"Minutes, Special General Assembly of the National Indian Brotherhood," Windsor, Ontario, March 7,8,9, 1970.

"Minutes of the General Assembly Meeting of the National Indian Brotherhood," March 26, 1970, Montreal, Quebec.

"Minutes of Meeting of National Indian Brotherhood," Vancouver, B.C., August 21, 1970.

Delisle, Chief Andrew Tanahokate, "Letter to Harold Cardinal, President, Indian Association of Alberta," (re withdrawal from committee), unpublished, January 14, 1971.

"Minutes of the General Assembly Meeting of the National Indian Brotherhood, Fredericton, New Brunswick," March, 1971.

"Report of the National Indian Brotherhood, a report submitted for the consideration of the General Assembly by the Indian

Association of Alberta, National Indian Brotherhood Meeting, Fredericton, New Brunswick," March 2-5, 1971.

"Minutes to Annual General Assembly National Indian Brotherhood, Regina Inn, Regina, Saskatchewan," July, 1971.

"Report to the General Assembly of the National Indian Brotherhood: The Negotiating Committee: Proposed Organization and Structure to facilitate Negotiations between the Federal Government and the Indian People of Canada," Indian Association of Alberta, July 14, 1971.

"President's Report (George Manuel) to the General Assembly on the activities of the National Indian Brotherhood for Fiscal 1970," July 14-16, 1971.

"Resolutions Passed at the Annual General Assembly of the National Indian Brotherhood at the Regina Inn, Regina, Saskatchewan, on July 14, 15 and 16, 1971.

Press Release -- National Indian Brotherhood, General Assembly, Union of B.C. Chiefs, Regina, Saskatchewan, July 16, 1971. (I.A.A. activities.)

Wacko, William J., "Report on the Indian Brotherhood of NWT: problems and Challenges Facing the Indian Brotherhood of NWT and its need for help from other native organizations in Canada in 1971," unpublished manuscript, Indian Association of Alberta, 1971.

"Indian Brotherhood of North West Territories proposal for a Regional Director for Indian Affairs in the North West Territories," unpublished manuscript, Indian Brotherhood of the North West Territories, January 1972. 9 p.

"President's Report," (A.E. Belcourt) First Annual General Assembly, Native Council of Canada, Ottawa, March 23, 1972, 8 pp.

"Constitution and By Laws," Ottawa, unpublished manuscript, Native Council of Canada, March 23, 1972, 7 pp.

"Minutes First Annual General Assembly, Native Council of Canada, Ottawa, March 23-25, 1972, 9 pp.

"What is Inuit Tapirisat of Canada?," Ottawa, unpublished manuscript.

"President's Report (George Manuel) to the General Assembly on the Activities of the National Indian Brotherhood for Fiscal 1971-1972," Ottawa, National Indian Brotherhood, July, 1972.

"Minutes to Founding Meeting for Consultation Mechanism of National Indian Brotherhood Executive Council and Ministerial Consultation Committee," Ottawa, July 7, 1972.

"Minutes of General Assembly of National Indian Brotherhood," Edmonton, Alberta, August 8-10, 1972.

"Native youth conference," Native Youth News, (Ottawa), August-September 1972, volume 1 (3-4).

McElroy, Ann P., "The origins and development of Inuit (Eskimo) alliance movements in the Eastern Canadian Arctic," paper presented to the Symposium, International Culture Change Among North American Indians, XL International Congress of Americanists, Rome, September 1972, 17 pp.

"North American Indians, XL International Congress of Americanists," Rome, September 1972, 17 pp.

"President's Report (A.E. Belcourt)," Second Annual General Assembly, Native Council of Canada, Ottawa, March 28, 1973, 5 pp.

C -- Provincial Associations

C 1 -- The Maritimes

"Minutes of organizational meeting," Amherst, N.S., Nova Scotia Union of Indians, May 13, 1969, 3 pp.

"Minutes of organizational meeting," Halifax, N.S., Union of Nova Scotia Indians, July 11-13, 1969, 8 pp.

"Minutes of second organizational meeting," Halifax, N.S., Union of Nova Scotia Indians, September 12, 13, 1969, 15 pp.

"Minutes, General Board of Directors Meeting," Union of Nova Scotia Indians, Halifax, N.S., August 8-9, 1970, 21 pp.

"Minutes, Union of Nova Scotia Indians, Second Annual Conference," February 26-28, 1971, 6 pp.

"The Founding Conference, New Brunswick Association of Non-Status Indians," Fredericton, New Brunswick, August 26, 1972.

C 2 -- Quebec

"Annual Conference, Quebec Metis and Non-Status Indian Association," Montreal, Quebec, June 24 and 25, 1972, Constitution and Resolutions.

LaRusic, Ignatius E., "The influence of the Indians of Quebec Association in Waswanipi," A report prepared for the Department of Secretary of State, September 1972, 59 pp.

C 3 -- Ontario

"Minutes of the Grand General Council of the Chippewas, Muncey, Six Nations, etc," June 25 -- July 3, 1871, Sarnia Reserve.

"Minutes of the 16th Grand Indian Council in the Province of Ontario, June 7-12, 1900.

"Minutes and proceedings of the 57th convention of the Grand Indian Council of Ontario, Section 9, 1930, Shawanaga.

"Minutes of 13th Grand General Indian Council," October 16-20, 1944, Moraviatown.

"Union of Ontario Indians Convention," August 24, 1961, Garden River Reserve.

"Minutes of a meeting of the board of directors of the Ontario Metis and Non-Status Indian Association," (Constitution and By-Laws), Toronto, April 16, June 1972, 8 pp.

"Report, Union of Ontario Indians," Toronto, September 1972, 68 pp.

"Annual Conference, Ontario Metis and Non-Status Indian Association," Sault Ste. Marie, Ontario, June 17 and 18, 1972, Constitution and Resolutions.

C 4 -- Manitoba

Beaulieu, Isaac, "Organizational Aspects of the Manitoba Indians," Winnipeg, Manitoba Indian Brotherhood, January 1968, 51 pp.

Clipsman, Muriel, "Report on the Native Brotherhood Society, Regina, Saskatchewan," unpublished manuscript prepared for the Conference on the Indian in the Community, May 1957, 4 pp.

"Conference on Indians and Metis in Manitoba," Welfare Council of Greater Winnipeg, October, 1954.

"Second Annual Meeting, Indian and Metis Conference," Welfare Council of Greater Winnipeg, 1955.

"Fifth Annual Meeting, Indian and Metis Conference," Winnipeg, February, 1959.

"Proceedings: 6th Annual Conference on Indian and Metis; Operation Council Fire, Teamwork in solving Community Problems," Welfare Council of Greater Winnipeg, February, 1960.

"Indian and Metis 9th Annual Conference," Winnipeg, Sponsored by the Community Welfare Planning Council, February, 1963.

"10th Annual Indian and Metis Conference," Sponsored by the Community Welfare Planning Council of Greater Winnipeg, February, 1964.

"11th Annual Indian and Metis Conference," Winnipeg, Community Welfare Planning Council, February 5-8, 1965.

"Indian and Metis Conference," January 14, 1966, Winnipeg.

"14th Annual Manitoba Indian and Metis Conference," Winnipeg, April, 1968.

"Constitution, The Manitoba Metis Federation," 1968.

"Annual Report, 1969-1970," Winnipeg, Manitoba Indian Brotherhood, 65 pp.

"Manitoba Indian Brotherhood, Two Years of Progress, Annual Report 1970,"Winnipeg, Manitoba Indian Brotherhood, April 1970, 46 pp.

"New Directions for Manitoba Indians, Annual Report, 1970-1971," Winnipeg, Manitoba Indian Brotherhood.

"Annual Conference Manitoba Metis Federation Inc.," Rivers, Manitoba, March 2, 3 and 4, 1972, Constitution and Resolutions.

C 4 -- Saskatchewan

Douglas, Hon. Thomas C., The Union of Saskatchewan Indians: the Record of the establishment of Indian unity in Saskatchewan, Regina, Saskatchewan, March 1946, 73 pp.

Conference Between the Province of Saskatchewan and the People of Indian Ancestry, Saskatoon, September 22-25, 1964.

"Federation of Saskatchewan Indians, Annual Conference," Valley Centre, Fort Qu'appelle, Sask., February 9, 10, 11, 1965.

"Federation of Saskatchewan Indians, Annual Conference," Prince Albert, November, 1967.

Barbarash, John and Johnny Yesno, "Federation of Saskatchewan Indians," Indian Magazine, broadcast March 28, 1969, Canadian Broadcasting Corporation.

"Progress Report 1969-70," Federation of Saskatchewan Indians.

"Annual Conference, Metis Society of Saskatchewan," Batoche, Saskatchewan, June 25-28, 1972, Constitution and Resolutions.

C 5 -- Alberta

"Minutes of the Annual General Meeting," Indian Association of Alberta, LeGoff Reserve, June 23, 24, 1948, 6 pp.

Minutes of the Council Meeting," Indian Association of Alberta, February 4, 1950, 6 pp.

Laurie, John, "General Meeting 1950," Canadian Cattlemen (Calgary), July, 1950.

"Minutes of the General Meeting," Indian Association of Alberta, June 14, 15, 1951, Good Fish Lake Reserve, 13 pp.

Laurie, John, "General Meeting 1951," Canadian Cattlemen (Calgary), August, 1951.

"Minutes of the Provincial Council," Indian Association of Alberta, February 23, 1952, 4 pp.

"Minutes of General Meeting," Indian Association of Alberta, June 12, 13, 1952, Gleichen Reserve, 9 pp.

Laurie, John, "General Meeting 1952," Canadian Cattlemen (Calgary), July, 1952.

"Minutes of the General Meeting," Indian Association of Alberta, June 24, 25, 1953, 14 pp.

Laurie, John, "Indian Association to hold 10th Annual Meeting," Canadian Cattlemen (Calgary), June, 1953.

Laurie, John, "The Indians Organize," Canadian Cattlemen, (Calgary), June, 1953.

Laurie, John, "General Meeting," Canadian Cattlemen (Calgary), August, 1953.

"Minutes of General Meeting," Indian Association of Alberta, June 9, 10, 1954, Sarcee Reserve, 9 pp.

Laurie, John, "Our Eleventh Annual Convention, The Indian Association of Alberta, Never Rained Out, Still Carried On," Canadian Cattlemen (Calgary), July, 1954.

"Minutes General Meeting," Indian Association of Alberta, June 20, 22, 1955, 10 pp.

"Minutes of the General Meeting," Indian Association of Alberta, Hobbema, Alberta, June 18, 19, 1957, 12 pp.

"Annual Meeting," Indian Association of Alberta, June 1968, 6 pp.

"Executive Meeting," Indian Association of Alberta, August 23, 1968, 6 pp.

"Report," (Harold Cardinal), Annual Meeting, Indian Association of Alberta, Sucker Creek, Alberta, 1969, 13 pp.

"Motions and Resolutions of The Indian Association of Alberta," Sucker Creek Reserve, June 19-21, 1969, 18 pp.

Cardinal, Harold, "Address," Alberta All Chiefs Conference and distinguished representatives of Canadian Provincial Associations, Lake Isle, Alberta, April 13, 1970, 12 pp.

Dempsey, Hugh A., "The History of the Indian Association," Kainai News (Cardston, Alta.), June 15, 1970.

"Report," (Harold Cardinal), 26th Annual Convention, Standoff, Alberta, June 17, 1970, 9 pp.

"Minutes of 27th Annual Meeting," Indian Association of Alberta, June 17-19, 1970, 108 pp.

"Memorandum, Recovery of Unity and Power to the People in the locals," Edmonton, unpublished manuscript, Metis Association of Alberta, August 1, 1970.

"Annual Meeting," Indian Association of Alberta, Hobbema, June, 1971.

"Native Youth Alliance," Edmonton, Alberta, 1971, By-Laws (draft).

"Annual Meeting," Indian Association of Alberta, Saddle Lake, Alberta, June, 1972.

"Annual Conference," Metis Association of Alberta, High Prairie, Alberta, July 8 and 9, 1972.

C 6 -- British Columbia

Report on Conference on Native Indian Affairs, B.C., Arts and Welfare Society, Vancouver, 1948.

"Annual Report," Indian Advisory Committee, Department of Provincial Secretary, Victoria, British Columbia, 1950 to present.

"Minutes, North American Indian Brotherhood," June 11, 1961, Hope, B.C.

"The Seventh Annual Meeting of Members," (N.A.I.B.), B.C. December, 1966.

"Indian Advisory Committee Newsletter," Victoria, B.C., February, 1968.

"First Annual Conference, B.C. Association of Non-Status Indians," Burnaby, B.C., November 1969, 4 pp.

"Minutes, North American Indian Brotherhood," February 15, 1970, Lillooet, B.C.

"Union of British Columbia Chiefs, 2nd Annual Convention," Vancouver, B.C., November 16-21, 1970.

Smitheram, Henry (Butch) Arthur, "Statement of intent regarding the organization and future of the B.C. Association of Non-Status Indians," Vancouver, B.C., Presidential Address at the annual meeting of the B.C. Association of Non-Status Indians, 1971, 20 pp.

"Minutes of the Special General Meeting," Prince George, B.C., Union of British Columbia Chiefs, March 23-26, 1971.

"Report of Executive Director (Len Maracle) to the Third Annual Conference of the B.C. Association of Non-Status Indians," Victoria, B.C., November, 1971, 10 pp.

"Cultural Unity Conference," Sechelt, B.C., Sechelt Local, B.C., Association of Non-Status Indians, October 7, 1972, 8 pp.

C 7 -- Yukon and Northwest Territories

"Annual Meeting," Yukon Native Brotherhood, Whitehorse, February 24-26, 1970, 13 pp.

"The Founding Conference, Yukon Association of Non-Status Indians," Whitehorse, Yukon Territory, February 18, 19, and 20, 1972. Constitution and Resolutions.

"Annual Meeting," of the Yukon Native Brotherhood, Whitehorse, Yukon Territory, May 9-11, 1972, 19 pp.

D --- **Non-Native (e.g. National Commission on the Indian Canadian 1957-1960 -- Indian-Eskimo Association of Canada 1960-1972 -- Canadian Association in support of Native People, 1972)** by date of publication.

"The way we have come ... " Indian Eskimo Association of Canada, Bulletin, March 1960, 1:

"Annual Report, Fifth Annual Meeting," Indian-Eskimo Association of Canada, London, Ontario, November 21, 1964, 18 pp.

"First Provincial Conference," Ontario Division, Indian-Eskimo Association of Canada, 1964

"Interpreting the work of Indian-Eskimo Association of Canada," Toronto, Indian-Eskimo Association of Canada, 1965.

"Report of Executive Director (E.R. McEwen) to the Sixth Annual Meeting, Indian-Eskimo Association of Canada," Toronto, October 21, 1965, 11 pp.

"Guidelines to Regional Organization," Indian-Eskimo Association of Canada, Toronto, June 1966, 19 pp.

Kerr, Wendie (reporter), "A white man fights for the Indians: as an economist and a Canadian he cannot tolerate the inequality under which the Indian citizen is forced to live," (Martin O'Connell), Don Mills -- North York Mirror (Ontario), October 12, 1966.

O'Connell, Martin P., "Address of Retiring Ontario Division President," 2nd Annual Meeting, Ontario Division, Indian-Eskimo Association of Canada, Toronto, November 24, 1967, 20 pp.

"Report of Executive Director (E.R. McEwen) to the Seventh Annual Meeting, Indian-Eskimo Association of Canada," Vancouver, B.C., December 2, 1966, 14 pp.

"Report of the Executive Secretary (James H. Buller) to the Second Annual Meeting of the Ontario Division," Indian-Eskimo Association of Canada, November 25, 1967, 8 pp.

"A Report on the First Regional Conference Held at Yellowknife, N.W.T.," Indian-Eskimo Association, N.W.T. Division, Yellowknife, January 6, 7, 1968, 24 pp.

"President's (Jack Boyd) Report, Indian-Eskimo Association of Canada, N.W.T. Division, Yellowknife," N.W.T., September 18, 1968, 42 pp.

"Third Annual Meeting and Conference, Ontario Division, Indian-Eskimo Association of Canada," London, Ontario, September 1968, 42 pp.

"Report of Executive Director (E.R. McEwen) to the Ninth Annual Meeting of Members, Indian-Eskimo Association of Canada," Toronto, September 28, 1968, 33 pp.

"National Indian Brotherhood, Canadian Metis Society, Indian-Eskimo Association: Report of a Joint Meeting of the Boards of Directors of the Above Organizations for purpose of Reviewing and redirecting the role of the Indian-Eskimo Association," Toronto, Indian-Eskimo Association, September, 1968, 56 pp.

"Agenda, Indian-Eskimo Association of Canada, Alberta Division, Annual Meeting, Edmonton, November 21, 1969.

"Report and Minutes, 4th Annual Meeting of Members, Ontario Division, Indian Eskimo Association of Canada," Toronto, December 6, 1969, 10 pp.

"Report of the Executive Director (E.R. McEwen) to the Tenth Annual Meeting of Members," Indian-Eskimo Association of Canada, Winnipeg, June 13, 1969, 22 pp.

Banff Conference, Sponsored by the Indian-Eskimo Association, May, 1970.

"Report of Executive Director (G. Allan Clark) to the Eleventh Annual Meeting of Members, Indian-Eskimo Association of Canada," Ottawa, National Library and Archives, June, 1970, 10 pp.

"Report of Executive Director (G. Allan Clark) to the Twelfth Annual Meeting of Members, Indian-Eskimo Association of Canada," Toronto, June 1971, 10 pp.

"Report of the Executive Director (G. Allan Clark) to the thirteenth Annual Meeting of Members, Indian-Eskimo Association of Canada," Rexdale, Ontario, June 1972, 20 pp.

Symons, Thomas H.B., "A message from the new president: the role of a national citizens' organization in support of native people," Bulletin (Indian-Eskimo Association of Canada), July, 1972, 13:

Ketchum, W.Q. (reporter), "Faces of Ottawa: Ernie McEwen," Ottawa Journal, November 25, 1972.

E -- Directories

Second Annual Tribal Leaders Conference Report, December 3, and 4, 1962, Duluth, Minnesota," 24 pp.

<u>Midwest Directory</u>: 1967: <u>Organizations</u>, <u>Agencies</u> <u>and</u> <u>Institutions</u> <u>Relating</u> <u>to</u> <u>Indian</u> <u>Affairs</u>, Institute of Indian Studies, The University of South Dakota, Vermillion, 1967, 44 p.

MacDonald, Nancy L., "A List of Indian Associations," Ottawa, unpublished manuscript, Social Research and Documentation Service, Department of Secretary of State, August 8, 1967.

MacDonald, Nancy L., "A List of Indian Publications, Newspapers and Bulletins," Ottawa, unpublished manuscript, Social Research and Documentation Service, Department of Secretary of State, August 8, 1967, 3 pp.

<u>Governing</u> <u>Bodies</u> <u>of</u> <u>Federally</u> <u>Recognized</u> <u>Indian</u> <u>Groups</u> (<u>excluding</u> <u>Alaska</u>), U.S. Dept. of the Interior, Bureau of Indian Affairs, January, 1969.

Price, John A., "U.S. and Canadian Indian Periodicals," Toronto, unpublished manuscript, York University, June, 1971.

"Current North American Periodicals," Washington, D.C., Centre for the Study of Man Smithsonian Institution, 1972, 15 pp.

"Listing of Native Newspapers," Ottawa, National Indian Brotherhood, 1972, 2 pp.

<u>Opposition</u> <u>to</u> <u>ethnocide</u>: <u>index</u> <u>of</u> <u>groups</u> <u>concerned</u> <u>with</u> <u>the</u> <u>defense</u> <u>of</u> <u>tribal</u> <u>minorities</u>, Rennes, France, Groupe d'Etudes les Minorités Ethniques, Université de Haute-Bretagne, February 1972, 53 pp.

"Agenda," National Archives Conference on Research in the History of Indian-White Relations, June 15, 16, 1972, Washington, D.C.

"Metis and Non-Status Indian Associations in Canada," Ottawa, Native Council of Canada, November, 1972.

PART XI

RESISTANCE

A -- Philosophy and resistance (passive and violent)
B -- Wars

A -- Philosophy and Resistance

Adams, Howard J., "A better deal for the Indians," The Cutting Edge, (United Church Publishing House), 1968.

Adams, Howard J., "The Cree as a colonial people," The Western Canadian Journal of Anthropology, 1969, 1:120-124.

Adams, Howard J.,, "Three views of Canada's third world people," (Book reviews), Canadian Dimension Magazine, 1970, pp. 43-46.

Adams, Howard J., "Red power: an interview with Howard Adams," Canadian Dimension Magazine, circa 1970.

Adams, Howard J., "Its inevitable: Indians and Metis will use violence," Toronto Daily Star, November 5, 1971.

Anglin, Perry (reporter), "Protest: how they organized the march that killed Kenora's apathy," Toronto Daily Star, November 27, 1965.

Armstrong, Virginia Irving, ed., I have spoken: American history through the voices of the Indians, Chicago, The Swallow Press, 206 pp.

Assheton-Smith, Marilyn I., and W. Bruce Handley, The Lac La Biche Native Sit-In, Lac La Biche, Alberta New Start, October, 1970, 12 pp.

Bachop, Bill (reporter), "In cultural minorities brief Japanese support Indians," Vancouver Sun, March 7, 1972.

Bachrach, William B., "An assault in the sixties," Humanist, September-December, 1967.

Bacon, Georges, "Presentation," recherches amerindiennes au quebec, November 1972, 2:9-11.

Bell, Dennis, (reporter), "Geronimo lives! ... as the spirit of red power in Canada," (NARP Native Alliance for Red Power), Examiner (Peterborough, Ont.) July 3, 1969.

Benedict, Ernest, "Information for the people of Akwesasne about the Jay Treaty and customs," St. Regis, unpublished manuscript, 1968, 5 pp.

Benedict, Ernest, "Indians and a treaty," in Waubageshig, ed., The only good Indian: essays by Canadian Indians, Toronto, New Press, 1970, pp. 157-160.

Bennett, Lerone Jr., "Red and black: Indians and Africans," _Ebony_, December, 1970 (reprinted in _Akwesasne Notes_, (Rooseveltown, N.Y.), December 1971, 3:44.)

Bigart, Homer (reporter), "Militancy of urban Indians spurs hope for change," _The New York Times_, February 10, 1972.

Billotte, Roger, "Prof. and students arrested: American Indians protest anthro. studies," _The Rocky Mountain Collegian_, (Colorado State University), September 28, 1971, (reprinted in _Akwesasne Notes_, (Rooseveltown, N.Y.), Autumn, 1971, 3:14.)

Blackned-Watt, Gertrude, "This land was our land," _Human Relations_ (Toronto), June, 1966.

Bongartz, Roy (reporter), "The New Indian," _Esquire_, August, 1970.

Burns, Wayne (reporter), "Chief Smallboy opts out: they seek dignity in nature and isolation. To escape the white man and his unwanted influence, they live in tents through the vicious foothills winter," _Canadian Magazine_, (Toronto), February 1, 1969.

Caibaiosai, Lloyd Roland, "Politics of patience," in Waubageshig, ed., _The only good Indian: essays by Canadian Indians_, Toronto, New Press, 1970, pp. 143-155.

Calamai, Peter (reporter), "Indians appeal for world aid in compensation fight," _The Ottawa Citizen_, June 14, 1972.

Cameron, William (reporter), "A long afternoon," _Toronto Daily Star_, May 23, 1969, (reprinted in N. Sheffe, ed., _Issues for Seventies: Canada's Indians_, Toronto, McGraw-Hill, 1970, pp. 32-34).

Cardinal, Harold, _The unjust society: the trágedy of Canada's Indians_, Edmonton, M.G. Hurtig, Co., 1969, 171 pp.

Cardinal, Harold, "Canadian Indians and the Federal Government," (originally presented as an address to the Glendon Forum on Canadian Indians, Glendon College, York University, October, 1968) _The Western Canadian Journal of Anthropology_, 1969, 1:90-97.

Castellano, Marlene, "Vocation or identity: the dilemma of Indian youth," in Waubageshig, ed., _The only good Indian: essays by Canadian Indians_, Toronto, New Press, 1970, pp. 52-60.

Cawley, Janet (reporter), "Kahn-Tineta Horn declares she's a racist and proud of it," _The Ottawa Journal_, May 29, 1971.

Cohen, Felix S., "Americanizing the white man," reprinted in _The ignorant society: White? or Indian?_, Proceedings of a Seminar held at Paradise Lake Camp, St. Clements, Ontario, October, 1967.

Collier, John, "Indians come alive: new hope for native Americans," _Atlantic Monthly_, Spring, 1942, 170:

Collier, John, "Back to dishonor," Christian Century, May 12, 1954, 71:

Collier, John, "Indian takeaway," Nation, October, 1954, 179:

Collier, Peter (reporter), "The Red Man's burden," Ramparts Magazine, February, 1970, 8:

Collier, Peter (reporter), "Salmon fishing in America: the Indians vs. the State of Washington," Ramparts Magazine, April, 1971, 9:

Courchene, Dave, "Address of welcome to H.M. Queen Elizabeth II," The Pas, Manitoba, 1970, 2 pp.

Craig, Barrie (reporter), "Indian protest of housing, schools, may spread," (Cold Lake, Alberta), The Globe and Mail, (Toronto), October 23, 1971.

Currie, Walter, "Who are you? I am an Indian," MicMac News, (Sydney, N.S.), December, 1972.

Debo, Angie Elbertha, The road to disappearance, Norman, University of Oklahoma Press, 1941.

Deloria, Vine Jr., Custer died for your sins: an Indian manifesto, Collier-Macmillan, 1969, 279 pp.

Deloria, Vine Jr., "Custer died for your sins," Playboy, August, 1969.

Deloria, Vine Jr., "This country was a lot better off when the Indians were running it," New York Times Magazine, March 8, 1970.

Deloria, Vine Jr., We Talk You Listen: new Tribes, new Turf, New York, MacMillan, 1970, 227 pp.

Demarine, Guy (reporter), "Metis vent century of resentment against white man," The Ottawa Citizen, March 27, 1972.

Dirthrower, Anderson, "Nationalism," in Ralph Osborne, ed., Who is chairman of this meeting? A collection of essays, Toronto Neewin Publishing Co., 1972, pp. 79-96.

Donovan, Walter, "Separatism and the Indians," Human Relations, (Toronto), June, 1966.

Dozier, Edward P., "Resistance to acculturation and assimilation in an Indian pueblo," American Anthropologist, 1951: 53:56-66.

Dufour, Joseph (reporter), "The Ontario Indian -- low man on totem pole," Toronto Daily Star, May 24, 1969, (reprinted in N. Sheffe, ed., Issues for the Seventies: Canada's Indians, Toronto, McGraw-Hill, 1970, pp 24-40).

Duran, James A. Jr., "Why Indians demonstrate," Sentinel, (Washington, D.C.) Winter-Spring, 1969, pp. 19-22.

Embry, Carlos B., America's concentration camps: the facts about our Indian reservations today, David McKay Co., 1956, 242 pp.

Farb, Peter, "The American Indian: a portrait in limbo," Saturday Review, October 12, 1968.

Favel, Fred, "Wabasca ... a lesson in politics," Ottawa, unpublished manuscript, 1967.

Fidler, Dick (reporter), "Canada's new 'Indians': toward nationhood," Labor Challenge, April 6, 1970.

Filler, Louis and Allen Guttman, eds., The removal of the Cherokee Nation, Boston, 1962.

Forbes, Jack D., ed., The Indian in America's past, Prentice-Hall, 1964, 181 pp.

Forbes, Jack D., "Who speaks for the Indian?," The Humanist, September-December, 1967.

Forbes, Jack D., "Alcatraz: what its seizure means to Indian people," The Warpath (San Francisco), 1970, 2:5.

Forbes, Jack D., "The New Indian Resistance?," Akwesasne Notes, (Rooseveltown, N.Y.), Late Spring, 1972, 4:20-22.

Ford, Thomas (reporter), "'Neglected', Canadian Indians seek UN help," The Toronto Daily Star, February 5, 1964.

Foreman, Grant, Indian Removal: the emigration of the Five Civilized Tribes of Indians, rev. ed., Norman, University of Oklahoma Press, 1953.

Foster, Laurence, Indian-Negro relationships in the southwest, University of Pennsylvania Press, 1935, 86 pp.

Freilich, Morris, "Cultural persistence among the modern Iroquois," Anthropos, 1958, 53:473-483.

Friedl, Ernestine M., An attempt at directed culture change: leadership among the Chippewa, 1640-1948, Ph D dissertation, Columbia University, 1950, 362 pp.

Gagne, Raymond C., "Amerindian cultural survival: a dilemma," Ottawa, Department of Indian Affairs and Northern Development, June, 1969, 15 pp.

Gaillard, Frye, "North Carolina's Lumbees and Haliwas: Indians, blacks eye possible coalition," (reprinted in Akwesasne Notes, (Rooseveltown, N.Y.), Late Autumn 1971, vol. 3:35).

Gambill, Jerry T., "Indians, white men and I," The Humanist, September-December, 1967.

Gambill, Jerry T., "The Thunder Water movement: an anthropological examination of the Indian Affairs Branch reaction to stress," Akwesasne Notes, (Rooseveltown, N.Y.), Autumn 1971.

Gambill, Jerry T., "How democracy came to St. Regis," Cornwall, Ont. unpublished manuscript, 1968, 16 p.

George, Chief Dan, "Confederation Lament," Address, Centennial Birthday Party, Empire Stadium in Vancouver, 1967.

George, Chief Dan, "our sad Winter has passed," Indian News (Ottawa), October 1968, (reprinted in Kent Gooderham, ed., I am an Indian, Toronto, J.M. Dent and Sons, 1969).

George, Chief Dan, "My very good dear friends," Address, Banff Conference on Indian Education, May, 1970, (reprinted in Waubageshig, ed., The only good Indian: essays by Canadian Indians, Toronto, New Press, 1970).

Gilbert, William H. Jr., "The Cherokees of North Carolina: living memorials of the past," Smithsonian Report for 1956, 1957, pp. 529-555.

Gill, Dennis, "Change," recherches amerindiennes au quebec, November, 1972, 2:69-69.

Goedhart, Bernie (reporter), "Rebel Chief Smallboy plans to lead band to public land," Edmonton Journal, April 28, 1971.

Greenway, John, "Will the Indians get whitey?," The National Review, (reprinted in Waubageshig, ed., The only good Indian: essays by Canadian Indians, Toronto, New Press, 1970).

Grescoe, Paul (reporter), "A gallant band of Indians fights for its tribal life," Canadian Magazine, (Toronto), February 22, 1969.

Gulick, John, "Language and passive resistance among the eastern Cherokee," Ethnohistory, Winter 1958, 5:61-77.

Hall, Louis, "Chronic mental ailment strikes again," Longhouse News, (Kahnawake Branch of the Six Nation Confederacy), No. 30, May 15, 1968.

Halpin, Lester A., "Massacres not new to U.S.," Edmonton Journal, December 13, 1969.

Hammersmith, Jerry, "The New Breed: an interview with Dr. Howard Adams," The Northian, (Saskatoon), Volume 7.

Hannula, Don, "Indians again try to occupy Fort Lawton: 80 detained, storm Fort for 3rd time," The Seattle Times, April 2, 1970.

Harding, Jim (reporter), "Two padlocks on the doors: council house locked again," Brantford Expositor (Brantford, Ontario), July 13, 1970.

Hogg, Carol (reporter), "Aboriginal unity proposed," (George Manuel), Calgary Herald, May 20, 1971.

Hogg, Carol (reporter), "More Indians joining back-to-wilds movement: important for youngsters," Calgary Herald, February 14, 1972.

Horn, Kahn-Tineta, "Indians seek to regain their rightful status," Human Relations (Toronto), 1963, 4:4.

Howard, James H., "Pan-Indian culture of Oklahoma," The Scientific Monthly, November, 1955, 23:215-.

Hudson, Charles M., ed., Red, white, and black: symposium on Indians in the Old South, Southern Anthropological Society Proceedings, No. 5, University of George Press, Athens, 1971, 143 pp.

Hunter, Robert (reporter), "Revolution in the North: it would be easy to drive the white man out," The Vancouver Sun, June 25, 1970.

Hurst, John (reporter), "It isn't over yet: riot-ready police arrest 34 Indians near Big Bend," Record-Searchlight (Redding, Calif.), June 6, 1970.

Hurst, John (reporter), "Pit River Indians seize PG and E dam," Record-Searchlight, (Redding, Calif.), July 11, 1970.

Isaac, Morris, "Until I find an Indian name," Kanawake News (Caughnawaga), May, 1969.

Jack, Henry, "Native Alliance for Red Power," in Waubageshig, ed., The only good Indian: essays by Canadian Indians, Toronto, New Press, 1970, pp. 162-180.

Jacobs, Paul (reporter), "Hawaiian war chant: no more hula hula, no more primo warriors, no more Aloha," Rolling Stone, July 22, 1971 (reprinted in Akwesasne Notes, Early Autumn, 1971, 328).

Jarrett, Walter, "Tecumseh, The First Advocate of Red Power," Mankind, 2:20-23, 60-62.

Johnston, Basil, "Bread before books or books before bread," in Waubageshig, ed., The only good Indian: essays by Canadian Indians, Toronto, New Press, 1970, pp. 126-141.

Johnston, Greg, "MicMac sovereignty vs. Indian Affairs," MicMac News (Sydney, N.S.), December, 1972.

Josephy, Alvin, M. Jr., "Indians in history," Atlantic, 1970, 225:

Josephy, Alvin M. Jr., Red power: the American Indian's fight for freedom, New York, McGraw-Hill, 1972, 259 pp.

Keen, Ralph, "The question what is an Indian?," Many Smokes, (Los Angeles), 1966, 1:

Kelly, Fred, "The fresh assertiveness -- red power," The Telegram (Toronto), September 27, 1969.

Kennedy, Fred, "The Indian ride to nowhere," The Native People, (Edmonton), May, 1969, (reprinted in N. Sheffe, ed., Issues for the Seventies: Canada's Indians, Toronto, McGraw-Hill, 1970 pp. 29-31).

Knirck, Mrs. Carola, "The story of 'Set OK' the son of a Polish emigrant and a Canadian Indian," Ottawa, unpublished manuscript, December 15, 1967.

Lahr, John, "Arthur Kopit's 'Indians' dramatizing national amnesia," Evergreen Review, October, 1969.

Lake, Stuart (reporter), "Native leader Nellie Cournoyea: many whys, much bitterness," The Ottawa Citizen, August 30, 1972.

LaRoche, Emma, "The Indian in society today -- an opinion: Part 1," The Native People (Edmonton), June 1970, 3 (1) :7.

LaRoche, Emma, "The Indian in society today -- an opinion: Part 2," to be or not to be an Indian," The Native People (Edmonton), June 1970, 3 (2) :11.

Lemert, Edwin M., "The life and death of an Indian state," Human Organization, Fall 1954, 13:23-27.

Levine, Stuart, "The Indian as American: some observations from the editor's notebook," Midcontinent American Studies Journal, 1965, 6:5-22.

Levitan, Sar A., and Barbara Hetrick, "Big brother's last stand," Poverty and Human Abstracts, May-June, 1970, 8 pp.

Lind, Loren (reporter), "Common sense in Iroquois land," The Globe and Mail (Toronto), January 1, 1969 (reprinted in N. Sheffe, ed., Issues for the Seventies: Canada's Indians, Toronto, McGraw-Hill, 1970, pp 66-69).

Loutitt, Neil (reporter), "Red power not militant say Indians: young people define phase as movement for recognition," (Canadian Indian Youth Council) Winnipeg Free Press, October 10, 1967.

Lumpkin, Wilson, Removal of the Cherokee Indians from Georgia, 2 vols. Savahnah, 1907.

Lurie, Nancy Oestreitch, "An American Indian renaissance?" in Stuart Levine and Nancy O. Lurie, eds., The American Indian Today, Baltimore, Md., Penquin Book, 1970, pp. 295-337.

Magowan, N. (Littlefoot), "Indians attack army," (Fort Lawton, Wash.) Los Angeles Free Press, (reprinted in Akwesasne Notes, (Rooseveltown, N.Y.), May 1970).

Malling, Eric, "Regina's Indians: the hate is rising in 'whitey's' town," Toronto Daily Star, June 22, 1972.

Mandamin, Tony, "On education," in Ralph Osborne, ed. Who is the chairman of this meeting? A collection of essays, Toronto, Neewin Publishing Co., 1972, pp. 21-25.

Manuel, George, "Discussion paper on the Cold Lake Issue," Ottawa, unpublished manuscript, National Indian Brotherhood, October, 1971, 9 pp.

Manuel, Chief George and Michael Posluns, The Fourth World: social change and the Indian reality, Toronto, Collier-MacMillan (forthcoming).

McNickle, D'Arcy, "Definition of a problem," Address to Resolving Conflicts -- a Cross-Cultural Approach, February 10--May 14, 1967, Kenora, Ontario, pp. 6-15.

Meyer, William (yonv ut sisla), Native Americans: the new Indian resistance, New York, International Publishers, 1971, 95 pp.

Milord, James E., "Genocide in Canada: we call it integration," The United Church Observer, (Toronto), August, 1970, pp. 24-26.

Morrison, Walter M. (reporter), "Old Coast Guard Station occupied by militants," Milwaukee Journal, August 14, 1971, (reprinted in Akwesasne Notes, (Rooseveltown, N.Y.), Early Autumn, 1971, 3:19).

Munroe, George, "Indian revolution?" editorial, The New Nation (Winnipeg), February, 1973.

Nabess, Archie J., "Indians on the march," Letter to the Editor, Winnipeg Free Press, October 26, 1972.

Nicholas, Andrew, "New Brunswick Indians -- conservative militants," in Waubageshig, ed., The only good Indian: essays by Canadian Indians, Toronto, New Press, 1970, pp. 42-50.

Novack, George, Genocide against the Indians: its role in the rise of U.S. capitalism, New York, A Merit Pamphlet, Pathfinder Press, June, 1970, 31 pp.

Nujoweket, "Indians plan research on whites," Micmac News (Sydney, N.S.), January, 1973.

Nyerere, Julius K., "Press Statement," Dodoma, Tanzania, July, 1971.

Pelletier, Wilfred, "Organization," The ignorant society: white? or Indian?, Proceedings of a seminar held at Paradise Lake Camp, St. Clements, Ontario, October, 1967.

Pelletier, Wilfred, (Wawashkesh), "Dumb Indian," in Ralph Osborne, ed. Who is the chairman of this meeting? A collection of Essays, Toronto, Neewin Publishing Co., 1972, pp. 1-20.

Peterson, John H., Jr., "The Indians in the Old South," in Charles M. Hudson, ed., Red, white, and black: symposium on Indians in the Old South, Southern Anthropological Society Proceedings, Athens, No. 5, University of Georgia Press, 1971, pp. 116-133.

Platiel, Rudy (reporter), "Breaking the chain," The Globe and Mail, (Toronto), December 25, 1968, (reprinted in N. Sheffe, ed., Issues for the Seventies: Canada's Indians, Toronto, McGraw-Hill, 1970, pp. 40-45).

Platiel, Rudy (reporter), "Reclaimed by Mohawks: all is quiet on occupied Stanley Island," The Globe and Mail (Toronto), May 18, 1970.

Poole, Ted, "Conversations with North American Indians," in Ralph Osborne, ed., Who is chairman of this meeting? A collection of Essays, Toronto, Neewin Publishing Co., 1972, pp. 39-52.

Porter, Kenneth, W., "Negroes and the Seminole War, 1835-1842," Journal of Southern History, 1964, 30:427-440.

Posluns, Michael, "Conflict at Akwesasne," Canadian Welfare, (Ottawa), March-April, 1971, 49:4-9, 27.

Quig, James (reporter), "Trouble in the land where the partridge drums," Weekend Magazine, (Montreal), April 19, 1969.

Reguly, Robert (reporter), "Angry Indians threaten to fight 'like U.S. Negro'," Toronto Daily Star, August 15, 1963.

Richardson, Boyce (reporter), "The struggle for equality," Montreal Star, October 16, 1971.

Richardson, Boyce (reporter), "Angry Crees burn hundreds of James Bay ecology reports," Montreal Star, February 24, 1972.

Richardson, Boyce (reporter), "Metis showing leadership in fight for native rights," Montreal Star, April 8, 1972.

Richardson, Boyce (reporter), "Natives start to fight back, oppose development schemes: protest from one end of Canada to the other," Montreal Star, June 5, 1972.é

Richmond, Robin, "Rediscovery of the Redman," Life, 1967, 63:52-72.

Robertson, Heather, Reservations are for Indians, Toronto, James Lewis and Samuel Co., 1970, 303 pp.

Ruddy, Jon (reporter), "This is Harold Cardinal, a Cree and perhaps the most charismatic Indian leader since Cochise. He is telling you what the Canadian Indian wants from you," Maclean's Magazine, (Toronto), December, 1969.

Russell, Frances (reporter), "Reason wears a steel will," Weekend Magazine (Montreal), June 7, 1969 (reprinted in N. Sheffe, ed., Issues for the Seventies: Canada's Indians, Toronto, McGraw-Hill, 1970, pp. 61-62).

Schlesier, Karl H., The Indians of the United States: an essay on cultural resistance, Wichita, Kansas, Wichita State University Bulletin, University Studies No. 81, November, 1969, 27 pp.

Schmidt, John T. (reporter), "Lo, the poor, irresponsible, lazy Indian," Saturday Night, (Toronto), November 21, 1959, (reprinted in Richard Laskin, ed. Social Problems: a Canadian profile, McGraw-Hill, 1964, 109-111).

Schusky, Ernest L., The right to be Indian, San Francisco, California, The Indian Historian Press, 1970, 67 pp.

Scott, John (reporter), "Peaceful invasion: Indian militants land at second site," (Loon Island), The Globe and Mail (Toronto), May, 1970.

Sioui, Georges, "Food for thought for whites of America and other strangers," recherches amerindiennes au quebec, November, 1972, 2:65-68.

Sioui, Jules, "War ... ...Peace in Canada: The invader responsible for the death of the patriot Louis Riel, Innocence ... and ... Silence what success will crown the efforts of the Patriot who implored the Chiefs of our Nation to rise and unite, in assembly in Ottawa?" Comité de Protection des droits Indiens, Village Huron de Lorette, 1943, 26 pp.

Smallboy, Chief Robert, "Decision to leave Hobbema," The Western Canadian Journal of Anthropology, 1969, 1:112-118.

Spinks, Sarah, "Some O.I.S.E. projects," This Magazine is About Schools, (Ontario), 1970, 4:28-54.

St-Onge-Andre, Anne-Marie, "Where will they move us to next?" recherches amerindiennes au quebec, November, 1972, 2:61-63.

Staebler, Edna, "The unconquered warriors of Ohswaken," MacLean's Magazine, (Toronto), November 12, 1955, pp. 24-25, 92-98.

Steiner, Stan, The New Indians, Dell Publishing Co. (A Delta Book), 1968, 348 pp.

Stockand, Dave (reporter), "Indian just lumped in with coal, ore,: Quilt probe observer Gloria Gabert wants rid of Indian Affairs Department," The Vancouver Sun, August 2, 1972.

Strynadka, Arnold, "Misunderstood and misrepresented," The Native People (Edmonton), October, 1971, 4 (3):16.

Sun Bear, "The Indian renaissance," Many Smokes, (Los Angeles), 1966, 1:

Tax, Sol, "The freedom to make mistakes," American Indigena, June, 1956, 16:171-177.

Thomas, Robert K., "Colonialism: classic and internal," New University Thought, 1966, 4:37-44.

Thomas, Robert K., "Powerless politics," New University Thought, 1966, 4:44-

Thomas, Robert K., "Pan Indianism," American Studies Journal 6: (reprinted in Stuart Levine and Nancy O. Lurie, ed., The American Indian Today, Baltimore, Md., Penguin Books, 1970, pp. 128-140).

Tierney, Ben (reporter), "Mohawk claim denied," (reprinted in Indian Record (Winnipeg), September-October, 1970).

Trimble, Charles, et. al., Shove it, buster we'd rather have our land, a candid look at modern Indian history in the making, Denver, American Indian Press Association, 1972.

Trustian, Tom, "Where's your rent whiteman?," The Silhouette, December 5, 1969, (reprinted in N. Sheffe, ed., Issues for the Seventies: Canada's Indians, Toronto, McGraw-Hill, 1970, pp. 63-66).

Unseem, John, J.D. Donogue and Ruth Hill Unseem, "Men in the middle of the third culture," Human Organization, 1963, 22:169-179.

Vallee, Frank G., "Unrest at Brantford," National Commission on the Indian Canadian, Bulletin 7.June, 1959,

Van Every, Dale, Disinherited: the lost birthright of the American Indian, New York, Avon Books, 1966, 302 pp.

Wainman, Helen (reporter), "Conference warned of Indian violence," (A. Belcourt), Toronto Daily Star, June 22, 1972.

Walker, Deward E. Jr., "Some limitations of the renaissance concept in acculturation: the Nez Perce case," in Stuart Levine and Nancy O. Lurie, eds., The American Indian Today, Penguin Books, Baltimore, Md. 1970, pp. 236-256.

Warhrhftig, Albert L. and Robert K. Thomas, "Renaissance and repression: the Oklahoma Cherokee," Trans-action, February, 1969.

Warrior, Clyde, "Poverty, community and power," New University Thought, 1965, 3:

Waterman, T.T., "All is trouble along the Klamath," in Elsie Clews Parsons, ed., American Indian Life, 1922, (University of Nebraska Press, 1967, pp. 289-296).

Weaver, Sally Mae, Health, culture and dilemma: a study of the non-Conservative Iroquois, Six Nations Reserve, Ontario, Ph D dissertation, University of Toronto, 1967, 435 pp.

Whiteside, Don, "Guest editorial," Human Concern, (Alberta Human Rights Commission,Edmonton), Autumn, 1969, 1 (2):1.

Whiteside, Don, "Two facts of life and a viable alternative to revolution," Address, Unitarian Church, Edmonton, May 17, 1970, 14 pp.

Whiteside, Don, (sin a paw), "The necessity of alliances in the timeless struggle by Amerindians for freedom and dignity," Ottawa, unpublished manuscript, July 7, 1972, 15 pp.

Whiteside, Don, (sin a paw), "New pathways in the timeless struggle for freedom and dignity by North American Indians," recherches amérindiennes au Québec, November, 1972, 2:71-78.

Whiteside, Don, "Brief Survey of Articles in the Press, etc., on the 1965 Kenora (Ontario) March, and Some Consequences,"

Ottawa, unpublished manuscript, Strategic Planning, Citizenship Branch, Department of Secretary of State, January 1, 1973, 5 pp.

Whiteside, Don, "Brief survey of articles in the Press, etc., on the 1971-1972 Cold Lake (Alberta) Boycott and sit-in," Ottawa, unpublished manuscript, Strategic Planning, Citizenship Branch, Department of Secretary of State, January 3, 1973, 7 pp.

Willhelm, Sidney M., Who needs the negro? ("Black man, red man and white America: the constitutional approach to genocide,"), (reprinted in Akwesasne Notes, December, 1971, 3:44).

Willis, William S., Jr., "Divide and rule: red, white and black in the southeast," Journal of Negro History, July, 1963, 48:157-176 (reprinted in Charles M. Hudson, ed. Red, white, and black: Symposium on Indians in the Old South, Athens, University of Georgia Press, 1971).

Wuttunee, William Ivan Clark, "Integration -- the best solution," The Manitoba Teacher, 1968, 46:6-8.

Young, Scott (reporter), "New deal smoke signals read clearly," The Globe and Mail (Toronto), July 4, 1969 (reprinted in N. Sheffe, ed., Issues for the Seventies: Canada's Indians, Toronto, McGraw-Hill, 1970, pp. 22-25).

Zionty, Alvin J., "New Consciousness: the Indian uprising," Civil Liberties, (American Civil Liberties Union), December, 1972, Number 291, pp. 13-14.

Miscellaneous Reports by date of publication

The story of Louis Riel the rebel chief, Ottawa, Hunter Rose and Co., 1885 (reprinted by J.S. Robertson and Bros., Toronto, 1970, 192 pp).

"White man has made 'a mess' of this country, Indians are told: His ways lead only to strife and trouble, declares Chief at solemn Pow-wow of braves at Caughnawaga, demand right to govern reservations by tribal laws," Ottawa, February 28, 1938.

"Chief advises Indians, approach UN for help," The Globe and Mail(?) (Toronto), August 16, 1948.

"Mounties invade reserve of Six Nations 'rebels'," Ottawa Citizen, March 13, 1959.

"New Nation, Indian aim at pow-wow," Ottawa Citizen, March 28, 1959.

Declaration of Indian purpose: the voice of the American Indian, American Indian Congress Conference, University of Chicago, June 26, 1961, 50 pp.

"Indians, black power form alliance," (Black Liberation Front of Canada and Fred Kelly), Toronto Daily Star, February 22, 1966.

"Art Buchwald explores a new controversy: what Indian discovered Columbus?," Winnipeg Free Press, November 20, 1965.

"Indians denounce French," (Caughnawaga Defence Committee (Frank Horne)), Winnipeg Free Press, December 1, 1965.

"Indians deny they won't talk French," (Andrew Delisle), Winnipeg Free Press, December 4, 1965.

"Indians, Metis stage march," Edmonton Journal, July 30, 1966.

"Indian power reaches Alberta (PANE, Protest Alliance Against Native Extermination), Edmonton Journal, October 23, 1968.

"Western hemisphere meeting of Indians called," (Native aboriginals of the Americas Unity Conference), January, 1969, (reprinted in Akwesasne Notes, (Rooseveltown, N.Y.), February, 1969).

"R.C.M.P. links Indian disturbances to agitators from U.S.," (W.H. Kelly), The Globe and Mail, (Toronto), March 7, 1969.

"Mother confronts Edmonton authority: erects teepee outside City Hall," (Lillian Piche), Edmonton Journal, March 31, 1969.

"My country 'tis of thy people you are dying," (Buffy Saint Marie) Akwesasne Notes, (Rooseveltown, N.Y.), July, 1969.

"Indians: to end a bitter heritage," Time, July 4, 1969.

"Indian reforms begin -- at last," Toronto Daily Star, June 25, 1968, (reprinted in N. Sheffe, ed., Issues for the Seventies: Canada's Indians, McGraw-Hill, 1970, pp. 21-22).

"Today, next month, next year," World Review, (United Nations), November, 1968, (reprinted in N. Sheffe, ed., Issues for the Seventies: Canada's Indians, McGraw-Hill, 1970, pp. 11-15).

"We will close with a prayer," The Calumet (Toronto), November 30, 1968, (reprinted in N. Sheffe, ed., Issues for the Seventies: Canada's Indians, McGraw-Hill, 1970, p. 62).

"Amerindians who live, work and train in London: a preliminary report," N'Amerind, (London, Ont.), January-February 1969, (reprinted in N. Sheffe, ed., Issues for the Seventies: Canada's Indians, McGraw-Hill, 1970, pp. 79-86).

"Going South is no answer," Toronto Daily Star, June 14, 1969, (reprinted in N. Sheffe, ed., Issues for the Seventies: Canada's Indians, McGraw-Hill, 1970, pp. 58-59).

"A time to act," Kenomadiwin News, (Thunder Bay, Ont.), June 15, 1969, (reprinted in N. Sheffe, ed., Issues for Seventies: Canada's Indians, McGraw-Hill, 1970, p. 70).

Survivl of American Indians Association Magazine, Tacoma. Washington, 1970.

"NARP eight point program," NARP Newsletter (Native Alliance for
Red Power, Vancouver), (reprinted in N. Sheffe, ed., Issues for
the Seventies: Canada's Indians, McGraw-Hill, 1970, pp. 65-65).

"Native sit-in at New Start," The Native People, (Edmonton),
January 1970, 2:1-2.

"The angry American Indian: starting down the protest trail,"
Time, February 9, 1970.

"Canada's Indian Problem," San Francisco Chronicle, September 29,
1969 (reprinted in The Warpath (San Francisco, California),
Spring 1970, 2(1):(6).

"Canadian and U.S. Indians move onto Stanley Island," Standard-
Freeholder (Cornwall), May 11, 1970.

"Indians demand control over education: sit-in slated at Blue
Quills School," The Native People (Edmonton), July, 1970.
3(3)1-2.

"Blue Quills taken over by Indians," The Native People (Edmonton),
August, 1970, 3(4):2.

"Blue Quills -- Another first for Indians," The Native People,
(Edmonton), September, 1970, 3(5):1-2.

Chronicles of American Indian protest, Greenwich, Conn., Fawcett
Premier Book, 1971, 376 pp.

"Guest editorial: by Phil Thompson: the Indian, his home and
money," The Native People, (Edmonton), January, 1971, 3(8):5.

"All treaty Indians free from medicare premiums," The Native
People (Edmonton), May, 1971, 3(12):1.

"Indians 'eliminate' Hogansburg," The Ottawa Citizen, May 17,
1971.

"Indians lose hold on Alcatraz," The Ottawa Citizen, June 14,
1971.

"Canada-U.S. crossing: Indian rights march over border bridge,"
Montreal Star, July 19, 1971.

"Indians 'secede' from township," Toronto Daily Star, August 7,
1972.

"Indians plan toll gates on Trans-Canada land," The Ottawa
Citizen, August 12, 1971.

"Judge in a quandry: young Indian challenges legality of skyway
toll," St. Catherines Standard (Ontario), August 21, 1971.

"All-white school burned," (Restigouche, P.Q.), Montreal Star,
September 23, 1971.

"Cold Lake school dispute may become national issue," The Edmonton
Journal, September 30, 1971.

"Coalition of Groups Proposed," (Black United Front and Union of Nova Scotia Indians), Chronicle-Herald, (Halifax), November 3, 1971.

"Caughnawaga band refuses use of land to widen road," Montreal Gazette, November 15, 1971.

"Indian Affairs and Northern Development," (Cold Lake, Cultural-Educational Centres, etc.), House of Commons Debates, November 24, 1971, 115:9843-9867.

"Northeastern Alberta -- action by Minister to solve school dispute -- discussion of long range educational program," House of Commons Debates, November 26, 1971, 115:9922-9923.

"Alberta Indian leader quits to end his feud with Chrétien," (Harold Cardinal), Toronto Daily Star, December 22, 1971.

"Minority and human rights," Indian News, (Ottawa), 1972, 14(9):1-4.

"40 million yearly big-city relocation policy re-focused, U.S. Indians shun melting pot," Calgary Herald, January 17, 1972.

"Alberta Indians: the 110-day sit-in," The Globe and Mail (Toronto), January 28, 1972.

"Indians threaten to raid RCMP HQ in bid to get historic wampum belts," The Ottawa Journal, February 7, 1972.

"1,000 Indians invade town in Nebraska," The Globe and Mail (Toronto), March 8, 1972.

"Nebraska Indian protest ends in 'complete victory'," The Edmonton Journal, March 9, 1972.

"Indians told to find own financial security," (Arthur Manuel), The Ottawa Citizen, March 9, 1972.

"Indian protestors storm, loot post," Vancouver Sun, March 10, 1972.

"Indian, white kids battle in N.B.," The Montreal Star, March 15, 1972.

"Chrétien signs Cold Lake agreement: Alberta Indians get their school, end six-month sit-in," The Globe and Mail (Toronto), April 22, 1972.

"Racial conflict flares up in N.B. village," The Globe and Mail (Toronto), April 22, 1972.

"Indians and blacks meet on O.F.Y.," MicMac News, (Sidney, N.S.), June, 1972, 2(6):7.

"The latest in the 'social genocide' field: adoption of Indian children by white families," Akwesasne Notes, (Rooseveltown, N.Y.), Summer 1972, p. 10.

"Legal challenge brewing against schools for Hawaiians only," _Wausau_ _Daily_ _Record-Herald_ (Wisconsin), August 3, 1972.

"Canadian Indians seek membership in U.N.," (George Manuel), _The_ Ottawa _Citizen_, August 10, 1972.

"White people are too greedy," (Nellie Cournoyea), _The_ _Globe_ _and_ _Mail_ (Toronto), September 9, 1972.

"Shots quell Indian reserve riot," _The_ _Ottawa_ _Citizen_, September 11, 1972.

"Indians march for freedom," _The_ _New_ _Nation_ (Winnipeg), October, 1972, 1(5):1.

"Manifesto of the National Indian Movement of Canada, Winnipeg, unpublished manuscript, October, 1972 4 pp.

"Traditionalists oppose Ottawa: Mohawks set up Longhouse School," _The_ _Gazette_ (Montreal), October 25, 1972.

"Indians plan Washington demonstrations seeking benefits due 'first citizens of land'," _The_ _Globe_ _and_ _Mail_ (Toronto), October 31, 1972.

"U.S. Indians continue to occupy building," _Ottawa_ _Citizen_, November 4, 1972.

"U.S. Indians end occupation after seizing documents," _The_ _Globe_ _and_ _Mail_ (Toronto), November 9, 1972.

"Union Jack burned at Plymouth Rock," _The_ _Vancouver_ _Sun_, November 27, 1972.

"Indians: drums on the Potomac," _Time_, December 18, 1972.

"Trail of broken treaties," (Special issue) _Akwesasne_ _Notes_ (Rooseveltown, N.Y.), January, 1973, Volume 5(1).

"Plunk, the natives are counting too," _Canadian_ _Magazine_, (Toronto), January 6, 1973.

Indians, police clash at Custer," (South Dakota) _Mail_ - _Star_ (Halifax), February 10, 1973.

"Shots exchanged with F.B.I., Indians hold 10 hostages in Wounded Knee," (South Dakota) _The_ _Globe_ _and_ _Mail_, (Toronto), March 1, 1973.

"Native sit-in in Saskatoon," _The_ _Leader-Post_, (Regina), March 13, 1973.

"American Indian Movement, Custer gets it again," _The_ _New_ _Breed_, (Regina), March, 1973.

"Metis extend school boycott in Manitoba," (Camperville), _The_ _Globe_ _and_ _Mail_, (Toronto), March 23, 1973.

"The first month at Wounded Knee" (Special Issue) <u>Akwesasne</u> <u>Notes</u> (Rooseveltown, N.Y.), April 1973, Volume 5(2).

B -- Wars, etc.

Abel, Annie Heloise, <u>The</u> <u>American</u> <u>Indian</u> <u>as</u> <u>Slaveholder</u> <u>and</u> <u>Secessionist</u>, Cleveland, Ohio, The Arthur H. Clark Co., 1915.

Abel, Annie Heloise, <u>The</u> <u>American</u> <u>Indian</u> <u>as</u> <u>participant</u> <u>in</u> <u>the</u> <u>Civil</u> <u>War</u>, Cleveland, Ohio, The Arthur H. Clark Co., 1919.

Ahenakew, Edward, "An opinion of the Frog Lake massacre," <u>Alberta</u> <u>Historical</u> <u>Review</u>, 1960, 8:9-15.

Akweks, Aren (Ray Fadden), <u>Six</u> <u>Nations</u> <u>Iroquois</u> <u>Confederacy</u> <u>record</u> (World War II), Akwesasne Mohawk Counsellor Organization, St. Regis Reservation, Hogansburg, N.Y., Potsdam, N.Y., <u>The</u> <u>Potsdam</u> <u>Herald</u>, 1949.

Annett, William S., "Massacre: when they could find no more white men to murder, the Indians put a torch to every Frog Lake building," <u>The</u> <u>Star</u> <u>Weekly</u>, October 15, 1960.

Arnold, Ross, R., <u>Indian</u> <u>Wars</u> <u>of</u> <u>Idaho</u>, Caldwell, Idaho, Claxton Printers, 1932.

Bailey, L.R., <u>Indian</u> <u>slave</u> <u>trade</u> <u>in</u> <u>the</u> <u>southwest</u>, N.Y., Tower Publications, 1966, 204 pp.

Bingaman, Sandra Elizabeth, The North-West Rebellion trials, <u>1885</u>, <u>Regina</u>, Masters Thesis (<u>History</u>), University of Saskatchewan, 1971.

Brant, C.S., <u>A</u> <u>history</u> <u>of</u> <u>the</u> <u>great</u> <u>massacre</u> <u>of</u> <u>the</u> <u>Sioux</u>, Cincinnati, Rickey and Carra, 1954.

Brimlow, George Francis, <u>The</u> <u>Bannock</u> <u>Indian</u> <u>War</u> <u>of</u> <u>1878</u>, Caldwell, Idaho, Claxton Printers, 1938.

Brown, Dee Alexander, <u>Showdown</u> <u>at</u> <u>Little</u> <u>Big</u> <u>Horn</u>, New York, G.P. Putnam's Sons, 1964 (reissued Berkley Medallion Book, 1971), 190 pp.

Brown, Dee Alexander, <u>Bury</u> <u>my</u> <u>heart</u> <u>at</u> <u>Wounded</u> <u>Knee</u>, Holt, Rinehart and Winston, 1971, 487 pp.

Coulter, John, <u>The</u> <u>trial</u> <u>of</u> <u>Louis</u> <u>Riel</u>, Toronto, Oberson Press, 1968, 66 pp.

Cunningham, Frank, <u>General</u> <u>Stand</u> <u>Watie's</u> <u>Confederate</u> <u>Indians</u>, San Antonio, Texas, The Naylor Co., 1959.

Custer, Col. George Armstrong, <u>Wild</u> <u>life</u> <u>on</u> <u>the</u> <u>plains</u>, St. Louis Mo., Royal Publishing Co., 1891.

Downey, Fairfax, _Indian-Fighting army_, New York, Charles Scribner's Sons, 1941.

Downey, Fairfax, General Crook: Indian fighter, Philadelphia, Pa., The Westminster Press, 1957.

Downey, Fairfax, Indian Wars of the U.S. Army, 1776-1865, New York, Charles Scribner's Sons, 1963.

Drimmer, Frederick, ed., Scalps and tomahawks: narratives of Indian captivity, New York, Coward-McCann, 1961 378 pp.

Emmitt, Robert, The last war trial, Norman, University of Oklahoma Press, 1954.

Greighton, D.G., "The employment of the Indians in the War of 1812," Report of the American Historical Association, 1895, pp. 321-335.

Hart, George, "Geronimo's last fight," Real West Magazine, March, 1971.

Howard, Joseph Kinsey, The strange empire of Louis Riel, Toronto, Swan Publishing Co., 1970, 480 pp.

Hunt, G.T., The wars of the Iroquois: a study on intertribal trade relations, Madison, University of Wisconsin Press, 1940.

Johnston, A., "The battle at Belly River: stories of the last great Indian battle," Historical Society of Alberta, Lethbridge, 1966.

Merritt, Gen. Wesley, "Three Indian campaigns," Harper's Magazine, April, 1890.

Mishkin, B., "Rank and warfare among plains Indians," American Ethnological Society Monograph, 1940.

Oehler, C.M., The great Sioux uprising, Oxford University Press, 1959, 272 pp.

Parkhill, Forbes, The last of the Indian Wars, New York, Crowell-Collier, 1961.

Peckham, H.H., Pontiac and The Indian uprising, Princeton, N.J., Princeton University Press, 1947, 346 pp.

Porter, C. Fayne, The battle of the 1,000 slain and other stories selected from our Indian heritage, Richmond Hill, Ontario, Scholastic Book Services, 1967, 256 pp.

Robertson, R.W.W., The execution of Thomas Scott, Toronto, Burns and MacEachern Lt. 1968.

Rousseau, Jacques, "Le dernier des peaux-rouges," _Cahiers des Dix_, 1962, 27:47-76.

Shields, Roy, "He set the West aflame: it was Gabriel Dumont, a bull-shouldered buffalo hunter with the look of the fiery Metis coursing his wins, not Louis Riel, who touched off the famous Canadian rebellion," _The Star Weekly Magazine_, December 24, 1960.

Stanley, George F.G., "The significance of the Six Nations participation in the War of 1812," _Ontario History Quarterly_, 1963, 60:215-231.

Stanley, George F.G., _The birth of western Canada, a history of the Riel Rebellion_, University of Toronto Press, 1960, 452 p.

Stanley, George F.G., "The Metis and the conflict in western Canada," _The Canadian Historical Review_, 1947, 28:

Stanley, George F.G., "Louis Riel: patriot or rebel," _Canadian Historical Association Booklet 2_, Ottawa, 1970.

Tebbel, John, _The compact history of the Indian wars_, New York, Tower Publications, 1966, 318 pp.

Thevenin, R. and P. Coze, _Moeurs et histoire des Peaux-Rouges_, Paris, Payot, 1952, 300 pp.

Trigger, Bruce Graham, "Trade and tribal warfare on the St. Lawrence in the Sixteenth Century," _Ethnohistory_, 1962, 9:240-256.

Trudel, Marcel, _L'es clavage au Canada-français,_ Quebec City, Presse de l'Université Laval, 1960.

Turney-High, H.H., _Primitive warfare, its practices and concepts_, Columbia, University of South Carolina Press, 1949.

Woolworth, Alan R., "A disgraceful proceeding: intrigue in the Red River country in 1864," _The Beaver_, 1969, 299:54-59.

Miscellaneous Reports by date of publication

"The North-West disturbance," _House of Commons Debates_, March 8, 1886, p. 61.

"Execution of Louis Riel," _House of Commons Debates_, March 11, 1886, pp. 68-368.

PART XII

COMMUNITY DEVELOPMENT and INTERNAL ORGANIZATION
(see also Economic Development)

Baker, W.B., "Some Observations on the Application of Community Development to the Settlements of Northern Saskatchewan," Toronto, Indian-Eskimo Association of Canada, 1961, 14 pp.

Ball, Nelson E., "Profile of Indian Community: Burnt Church," (New Brunswick), unpublished manuscript, 1964. 14 pp.

Ball, Nelson E., "Burnt Church, A Canadian Indian Community," unpublished term paper, Michigan State University, November, 1965, 33 pp.

Bernard, Jessie, "Political Leadership Among North American Indians," American Journal of Sociology, 1928, 34:

Blackmar, Frank W., "The Socialization of the American Indian," American Journal of Sociology, 1928, 34:

Bock, Philip K., The Social Structure of a Canadian Indian Reserve, Ph.D. Dissertation, Harvard University, 1964.

Boggs, S.T., Objibwa Socialization: Some Aspects of Parent Child Interaction in a Changing Culture, Seattle, Ph.D. Dissertation, University of Washington, 1954.

Brasser, T., "Leadership Among the Northeastern Algonkians of Canada," Kula, December, 1962, 3:4-17.

Buckley, Helen, J.E.M. Kew and John B. Hawley, The Indians and Metis of Northern Saskatchewan: A report on economic and social development, Saskatoon Centre for Community Studies, 1963, 114 pp.

Castellano, Marlene, "Out of Paternalism and Into Partnership: An Exploration of alternatives in Social Service to Native People," in James A. Draper, ed., Citizen Participation: Canada, a Book of Readings, Toronto, New Press, 1971, pp. 351-361.

Cohen, R., An Anthropological Survey of Communities in the MacKenzie-Slave Lake Region of Canada, Ottawa Northern Coordination and Research Centre, Department of Northern Affairs and Natural Resources, 1962, 119 pp.

Colley, Louise, "Community Recreation on Christian Island," Ora (Ontario Recreation Association), December, 1962.

Connor, Desmond, "Report No. 9, Workshop for Manitoba Metis Federation," Gimli, Manitoba, Developmental Services Unit, Rural Development Branch, December, 1968, 4 pp.

Corbiere, Jeanette and Wilfred Pelletier, "Canada's Indians and the Company of Young Canadians," Ottawa, unpublished manuscript, April 1967.

Courchene, Dave, "It takes an Indian to help an Indian," Involvement, (Newmarket, Ont.), Fall 1971, 4:7-13.

Damas, David, "Diversity in White-Eskimo Leadership Interaction," Anthropologica, 1966, 8:45- (reprinted in Mark Nagler, ed., Perspectives on the North American Indian, Toronto, McClelland and Stewart, 1972).

de Cocq, Gustave, Northeast Edmonton Youth Survey, Edmonton Council of Community Services, 1962.

Dobyns, Henry, F., "Therapeutic Experience of Responsible Democracy," in Stuart Levine and Nancy O. Lurie eds., The American Indian Today, Baltimore, Md., Penguin Books, 1970, pp. 268-291.

Drucker, Philip, "Rank, Wealth, and Kinship in Northwest Coast Society," American Anthropologist, 1939, 41:55-65.

Dunning, Robert William, "Some problem of Reserve Indian Communities; a Case Study," Anthropologica, 1964, 6:3-38.

Dunphy, Pat, "Developments Which Have Taken Place on the Roseau River Reserve and Buffalo Point Reserve Since January 1966," unpublished manuscript, January 1969, 6 pp.

Erikson, Erik Homburger, "Observations on Sioux Education," Journal of Psychology, 1939, 7:

Erikson, Erik Homburger, "Hunters Across the Prairie," Childhood and Society, W.W. Norton, 1950, pp. 98-140.

Erikson, Erik Homburger, "Fisherman Along a Salmon River," Childhood and Society, W.W. Norton, 1950, pp. 141-160.

Forbes, Jack D., "A Comprehensive Program for Tribal Development," Human Organization, Summer, 1965, 24:159-161.

Fried, Jacob, "White Dominant Settlements in the Canadian Northwest Territories," Anthropologica, 1963, 5:57-63.

Gambill, Jerry, T., "The Company of Young Canadians and Indians of Canada,", Ottawa: unpublished manuscript, June, 1967.

Gearing, Fred, "Today's Mesquakies," The American Indian, 1955, 7:24-37.

Gibson, Gayll and Don Whiteside, "Linkages between action groups in the community," Ottawa, unpublished manuscript, November 1, 1972, 9 pp.

Goodwill, Jean Ida, "A New Horizon for Native Women in Canada," in James A. Draper, Citizen Participation: Canada, a Book of Readings, Toronto, New Press, 1971, pp. 362-370.

Grafton, Bernie, "Family Development Project, Duck Bay, Manitoba," Manitoba School Journal, January-February, 1962.

Grant, Dale (reporter), "Who But an Indian Know's What is Best for an Indian?," Weekend Magazine (Montreal) May 22, 1971.

Hanley, David W., "Report to Bosco Centre Study Committee on Some Models for Community Based Services," unpublished manuscript, April, 1968, 32 pp.

Harmsworth, Harry C., "Family Structure on the Front Hall Indian Reservation," The Family Life Coordinator, 1965, pp. 7-9.

Harvey, Ian, Harold Huston, and James R. Whitford, et. al., "Steps in Problem Solving," Winnipeg, Community Development Service, Department of Health and Public Welfare, 1961, 9 pp.

Hatt, Fred Kenneth, "Appendix A. Metis of the Lac La Biche Area," Edmonton Community Opportunity Assessment Human Research and Development Government of Alberta, March 1967, 229 pp.

Hatt, Judy Lynn Keever, "History Social Structure and Life Cycle of Beaver Metis Colony," The Western Canadian Journal of Anthropology, 1969, 1:19-32.

Hawthorn, Harry Bertram, "Epilogue: The Indian Decides," in Arthur Kent Davis, et. al., eds., A Northern Dilemma: Reference Papers, Bellingham, Western Washington State College, August, 1966, Volume 2, pp. 578-585.

Hertzberg, Hazel W., The search for an American Indian Identity.

Hill, Bernard and Wilma J. Hill, "The Buffalo Narrows Project," Regional Services Branch, Department of Social and Welfare and Rehabilitation, Province of Saskatchewan, October 1, 1958, 29 pp.

Hinckley, Edward C., "Indian Participation in Community Development Programs, Washington, D.C., U.S. Department of Health, Education and Welfare, n.d. 5 pp.

Hiroko, Sue, Pre-School Children of the Hare Indians, Ottawa Northern Co-ordination and Research Centre, Dept. of Northern Affairs and National Resources, March, 1965, 50 pp.

Hlady, Walter M., "A Community Development Project Amongst the Churchill Band at Churchill, Manitoba, September, 1959--March, 1960, Saskatoon, December, 1960, 38 pp.

Honigmann, John Joseph, Social Networks in Great Whale River, National Museum of Canada, Bulletin, Anthropological Series No. 178, 1962.

Honigmann, John Joseph, and Irma Honigmann, "Frobisher Bay Eskimo Childhood," Ottawa, Department of Indian Affairs and Northern Development. n.d. 7 pp.

Hope, Adrian, "Brief History of Kikino Settlement," Edmonton, unpublished manuscript, April, 1970, 2 pp.

Hughes, Daniel T., "Democracy in a traditional society: two hypothesis on role," (Micronesian Islands), American Anthropologist, February, 1969, 71:36-45.

Hulbert, Janice, Age as a Factor in the Social Organization of the Hare Indians of Fort Good Hope, N.W.T., Ottawa, Department of Northern Affairs and National Resources, 1962, 80 pp.

Hynam, Charles A.S., "Community Development and the White-Indian Problem," in James A. Draper, ed., Citizen Participation: Canada, a Book of Readings, Toronto, New Press, 1971, pp. 371-381.

Keeper, Joseph Irwin, "Community Development Methods," Winnipeg, unpublished manuscript, Community Development Branch, Government of Manitoba, December, 1964, 4 pp.

Kerr, A.J., Subsistence and Social Organization in a Fur Trade Community: anthropological Report on the Ruperts House Indians, Ottawa, The National Committee for Community Health Studies, 1950, 260 pp.

Kerri, James, N., "Inuvik Town: Structural Functional Analysis of the Effectiveness of a Native Organization," Research proposal Prairie Region, Department of Manpower and Immigration, Winnipeg, Manitoba, 1971, 28 pp.

Knight, Rolf, "Big Beaverhouse and Wunnumen Lake Project," unpublished manuscript, n.d.

Kopas, Clifford Leslie, Political action of the Indians of British Columbia, Vancouver, Master's Thesis, University of British Columbia, 1972.

Lagasse, Jean-Henry, "Community Development in Manitoba," Human Organization, 1961, 20:232-237.

Lagasse, Jean-Henry, "A Community Development Program for Manitoba," unpublished manuscript, January, 1962. 5 pp.

Lagasse, Jean-Henry, "Indians and Social and Cultural Development: co-ordination of Social and Cultural Development Programmes for Indians," Ottawa, unpublished manuscript, Citizenship Branch, Department of Secretary of State, August, 1967. 3 pp.

Laing, Hon. Arthur, "Program for Physical Development of Indian Communities," Press Release, Ottawa, Northern Affairs and National Resources, n.d 8 pp.

Laing, Hon. Arthur, "Role of Other Citizens in Indian Affairs," Ottawa, Selections from Speeches by the Minister of Indian Affairs, March 16, and October 16, 1967. 3 pp.

Lal, Ravindra, "Some Observations on the Social Life of the Chipewyans of Camp 10, Churchill and their Implication for Community Development," Musk Ox, 1969, 6:14-21.

Lavallee, Mrs. Mary Ann, "Problems that concern Indian women," Address, Saskatchewan Indian Women's Conference, Fort Qu'Appelle, November 7, 1967, pp. 10-15.

Lloyd, Anthony John, Community Development in Canada, Ottawa, Document: 1, Canadian Research Centre for Anthropology, St. Paul University, 1967, 98 pp.

Lotz, James R., "The Community Developer: Outsider in the Middle," International Review of Community Development, 1969, 21-22:261-278.

Luebben, Ralph A., "Navajo Status and Leadership in a Modern Mining Situation," Plateau, (The Quarterly of the Museums of Northern Arizona), Summer 1962, 35:1-14.

MacGregor, Gordon, Warrior Without Weapons: A Study of the Society and Personality Development of the Pine Ridge Sioux, University of Chicago Press, 1946.

MacGregor, Gordon, "Community Development and Social Adaptation," Human Organization, 1961, 20:238-242.

MacNeish, June Helm, "Leadership Among the Northeastern Athabascans," Anthropologica, 1956, 2:131-163.

Mailhot, Jose, Inuvik Community Structure -- Summer, 1965, Ottawa, Northern Science Research Group, Department of Indian Affairs and Northern Development, May, 1968, 38 pp.

Majowicz, Mrs. Tricia, "The Native People and the Media," Toronto, unpublished term paper, Department of Sociology, Atkinson College, York University, April 1, 1972, 6 pp.

Manning, Ernest C., A White Paper on Human Resources Development, Edmonton, Government of Alberta, March, 1967. 100 pp.

Mansell, R.L., "A socio-economic survey of isolated communities in Northern Alberta," Edmonton, Human Resources Development Authority, Government of Alberta, July, 1970, 120 pp.

McEwen, Ernest Roy, Community Development Services for Canadian Indians and Metis Communities, Toronto: Indian-Eskimo Association, January 31, 1968, 52 pp.

Melling, John, "Canadian Indian Affairs and Derogated Authority," Canadian Journal of Political Science. 29 pp.

Michelson, Truman, "How Meskwaki Children should be Brought Up," in Elsie Clews Parsons ed., American Indian Life, 1922, (University of Nebraska Press, 1967, pp. 81-86).

Miller, Frank C. and D.D. Caulkins, "Chippewa Adolescents: A Changing Generation," Human Organization, Summer, 1964, 23:150-159.

Mills, Mrs. R.S., Family Life in Indian Communities in Ontario, Ottawa Canadian Conference on the Family, 1964, 61 pp.

Morris, William J., "Indian Integration Into the Community; Community Study," (Red Lake, Ontario), Province of Ontario, n.d.

Morris, William J., "Policies of Integration of Agencies Responsible for Canadian Indians," Province of Ontario, n.d.

Mulvihill, Father James P., "Indian Leadership," Oblate News, September, 1962, (reprinted in Seven Articles on Indian Affairs and The Dilemma, 1963).

O'Brien, Andy (reporter), "Anyone for Ipirautaqturnig?," Weekend Magazine, (Montreal), February 19, 1972.

O'Connell, Martin P., "Brief to the Hon. Lester B. Pearson: Failure of Community Development Program on Indian Reserves," Toronto Indian-Eskimo Association of Canada, January 4, 1968, 11 pp.

Pattillo, Miss M.H., "Women in Groups -- Community Work," Address to the Saskatchewan Indian Women's Conference, Valley Centre, Fort Qu'Appelle, Saskatchewan, November 6-10, 1967, pp. 24-27.

Pelletier, Wilfred and Duke Redbird, "Some views on Indian personality and organization," in Frank G. Vallee, Indians and Eskimos of Canada, an overview of studies of relevance to the Royal Commission on Bilingualism and Biculturalism, Ottawa, September, 1966, Volume 1, pp. 94-111.

Peterson, Helen L., "American Indian Political Participation," The Annals of The American Academy of Political and Social Science, May, 1957, 311-116-126.

Petkau, Henry, "Report on Community Development in Indian Communities of Northwestern Ontario," Dryden, Ontario, Youth and Recreation Branch, Ontario Department of Education, 1968, 8 pp.

Pilson, Susan, "Essay for Native People of Canada Course," Toronto, unpublished term paper, Sociology Department, Atkinson College, York University, April, 1972, 9 pp.

Pothier, Roger and Hedley Dimock, eds., "Report of the Seminar on Indian Community Government," Project Report Number 9, Centre for Human Relations and Community Studies, Sir George Williams University, Montreal, October 8-13, 1967, 18 pp.

Read, Margaret, "The Tribal Areas in India and the Community Development Program," Address, Research Seminar, Kingston, Ontario, June 12-15, 1960, 14 pp.

Renaud, Andre, A Study of the Best Ways of Fostering Native Community Development Among Canadian Indians, Ottawa, School of Psychology and Education, University of Ottawa, 1958-1959.

Ricciardelli, Alex Frank, Factionalism at Oneida, An Iroquois Indian Community, Ph.D. Dissertation, University of Pennsylvania, 1961, 298 pp.

Roger, Maysie, "A Radio Address on the Indian and Metis Conference in Manitoba," Winnipeg, October 16, 1954, 8 pp.

Rogers, Edward S., "Leadership Among the Indians of Eastern Subarctic Canada," Anthropologica, 1965, 7: (reprinted in Mark Nagler, ed., Perspectives on the North American Indian, Toronto, McClelland and Stewart, 1972).

Rogers, Edward S., "The Indian and Euro-Canadian Society," in James A. Draper, ed., Citizen Participation: Canada, A Book of Readings, Toronto, New Press, 1971, pp. 331-350.

Rosenthal, Elizabeth Clark, "Culture and the American Indian Community," in Stuart Levine and Nancy O. Lurie eds. The American Indian Today, Baltimore Md. Penguin Books, 1970, pp. 82-89.

Sapir, Edward, A Sketch of the social organization of the Nass River Indians, Ottawa, Museum Bulletin No. 19, Anthropological Series No. 7, Department of Mines, October 15, 1915, 30 pp.

Schusky, Ernest L., Politics and Planning in a Dakota Indian Community: A case study of views on termination and plans for rehabilitation on the Lower Brule Reservation in South Dakota, Institute of Indian Studies, State University of South Dakota, April, 1959. 89 pp.

Serl, Vernon C., "Action and Reaction: An Overview of Provincial Policies and Programs in Northern Saskatchewan," in Arthur Kent Davis, et. al., eds., A Northern Dilemma: Reference Papers, Bellingham, Western Washington State College, April, 1967, Volume 1, pp. 8-68.

Showalter, Don, "Report on Recreation Programs at Round Lake," (Ontario), Dryden, Ontario, Youth and Recreation Branch, Ontario Department of Education, 1968, 3 pp.

Sim, R. Alexander, Report to Indian Affairs Branch on community development training project, Ottawa, Department of Citizenship and Immigration, 1963.

Sim, R. Alexander, A radio forum project for the Canadian North, Toronto, Indian-Eskimo Association of Canada, 1966, 63 pp.

Sim, R. Alexander, "A Foundation for Indian and Metis People in Western Canada; a Feasibility Study," unpublished manuscript, Strathmere Associates, May, 1968, 26 pp.

Slobodin, Richard, Band Organization of the Peel River Kutchin, Ph.D. Dissertation, Columbia University, 1959 (also Bulletin of The National Museum of Canada, Ottawa, 1962, Vol. 179, Series No. 55).

Slobodin, Richard, Metis of the MacKenzie District, Ottawa, Canadian Research Centre for Anthropology, St. Paul University 1966, 175 pp.

Smitheram, Henry (Butch) Arthur, "Recommendations for Self-Help Programmes for the Native Indians of British Columbia," Vancouver, B.C., unpublished manuscript, 1971, 6 pp.

Spaudling, Philip, "The Social Integration of a Northern Community: White Mythology and Metis Reality," in Arthur Kent Davis, et. al., eds., A Northern Dilemma: Reference Papers, Bellingham, Western Washington State College, April, 1967, Volume 1, pp. 90-111.

Spence, Ahab, "Challenges to today's Indian women," Address, Saskatchewan Indian Women's Conference, Fort Qu'Appelle, November 6, 1967, pp. 4-8.

Spingarn, Lawrence P., "Children of Uncas -- The New England Indian Today," The American Indian, 1958-1959, 8:

Steinbring, Jack, "Recent Studies among the Northern Ojibwa," Manitoba Archaeological Newsletter, Winter, 1964, 1:9-12.

Steinhauer, Eugene, "Alberta Native Communications Society: Role and Structure," Edmonton, unpublished letter to members, April 3, 1969, 5 pp.

Stewart, W.D., and Doug Schweitzer, "The Definition and Evaluation of Values and Goals in a Cross-Cultural Region," The Musk Ox, 1970, 7:32-52.

Stipe, Claude E., "Eastern Dakota clans: the solution of a problem," American Anthropologist, October, 1971, 73:1031-1035.

Streib, Gordon Franklin, Patterns of Communication Among the Navaho Indians, Ph.D. Dissertation, Columbia University, 1954.

Suttles, Wayne P., "Persistance of Intervillage Ties Among the Coast Salish," Ethnology, October, 1963, 2:512-525.

Suttles, Wayne P., "Affinal Ties, Subsistence, and Prestige Among the Coast Salish," American Anthropology, April, 1960, 62:296-305.

Tarasoff, Koozma John, "Pine Creek Study, and Camperville and Duck Bay Areas, Manitoba," Winnipeg, unpublished memorandum Western Region, Department of Regional Economic Expansion, January 16, 1970, 29 p.

Taylor, Herbert C., Jr., "The Parameters of a Northern Dilemma," in Arthur Kent Davis, et. al., eds., A Northern Dilemma: Reference Papers, Bellingham, Western Washington State College, April, 1967, volume 1, pp. 1-7.

Thompson, Charles Thomas, Patterns of Housekeeping in Two Eskimo Settlements, Ottawa, Northern Science Research Group, Department of Indian Affairs and Northern Development, May, 1969, 59 pp.

Tiedke, Kenneth E., "A Study of the Hannahville Indian Community, Menominee County, Michigan," Special Bulletin 369, Michigan

State College, Agricultural Experiment Station, East Lansing, April, 1951, 43 pp.

Tooker, Elizabeth, "Brief communications: northern Iroquoian sociopolitical organization, American Anthropologist, February, 1970, 72:90-97.

Uppal, Krishan Dev., Community Development Institute for Assistance, Indian Agency at Valley Centre, Fort Qu'Appelle, Saskatoon, Saskatchewan Indian Affairs Branch, December 5, 1965 to December 16, 1965, 109 pp.

Uppal, Krishan Dev., "Training in Community and Staff Development," Regina, unpublished manuscript, Saskatchewan Indian Affairs Branch, November, 1966, 8 pp.

Vallee, Frank G., "Differentiation among the Eskimo in some Canadian Arctic Settlements," Sociological Research in the Arctic, Northern Coordination and Research Centre, Department of Northern Affairs and National Resources, 1962, (reprinted in W.E. Mann, ed., Canada: a Sociological Profile, 2nd ed., Copp Clark Publishing Co. (Canada), 1971, pp. 277-286).

Warren, Roland and Ed Moe, "Dimensions of Community Analysis," unpublished manuscript, n.d. 7 pp.

White, Hilary, J., Three Yukon Settlements Based on Mining -- A Study of Social Adaptation to Northern Isolation, Ottawa, June, 1969, 302 pp.

Whiteside, Don, Willie Parasuik, et. al., "Information communication program, The Pas, (Manitoba), Special Area," Ottawa, unpublished proposal, Social and Human Analysis Branch, Department of Regional Economic Expansion, October 29, 1970, 10 pp.

Wilson, Stan, "Message from the chairman of the board of directors," Miskamok News (The Pas, Manitoba), June 30, 1972, Volume 1, No. 1.

Witherspoon, Gary, "A new look at Navajo social organization," American Anthropologist, February 1970, 72:55-65.

Worth, Sol and John Adair, "Navajo filmmakers," American Anthropologist, February, 1970, 72:9-34.

York, Mrs. Cecilia, "Proud to be Indian," Involvement, (Newmarket, Ont.), Fall, 1971, 4:15-17, 54-55.

Miscellaneous Reports by date of publication

"Indian Self-Government," The American Indian, 1949, 8 pp.

"St. Mary's Home and School Association, Fredericton," Citizen, June, 1960.

A program for Indian Citizens (a summary report), Albuquerque, NM, Commission on the Rights, Liberties and Responsibilities of the American Indian, established by The Fund for the Republic, 1961, 45 pp.

"Indian Particpate in Leadership Training Conference," Citizen, October, 1961.

"We hunt together, notes on Indian Communities in North-Western Region," Toronto, Indian-Eskimo Association of Canada. Ontario Division, 1964.

"Indian-Eskimo Association of Canada, Report on the program of We hunt together," Thunderbird, (Toronto), July, 1964, 1(8):

"Brief on Indian Youth of Ontario for Consideration of the Ontario Legislative Assembly Select Committee on Youth," Toronto, Ontario Division of the Indian-Eskimo Association of Canada, October 27, 1964, 15 pp.

"Notes on Indian Communities in South-Western Ontario," Toronto, Indian-Eskimo Association of Canada, Ontario Division, October, 1964.

"A memorandum to provincial premier expressing the views of the Indian-Eskimo Association," Toronto, Indian-Eskimo Association of Canada, October 14, 1964.

"We hunt together; notes on Indian communities in North-Eastern Ontario region," Toronto, Indian-Eskimo Association of Canada, Ontario Division, 1964.

"We hunt together, a three year plan of Ontario Division of Indian-Eskimo Association of Canada," Toronto, Indian-Eskimo Association of Canada.

"We hunt together, Georgian Bay regional workshop," Toronto, Indian-Eskimo Association of Canada, 1965.

"The Indian and Metis -- A Modern Solution," Winnipeg, Department of Industry and Commerce, n.d., 94 pp.

"Canadian Indian Youth Council," Bulletin, (Winnipeg), March 1, 1966.

"Brief on Recreation Needs of Indian Youth of Ontario," Prepared by the Indian Recreation Committee of The Ontario Recreation Association, January 7, 1965, 8 pp.

"The Northern Community Action Program (NORCAP)," Toronto, Indian-Eskimo Association of Canada, March, 1967, 4 pp.

"Community Development on Reserve Lands, Ottawa, Selection from speeches by Ministers of Indian Affairs and Senior Departmental officials," Ottawa, Department of Indian Affairs and Northern Development, 1967, 7 pp.

"What happened to the Indian before you volunteered: for the Company of Young Canadians volunteer who is planning to live with Indian people, this is a description of previous relationships which Indians have had with others, What will yours be like?," Ottawa, unpublished manuscript, Company of Young Canadians, March, 1967, 10 pp.

Saskatchewan Indian Women's Conference, Valley Centre, Fort Qu'Appelle, Saskatchewan, November 6, 1967, 43 pp.

"Self-Government in Indian Communities, Selections from speeches by Ministers of Indian Affairs and Senior Departmental officials," Department of Indian Affairs and Northern Development, Ottawa 1968, 6 pp.

"Study and Field Research on Indian Women," Ottawa, unpublished report, Royal Commission on the Status of Women, c 1968, 141 pp.

"Indian Projects Approved by ARDA, April 1, 1967--March 31, 1968," Ottawa, unpublished manuscript, ca 1968, 3 pp.

Past, present and future, report of First Alberta Native Women's Conference, Edmonton, March 12-15, 1968, 52 pp.

"The role of film in community development," report on the Newfoundland film workshop, May 31 to June 28, 1968, 24 pp.

Third Annual Conference, Saskatchewan Indian Women, North Battleford, October 7-10, 1968

"How to Negotiate," Edmonton, unpublished manuscript, Alberta Metis Association, 1969, 9 pp.

Summary Report on the Field Study of American and Mexican Indian Development. Rural Development Branch, Department of Forestry and Rural Development, Ottawa, January, 1969.

"Y-Teen Intercultural Development Projects: in Indian and urban communities in Ontario and Quebec: Complation of the 1968 Projects and New Developments in 1969," Submission to Secretary of State, Young Women's Christian Association of Canada, January, 1969.

Round Lake Interim Report, Ontario Department of Lands and Forest, March, 1969.

"Success with unity -- we are responsible," Second Alberta Native Women's Society Conference, Edmonton, March 1969, 53 pp.

"Saddle Lake," H.R.D.A. in Alberta, Volume 1, 1969.

"Progress Reports, C.D. 12," H.R.D.A. in Alberta, Volume VI, 1970.

"Community Development Program," Union of Nova Scotia Indians, January 30, 1970, 12 pp.

"Brief to the Canadian Radio Television Commission: Radio and Television Service for Indian, Eskimo and Metis Communities," Jointly prepared by the National Indian Brotherhood of Canada,

The Canadian Metis Society, The Indian-Eskimo Association of Canada, February, 1970, 23 pp.

"Progress Report," Edmonton, Alberta Native Communications Society, November 15, 1970, 10 pp.

"The Need to Improve Radio Services for Alberta Native Communities," Edmonton, Brief presented to the Canadian Radio-Television Commission and the Canadian Broadcasting Corporation, The Alberta Native Communications Society, December 2, 1970, 6 pp.

"Native Indians in politics," Vancouver, B.C., BC Association of Non-Status Indians, 1971, 1 p.

"Indian Sport Olympic (INSPOL) Concept: An Alberta Indian Sports and Recreation Development Proposal," Edmonton, unpublished proposal, Indian Association of Alberta, ca 1971, 8 pp.

"Indian and Eskimo Programming: Northern Service Shortwave Service," Ottawa, Canadian Broadcasting Corporation, February 9, 1971, 6 pp.

First National Native Women's Conference, Edmonton, March 22, 23, 1971, 48 pp.

"Let Indians control own destiny: excerpt from the Official Report of Debates Legislature of Ontario," Involvement (Newmarket, Ont.), Fall, 1971, 4:19-20.

"Indian Sports and Recreation Directorate," Regina, unpublished proposal to the National Indian Brotherhood, by the Federation of Saskatchewan Indians, ca 1972, 23 pp.

Report, Workshop on Communications Held at Coqualeetze Centre, Sardis, B.C., January 12-14, 1972, Ottawa, unpublished manuscript, Department of Secretary of State, January, 1972.

"1972 Western Native Winter Games," Edmonton, unpublished proposal by the Governing Council, February 4, 1972, 30 pp.

"Indian communications in Canada," prepared for the National Indian Brotherhood by the Federation of Saskatchewan Indians and National Communications Workshop Members, February, 1973, 36 pp.

PART XIII

ECONOMIC DEVELOPMENT (see also Community Development)

Abrahamson, G., Tuktoyaktuk-Cape Parry: an Area Economic Survey, Ottawa, Industrial Division, Northern Administration Branch, Department of Indian Affairs and Northern Development, June, 1968, 83 pp.

Allan, D.J., "Indian Land Problems in Canada," in Charles T. Loram and Thomas F. McIlwraith, eds., The North American Indian Today, University of Toronto Press, 1943, pp. 184-198.

Andres, G. and J. Morissett, Rae -- Lac La Marte: an Area Economic Survey, Ottawa, Industrial Division, Northern Administration Branch, Department of Indian Affairs and Northern Development, June, 1969, 113 pp.

Barnes, Peter, "The Potential for Rational Land Use: Unfreezing Alaska," The New Republic, September 11, 1971, 165:15-17.

Bauer, George W., "James Bay: the last massacre of Indian rights, to make its power dams, Quebec is drowning lands that the Indians own," Saturday Night, (Toronto), January, 1973.

Bennett, Robert L., "Building Indian Economies with Land Settlement Funds," Human Organization, 1961, 20:159-163.

Bennett, Robert L., "Problems and Prospects in Developing Indian Communities," Arizona Law Review, Winter, 1968, 10:649-660.

Berger, Edward B., "Indian Mineral Interest -- Potential for Economic Advancement," Arizona Law Review, Winter, 1968, 10:675-690.

Bissett, Don, Resolute: an Area Economic Survey, Ottawa, Industrial Division, Northern Administration Branch, Department of Indian Affairs and Northern Development, November, 1968, Vol. 2, 175 pp.

Bissett, Don, Northern Baffin Island: an Area Economic Survey, Ottawa, Industrial Division, Northern Administration Branch, Department of Indian Affairs and Northern Development, November, 1968, Vol. 1, 131 pp.

Bissett, Don, Northern Baffin Island: an Area Economic Survey, Ottawa, Industrial Division, Northern Administration Branch, Department of Indian Affairs and Northern Development, November, 1969, Vol. 2, 209 pp.

Bonnycastle, R.H.G., "The Role of the Trader in Indian Affairs," in Charles T. Loram and Thomas F. McIlwraith, eds., The North American Indian Today, University of Toronto Press, 1943, pp. 59-78.

Bourne, L.S., Yellowknife, N.W.T.: A Study of Its Urban and Regional Economy, Master's Thesis, University of Alberta, (reprinted by Northern Co-ordination and Research Centre,

Department of Northern Affairs and National Resources, Ottawa, September, 1963, 160 pp.).

Buckley, Helen and Sheridan Campbell, "The Farm Potential on Two Saskatchewan Indian Reserves and a Proposal for ARDA Program," Centre for Community Studies, Saskatoon, 1966, 53 pp.

Buckley, Helen, "Farming for Canadian Indians? An Economist's View," 1970, 7 pp.

Carr, D. William and Associates, The Yukon Economy, Its Potential for Growth and Continuity, 8 volumes, 1968:

Vol. 1   Final Report
Vol. 2   Analysis of Statistics and Needs
Vol. 3   A Model Simulation of the Yukon Economy
Vol. 4   Reference Studies on Social Services
Vol. 5   Reference Study on Minerals
Vol. 6   Reference Study on Power
Vol. 7   Reference Study on Transportation
Vol. 8   Reference Study on Forest Resources.

Charley, Robert, "The Native People reply: response of the Native People to Mr. Chrétien's address," in Douglas H. Pimlott, Kitson M. Vincent and Christine E. McKnight, eds., Arctic Alternatives a national workshop, Canadian Arctic Resources Committee, 1973, pp. 41-45.

Chatain, Dennis, "Task Force for action research in socio-economic development using the total community approach: preliminary draft," Ottawa, Department of Indian Affairs and Northern Development, November, 1972, 58 pp.

Chrétien, Hon. Jean, "Pipeline Guidelines," Address, National Press Club, Ottawa, June 28, 1972, 8 pp.

Chrétien, Hon. Jean, "Northern development for northerners," in Douglas H. Pimlott, Kitson M. Vincent and Christine E. McKnight, eds., Arctic Alternatives, a national workshop, Ottawa, Canadian Arctic Resources Committee, 1973, pp. 27-35.

Cooper, P.F. Jr., The Mackenzie Delta-Technology, Ottawa Northern Co-ordination and Research Centre, Department of Indian Affairs and Northern Development, July, 1967, 69 pp.

Cowan, Edward (reporter), "Good-doing Won't Replace Traplines," Weekend Magazine, (Montreal), January 18, 1969.

Cox, Bruce, "Environmental disturbances in northern peoples' lands," Paper presented at the 40th International Congress of Americanists, Rome, 1972, 23 pp.

Crowe, Keith J., A Cultural Geography of Northern Foxe Basin, N.W.T., Ottawa, Northern Science Research Group, Department of Indian Affairs and Northern Development, October, 1969, 130 pp.

Cummings, Peter A., "Our land -- our people: Native rights north of '60," in Douglas H. Pimlott, Kitson M. Vincent, and Christine

E. McKnight, eds., Arctic Alternatives, a national workshop, Ottawa, Canadian Arctic Resources Committee, 1973, pp. 87-110.

Currie, R.D., Western Ungava: an Area Economic Survey, Ottawa, Industrial Division, Northern Administration Branch, Department of Indian Affairs and Northern Development, 1968, 93 pp.

Diamond, David, "James Bay and the Cree," recherches amerindiennes au quebec, November, 1972, 2:33-35.

Dorner, Peter P., The Economic Position of the American Indians: Their Resources and Potential for Development, Ph.D. Dissertation, (Economics), Harvard University, 1959.

Dunne, Mrs. N.R., "Economic Possibilities for Native Communities," Toronto, unpublished manuscript, Indian-Eskimo Association of Canada, September, 1968, 8 pp.

Dunning, Robert William, "Some Implications of Economic Change in Northern Ojibwa Social Structure," Canadian Journal of Economics and Political Science, 1958, 24:562-566.

Edwards, Newton, "Economic Development of Indian Reserves," Human Organization, 1961, 20:197-202.

Eicher, Carl K., "An Approach to Income Improvement on the Rosebud Sioux Indian Reservation," Human Organization, 1961, 20:191-196.

Euler, Robert C. and Henry F. Dobyns, "Ethnic Group Land Rights in the Modern State: Three Case Studies," Human Organization, 1961, 20:203-207.

Evans, Jon, Ungava Bay: an Area Economic Survey, Ottawa, Industrial Division, Northern Administration Branch, Department of Indian Affairs and Northern Development, 1968, 72 pp.

Ferguson, Jack D., The Human Ecology and Social Economic Change in the Community of Tuktoyaktuk, N.W.T., Ottawa, Northern Coordination and Research Centre, Department of Northern Affairs and National Resources, February, 1961, 80 pp.

Fransen, Jack Jacob, Employment Experiences and Economic Position of a Selected Group of Indians in Metropolitan Toronto, Master of Social Work Thesis, University of Toronto, 1964, 105 pp.

Getty, Harry Thomas, "San Carlos Apache Cattle Industry," Human Organization, 1961, 20:181-186.

Gimmer, David, "Milady's Fur: the Trapper," in Maja Van Steensel, ed., People of Light And Dark, Ottawa, Department of Indian Affairs and Northern Development, 1966.

Glooschenko, Valanne, "The James Bay Power proposal," Native Canada, (Canadian Native Federation) January-March, 1973.

Godt, P., "Co-operatives Among Indian People in Canada -- First National Statistical Report," Department of Indian Affairs and Northern Development, 1967, 4 pp.

Gordon, John H., "Northern Indians: their Economic Future," North (Ottawa) September-October, 1962, 9:28-34.

Gourdeau, Eric, "The people of the Canadian north," in Douglas H. Pimlott, Kitson M. Vincent and Christine E. McKnight, eds., Arctic Alternatives, a national workshop, Ottawa, Canadian Arctic Resources Committee, 1973, pp. 71-85.

Greenwood, Martin H., Big Trout Lake -- a Pilot Study of an Indian Community in Relation to its Resource Base, Ottawa, Economic and Social Division, Department of Citizenship and Immigration, February, 1964.

Gunther, Erna, "Indian Craft Enterprises in the Northwest," Human Organization, 1961, 20:216-218.

Harper, Allan G., "Indian Land Problems in the United States," in Charles T. Loram and Thomas F. McIlwraith, eds., The North American Indian Today, University of Toronto Press, 1943, pp. 170-183.

Hawthorn, Harry Bertram and A. Laforet, "Paper presented at the Seminar on Guidelines for Scientific Activities in Northern Canada," ca 1971, 65 pp.

Helm, June and Nancy Oestreich Lurie, The Subsistence Economy of the Dogrib Indians of Lac La Martre in the Mackenzie District of the N.W.T., Ottawa, Northern Coordination and Research Centre, Department of Northern Affairs and National Resources, 1961.

Higgins, G.M., South Coast Baffin Island: an Area Economic Survey, Ottawa, Industrial Division, Northern Administration Branch, Department of Indian Affairs and Northern Development, June, 1968, 235 pp.

Hlady, Walter M., Sandy Bay, Saskatchewan: A Social and Economic Study, Department of Natural Resources, Province of Saskatchewan, September, 1959, 143 pp.

Hlady, Walter M. and Frank E. Price and Associates, A Sociological Study of the Saskatchewan River Delta: A Study of Indian and Metis Attitudes to Potential Development in the Cumberland House Area, Winnipeg, Manitoba, February, 1967, 90 pp.

Hlady, Walter M., "The Cumberland House Fur Project: the First Two Years," Western Canadian Journal of Anthropology, 1969, 1:124-139.

Horn, Kahn-Tineta, "James Bay," News Bulletin (Caughnawaga), January, 1973.

Howard, S.H., "New day on James Bay dawning for Indians," Saturday Night, (Toronto), April 17, 1948, pp. 12-13.

Jamieson, Stuart, "Native Indians and the Trade Union Movement in B.C.," Human Organization, 1961, 20:219-225.

Jeness, R.A., Great Slave Lake Fishing Industry, Ottawa, Northern Coordination and Research Group, Department of Northern Affairs and National Resources, 1963.

Josephy, Alvin M. Jr., "Here in Nevada a terrible crime," (Pyramid Lake), American Heritage, 1970.

Kelly, William H., "The Economic Basis of Indian Life," Annals of the American Academy of Political and Social Science, 1957, 311:71-79.

Kemp, William B., "The Flow of Energy in a Hunting Society," Scientific American, 1971, 224:104-115.

Kennard, Edward A., "Post-War Economic Changes Among the Hopi," unpublished manuscript, n.d. 7 pp.

Kennedy, Alex, et al., "Agricultural development on Indian reserves in Saskatchewan," draft report presented to the Chief's Conference, Saskatoon, October 17, 1972, by the Agricultural Development Committee, Federation of Saskatchewan Indians, 70 pp.

Lang, Gottfried O., "Economic Development and Self-Determination, The Northern Ute Case," Human Organization, 1961, 20:164-171.

Levy, Jerrold E., "South Tuba: A Western Navajo Wage Work community," Window-Rock, Arizona, unpublished manuscript, U.S. Public Health Service, 1962, 11 pp.

Lotz, James R., "The Chilkoot Trail To-day -- Dyea to Bennett, A Guide to the Trail," No. 4 in Yukon Research Project Series, Northern Co-ordination and Research Centre, Department of Northern Affairs and National Resources, December, 1965, 11 pp.

Lotz, James R., The Squatters of Whitehorse: an Area Economic Survey, Ottawa, Industrial Division, Northern Administration Branch, Department of Indian Affairs and Northern Development, 1968.

MacDonald, A.H., "Co-operatives and People of Indian Ancestry," Canadian Co-operative Digest, Spring, 1960.

MacLeod, William C., "Big Business and the North American Indian," American Journal of Sociology, 1929, 34:

Martin, Harry W. and Robert L. Leoh, "Report on Alaskan Consultation with Employment Assistance Branch, Bureau of Indian Affairs," Dallas, Southwestern Medical School, University of Texas, January, 1964, 48 pp.

Matthiasson, John S., "Caught in the middle, two Cree communities and the southern Indian Lake Hydro Electric Power controversy," Paper presented to the International Culture Change among North American Indians Symposium, 40th International Congress of Americanists, Rome, September, 1972, 12 pp.

McFeat, Thomas, "Two Malecite Family Industries: a Case Study," Anthropologica, 1962, 4:233-271.

Metzler, William, "Relocation of the Displaced Worker," <u>Human Organization</u>, Summer, 1963, 22:142-145.

Mortimore, George E., <u>The Indian in Industry</u>, <u>Roads to Independence</u>, Ottawa: Department of Indian Affairs and Northern Development, 1965, 29 pp.

Nablo, Ron., "Kainai Industries," Ottawa, unpublished memorandum, Department of Regional Economic Expansion, August 25, 1970, 16 pp.

Nablo, Ron, "Department of Indian Affairs and Northern Development (summary of programs conducted on behalf of registered Indians and Eskimos), Ottawa, Department of Regional Economic Expansion, December 11, 1970.

Naysmith, John K., "Management of Polar Lands," Ottawa, unpublished paper presented at the 12th Technical Meeting of the International Union for Conservation of Nature and National Resources, Banff, September, 1972, 20 pp.

Nolet, Jean-Paul, "The James Bay development project," <u>recherches amerindiennes au quebec</u>, November, 1972, 2:37-38.

O'Brien, F.X., "Compensatory employment practices for Native Peoples in Canada's north," Ottawa, unpublished manuscript, March 12, 1972, 22 pp.

O'Connell, Martin P., "An Economic Development Plan for Indian Reserve Communities in Canada," Toronto, Indian-Eskimo Association of Canada, 1964.

Paust, Gil, "Welcome Paleface!," <u>Argosy</u>, June 1966, pp. 53-56, 100-101.

Pimlott, Douglas H., Kitson M. Vincent and Christine E. McKnight, eds., <u>Arctic Alternatives</u>, <u>a national workshop on people</u>, resources, and environment North of '60. (May, 1972), Ottawa, Canadian Arctic Resources Commitee, 1973, 391 p.

Radojic, D. and G. Anders, eds., <u>Great Slave Lake -- South Shore: an Area Economic Survey</u>, Ottawa, Industrial Division, Northern Administration Branch, Department of Indian Affairs and Northern Development, July, 1968, 126 pp.

Richardson, Boyce (reporter), "The Indians: Canadian racism in full flower," (James Bay), <u>Montreal Star</u>, February 5, 1972.

Roe, Frank Gilbert, "The Hudson's Bay Company and the Indians," <u>The Beaver</u>, September, 1936, 8-14, 64-65.

Rogers, Edward S., <u>The Hunting Group -- Hunting Territory Complex Among Misstassini Indians</u>, Ottawa: National Museum of Canada, Bulletin No. 195, Anthropological series No. 63, 1963, 95 pp.

Rogers, Edward S. and Jean Shawana, "Programme for Ontario Indians -- action and reaction," Paper presented to the 40th International Congress of Americanists, Rome, 1972, 22 pp.

Sasaki, Thomas and Harry W. Basehart, "Sources of Income Among Many Farms -- Rough Rock Navajo and Jicarilla Apache: Some Comparisons and Comments," Human Organization, 1961, 20:187-190.

Sauve, Clayton, "Theoretical Considerations for Socio-Economic Development among Native People," Edmonton, unpublished manuscript, Rural Development Research Branch, Department of Agriculture, Alberta, 1969, 15 pp.

Smith, Derek, G., The Mackenzie Delta -- Domestic Economy of the Native People: a Preliminary Study, Ottawa, Northern Co-ordination and Research Centre, Department of Indian Affairs and Northern Development, 1967, 59 pp.

Smith, Gordon W.,"Territorial Sovereignty in the Canadian North: a Historical Outline of the Problem," Ottawa, Northern Co-ordination and Research Centre, Department of Northern Affairs and National Resources, July, 1963, 12 pp.

Stern, Theodore, "Livelihood and Tribal Government on the Klamath Reservation," Human Organization, 1961, 20:172-180.

Stevenson, David S., Problems of Eskimo Relocation for Industrial Employment, Ottawa, Northern Science Research Group, Department of Indian Affairs and Northern Development, May, 1968, 25 pp.

Stewart, James (reporter), "Indian crew ignores native protest; power project tightens grip on James Bay area," Montreal Star, December 21, 1972.

Stylt, R., "Report IE2 Social Correlates of Economic Development," Ottawa Economic and Social Research Division, Department of Citizenship and Immigration, October, 1960, 21 pp.

Tanner, A., Trappers, Hunters and Fishermen, Yukon Research Project, Ottawa, Department of Indian Affairs and Northern Development, 1966.

Tarasoff, Koozma John, The Broadview Rural Development Area Study, Regina, Research and Planning Branch, Saskatchewan, Department of Welfare, January, 1968, 142 pp.

Tarasoff, Koozma John, "Problems and Prospects for Development in Northern Saskatchewan, Visit No. 1, (July, 1968)," unpublished manuscript, Western Regional Office, Rural Development Branch, Department of Forestry and Rural Development, August 23, 1968, 44 pp.

Tarasoff, Koozma John, Some Trends in the Development of Canadian Indian Handicrafts -- A Résumé of Selected Sources, Winnipeg, Department of Regional Economic Expansion, Western Region, August, 1969.

Tarasoff, Koozma John, et. al., A Socio-Economic Review of the Garment Plant -- Fisher River and Peguis Communities, Winnipeg, Department of Regional Economic Expansion, Manitoba, April, 1970, 95 pp.

Tarasoff, Koozma John, "An evaluation of the Opportunity corps program, Lesser Slave Lake Special Area, Alberta," Ottawa, unpublished manuscript, Social and Human Analysis Branch, Department of Regional Economic Expansion, September, 1972, 148 pp.

Taylor, Benjamin J., "Indian Manpower Resources: The Experiences of Five Southwestern Reservations," Arizona Law Review, Winter, 1968, 10:579-596.

Taylor, Walter, "The defense of James Bay -- an emergency for all Native people and other residents of North America," Penticton B.C., unpublished manuscript, January, 1973, 28 pp.

Usher, Peter Joseph, Banks Island: An Area Economic Survey, Ottawa, Industrial Division, Northern Administration Branch, Department of Indian Affairs and Northern Development, April, 1966, (reprinted 1968), 91 pp.

Usher, Peter Joseph, The Bankslanders: Economy and Ecology of a Frontier Trapping Community, Volume I -- History, Ottawa, Northern Science Research Group, Department of Indian Affairs and Northern Development, February, 1971, 124 pp.

Usher, Peter Joseph, The Bankslanders: Economy and Ecology of a Frontier Trapping Community, Vol. II: Economy and Ecology, Ottawa, Northern Science Research Groups, Department of Indian Affairs and Northern Development, February, 1971, 169 pp.

Usher, Peter Joseph, The Bankslanders: Economy and Ecology of a Frontier Trapping Community, Vol. III: The Community, Ottawa, Northern Science Research Group, Department of Indian Affairs and Northern Development, October, 1971, 88 pp.

Van Stone, James W., The Economy of a Frontier Community, Ottawa, Northern Coordination and Research Centre, Department of Northern Affairs and National Resources, 1961.

Villiers, Desme, Central MacKenzie: an area economic survey, Ottawa, Industrial Division, Department of Indian Affairs and Northern Development, 1968.

Villiers, Desme, The Central Arctic: an area economic survey, Industrial Division, Department of Indian Affairs and Northern Development, August, 1969.

Voget, Fred, "Introduction and commentary," Human Organization, (American Indians and their economic development), 1961, 20:157-158, 243-248.

Whiteside, Don, "Brief bibliography of articles in the press, etc., on the James Bay hydro-electric project, P.Q., April 24, 1971 -- May 1, 1973," Ottawa, National Indian Brotherhood, May 31, 1973, 76 pp.

Wolf, Roger, C., "Needed: a System of Income Maintenance for Indians," Arizona Law Review, Winter, 1968, 10:597-616.

Woods, Richard G. and Arthur M. Harkins, Indian Employment in Minneapolis, Training Centre for Community Programs, University of Minnesota, Minneapolis, April, 1968, 44 pp.

Wyant, William K. Jr., "Sharing the Wealth of Alaska: The Oil Rush," The New Republic, February 14, 1970, 162:19-21.

Miscellaneous Reports by date of publication

"Northern Co-Operatives," unpublished list? n.d. 4 pp.

"Indian Reserve Lands," Ottawa, unpublished manuscript, Department of Indian Affairs and Northern Development, n.d. 4 pp.

"National Native Development Fund," Toronto, unpublished draft, Indian-Eskimo Association of Canada, n.d. 56 pp.

"Co-ops are changing the Northland," Regina, Department of Industry and Information, Province of Saskatchewan, n.d. 4 pp.

Reports from Committees, Hudson's Bay Company, Eleven Volumes, Session 2, 1857.

Native Canadians, a Plan for the Rehabilitation of Indians, Oliver, B.C.: Okanagan Society for the Revival of Indian Arts and Crafts, Okanagan Society, 1942-3.

"The Fur Trade," Canadian Imperial Bank of Commerce, February, 1953, 5 pp.

A Conference of Indian Business Men: Report of the Second Decenial Conference on Native Indian Affairs, Vancouver, University of British Columbia, April, 1958, 43 pp.

"Placing Indians Who Live on Reservations: a Co-operative Program," Employment Security Review, January, 1959, pp. 27-29.

"Brief to the Parliamentary Committee on Indian Affairs," Cooperative Union of Canada, December, 1959, 34 pp.

"Report IE2-Social Correlates of Economic Development with Special Reference to the Problems of the Canadian Indian," Ottawa, Economic and Social Research Division, Department of Citizenship and Immigration, October, 1960, 21 pp.

Human Organization, (American Indians and their Economic Development), 1961, Vol. 20.

"Role of Native People in the North in Industrial Development," Report of the Committee on Manitoba's Economic Future, Winnipeg, 1963, Part 11:1-18.

A Socio-Economic Survey of the Lake Winnipeg Channel and Narrows Area, Winnipeg, Community Development Services, Department of Welfare, Province of Manitoba, March, 1963, 23 pp.

"Indian Division Programs, Office of Operations, Office of Economic Opportunity," Washington, D.C., U.S. Gov't Printing Office, ca 1965.

The Development of Indian and Eskimo Art and Crafts in the Far North, Toronto: Indian-Eskimo Association of Canada, May 3, 1965.

Vocational Opportunity and the Canadian Indian, Ottawa: Indian Affairs Branch, Department of Citizenship and Immigration, 1966.

Canadian Indian Crafts Limited: a Proposed Program for Developing Indian Arts and Crafts in Canada, Toronto, Canadian Consociates Ltd., June, 1966.

First Annual Report, Teamwork Enterprises of Alberta and Mackenzie, September 21, 1966.

"Equal Opportunity in our Land," Vancouver, Indian-Eskimo Association of Canada, December 2-4, 1966.

"The Seal Hunt," North, (Ottawa), November--December 1966.

"Considerations in a Program for Expanding Economic Opportunities of the Indians and Metis of Manitoba," Menlo Park, CA, Sanford Research Institute Project 6304, 1967, 39 pp.

Round Table Conference on Job Opportunities and Vocational Training, Edmonton, University of Alberta, May 5-6, 1967, 47 pp.

Indian Resources Development Act of 1967, Hearings before the Sub-committee on Indian Affairs of the Committee on Interior and Insular Affairs, House of Reps., 90th Congress, 1st Session on H.R. 19560, July 13, 14, 1967, 94 pp.

"An Action Project to Help Canadians of Native Ancestry to Get Adequate Vocational Training and Suitable Jobs," Brief presented to the Hon. A. Laing, by the Indian-Eskimo Association of Canada, Toronto, September, 1967, 11 pp.

Co-Op Commentary, October 5, 1967, Vol. 20, 5 pp.

"Trappers Assistance Program: a Brief to the Government of the N.W.T.," Yellowknife, Indian-Eskimo Association of Canada, N.W. Territories Division, November, 1967, 5 pp.

"Indian Opportunities: A Summary of Indian participation in OEO Programs," Washington, D.C., Office of Economic Opportunity, ca 1968.

"Physical Improvement on Reserve Lands," Selections from Speeches by Ministers of Indian Affairs and Senior Department Officials, Department of Indian Affairs and Northern Development, Ottawa, ca 1968, 8 pp.

"Economic Development on Reserve Lands," Selections from Speeches by Ministers of Indian Affairs and Senior Departmental

Officials, Department of Indian Affairs and Northern Development, Ottawa, ca 1968, 8 pp.

"Report of Lennox Island Band Workshop held at Summerside, P.E.I.," unpublished manuscript, February 6-8, 1968, 12 pp.

Report of Working Group 1 -- Indians -- to the Executive Committee, Rural Development Branch, Ottawa, Department of Forestry and Rural Development, Vol. 1, Revised: Vol. 2, Appendices, June, 1968, 149 pp.

"Bill C-30, An Act to Preserve and Promote Native Indian and Eskimo Arts and Crafts," The House of Commons of Canada, September 20, 1968.

Mines and Minerals North of 60, Activities 1969, Ottawa, Northern Economic Development Branch, Department of Indian Affairs and Northern Development, 1969, 34 pp.

Fourth Annual Report, Team Products, Edmonton, Alberta, October 17, 1969.

"South Indian Lake: people and progress -- must there be conflict?," Winnipeg, Community Welare Planning Council, February 10, 1969, 5 pp.

Indian Arts and Crafts -- Retail Outlets, Ottawa, Department of Indian Affairs and Northern Development, 1969.

"Indian Economic Development Fund Program Draft Operating Policies," Ottawa, unpublished draft, Department of Indian Affairs and Northern Development, February 18, 1970, 15 pp.

"Conference on Economic Development," Union of Nova Scotia Indians, May 14, 1970.

"Minutes of Meeting of June 29, and 30, 1970, at Regina, Saskatchewan, between representatives of the Indian and Metis organizations of the Three Prairie Provinces and Representatives of the Department of Regional Economic Expansion," Ottawa, unpublished manuscript, Department of Regional Economic Expansion, ca 1970, 15 pp.

"Indian Affairs Minister Jean Chrétien Releases MacKenzie Delta Task Force Report," Ottawa, Press Release, Department of Indian Affairs and Northern Development, June 29, 1970, 10 pp.

"Economic Opportunities and Human Resources Development: a Planning Study," unpublished proposal, Union of B.C. Indian Chiefs, July, 1970, 10 pp.

"Brief to the Department of Regional Economic Expansion, Government of Canada," unpublished proposal, Indian and Metis Association, Lac La Loche, Saskatchewan, July 13, 1970, 3 pp.

"National Council on Indian Opportunity," Washington, D.C., Office of the Vice-President, September 28, 1970, 3 pp.

"100,000 New Indians Suggested as Way to End Unemployment," The Toronto Daily Star, November 23, 1970.

"A Model for a Community Project Designed in and for Sandy Lake, (Ontario), to provide a Structure for the Development of Sandy Lake as a Viable Indian Community in the 1970's and Beyond," unpublished manuscript, December, 1970, 8 pp.

A Socio-Economic and Resource Evaluation Study of the Sarcee Indian Reserve, Edmonton, Stanley Associates Engineering Ltd., December, 1970, 84 pp.

"Indian Affairs: Alleged Approval of Route of Pipeline through lands covered by Treaties 8 and 11," House of Commons Debates, December 1, 1970, 115:10062.

"Oil Favored over Eskimos report says," Toronto Daily Star, February 1, 1972.

James Bay development: progress or disaster? Le comité pour la defense de la baie James, Montreal, P.Q., July, 1972, 38 pp.

"Is This Our Land?," Inuvik, N.W.T., unpublished manuscript, Committee for Original Peoples Entitlement, October 10, 1972, 11 pp.

"Native Peoples reaffirm their claims: a symposium on Native rights," in Douglas H. Pimlott, Kitson M. Vincent and Christine E. McKnight, eds., Arctic Alternatives, a national workshop, Ottawa, Canadian Arctic Resources Committee, 1973, pp. 111-129.

"Treaty Indians win temporary land freeze," (N.W.T.), The Ottawa Citizen, April 4, 1973.

PART XIV

OTHER SOCIAL AND CULTURAL CHANGES

Adair, John and Evon Z. Vogt, "Navaho and Zuni Veterans: A Study in Contrasting Modes of Culture Change," American Anthropologist, 1949, 51:547-561.

Arbess, Sault E., Social Change and the Eskimo Co-operative at George River, Quebec, Ottawa, Northern Co-ordination and Research Centre, Department of Northern Affairs and National Resources, August, 1966, 79 pp.

Balikci, Asen, Vunta Kutchin Social Change: A Study of the People of Old Crow, Yukon Territory, Ottawa, Northern Co-ordination and Research Centre, Department of Northern Affairs and National Resources, February, 1963.

Balikci, Asen, "Some Acculturative Trends Among the Eastern Canadian Eskimos," Anthropologica 1960, 2:139-153 (reprinted in Mark Nagler, ed., Perspectives on the North American Indian, Toronto, McClelland and Stewart, 1972).

Barbeau, Charles Marius, "Our Indians -- Their Disappearance," Queen's Quarterly, (Kingston), 1931, 38:691-701.

Barnett, M.L. and D.A. Baerreis, "Some Problems Involved in the Changing Status of the American Indian," in D.A. Baerreis, ed., The Indian in Modern America, Madison, State Historical Society of Wisconsin, 1956, pp. 50-70.

Barnouw, Victor, "Acculturation and Personality Among the Wisconsin Chippewa," American Anthropological Association: Memoir No. 72, October, 1950, 152 pp.

Beatty, Willard W., "The Goal of Indian Assimilation," The Canadian Journal of Economics and Political Science, August, 1946, 12:395-404.

Bee, Robert L., "Changes in Yuma Social Organization," Ethnology, January, 1963, 2:207-227.

Bell, Dennis (reporter), "Same Class: Equal Chance? St. Catherine Standard (Ontario), (also in N. Sheffe ed., Issues for the Seventies: Canada's Indians, McGraw-Hill, 1970, pp. 53-54).

Bennett, John William (in collaboration with Niels Braroe), Northern Plainsmen: Adaptive Strategy and Agrarian Life, Chicago, Aldine Publishing Co., 1969.

Briggs, Jean L., "Kapluna Daughter: Living with Eskimos," Trans-Action, June, 1970, pp. 12-24.

Bruner, Edward M., "Primary Group Experience and the Process of Acculturation," American Anthropologist, 1956, 58:605-623.

Bruner, Edward M., "Assimilation Among Fort Berthold Indians," The American Indian, 1953, 6:21-29.

Chance, Norman A., "Culture Change and Integration: An Eskimo Example," American Anthropologist, December, 1960, 62:1028-1044.

Chance, Norman A. and Jean Trudeau, "Social Organization, Acculturation and Integration among the Eskimo and the Cree: A Comparative Study," Anthropologica, 1963, 5:47-56.

Chance, Norman A., "Acculturation, Self-identification and Personality Adjustment," American Anthropologist, April, 1965, 67:

Chance, Norman A., ed., Conflict in Culture: Problems of Developmental Change Among the Cree, Ottawa, Document: 2, Canadian Research Centre for Anthropology, St. Paul University, 1968, 104 pp.

Chance, Norman A. et. al., "Developmental Change Among the Cree Indians of Quebec," Montreal, McGill Cree Project (ARDA Project No. 34002), DREE, August, 1970.

Clifton, James A., "Factional Conflict and the Indian Community -- The Prairie Potawatomi Case," in Stuart Levine and Nancy O. Lurie, eds., The American Indian Today, Baltimore, Penguin Books, 1970, pp. 184-211.

Collier, John, "Comments on the Essay of Robert A. Manners, Pluralism and the American Indian," American Indigena, 1972, 22:205-208.

Cressey, Paul F., "The Anglo-Indians: A Disorganized Marginal Group," Social Forces, December, 1935, 14:

Cruikshank, Julia M., The Role of Northern Canadian Indian Women in Social Change, Master of Arts Thesis, (Anthropology and Sociology), University of British Columbia, April, 1969, 137 pp.

Cujes, Rudolf P., "Contribution of Slovenes to the Socio-Cultural Development of the Pre-Charter Canadians, The Canadian Indians," paper presented at the 2nd National Conference on Canadian Slavs, University of Ottawa, June 9-11, 1967, 14 pp.

De Pena, Joan F., "Contributions of Anthropology and Other Social Sciences in Method and Theory to Such Problems: Pertinent Concepts of Anthropology," Address, Resolving Conflicts -- a Cross-Cultural Approach, Kenora, Ontario, April 3, 1967, pp. 98-116.

Dirthrower, Anderson, "The white man's rule," in Ralph Osborne, ed., Who is the chairman of this meeting? A collection of Essays, Toronto, Neewin Publishing Co., 1972, pp. 26-33.

Dirthrower, Anderson, "The prophecy," in Ralph Osborne, ed., Who is the chairman of this meeting? A collection of Essays, Toronto, Neewin Publishing Co., 1972, pp. 34-38.

Dowling, John H., "The Evolution of Funerary Customs in Oneida Society," Human Organization, 1968.

Dozier, Edward P., George E. Simpson and J. Milton Yinger, "The Integration of Americans of Indian Descent," The Annals of the American Academy of Political and Social Science, May, 1957, 311:158-165.

Duff, Wilson, The Indian History of British Columbia, Vol. 1., The Impact of the White Man, Victoria, Anthropological Memoir No. 5, Provincial Museum of B.C., 1964, 117 pp.

Dunning, Robert William, Social and Economic Change among the Northern Ojibwa, Toronto, University of Toronto Press, 1959, 213 pp.

Eggan, Fred, The American Indian: Perspectives for the Study of Social Change, Chicago, Aldine Publishing Co., 1966.

Eiseley, Loren C., "The Paleo Indians: Their Survival and Diffusion," New Interpretations of Aboriginal American Culture History, (1955), pp. 1-11.

Ervin, Alexander M., New Northern Townsmen in Inuvik, Ottawa, Northern Science Research Group, Department of Indian Affairs and Northern Development, May, 1968, 25 pp.

Ewers, John Canfield, The Horse in Blackfoot Culture -- With Comparative Material from other Western Tribes, Bulletin 159, United States Bureau of American Ethnology.

Fall, Thomas, The Ordeal of Running Standing, New York, Bantam Book, 1970, 312 pp.

Freedman, Jan., "A Review of the Changes Among the Indians and Metis of Northern Saskatchewan," unpublished manuscript, University of Saskatchewan, ca 1968, 25 pp.

Frisch, Jack A., "Conflict, Confrontation, and Social Change on the St. Regis Indian Reserve," Paper presented at the annual meeting of the Society for Applied Anthropology, Miami, Florida, April 15, 1971, 10 pp.

Gladwin, Thomas, "Personality Structure in the Plains," Anthropological Quarterly, October, 1957, 30:111-124.

Gold, Dolores, "Psychological Changes Associated with Acculturation of Saskatchewan Indians," The Journal of Social Psychology, 1967, 71:177-184.

Goldfrank, E.S., "Historical Change and Social Character, a Study of the Teton Dakota," America Anthropologist, 1943, pp. 67-83.

Goldfrank, E.S., "Changing Configurations in the Social Organization of a Blackfoot Tribe During the Reserve Period," American Ethnological Society Monograph, 1945.

Goldfrank, E.S., "The Different Patterns of Blackfoot and Pueblo Adaption to White Authority," in Sol Tax, ed., Acculturation in the Americas, Chicago, University of Chicago Press, 1952.

Hagan, William T., "Private Property, The Indian's Door to Civilization," Ethnohistory, 1955, 3:126-137.

Hagen, Everett E., "A Case in Point: Sioux on the Reservations," On the Theory of Social Change, Dorsey Press, 1962, Chapter 19, pp. 471-502.

Hallowell, Alfred Irving, "American Indians, White and Black: The Phenomenon of Transculturalization," Current Anthropology, 1963, pp. 519-531.

Hatt, Fred Kenneth, The Response to Directed Social Change on an Alberta Métis Colony, Edmonton, Ph.D. Dissertation, (Sociology), University of Alberta, 1969, 290 pp.

Hawthorn, Harry Bertram, "The Maori: A Study in Acculturation," American Anthropological Association, Memo 64.

Hawthorn, Harry Bertram, "Enter the European, -- Among the Indians of Canada," Part IV, The Beaver, June, 1954, 285:3-7.

Hawthorn, Harry Bertram, et. al., The Indians of British Columbia, a Study of Contemporary Social Adjustment, University of Toronto Press, 1958, 499 pp.

Hawthorn, Harry Bertram, "Problems of cultural adjustment in relation to northern resources development," Address, Resources for Tomorrow Conference, 1961, 1:597-606.

Hawthorn, Harry Bertram, "The Survival of Small Societies," Anthropologica, 1971, n.s. 13:63-84.

Hellaby, Hilda Alice, "The Indian in Social Adjustment," North, (Ottawa), September-October, 1961, 8:22-23.

Helm, June and David Damas, "The Contact-Tradition All-Native Community of the Canadian North; The Upper Mackenzie Bush Athabaskans and the Iglulimiut," Anthropologica, 1963, 5:9-21.

Hill, Willard William, "Some Navaho Culture Changes During Two Centuries," Smithsonian Miscellaneous Collections, 1940, pp. 395-415.

Hirabayashi, Gordon K., "Apathy as a Mode of Adjustment: A Hypothesis," in Brigham Young Card, et al., eds., The Metis in Alberta Society, Edmonton, University of Alberta, 1963, Chapter 13, pp. 375-384.

Hlady, Walter M., "Directed Social Change and the Agencies Involved," Paper presented at the Learned Societies meeting, Queen's University, Kingston, Ontario, June 14, 1969, 8 pp.

Hoffman, Hans, "Culture Change and Personality Modification among the James Bay Cree," Alaska University Anthropological Papers, May, 1961, 9:81-91.

Holden, David E.W., "Modernization Among Town and Bush Cree in Quebec," Canadian Review of Sociology and Anthropology, 1969, 6:237-248.

Honigmann, John Joseph, "Community Organization and Patterns of Change Among North Canadian and Alaskan Indians and Eskimos," Anthropologica, 1963, 5:3-8.

Honigmann, John Joseph, "Arctic Town Life as a stimulus to Eskimo culture change," Paper presented to the Central State Anthropological Society, Lexington, Kentucky, April 16, 1965.

Honigmann, John Joseph, "Social Disintegration in Five Northern Communities," The Canadian Review of Sociology and Anthropology, 1965, 2:199-214.

Honigmann, John Joseph, "Deculturation and Protelarization of Canada's Far Northern Native People," Paper presented at the Canadian Sociological and Anthropological Association Meeting, Toronto, 1969, 19 pp.

Honigmann, John Joseph and Irma Honigmann, Arctic Townsmen: Ethnic Backgrounds and Modernization, Ottawa, Canadian Research Centre for Anthropology, St. Paul University, 1970, 303 pp.

Hughes, Charles C., "Observations on Community Change in the North: An Attempt at Summary," Anthropologica, 1963, 5:70-79.

Hunter, Guy, Modernizing Peasant Societies: a comparative study in Asia and Africa, New York, Oxford University Press, 1969, 324 pp.

Iglaver, Edith, The New People: The Eskimos Journey into our Time, Garden City, New York, Doubleday and Co., 1966, 205 pp.

James, Bernard J., "Social-psychological dimensions of Ojibway Acculturation," American Anthropologist, 1961, 63:721-746, (see also "Comment", American Anthropologist, 1962, 826-833.)

Jenness, Diamond, "Enter the European ... Among the Eskimos," The Beaver, Winter, 1954, 285:24-30.

Johnson, Guy B., "Personality in a White-Indian-Negro Community," American Sociological Review, 1939, 4:516-523.

Jones, Dorothy V., "A Potawatomi Faces the Problem of Cultural Change: Joseph N. Bourassa in Kansas," Kansas Quarterly, Fall, 1971, 3:47-55.

Kelly, William H., "The Changing Role of the Indian in Arizona," Circular 263, Agricultural Extension Service, University of Arizona, 26 pp.

Knight, R., Changing Social and Economic Organization Among the Rupert House Cree, Master of Arts Thesis, University of British Columbia, 1962, 212 pp.

Koolage, William W. Jr., "Relocation and culture change: a Canadian subarctic case study," Paper presented to 40th International Congress of Americanists, Rome, September, 1972, 7 pp.

Kraenzel, Carl F., The Great Plains in Transition, Norman, University of Oklahoma Press, 1955, 428 pp.

Kupferer, Harriet J., "Cherokee Change: A Departure from Lineal Models of Acculturation," Anthropologica, 1963, 5:187-198.

Kurtz, Ronald J., Role Change and Culture Change: The Canyoncito Case, Ph.D. Dissertation, University of New Mexico, 1963.

Lafarge, Oliver, ed., The Changing Indian, Norman, University of Oklahoma Press, 1942.

La Rusic, Ignatius E., "The New Auchimau: A Study of Patron-Client Relations Among the Waswanipi Cree," Cree Development Change Program, Montreal, McGill University, April, 1968, 63 pp.

La Rusic, Ignatius E., "From Hunter to Proletarian -- The Involvement of Cree Indians in the White Wage Economy of Central Quebec," in Norman A. Chance, et al., Developmental Change Among the Cree Indians of Quebec, Ottawa, Department of Regional Economic Expansion, August, 1970.

La Rusic, Ignatius E., "Indian Power in Waswanipi Political Process and Social Change in an Encapsulated Society," Montreal, unpublished, Ph.D. dissertation proposal, December 10, 1970.

La Violette, Forrest Emmanuel, The Struggle for Survival: Indian Cultures and the Protestant Ethnic in British Columbia, University of Toronto Press, 1961, 325 pp.

Leacock, Eleanor Burke, The Montagnais Hunting Territory and the Fur Trade, Minasha, Wis., Memoirs of American Anthropology Association, 1954, Vol. 78, 54 pp.

Levine, Stuart, "The Survival of Indian Identity," in Stuart Levine and Nancy O. Lurie, eds., The American Indian Today, Baltimore, Md., Penguin Books, 1970, pp. 9-45.

Lewis, C.L., A Study of the Impact of Modern Life on a Canadian Indian Band, Ph.D. Dissertation, Columbia University, 1959.

Lewis, Claudia, Indian Facilities of the Northwest Coast: The Impact of Change, University of Chicago Press, 1970, 224 pp.

Lewis, Oscar, The Effects of White Contact upon Blackfoot Culture: with Special Reference to the Role of the Fur Trade, New York, Monographs of the American Ethnological Society, 6, New York, 1942, 73 pp.

Liebow, Elliott and Jean Trudeau, "A preliminary Study of Acculturation among the Cree Indians of Winisk, Ontario," Arctic, September, 1962, 15:190-204.

Linton, Ralph, ed., Acculturation in Seven American Indian Tribes, New York, Appleton-Century-Crofts 1940 (reprinted 1963).

Loree, Don, "The Marginal Situation of Canadian Indians: The Dogrib Tribe of the Northwest Territories," Edmonton, unpublished Thesis Prospectus, Department of Sociology, University of Alberta, January, 1970, 20 pp.

MacDonald, A.A., Community Resources and Dimensions of Alienation on Indian Reserves, Antigonish, Nova Scotia, Extension Department, St. Francis Xavier University, May, 1967, 76 pp.

Malan, Vernon D., "Acculturation of the Dakota Indians," Pamphlet 119, Agricultural Experiment Station, South Dakota State College, Brookings, S.D., June, 1956, 82 pp.

Manuel, Chief George, "Canadian Indians and Maoris Share Common Problems," The Black i, (Ottawa), March, 1972, 1:14-17.

Masson, Leonard, The Swampy Cree: A Study in Acculturation, Ottawa, National Museum, Anthropology Paper No. 13, January, 1967, 75 pp.

Matthiasson, John S., "Forced Relocation: An Evaluative Case Study," (Easterville, Man.), unpublished manuscript, Department of Anthropology, University of Manitoba, n.d. 18 pp.

McClelland, Joseph (reporter), "The Indian: Challenge of 70's," The London Free Press, (Anglican Church of Canada), n.d. (ca 1970) series of articles.

McFee, Malcolm, Modern Blackfeet: Contrasting Patterns of Differential Acculturation, Stanford, California, Ph.D. Dissertation, Stanford University, 1962.

McGee, John T., Cultural Stability and Change Among the Indians of the Lake Melville Region of Labrador, Washington, D.C., The Catholic University of America Press, Anthropological Series No. 19, 1961, 159 pp.

McKenzie, Fayette A., "The Assimilation of the American Indian," American Journal of Sociology, 19:761-772.

Mead, Margaret, The Changing Culture of an Indian Tribe, New York, Columbia University Press, 1932.

Mortimore, George E. (reporter), "Caught Between Cultures," Weekend Magazine, (Montreal) (also in N. Sheffe, ed., Issues for the Seventies: Canada's Indians, McGraw-Hill, 1970, pp. 46-50).

Mulvihill, Father James P., "Twilight Zone, Looking at Reserves Through the Eyes of the Indians," Oblate News, January, 1962, (reprinted in Seven Articles on Indian Affairs, and The Dilemma, 1963).

Nagler, Mark, "North American Indians and Intermarriage," Address, Department of Sociology, Atkinson College, York University, February, 1972, 19 pp.

Newcomb, W.W., Culture and Acculturation of the Delaware Indians, Ann Arbor, University of Michigan Press, 1956, 141 pp.

Nickols, Peter, "Since the Days of Barter," North, (Ottawa), November-December, 1966, pp. 20-23.

Oswalt, Wendall and James Vanstone, "The Future of the Caribou Eskimo," Anthropologica, 1960, 2:

Oswalt, Wendall and James Vanstone, "Partially acculturated communities -- Canadian Athabaskan and West Alaskan Eskimos," Anthropologica, 1953, 5:

Parman, Donald L., "J.C. Morgan: Navajo Apostle of Assimilation," Prologue, (Washington, D.C.), Summer, 1972, 4:83-98.

Parsons, George F., Retreatists and innovators in an Indian community, Hamilton, Master's Thesis, (Sociology and Anthropology), McMasters University, October 1968.

Peacock, F.W., Some Psychological Aspects of the Impact of the White Man upon the Labrador Eskimo, Masters Thesis, University of Montreal, 1948.

Pearce, Terry, "Human Problems in Canada's North," The Labour Gazette, (Ottawa), June, 1970, pp. 416-420.

Peretti, Peter O., "Enforced acculturation and Indian-White relations," The Indian Historian, Winter 1973, 6:38-52.

Plambeck, Hans H., "Culture and Social Change," part of Final Report, Vol. 1, Warm Springs Research Project, Corvallis, Oregon State College, December, 1960.

Pothier, Roger, "Community Complexity and Indian Isolation," in Norman Chance, ed., Conflict in Culture Problems of Developmental Change Among the Cree, Ottawa, Working Papers of the Cree Developmental Change Project, Canadian Centre for Anthropology, St. Paul University, 1968, pp. 33-45.

Provinse, John, et al., "Wenner-Gren Foundation Supper Conference: The American Indian in Transition," American Anthropologist, June, 1954, 56:387-394.

Reifel, Benjamine, "To Die or to Become?: Cultural Factors in Social Adjustment of Indians," Indian Education, April, 1957.

Ricciardelli, Alex Frank, "The Adoption of White Agriculture by Oneida Indians," Ethnohistory, Fall, 1963, 10:309-328.

Richards, C.A., The Role of Iroquois Women: A Study of the Onondaga Reservation, Ithaca, New York, Ph.D. Dissertation, Cornell University, 1957.

Richardson, Boyce, James Bay: the plan to drown the North woods, Toronto, Clarke Irwin and Co., 1972, 190 pp.

Richardson, Robert Alan, Acculturation among the Seven Island Montagnais, Montreal, Master of Arts Thesis, (Anthropology), McGill University, 1961.

Roe, Frank Gilbert, The North American Buffalo, University of Toronto Press, 1951, 957 pp.

Roe, Frank Gilbert, The Indian and the Horse, Norman, University of Oklahoma Press, 1955, 433 pp.

Rogers, Edward S., "Changing Settlement Patterns of the Cree-Ojibwa of Northern Ontario," Southwestern Journal of Anthropology, Spring, 1963, 19:64-88.

Rosenthal, Eric, "Acculturation without Assimilation," American Journal of Sociology, 1960, 66:275-288.

Rowley, Graham W., "The Canadian Eskimo Today," The Polar Record, 1972, 16:201-205.

Saum, O. Lewis, The Fur Trader and the Indian, Seattle, University of Washington Press, 1965, 324 pp.

Secoy, Frank Raymond, Changing Military Patterns on the Great Plains, Monographs of the American Ethnological Society, No. 21, (1953).

Shepardson, Mary and Blodwen Hammond, "Change and Persistence in an Isolated Navajo Community," American Anthropologist, 1964, 66:1029-1050.

Shimpo, Mitsuru and Robert Williamson, Socio-cultural Disintegration Among the Fringe Saulteaux, Saskatoon, Centre for Community Studies, University Campus, April, 1965, 291 pp.

Siegel, Bernard J., Acculturation. Stanford, California, Stanford University Press, 1955, 231 pp.

Siegel, Bernard J., "Some Recent Developments in Studies of Social and Cultural Change," Annals of the American Academy of Political and Social Science, January, 1966, 323:137-153.

Siegel, Bernard J., "Some Recent Developments in Studies of Social and Cultural Change," Annals of the American Academy of Political and Social Science, September, 1969, 326:157-174.

Sindell, Peter Samuel, "Continuity and change in Micmac Values," Bachelor of Art Paper (Honors), (Anthropology), Harvard College, March, 1963, 96 pp.

Smith, Derek G., "The Implications of Pluralism for Social Change Programs in a Canadian Arctic Community," Anthropologica, 1971, n.s. 13:193-214.

Smith, June E., Anomie and Acculturation: A Case Study Among the Ojibway, Hamilton, Master of Arts Thesis, (Sociology), McMaster University, 1962, 125 pp.

Smith, Robert J., ed., "Culture Change and the Small Community," The Journal of Social Issues, 1958, 14:

Smitheram, Henry (Butch) Arthur, "Cultural Conflict -- General and Specific," Exploration, November, 1969, 10:33-36.

Sparks, Joseph P., "The Indian Stronghold and the Spread of Urban America," _Arizona Law Review_, Winter, 1968, 10:706-724.

Speck, Frank Gouldsmith, "Cultural Problems in Northeastern North America," _Proceedings of the American Philosophical Society_, 1926, 65:272-311.

Spence, Ian, _Human adaptation in the Mackenzie Delta, a study in facilitating the adjustment of the northern Indian and Eskimo to rapid social change_, Montreal, Master of Social Work Thesis, McGill University, 262 pp.

Spicer, Edward Holland, ed., _Perspectives in American Indian Culture Change_, University of Chicago Press, 1961, 544 pp.

Spindler, George Dearborn, "Socio-Cultural and Psychological Processes in Menomini Acculturation," Berkeley, University of California _Publications in Culture and Society_, 1955, 267 pp.

Spindler, Louise Schauber, _Menomini Women and Culture Change_, Memoir 91, American Anthropological Association, 1952.

Spindler, Louise Schauber, _Women and Cultural Change: A Cast Study of the Menomini Indians_, Stanford, California, Ph.D. Dissertation, Stanford University, 1956.

Stanley, George F.G., "The Indians and the Brandy Trade During the Ancient Regime," _Revue d'Histoire de l'Amerique française_, Juin, 1952, 6:489-505.

Steen, Sheils C., _The psychological consequences of Acculturation among the Cape Breton Micmac_, 1951.

Still, Larry (reporter), "Collision of cultures; ancient Eskimo ways vs. mechanization," _Vancouver Sun_, December 30, 1972.

Tax, Sol. (ed.), _Acculturation in the Americas_ (29th Congress of Americanists), University of Chicago Press, 1952, 339 pp.

Toombs, Farrell C., "Psychological Aspects of Cultural Change, unpublished manuscript? May, 1960.

Usher, Jean, "The Long Slumbering Offspring of Adam: The Evangelical Approach to the Tsimshian," _Anthropologica_, 1971, n.s. 13:37-61.

Usher, Peter Joseph, _Fur Trade Posts of the Northwest Territories, 1870-1970_, Ottawa, Northern Science Research Group, Department of Indian Affairs and Northern Development, March, 1971, 180 pp.

Usher, Peter Joseph, "The Canadian Western Arctic a Century of Change," _Anthropologica_, 1971, n.s. 13:169-183.

Valentine, Victor Fortune and R.G. Young, "The situation of the Metis of Northern Saskatchewan in relation to his physical and social environment," _North_, (Ottawa), January-February, 1967, pp. 21-27.

Vallee, Frank G., _Kabloona_ and Eskimo in the Central Keewatin: trends and comparisons, Ottawa, Department of Northern Affairs and National Resources, May, 1962, 232 pp. (also published by the Canadian Research Centre for Anthropology, St. Paul University, Ottawa, 1967).

Voget, Fred, "Acculturation at Caughnawaga, A Note on the Native-Modified Group," _American Anthropologist_, 1951, 53:220-231.

Voget, Fred, "The American Indian in Transition: Reformation and Status Innovations," _American Journal of Sociology_, 1951, 62:369-378.

Voget, Fred, "The American Indian in Transition: Reformation and Accommodation," _American Anthropologist_, 1956, 58:249-260.

Vogt, Evon Z., "The Acculturation of American Indians," _The Annals of the American Academy of Political and Social Science, May,_ 1957, 311:137-146.

Wallace, Anthony F.C., "No. 4, Some psychological determinants of culture change in an Iroquoian community," in William N. Fenton ed., _Symposium on local diversity in Iroquois culture_, Washington, Smithsonian Institute, Bureau of American Ethnology, Bulletin 149, 1951, pp. 59-76.

Weaver, Thomas, "Social and economic change in the context of Pima-Maricopa history," Paper presented at the 40th International Congress of Americanists, Rome, September, 1972, 29 pp.

White, Lynn Carlton, _Assimilation of the Spokane Indians: on reservation versus off reservation residence_, Ph.D. Dissertation, Washington State University, 1968.

White, Robert, _The Assimilation of the Dakota Indians_, Master's Thesis, St. Louis University, 1959.

Wolcott, Harry Fletcher, _Acculturation Among the Indian Children of Western Canada: a Case Study_, Stanford, California, Ph.D. Dissertation, Stanford University, 1963.

Worsley, Peter M., Helen L. Buckley and Arthur Kent Davis, "Economic and Social Survey of North Saskatchewan," Saskatoon, Research Division, Centre for Community Studies, 1961, 50 pp.

Yawney, Carole Dianne, "The Indian Response to Change," _Sanity_, October, 1966.

Miscellaneous Reports

"The Threat to the Indian in the North West Territories," Brief presented by the President of the Indian Brotherhood of the N.W.T., to the National Indian Brotherhood at Regina, 1971.

A   --   General
B   --   Friendship Centres

A -- General

Ablon,   Joan,   Relocated American Indians in the San Francisco Bay
Area: Concepts of Acculturation, Success and Identity in the
City, Ph.D. dissertation, University of Chicago, 1963.

Ablon,   Joan,   "Relocated American Indians in the San Francisco Bay
Area: Social   Interaction   and   Indian   Identity,"   Human
Organization, 1964, 23:296-304.

Asimi,   A.D.,   "The Urban Setting," Address, Resolving Conflicts --
a Cross-Cultural Approach, Kenora, Ontario, March 27, 1967,
pp. 88-96.

Atwell,   Phyllis   Harryette,   Kinship and Migration Among Calgarian
Residents of Indian Origin, Master's Thesis, (Sociology and
Anthropology), University of Calgary, 1969, 85 pp.

Batan,   Jorge,   "Migrant Native Socio-economic Differences in Latin
American   Cities: a   Structural   Analysis,"   Latin   American
Research Review, 1969, 4:3-29.

Bear Robe, Andrew, "Indian Urbanization," Tawow, (Ottawa), Spring,
1970, 1:2-5, 28-31.

Beaulieu,   Isaac,   "Urbanizing   the   Indian,"   Ontario   Housing,
February, 1964, pp. 16-22.

Blumenfeld, Ruth, "Mohawks: Round Trip to the High Steel," Trans-
Action, 1965, 3:19-21.

Boe,   Robert L.,   "Changes in Yuma Social Organization," Ethnology,
1963, 2:207-222.

Bone, Robert M., "The Chippewyan Indians of Dene Village: an
Editorial Note," The Musk Ox, 1969, 6:1-4.

Braun,   Gordon   A.,   An   Analysis   of   the   Determinants of Labour
Mobility Among the Indian and Metis of Northern Manitoba,
Winnipeg,   Master of Arts Thesis, University of Manitoba, 1970,
143 pp.

Brody, Hugh,   Indians on Skid Row: The Role of Alcohol and
Community in the Adaptive Process of Indian Urban Migrants,
Ottawa, Northern Science Research Group, Department of Indian
Affairs and Northern Development, 1971, 86 pp.

Carter,   E.   Russell,   "Rapid   City,   South   Dakota,"   The American
Indian, 1963, 6:29-38.

Currie, Walter, "Indians and the City," Address Indians and the City Conference, Winnipeg, October 6-9, 1966, 8 pp.

Currie, Walter, "Urbanization of Indians," Address, Mid-Canada Development Corridor Conference, Lakehead University, August 20, 1969, 13 pp.

Davis, Arthur Kent and J.P. Brady, "Edging into Mainstream: Urban Indians in Saskatchewan," in Arthur Kent Davis, Vernon C. Serl and Philip Spaulding, eds., A Northern Dilemma: Reference Papers, Volume 2, Bellingham, Washington State College, 1966, pp. 338-577.

Davis, Arthur Kent, "Urban Indians in Western Canada: Implications for Social Theory and Social Policy," Transactions of the Royal Society of Canada, June, 1968, 6:217-228.

Denton, Trevor, Strangers in their land: a study of migration from a Canadian Indian reserve, Ph.D. Dissertation, (Anthropology), University of Toronto, 1970, 460 pp.

De Pena, Joan F., "Research Proposal: Indians in Urban Winnipeg," Winnipeg, unpublished proposal, Department of Anthropology, University of Manitoba, December 1, 1967.

Dickman, Phil, "Thoughts on Relocation," The Musk Ox, 1969, 6:21-31.

Dosman, Edgar Joseph, The urban dimension of the Indian problem in Canada, Ph.D. dissertation, Harvard University.

Dowling, John H., "A 'Rural' Indian Community in an Urban Setting," Human Organization, 1968, 27:236-240, (reprinted in Mark Nagler, ed., Perspectives on the North American Indian, Toronto, McClelland and Stewart, 1972).

Ebihara, May M. and Gail Margaret Kelly, A Survey of the Indian Population of Portland, Oregon, in the Summer of 1955, Portland, Oregon, Reed College, September, 1955, 71 pp.

Frantz, Charles, The Urban Migration and Adjustment of American Indians Since 1940, Haverford, Conn., Master's Thesis, Trinity College, 1951.

Freeman, Jan, "An examination and evaluation of the programs and services available to Native People through the various social service departments in Toronto and Vancouver," Toronto, Department of Sociology, York University, ca 1971, 26 pp.

Frum, Barbara (reporter), "Canadian Indians 1968: How Ottawa (and We) slept," Chatelaine, (Toronto), November, 1968.

Graves, Theodore D. and Minor Van Arsdale, "Values, Expectations and Relocation: The Navajo Indian Migrant to Denver," Human Organization, 1966, 25:300-307.

Graves, Theodore D., "The Personal Adjustment of Navajo Indian Migrants to Denver, Colorado," American Anthropologist, February, 1970, 72:35-54.

Hanson, Marshall Roy, <u>Plains Indians</u> and <u>Urbanization,</u> Stanford, California, Ph.D. Dissertation, Stanford University, June, 1960, 163 pp.

Harris, Michael, "American cities: the new reservations," <u>City,</u> (National Urban Coalition, Washington, D.C.), March-April, 1971, pp. 45-48.

Hillery, George A., "Navajos and Eastern Kentuckians: A Comparative Study in the Cultural Consequences of the Demographic Transition," <u>American Anthropologist</u>, 1966, 68:

Hodge, William H., "Navaho urban silversmiths," <u>Anthropological Quarterly</u>, 1967, 40:185-200.

Hodge, William H., "Urban Indian Bibliography: Canada and the United States," Milwaukee, unpublished manuscript, Department of Anthropology, University of Wisconsin, October, 1968, 17 pp.

Hogg, Carol (reporter), "Cities can be cruel, influx reveals native dilemma, some Indians can make it finding their own way, others can't," <u>The Calgary Herald</u>, May 16, 1970.

Hurt, Wesley, R. Jr., "The Urbanization of the Yankton Indian," <u>Human Organization</u>, 1961, 20:226-231.

Inglis, Gordon Bahan, "Urban Relocation: A Proposal for Research," unpublished proposal, Department of Anthropology, University of Toronto, December, 1967, 5 pp.

Johnson, William A. et al., "Adjustment Factors in the Indian Moving to the Urban Community: A Descriptive Study," The Family Service Association of Edmonton, ca 1965, 16 pp.

Jones, James (reporter), "Indian woes in cities called worse than on reservations," <u>The Minneapolis Star</u>, March 19, 1969.

Kerri, James N., <u>Adjustment of People of Indian Ancestry in Urban Centers: A Bibliography</u>, Citizenship Branch, Department of the Secretary of State, Winnipeg, August, 1971, 53 pp.

King, Hector, "Brief Presented to the Honourable Jean Chrétien," unpublished manuscript, Armstrong, (Ontario) Indian Association, October 3, 1968, 9 pp.

Korchinski, Emil, "Social Determinants of Rural to Urban Mobility Among Indian People as Compared to Non-Indians," Ottawa, Department of Indian Affairs and Northern Development, January, 1968, 34 pp.

Lal, Ravindra, "From Duck Lake to Camp 10: Old Fashioned Relocation," <u>The Musk Ox</u>, 1969, 6:5-13.

Latham, Carl H., <u>The Indian in the City</u>, Master's Thesis, 1962.

Lovrich, Frank, <u>The Assimilation of the Indian in Rapid City</u>, Master's Thesis, State University of South Dakota, 1951.

Lurie, Nancy Oestreich, "The Indian Moves to an Urban Setting," Address to Resolving Conflicts -- a Cross-Cultural Approach, March 20, 1967, Kenora, Ontario, pp. 72-86.

Madigan, LaVerne, "The American Indian Relocation Program," New York, The Association on American Indian Affairs, December, 1956, 22 pp.

Manitowabi, Edna, "An Ojibwa Girl in the City," This Magazine is About Schools, (Ontario), 1970, 4:8-24.

Marshall, John (reporter), "Ontario's Ghettos," Toronto Telegram, March 22, 1969.

Marshall, John (reporter), "Migration the Solution for our Indians: They're Far from Blameless when it comes to judging," Toronto Telegram, March 25, 1969.

Martin, Harry W., "Correlations of Adjustment Among Indians in an Urban Environment," Human Organization, 1964, 23:290-295.

McCaskill, Donald N., Migration Adjustment and Integration of the Indian into the Urban Environment, Ottawa, Master's Thesis, Carleton University, 1970.

McElroy, Ann P., "The Effects of Urbanization on Eskimo Child Life and Personality," Paper presented at the Canadian Sociology and Anthropology Association, Meeting, 1968, 83 pp.

McEwen, Ernest Roy, "An Action Research Project on the Problem of Migrating Native People," Toronto, Indian-Eskimo Association of Canada, n.d.

Mitchell, J., "The Mohawks in High Steel," The New Yorker, 1949, 25:33-52.

Morrison, William A., et al., "Urbanizing Indian Adjustment Project: A Study of Changing Individual Indians in Urban Settings," unpublished proposal, Sociology Research Unit, University of Winnipeg, November, 1967, 18 pp.

Nagler, Mark, Indians in the City, Ottawa, Canadian Research Centre for Anthropology, Saint Paul University, 1970, 107 pp.

Nagler, Mark, "Patterns of Urbanization of Indians in Canada," Paper presented at the Annual Meeting of the Canadian Association of Anthropology and Sociology, St. John's, Newfoundland, June, 1971, 12 pp.

Nagler, Mark, "Status and Identification Groupings Among Urban Indians," in Mark Nagler, ed., Perspectives on the North American Indians, Toronto, McClelland and Stewart, 1972, pp. 280-287.

Price, John A., "The Migration and Adaptation of American Indians to Los Angeles," Human Organization, Summer, 1968, 27:168-175.

Rasky, Frank (reporter), "Trapped in the Ghetto," Canadian Magazine, (Toronto), May 24, 1969.

Ritzenthaler, Robert and Mary Sellers, "Indians in an Urban Situation," The Wisconsin Archaeologist, 1955, 36:147-161.

Roy, Prodipto, and D.M. Walker, "Assimilation of the Spokane Indians," Bulletin 628, Washington Agricultural Experimental Station, Washington State University, May, 1961.

Roy, Prodipto, "The Measurement of Assimilation of the Spokane Indians," American Journal of Sociology, 1962, 67:541-551.

Schusky, Ernest L., "Contemporary Migration and Culture Change on Two Dakota Reservations," Plains Anthropology, (University of Nebraska), 1961, 7:178-183.

Shackleton, Doris, "The Indian as Newcomer," Canadian Welfare, (Ottawa), July-August, 1969, 45:7-9, 17, 18.

Shannon, Lyle and Patricia Morgan, "The Prediction of Economic Absorption and Cultural Integration Among Mexican, Indians and Negroes and Anglos in a Northern Industrial Community," Human Organization, 1966, 25:154-162.

Shepherd, Harvey L., "Indians in the City: Will Help Be Too Little and Too Late," The United Church Observer, April 1, 1967.

Sorokin, Alan L., "Some Aspects of American Indian Migration," Social Forces, December, 1969.

Stevenson, David S., "Proposals for an Eskimo Relocation Project," Ottawa, Northern Science Research Group, Department of Indian Affairs and Northern Development, May, 1970, 20 pp.

Tarasoff, Koozma John, Recent Experience of Geographic Mobility and Socialization on the Canadian Prairies, A Review, Winnipeg, Rural Development Branch, Department of Forestry and Rural Development, Canada, January, 1969, 133 pp.

Tarasoff, Koozma John, "Social Guidelines for the Conceptualization of 'Transition Centres' and Conflict Resolution Therein, With Particular Reference to the Proposed Special Areas of the Pas, Manitoba, and Meadow Lake, Saskatchewan," Winnipeg, Department of Regional Economic Expansion, Western Region, January, 1970, 51 pp.

Verdet, Paula, "Summary of Research on Indians in St. Louis and Chicago," Detroit, Michigan, unpublished manuscript, Anthropology Division, Monteith College, Wayne State University, 1969, 28 pp.

Villiers, Desme and Lorna Makepeace, "A Preliminary Report of a Review of the Literature on Migrating Indians," Ottawa, unpublished manuscript, Citizenship Branch, Department of Secretary of State, 1971, 42 pp.

Wall, Vincent H., A Report on the Canadian Family Project, Toronto, Central Neighbourhood House, October, 1965, 120 pp.

Miscellaneous Reports by date of publications

"The Reservation Indian Comes to Town," New York, National Social Welfare Assembly, c 1953, 15 pp.

The Indians in the Community, National Commission on the Canadian Indian, Canadian Association for Adult Education, Conference, Calgary, May 18, 1957, 38 pp.

"Our City Indians: Report of a Conference," October 30, November 1, 1958, Regina, Saskatchewan House, Centre for Continuing Education, 1959, 8 pp.

The Canadian Indian in an Urban Community, Community Chest and Councils of the Greater Vancouver Area, 1961.

The Indian and the Urban Community, Canadian Council of Christians and News, Brandon, Manitoba, February 26, 1964.

"A Guide to Agencies Working with Indians and Metis in the Cities and Larger Towns in Manitoba," Report in The Proceedings of the Eleventh Indian and Metis Conference, Winnipeg, 1965, 20 pp.

National Conference on Indians and the City, Indian-Eskimo Association of Canada, Winnipeg, Manitoba, October, 1966, 38 pp.

"An Action Research Project on 'Indians and the City'," Brief presented to the Honourable Arthur Laing, The Indian-Eskimo Association of Canada, Toronto, September, 1967, 13 pp.

"A Proposal for a Community Action Project -- Canadian Indians Migrating to Metropolitan Toronto," Social Planning Council of Toronto, December, 1967, 8 pp.

"Relocation and Indians in the City," Ottawa, Selections from Speeches by Ministers of Indian Affairs and Senior Departmental Officals, ca 1968, 3 pp.

"Where Do We Go From Here?, Report of Indian Study Tour," All Chiefs Conference, Alberta, April, 1968, 29 pp.

"Indians and the City," by an Ad Hoc Indian-Eskimo Association Committee, unpublished draft, Toronto, 1970, 13 pp.

"People on the Move," Ottawa, Report of the Ad Hoc Committee on Migrants and Immigrants, The Canadian Council on Social Development, March, 1972, 39 pp.

B -- Friendship Centres

Bear Robe, Study Tour of Canadian Native Friendship Centres, Ottawa, (under the Auspices of the Steering Committee for the

National Association of Friendship Centres), August, 1970, 600 pp.

Bear Robe, Andrew, Friendship Centres in Canada, Ottawa, (under the Auspices of the Steering Committee for the National Association of Friendship Centres), December, 1971.

Brouillard, Claude F., "Friendship Centres," Ottawa, unpublished manuscript, Citizenship Branch, Department of Secretary of State, June 30, 1965, 22 pp.

Coulter, E.J., Indians on the move, Friendship Centres, Beaver, outfit, 297, Summer, 1966, pp. 49-53.

Ewans, Marjorie, Fellowship Centres for Urban Canadian Indian, Vancouver, Master of Social Work Thesis, University of British Columbia, 1961.

Hirabayashi, Gordon K., et al., eds. The Challenges of Assisting The Canadian Aboriginal People to Adjust to Urban Environments, Edmonton, Report of the First Western Canadian Indian-Metis Seminar, 1962, 49 pp.

Keeper, Joseph Irwin, "Friendship Centres," Paper presented at the Sixth Annual Indian-Metis Friendship Centre Course, Saskatoon, Saskatchewan, 1968, 5 pp.

McLelland, Helen, "Our Indian and Metis Committee," The Journal (YWCA), January, 1963, pp. 13-16.

Sim, R. Alexander, "A Study on Friendship Centres," Ottawa, unpublished manuscript, Citizenship Branch, Department of Secretary of State, c 1966, 21 pp.

Williams, Guy, "Reports from Various Centres on Friendship Centres," in Gordon K. Hirabayashi, et. al., eds., The Challenges of Assisting the Aboriginal People to Adjust to Urban Environments, Report of the First Western Canadian Indian-Metis Seminar, Edmonton, 1962, pp. 8-17.

Miscellaneous Reports by date of publication

"Indian and Metis Friendship Centre, Winnipeg," Citizen, February, 1960.

"A Brief prepared by the Prince Albert Indian and Metis Service Council," Prince Albert, Saskatchewan, unpublished manuscript, 1960, 19 pp.

"Prince Rupert Friendship House," (condensed from the Report to the Community Chest and Councils of Greater Vancouver Area Committee for the Canadian Indian in an Urban Community, (Vancouver), May, 1961), 2 pp.

"Brief to the Government of Saskatchewan and Government of Canada," Regina Indian and Metis Centre, February-March, 1962, 7 pp.

"The Prairie Call," Published by the Indian Council of the Indian and Metis Friendship Centre, Winnipeg, Manitoba, May 24, 1963, Volume 3.

"The Moose Call," (Prince Albert Saskatchewan Indian and Metis Service Council), September 30, 1963, November-December, 1969.

"Brief to the Government of Saskatchewan and the Government of Canada," Leask Friendship Centre, Leask, Saskatchewan, June, 1964, 7 pp.

"Brief," Edmonton, unpublished manuscript, Canadian Native Friendship Centre, February, 1964, 9 pp.

"Annual Meeting," Regina, unpublished manuscript, The Indian and Metis Friendship Centre, January 29, 1964, 8 pp.

"Annual Report for the Year 1963," Winnipeg, Manitoba, Indian and Metis Friendship Centre, April 18, 1964, 16 pp.

"Brief," unpublished manuscript, Canadian Native Friendship Centre, Edmonton, February, 1964, 9 pp.

"Report on the Third Friendship Centre Training Course," Western Co-operative College, Saskatoon, Saskatchewan, November 8-13, 1965, 29 pp.

"Third Annual Report, Canadian Indian Centre of Toronto," (April 1, 1965 -- March 31, 1966), Toronto, Ontario, 1966.

"Annual Meeting," unpublished manuscript, The Indian and Metis Friendship Centre, Regina, January 29, 1966, 16 pp.

"Annual Report, 1966," Indian and Metis Friendship Centre, Winnipeg, Manitoba, April 16, 1966, 26 pp.

"Summary of discussions -- round table on Indians and the city," Northern Alberta Institute of Technology, Edmonton, September 17, 1966, Indian-Eskimo Association of Canada, 23 pp.

National Conference on Indians and the city, Winnipeg, October 6-9, 1966, Indian-Eskimo Association of Canada, 39 pp.

"Proceedings of the Indian-Metis Friendship Centre Course," Saskatoon, November 7-12, 1966, 21 pp.

"Newsletter," Indian and Metis Conference, Winnipeg, Manitoba, Winter, 1967, 7 pp.

"An action research project on Indians and the City," Brief presented to Hon. Arthur Laing, Minister of Indian Affairs and Northern Development, Indian-Eskimo Association of Canada, September, 1967, 13 pp.

"Summary Report of the Indian-Metis Friendship Centre Short Course," Saskatoon, Saskatchewan, October 30 -- November 3, 1967, 7 pp.

"Club 367 Newsletter," Winnipeg January 16, 1968, 3 pp.

"The Scout," Indian-Metis Friendship Centre Newsletter, Brandon, Manitoba, May-June, 1968, 10 pp.

"Report of the Sixth Annual Indian-Metis Friendship Centre Course," Saskatoon, Saskatchewan, November, 1968, 34 pp.

"Proposal for a Red Lake (Ontario) Indian Centre," unpublished manuscript, December, 1968, 9 pp.

"Projet de Centre d'Accueil, (document d'étude) pour Indiens de la réserve Mistassini à Chibougamau," Conseil de Bien-Etre Régional d'Abitibi, Inc., March, 1969, 15 pp.

"Alberta Native Friendship Centre's Workshop," Gold Eye Lake Camp, June 7-10, 1969, 18 pp.

"Quarterly Progress Report," Vancouver Indian Centre Society, October-December, 1969, 5 pp.

"List of Friendship Centres," Ottawa, unpublished manuscript, Citizenship Branch, Secretary of State, ca 1970, 5 pp.

"Final report, Indians and the city contract with Secretary of State," Toronto, Indian-Eskimo Association of Canada, March, 1971.

"Indian Affairs -- Closing of Friendship Centres -- Reason for Withdrawal of Funds," House of Commons Debates, May 16, 1972, 116:2299.

"Migrating Native People: the role of the Friendship Centres and the Native Organizations," Ottawa, Brief to the Secretary of State, Native Council of Canada, September, 1971, 8 pp.

PART XVI

FORMAL EDUCATION

A -- General
B -- Special cultural/educational programs

A -- General

Abu-Laban, Baha, "The Impact of Ethnicity and Occupational Background on the Aspirations of Canadian Youth," Sociological Inquiry, Winter, 1966, 36: (reprinted in Mark Nagler, ed., Perspectives on the North American Indian, Toronto, McClelland and Stewart, 1972).

Abu-Laban, Baha, "In-Group Orientation and Self-Conceptions of Indian and Non-Indian Students in an Integrated School," Alberta Journal of Educational Research, September, 1965, 11:118-194, (reprinted in Mark Nagler, ed., Perspectives on the North American Indians, Toronto, McClelland and Stewart, 1972).

Adams, Howard J., The Education of Canadians, 1800-1867: The Roots of Separatism, Montreal, Harvest House, c 1968, 145 pp.

Adams, Howard J., "Opening Remarks, and Comments," National Conference on Indian and Northern Education, Saskatoon, March 28-30, 1967, pp. 14-18, 40-41 and 100-102.

Adams, Howard J., "The outsiders: an educational survey of Metis and Non-Treaty Indians," Regina, Metis Society of Saskatchewan, June, 1972, 61 pp.

Adams, Ian, "Why Did Charlie Wenjack Die?," Maclean's Magazine (Toronto), (also in Ian Adams, The Poverty Wall, Toronto, McClelland and Stewart, 1970, pp. 27-44).

Anderson, Anne (Namoya Ayiman), Let's Learn Cree, Edmonton, 1970, 106 pp.

Anderson, James G. and Dwight Safar, "The Influence of Differential Community Perceptions on the Provision of Equal Educational Opportunities," Sociology of Education, Summer, 1967.

Baker, Marie, "School Program and Native Children," Address, National Conference on Indian and Northern Education, Saskatoon, March, 1967, pp. 54-59.

Barber, Lloyd, "University of Saskatchewan," Address, 7th Annual Conference of the Canadian Association for Indian and Eskimo Education, Ottawa, May, 1969, pp. 53-61.

Beatty, Willard W., "Indian Education in the United States," in Charles T. Loram and Thomas F. McIlwraith, eds., The North American Indian Today, University of Toronto Press, 1943, pp. 275-282.

Bishop, Roderick, "Integration," Address, National Conference on Indian and Northern Education, Saskatoon, March, 1967, pp. 50-53.

Bowman, Norman, "Progress in Navajo education," Address, the Canadian Club, Toronto, April 21, 1969, 6 pp.

Bradshaw, Thecla and André Renaud, "Here We Are -- Where Do We Go? The Indian Child and Education," The Canadian Home and School and Parent-Teacher Federation, 1967, 20 pp.

Brant, Charles Stanford and Charles W. Hobart, "Sociocultural Conditions and Consequences of Native Education in the Arctic: A Cross-National Comparison," unpublished manuscript, n.d.

Buller, James H., "Indian and Eskimo Education," Address, 6th annual conference of the Canadian Association for Indian and Eskimo Education, Toronto, May 23, 1968, 9 pp.

Caldwell, George, A Research Study of the Child Care Programs on Nine Residential Schools in Saskatchewan, Ottawa, The Canadian Welfare Council, January, 1967, 202 pp.

Caldwell, George, "An Island Between two Cultures: The Residential Indian School," Canadian Welfare, (Ottawa), 1967, 43:12-17.

Cameron, Sandy, "A Précis of 'Education for Self-Reliance'," Ottawa, unpublished manuscript, National Indian Brotherhood, 1972, 6 pp.

Carney, R.J. and W.O. Ferguson, A Selected and Annotated Bibliography on the Sociology of Eskimo Education, Edmonton, University of Alberta, 1965.

Carpenter, Mary, "Address," National Conference on Indian and Northern Education, Saskatoon, March, 1967, pp. 47-49.

Chalmers, J.W., "A New Deal in Indian Education," Quest, October, 1964, 2:

Clarkin, P.C., "The Teacher of Indian Pupils (Some points to consider)," Kenora, District School Superintendent, 1967, 3 pp.

Cobb, John C., Emotional performance of Indian students in boarding schools and related public schools, Albuquerque, N.M., Proceedings of a Workshop held at Albuquerque Indian School, April 11-30, 1960.

Coelho, G.V., Changing Images of America; A Study of Indian Students' Perceptions, Glencoe, Ill., Free Press, 1958.

Commes, Madison, L., "Implications of the Achievement Level of Indian Students," In Annual Conference of the co-ordinating Council for research in Indian Education, Phoenix, Division of Indian Education, Arizona State Department of Public Instruction, 1961.

Commes, Madison, L., <u>Doorway toward the Light: The Story of the Special Navajo education program</u>, Washington, D.C., Bureau of Indian Affairs, U.S. Department of the Interior, n.d.

Conde, Le Roy, "An Experiment in Second Language Instruction of Beginning Indian Children," <u>Education Research Bulletin of New Mexico Social Studies Education</u>, 1962, 1:8-11.

Connelly, Bob, "What's Lacking in the Integration Kit?," <u>The Saskatchewan Bulletin</u>, May, 1964, pp. 27-33.

Cowell, Mrs. V., "Kindergarten in Moosonee," Address, <u>7th Annual Conference of the Canadian Association for Indian and Eskimo Education</u>, Ottawa, May 28, 1969, 4 pp.

Cuthand, Rev. Stanley, "Integrated Schools Joint Agreements with the Government of Canada," <u>Report of the First Interprovincial Conference on the Schools in the Forest</u>, Northland School Division 61, Edmonton, 1963, pp. 20-23.

Dilling, Harold John, <u>Integration of the Indian Canadian in and through Schools with emphasis on St. Clair Reserve in Sarnia</u>, Master of Arts Thesis, (Education) University of Toronto, 1962.

Dilling, Harold John, <u>Educational Achievement and Social Acceptance of Indian Pupils Integrated in Non-Indian Schools of Southern Ontario</u>. Ed.D., University of Toronto, 1965, 440 pp.

Dumont, Robert V. Jr., and Murray L. Wax, "Cherokee School Society and the Intercultural Classroom," <u>Human Organization</u>, 1969, 28:

Eggan, Dorothy, "Instruction and Affect in Hopi Cultural Continuity," George Dearborn Spindler, ed., <u>Education and Culture, Anthropological Approaches</u>, Holt, Rinehard and Winston, 1963, pp. 231-350.

Elliott, John G., <u>Educational and Occupational Aspiration and Expectations: A Comparative Study of Indian and Non-Indians Youth</u>, Antigonish, N.S., Extension Department, St. Francis Xavier University, 1970.

Esche, Sandra, "Teaching in an Elemental Land: After nine months in Northern Labrador, two young teachers found that they were the ones who had much to learn," <u>Weekend Magazine</u>, (Montreal), September 30, 1972.

Fannin, Hon. Paul J., "Indian Education -- A Test Case for Democracy," <u>Arizona Law Review</u>, Winter, 1968, 10:661-674.

Fantini, Mario D. and Gerald Weinstein, "Taking Advantage of the Disadvantaged," N.Y., unpublished manuscript, 1967, 12 pp.

Fergusson, Hattie, Mrs., "Problems and its Phases," Address, <u>National Conference on Indian and Northern Education</u>, Saskatoon, March, 1967, pp. 35-39.

Fineday, Sidney, "School Integration: Whys and Wherefores," Address, <u>National Conference on Indian and Northern Education</u>, Saskatoon, March, 1967, pp. 18-20.

190

Fisher, Anthony Dwight, "Education and Social Progress," Alberta Journal of Educational Research, 1966, 12:257-268.

Fisher, Anthony Dwight, "Decolonization of Indian Education: Canada and Latin America," unpublished Research Proposal to Canada Council, October 20, 1971, 21 pp.

Foster, Ashley, "Changing Predispositions to Academic Success by Alaska Native People," in William W. Brickman and Stanley Lehrer, eds., Education and the Many Faces of the Disadvantaged: Cultural and Historical Perspectives, John Wiley and Sons, 1972, pp. 168-174.

Foster, Douglas Ray, The Canadian Indian: A Study of the Education of a Minority Group and its Social Problems, Madison, Master of Science Thesis, University of Wisconsin, 1963.

French, Cecil L., "Social Class and Motivation," in Brigham Young Card, et. al., eds., The Metis in Alberta Society, Edmonton, University of Alberta, 1963, Chapt. 11, pp. 313-354.

Gaddes, W.H., Audrey McKenzie, and Roger Barnsley, "Psychometric Intelligence and Spatial Imagery in two northwest Indian and two groups of children," The Journal of Social Psychology, 1968, 75:35-42.

Garber, Malcolm, Ethnicity and Measures of Educability Differences Among Navajo, Pueblo and Rural Spanish American First Grades on Measures of Learning Style, Hearing Vocabulary, Entry Skills, Motivation and Home Environment Processes, Los Angeles, CA, Ph.D. dissertation, University of Southern California, 1968.

Goucher, A.C., The Dropout Problem Among Indian and Metis Students, Calgary, Dome Petroleum, 1967, 50 pp.

Gue, Leslie Robb, "Reducing the Supply of Clueless Teachers," Address, 7th Annual Conference of the Canadian Association for Indian and Eskimo Education, Ottawa, May, 1969, pp. 62-67.

Handley, Bruce, "A Study of the Academic Program in Alberta Newstart," Alberta Newstart, Inc., Lac La Biche, Alta, November, 1970, 49 pp.

Hanley, David W., "School Integration in the Pas, Manitoba," unpublished manuscript, 1965, 16 pp.

Harrison, Fred, "Metis Society report on Education study," The Leader-Post, (Regina), June 30, 1972.

Havighurst, Robert James and Rhea R. Hilkevitch, "The Intelligence of Indian Children as Measured by Performance Scale," Journal of Abnormal and Social Psychology, 1944, 39:419-433.

Havighurst, Robert James and R.L. Neugarten, American Indian and White Children, University of Chicago Press, 1955, 335 pp.

Havighurst, Robert James, "Education Among American Indians: Individual and Cultural Aspects," Annals of the American Academy of Political and Social Sciences, 1957, 311:105-115, (reprinted in Mark Nagler, ed., Perspectives on the North American Indians, Toronto, McClelland and Stewart, 1972).

Havighurst, Robert James, "The National Study of American Indian Education," University of Chicago, unpublished proposal, Committee on Human Development, January, 1968, 4 pp.

Havighurst, Robert James, "National Study of American Indian Education: Progress Report," University of Chicago, unpublished manuscript, January, 1969, 8 pp.

Havighurst, Robert James, "National Study of American Indian Education: Progress Report," University of Chicago, unpublished manuscript, April 15, 1969, 3 pp.

Havighurst, Robert James, The National Study of American Indian Education: Summary Report and recommendations, Series 4, Number 6, University of Chicago, 1970.

Heshidahl, Gladys, et al., "How Well Do We Teach Indian Children?," Vancouver, unpublished manuscript, 1970, 11 pp.

Hobart, Charles W. and Charles Sanford Brant, "Eskimo Education, Danish and Canadian: A Comparison," in A. Malik, ed., Social Foundations of Canadian Education, Toronto, Prentice-Hall, 1969, pp. 68-87.

Homewood, E.L., "The Plight of Canada's Indians (Part 4), The Indian and Education," The United Church Observer, (Toronto), April 1, 1965.

Hopkins, Thomas R., "Secondary Education of Native North Americans," The Northian, (Saskatoon), 1970, pp. 5-9.

Horn, Kahn-Tineta, "Indian Education Crisis," Atlantic Advocate, May, 1966, 56:26-28.

Horn, Kahn-Tineta, "The Role of Church and School," Address, National Conference on Indian and Northern Education, Saskatoon, March, 1967, pp. 60-68.

Husby, P.J., Educational Effort in Five Resource Frontier Communities, Winnipeg, Center for Settlement Studies, University of Manitoba, 1971, 57 pp.

Jamieson, Elmer, E., Indian Education in Canada, Hamilton, Master of Arts Thesis, McMaster University, 1922.

Joblin, Elgin Ellingham Miller, The Education of the Indians of Western Ontario, London, Ontario, Master's Thesis, University of Western Ontario, 1946, 157 pp. (reprinted in Bulletin No. 13, Ontario College of Education, Department of Educational Research, 1947).

Jones, Thomas Jesse, "Essentials of Education for American Indians," in Charles T. Loram and Thomas F. McIlwraith, eds., The North American Indian Today, University of Toronto Press, 1943, pp. 299-312.

Kaegi, Gerda and Terry Bigwin, "The comprehensive view of Indian education," (reprinted by the Indian-Eskimo Association of Canada, March, 1972, 38 pp.

Kaplan, Robert B., "The Present Failure to Educate the American Indian," in William W. Brickman and Stanley Lehrer, eds., Education and the Many Faces of the Disadvantaged: Cultural and Historical Perspectives, John Wiley and Sons, 1972, pp. 153-163.

Katz, Sidney, "The Lost Children of British Columbia," MacLean's Magazine, (Toronto), May 11, 1957.

Keenleyside, David, "The Fallacy of Freedom: Education for the Adult Eskimo," Continuous Learning, September-October, 1968, 7:207-212.

Kennedy, Jacqueline Judith, Qu'Appelle Industrial School: White 'Rites' for the Indians of the Old Northwest, Ottawa, Master of Arts Thesis, Carleton University, 1970, 316 pp.

Kim, Yong C., "Social Origins of School Retardation among Indian Pupils, Summary Report," Saskatchewan, Research and Planning Branch, Department of Welfare, 1968, 10 pp.

King, Alfred Richard, A Case Study of an Indian Residential School, Stanford, California, Ph.D. Dissertation, Stanford University, 1964, 400 pp.

King, Alfred Richard, The School at Mopass, Holt, Rinehart and Winston, 1967, 91 pp.

Kinsella, Noel A., "Some Dimensions of Ego-Identity Among Acadians, Blacks, Indians and Whites in New Brunswick," Fredericton, N.B., Human Relations Study Centre, St. Thomas University, 1971.

Knill, William D. and Arthur Kent Davis, "Provincial Education in Northern Saskatchewan: Progress and Bog-Down, 1944-1962," in Arthur Kent Davis, et. al., eds., A Northern Dilemma: Reference Papers, Bellingham, Western Washington State College, April, 1967, Vol. 1, pp. 170-337.

Kronin, Kay, "Notes for an Address to the Conference for Principles of Roman Catholic Residential Schools," ca 1965.

Krush, Thaddeus P., John W. Bjork, Peter Sindell, and Noanna Nelle, "Some Thoughts on the Formation of Personality Disorder: Study of an Indian Boarding School Population," American Journal of Psychiatry, 1966, 122:868-876.

Laflesche, Francis, The Middle Five: Indian School Boys of the Omaha Tribe, Madison, University of Wisconsin Press, 1960 (reprinted 1963).

Laing, Hon. Arthur, "Educating Young Canadian Indians," (based on an address to the Northern B.C. Federal Teachers' Association, Terrace, B.C., October 6, 1967), in William W. Brickman and Stanley Lehrer, eds., Education and the Many Faces of the

Disadvantaged: Cultural and Historical Perspectives, John Wiley and Sons, 1972, pp. 175-178.

Laing, Hon. Arthur, "Address," Canadian Association for Indian and Eskimo Education, Royal York Hotel, Toronto, May 23, 1968, 12 pp.

Laronde, Louis, The Education of the Indian in Canada, Winnipeg, Master's Thesis, University of Manitoba, 1912, 33 pp.

Lavalle, Ed., "School Drop-Out," Address, National Conference on Indians and Northern Education, Saskatoon, March, 1967, pp. 69-73.

Lavallee, Mary Anne, "School Integration," Address, National Conference on Indian and Northern Education, Saskatoon, March, 1967, pp. 21-34.

Lesser, Alexander, "Education and the Future of Tribalism in the United States: The Case of the American Indians," Social Service Review, 1961, 35:135-143.

Levaque, Yvon, "The future of Indian Education," Indians of Maine, (Augusta), February, 1969.

Levaque, Yvon, "A reply to Mr. Roy Piepenburg," Bear Hill's Native Voice, (Hobbema, Alberta), May 7, 1971.

Levaque, Yvon, "A blueprint for Indian education: a look at the Parliamentary Report on Indian education," Northern, December 1971, 8:34-38.

Lewis, Michael L., "The Indian and Equality of Educational Opportunity," in Ralph W. Johnson, ed., Studies in American Indian Law, Georgetown University, June, 1970, pp. 326-374.

Locklin, G.R., A Study of Secondary School Pupils from an Indian Reservation and Their Problems Related to Guidance, Guidance Services Branch, Ontario Department of Education, 1958-59.

Loram, Charles T., "Church and State in Indian Education in the United States and Canada," in Charles T. Loram and Thomas F. McIlwraith, eds., The North American Indian Today, University of Toronto Press, 1943, pp. 294-298.

Lotz, James R., "Eskimos as Educators," Tapwe (Hay River, N.W.T.), August 4, 1969, pp. 2-7.

Lyon, Louise C., "Moms, Tots and Learning," Address, 7th Annual Conference of the Canadian Association for Indian and Eskimo Education, Ottawa, May 21, 1969, 9 pp.

MacArthur, R.S., "Some Congitive Abilities of Eskimo, White and Indian-Metis Pupils aged 9 to 12 years," Canadian Journal of Behavioural Science, 1969, 1:50-59.

MacLean, Hope, A Review of Indian Education in North America, Toronto, Ontario Teachers' Federation, 1972, 150 pp.

MacLeod, John, Indian Education in Canada, M. Ed. Thesis, University of New Brunswick, n.d.

MacPherson, Norm, "Recent developments in teacher training programs in intercultural Education," Address, 7th Annual Conference of the Canadian Association for Indian and Eskimo Education, Ottawa, May 28, 1969, pp. 39-47.

Mason, Evelyn P., "Cross validation study of personality characteristics of junior high students from American Indian, Mexican and Caucasian ethnic backgrounds," Journal of Social Psychology, 1969, 77:15-24.

McDiarmid, Garnet L., "The Challenge of Differential Curriculum: Ontario's Indian Children," Toronto, Ontario Institute for Studies in Education, 1971, 24 pp.

McGann, David, "More in Sorrow: Social Action and the Indian Boarding Home Program," Canadian Welfare, (Ottawa), 1967, 43:24-29.

McGrath, G.D., Robert Roessel, Bruce Meador, G.C. Heimstater, and John Barnes, Higher Education of southwestern Indians with reference to success and failure, Temple, Arizona State University (Co-operative research project No. 938), 1962.

Menarik, Elijah, "Education," Address, National Conference on Indian and Northern Education, Saskatoon, March, 1967, pp. 42-45.

Mitchell, Lonnie, E. and Leroy Jones, "New Careers: Training and Education for Career Development," Washington, D.C., National Institute for New Careers, University Research Corporation, 1970, 95 pp.

Molohon, Kathryn T., Abstracts of the Literature on the Psychological Testing of American Indians, Berkeley, University of California, 1965.

Mouat, W. Ivan, "Education in the Arctic Districts," The Musk Ox, 1970, 7:1-9.

Mulvihill, James P., "The Dilemma in Indian Education," Oblate News, January, 1963, 5: (reprinted in Seven Articles on Indian Affairs, The Dilemma and Studies and Documents, Ottawa Indianscon, Inc.).

Mulvihill, Father James P., "No 'Golden Rule', for Integration," Oblate News, June, 1961, (reprinted in Five Articles on Indian Affairs, (Vancouver)).

Mulvihill, Father James, "The Amalgamated School," Oblate News, November-December, 1961, (reprinted in Seven Articles on Indian Affairs and The Dilemma).

Murphy, H.B., Psychological test performance of children on the Caughnawaga Reserve: A pilot study, McGill University, 1965.

Nicholas, D.J., "An Indian Point of View on the Dispute at Assumption," Hay Lakes, unpublished manuscript, n.d., 5 pp.

Omar Born, David, Eskimo Education and the Trauma of Social Change, Social Science Notes, -1, Ottawa, Northern Science Research Group, Department of Indian Affairs and Northern Development, January 15, 1970.

O'Neill, Florence, "A Projected Plan for Indian Communities," Ottawa, Community Development Education Service, Educational Division, Indian Affairs Branch, Department of Citizenship and Immigration, 1963, 40 pp.

Orata, Pedro T., Fundamental Education in an Amer-Indian Community, Washington, D.C., Department of the Interior, Bureau of Indian Affairs, 1953.

Parmee, Edward A., Formal Education and Cultural Change: A Modern Apache Indian Community and Government Education Programs, Tucson, University of Arizona Press, 1968.

Parmee, Edward A., "Social Factors affecting the education of the San Carlos Apaches," in Annual Conference of the Co-ordinating Council for Research in Indian Education, Phoenix, Division of Indian Education, Arizona State Department of Public Instruction, 1961.

Peters, Omer, "Conference Evaluation," 7th Annual Conference, Canadian Association for Indian and Eskimo Education, Ottawa, May 30, 1969, pp. 108-113.

Peterson, Lester Ray, Indian Education in British Columbia, Vancouver, Master's Thesis, (Education), University of British Columbia, October, 1959, 143 pp.

Piepenburg, Roy L., "Indian Education in Alberta as I Viewed it: Part I, The Political-Administrative Superstructure of Indian Education," The Native People, (Edmonton), September, 1969, 2(4):8-11.

Piepenburg, Roy L., "Indian Education in Alberta as I Viewed it: Part II, Self-determination, Local Autonomy and the New Policy as it Affects Indian Education," The Native People, (Edmonton), October, 1969, 2(5):8-11.

Piepenburg, Roy L., "Indian Education in Alberta as I Viewed it: Part III, The Religious-Political Aspects of Indian Education," The Native People, (Edmonton), November, 1969, 2(6):16-20.

Piepenburg, Roy L., "Indian Education in Alberta as I Viewed it: Part IV, Indians in Provincial Integrated Schools -A Record of Racial Tension, Frustration, Discrimination and Marginal Academic Success," The Native People, (Edmonton), January, 1970, 2(8):13-16.

Piepenburg, Roy L., "Indian Education in Alberta as I Viewed it: Part V," The Native People, (Edmonton), February, 1970, 2(9):13-16.

Piepenburg, Roy L., "Indian Education in Alberta as I Viewed it: Part VI," The Native People, (Edmonton), March, 1970, 2(10):14-17.

Piepenburg, Roy L., "Indian Education in Alberta as I Viewed it: Part VII, Indian Education and Social Welfare Problems -- The Indians' Quest for Social and Political Power," The Native People, (Edmonton), April, 1970, 2(11):12-14.

Piepenburg, Roy L., "Indian Education in Alberta as I Viewed it: Part VIII," The Native People, (Edmonton), February, 1971, 3(9):10-11.

Rancier, C.J., "Present Curriculum Programs for Pupils of Indian Ancestry," Report of the First Interprovincial Conference on the Schools in the Forest, Edmonton, Northland School Division 61, 1963, pp. 30-38.

Randle, M.C., "Educational Problems of Canadian Indians," Food for Thought, March, 1953, 13:

Ray, Charles K., A Program of Education for Alaskan Natives, College, University of Alaska, 1958, (revised 1959).

Ray, Charles K., Joan Ryan, and Seymour Parker, Alaskan Native Secondary School Dropouts, College, University of Alaska, 1962, 411 pp.

Regan, Timothy F. and Jules Pagano, "The Place of Indian Culture in Adult Education," Adult Leadership, 1971, 4 pp.

Renaud, André, A Psychometric Study of Indian Residential School Students, Ottawa, School of Psychology and Education, University of Ottawa, Report, 1953 to 1955; 1956.

Renaud, André, "Indian Education Today, Anthropologica, 1958, 6:

Renaud, André, "Present Curriculum Programs for Pupils of Indian Ancestry," Report of the First Interprovincial Conferences on the Schools in the Forest, Edmonton, Northland School Division 61, 1963, pp. 39-43.

Renaud, André, "In Service and Pre-Service Training of Teachers," Address, Report of the First Interprovincial Conference on Schools in the Forest, Edmonton, Northland School Division, January, 1963.

Renaud, André, "Education from Within, Experiment in Curriculum Development With Children of Indian Background in Saskatchewan," Paper presented at the Ontario Division of the Indian-Eskimo Association Conference, November, 1964, 14 pp.

Renaud, André, and Howard Adams, eds., National Conference on Indian and Northern Education, Saskatoon, March 28-30, 1967, 128 pp.

Rosenthal, Robert and Lenore F. Jacobson, "Teacher Expectations for the Disadvantaged," Scientific American, April, 1968, 218:3-7.

Sagi, Douglas, "Should School Children Leave Reserve?," _The Globe and Mail_, (Toronto), (also in N. Sheffe, ed., _Issues for the Seventies_: _Canada's Indians_, McGraw-Hill, 1970, pp. 54-58).

St. Pierre, Paul, "Apartheid and the Indian," Address, _7th Annual Conference of the Canadian Association for Indian and Eskimo Education_, Ottawa, May 28, 1969, 8 pp.

Salisbury, Lee H., "A Conceptual Approach to the Speech Problems of Alaskan Natives," Address at National Society for the Study of Communication, Hillsdale College, Hillsdale, Michigan, August 23, 1965, 10 pp.

Salisbury, Lee H., _College Orientation Program for Alaskan Natives_ (COPAN), Program-Education for Survival, Bethseda, Md., Final Report, ERIC Document Reproduction Service, (#EDO 025225), 1968, 154 pp.

Schalm, Philip, "School administrator's perception of problems arising from the integration of Indian children in publicly supported schools in Saskatchewan," Saskatoon, University of Saskatchewan, 1968, 177 pp.

Shimpo, Mitsuru, "The Social Process of a Residential School as a Total Institution," Address, University of Regina, Saskatchewan, March 18, 1966, 28 pp.

Sim, R. Alexander, "Indian Schools for Indian Children," _Canadian Welfare_, (Ottawa), March-April, 1969, 45:11-16.

Sim, R. Alexander, _The Education of Indians in Ontario_, Strathmere, Ontario, unpublished report to the Provincial Committee on the Aims and Objectives of Education in Ontario Schools, 1969, 79 pp.

Simpson, D.W. and D.K.F. Wattie, et al., "The Role and Impact of the Educational Program in the Process of Change in Canadian Eskimo Communities," Paper presented at 19th Alaskan Science Conference, Whitehorse, Yukon Territory, August 26-30, 1968, 21 pp.

Sioui, Eleonore, "The right to exist," _recherches amerindiennes au quebec_, November, 1972, 2:39-41.

Slager, William R. and Betty M. Madsen, eds., _English for American Indians_, A Newsletter of the Office of Education Programs, Bureau of Indian Affairs, U.S. Department of the Interior, Spring, 1971.

Smith, Derek G., "Occupational Aspirations of Mackenzie Delta Students," Address, _7th Annual Conference of the Canadian Association for Indian and Eskimo Education_, Ottawa, May 30, 1969, pp. 68-75.

Snider, James G. and Arthur P. Coladarci, "Intelligence Test Performance of Acculturated Indian Children," _California Journal of Educational Research_, January, 1960, pp. 34-36.

Snider, James G., "Achievement Test Performance of Acculturated Indian Children," Alberta Journal of Educational Research, 1961, 7:29-41.

Solomon, Arthur, "A Brief to the Provincial Committee on the Aims and Objectives of Education in Ontario," Sudbury, Ontario, January 20, 1966, 4 pp.

Soonias, Rodney, "Selected findings of the Federation of Saskatchewan Indians education task force, 1970-1972, a preliminary report," Regina, April 11, 1972, 62 pp.

Soveran, Mrs. Marilylle, From Cree to English: Part One: The Sound System, Saskatoon, Indian and Northern Curriculum Resources Centre, College of Education, University of Saskatchewan, c 1970, 54 pp.

Spence, Ahab, Kahn-Tineta Horn, Celestino Makpah, Mary Anne Lavallée and Wilfred Tootoosis, "Symposium: Is the Contemporary Educational Program Failing the Native People?," National Conference on Indian and Northern Education, Saskatoon, March, 1967, pp. 74-90.

Spindler, George Dearborn, "Personality, sociocultural system and education among the Menomini," in George D. Spindler, ed., Education and Culture: Anthropological Approaches, New York, Holt, Rinehart and Winston, 1963.

Sydiara, D. and J. Rempel, "Motivational and Attitudinal characteristics of Indian School Children as Measured by the Thematic Apperception Test," Canadian Psychologist, 1964, 5:193-148.

Thompson, Hildegard, "Education Among American Indians: Institutional Aspects," The Annals of the American Academy of Political and Social Science, May, 1957, 311:95-104.

Thompson, Laura and Alice Joseph, "White Pressures on Indian Personality and Culture," American Journal of Sociology, 1947, 53:17-23.

Vallery, H.J., A History of Indian Education in Canada, Kingston, Master of Arts Thesis, Queen's University, 1942.

Walsh, Paul, "Dick and Jane on the Navaho Reservation," in William W. Brickman and Stanley Lehrer, eds., Education and the Many Faces of the Disadvantaged: Cultural and Historical Perspectives, John Wiley and Sons, 1972, pp. 164-167.

Warren, Dave, "American Indian Education in the United States: Indian Control of Education: The right of self determination," Paper presented by the United States Delegation to the VII Congress of the Inter-American Indian Institute, Brazilia, August 7-12, 1972, 17 pp.

Wattie, D.K.F., "Education in the Canadian Arctic," The Polar Record, (Great Britain), 1968, 14:293-304.

Wax, Murray L. and Rosalie H. Wax, "Publications on American Indians and Indian Education," unpublished manuscript, n.d., 2 pp.

Wax, Murray L., "American Indian Education as a Cross-cultural Transaction," Teachers College Record, 1963, 64:693-704.

Wax, Murray L. and Rosalie H. Wax, "Cultural Deprivation as an educational ideology," Journal of American Indian Education, 1964, 111:15-18.

Wax, Murray L. and Rosalie H. Wax, Dropout of American Indians At the Secondary Level, Co-operative Research Project S-099, USOE, Mimeo, 1964.

Wax, Murray L. and Rosalie H. Wax, "Indian Education for What?," Midcontinent American Studies Journal, 1965, 6:164-170, (reprinted in Stuart Levine and Nancy O. Lurie, eds., The American Indian Today, Baltimore, Md., Penguin Books, 1970, pp. 257-269).

Wax, Rosalie H., "The Warrior Dropouts," Trans-Action, 1967, 4:40-46.

Weitz, Jacqueline, Culture change and field dependence in two Native Canadian linguistic families, Ph.D. Dissertation, University of Ottawa, July, 1971.

Wenner, Lambert N., "The American Indian and Formal Education," in William W. Brickman and Stanley Lehrer, eds., Education and the Many Faces of the Disadvantaged: Cultural and Historical Perspectives, John Wiley and Sons, 1972, pp. 143-152.

Wescott, A.E., "Curricula for Indian Schools," in Charles T. Loram and Thomas F. McIlwraith, eds., The North American Indian Today, University of Toronto Press, 1943, pp. 283-293.

West, Lloyd, W., Assessing Intellectual Ability with a Minimum of Cultural Bias for Two Samples of Metis and Indian Children, Edmonton, Master of Ed. Thesis, University of Alberta, 1962.

Whelan, Mary E., Reading Achievement and Intelligence Scores of Indian Children, Master of Arts Thesis, University of Ottawa, 1956.

Wintrob, Ronald M., and Peter S. Sindell, Education and Identity Conflict Among Cree Youth: A Preliminary Report, Ottawa, McGill Cree Project, Rural Development Branch, Department of Forestry and Rural Development, October, 1968, 116 pp.

Wolcott, Harry Fletcher, A Kwakiutl Village and School, Holt, Rinehart and Winston, 1967, 131 pp.

Wolcott, Harry Fletcher, "Bibliography -- North American Indian and Eskimo Education: Anthropological Emphasis," Eugene, unpublished manuscript, University of Oregon, revised June, 1968, 5 pp.

Wolcott, Harry Fletcher, "The Teacher as an Enemy," unpublished manuscript, November, 1968, 24 pp.

Woodsworth, J.F., "Problems of Indian Education in Canada," in Charles T. Loram and Thomas F. McIlwraith, eds., The North American Indian Today, University of Toronto Press, 1943, pp. 265-274.

Wutzke, Richard and David Tanaka, Education and the Native Students: A Study of the Difficulties Encountered by Native Youth in Relation to Education, University of Lethbridge, ca 1969, 105 pp.

Yawney, Carole Diane, "Indian Youth: Education for What?," Sanity, February, 1967.

Young, John (reporter), "How our schools are teaching Indians to become failures," Vancouver Sun, March 17, 1973.

Zentner, Henry, "Parental Behaviour and Student Attitudes towards Further Training among Indian and Non-Indian Students in Oregon and Alberta," Alberta Journal of Educational Research, December, 1962, 8:212-219; March, 1963, 9:22-30.

Zentner, Henry, "Value Congruence Among Indian and Non-Indian High School Students in Southern Alberta," Alberta Journal of Educational Research, September, 1963, 9:168-178.

Zentner, Henry, "Cultural Assimilation Between Indians and Non-Indians in Southern Alberta," Alberta Journal of Educational Research, 1963, 9:79-86, (reprinted in Richard Laskin, ed., Social Problems: A Canadian Profile, Toronto, McGraw-Hill, 1964).

Zentner, Henry, "Reference Group Behaviour Among High School Students," Alberta Journal of Educational Research, September, 1964, 10:142-152.

Zentner, Henry, "Blackfoot Adolescents and Their Non-Indian Peers: A Comparative Study," Calgary, University of Alberta, n.d.

Miscellaneous Reports by date of publication

"Information for Teachers Going into Special Schools for the First Time," Winnipeg, Department of Education, Province of Manitoba, 1955, 12 pp.

Residential education for Indian acculturation. Workshop I. General Principles, Ottawa: Indian and Eskimo Welfare Commission, Oblate Fathers in Canada, 1958.

"The Canadian Eskimo," National Commission of the Indian Canadian, (the Canadian Association for Adult Education), Bulletin 6, April, 1959.

"Indian education in Canada 40 years behind time: Mistakes made in U.S. being repeated say Rev. C.J. Mersereau," The Daily Gleaner (Fredericton, N.B.), May 17, 1961.

Guidance in Indian Schools and Hostels, Ottawa, Indian Affairs Branch, Education Division, Department of Citizenship and Immigration, 1962.

Indian Education, Ottawa, Indian Affairs Branch, Department of Citizenship and Immigration, 1962.

"Education in Northern Canada," Canadian Education and Research Digest, June, 1963, 3:85-91.

"Fiscal Year 1964: Statistics Concerning Indian Education," Bureau of Indian Affairs, Branch of Education, U.S. Department of the Interior, 36 pp.

"Bibliography: Anthropology and Education, 1960-63," Review of Educational Research, February, 1964, 34: (5 pp.).

"Resolutions Approved at the Northeastern Regional Workshops of the Indian-Eskimo Association of Canada in Cooperation with the Sudbury Citizen's Committee," Sudbury, June 25-27, 1964, 2 pp.

"A Suggested Program of Education and Training: Aimed at the Social and Economic Integration of Young Alberta Indians," Edmonton, unpublished manuscript, ca 1965, 12 pp.

"Metis Acceleration and Retardation," Edmonton, unpublished manuscript, ca 1965, 2 pp.

"Presentation by the Canadian Home and School and Parent-Teacher Federation to the Hon. J.R. Nicholson, Minister of Citizenship and Immigration and Superintendent general of Indian Affairs," Toronto, April 28, 1965.

"Education for What?," Toronto, Indian-Eskimo Association of Canada, December 1, 1965.

The Education of Indian Children in Canada; a symposium written by members of the Indian Affairs Education Division with comments by the Indian Peoples, Toronto: Ryerson Press, 1965, 129 pp.

Teach in Canada's Northland: Handbook for Prospective Teachers, Ottawa, Educational Division, Northern Administration Branch, Department of Indian Affairs and Northern Development, 1966, 25 pp.

"Reports to the Canadian Union of Students on the Indian Tutoring Program at the University of Alberta," Edmonton, 1966.

"Briefs to the Committee on Aims and Objectives of Education in the Schools of Ontario," Toronto, The Indian-Eskimo Association of Canada, March, 1966, 7 pp.

"Quality Education for American Indians, A Report on Organizational Location," Washington, D.C., Prepared for the

Sub-committee on Labour and Public Welfare, U.S. Senate, 1967, 11 pp.

"Breakthrough in Eskimo Education," Ottawa, Department of Indian Affairs and Northern Development, 1967, 3 pp.

"An Analysis from an Indian Point of View," National Conference on Indian and Northern Education, Saskatoon, March, 1967, pp. 111-128.

"Indian Education," Selection from speeches by Ministers of Indian Affairs and Senior Departmental Officials, Ottawa, Department of Indian Affairs and Northern Development, 1968, 14 pp.

"Brief on Indian, Metis and Eskimo Education," Canadian Teachers' Federation, November 17, 1967, (also extracted in Bulletin, Canadian National Commission for UNESCO, February, 1968, 10:6-7).

"Indian Students' Handbook," Ottawa, Department of Indian Affairs and Northern Development, ca 1968, 12 pp.

"Factors Affecting the Education of Apache Youth," Extract from Hearings Before the Special Sub-committee on Indian Education of the Committee on Labour and Public Welfare, U.S. Senate, 90th Congress, 1st and 2nd Sessions on the Study of the Education of Indian Children, Part 3, March 30, 1968, pp. 70-118.

"Report of education committee, Thinkers conference," Aurora, Ontario, Ontario Division, Indian-Eskimo Association of Canada, May 17-21, 1968, 14 pp.

"Brief to the Minister of Education of the Province of Ontario," Committee for the Course for the Teachers of Indian Children, Toronto, December 20, 1968, 8 pp.

Indian Education: A National Tragedy -- A National Challenge, Washington, D.C., Special Sub-committee on Indian Education, Government Printing Office, 1969, 220 pp.

The Indian in Transition: Indian Education, Ottawa, Department of Indian Affairs and Northern Development, 1969, 20 pp.

"Brief, Preservation of the Indian Parents' Rights in the Field of Education to the Prime Minister of Canada," The Federation of Independent School Assocations, British Columbia, 1969, 11 pp.

"Proposed Study of Indian Education Program," Toronto, Indian-Eskimo Association of Canada, 1969, 3 pp.

"Report on Akaticho Hall, Yellowknife," unpublished manuscript, Company of Young Canadians, 1969, 24 pp.

"Give it back to the Indians: education on reservation and off," Carnegie Quarterly, (N.Y.), Spring 1969, 17:1-5.

"Colleges, pride of the reservation," Time, April 11, 1969.

"Value Conflicts: Barriers to Participation," 7th Annual Conference, The Canadian Association for Indian-Eskimo Education, Ottawa, May 30, 1969, pp. 76-90.

"Participation in Decision-Making," 7th Annual Conference, The Canadian Association for Indian and Eskimo Education, Ottawa, May 30, 1969, pp. 91-107.

The Memramcook Conference of North American Indian Young People, Memramcook, N.B., Teaching and Research in Bicultural Education, July, 1969, 162 pp.

The Education of American Indians: The Organization Question, Prepared for the Sub-committee on Indian Education of the Committee on Labour and Public Welfare, U.S. Senate, Vol. 4, November, 1969, pp. 433-925.

"Model Programs: Childhood Education Behaviour Analysis Model of a Follow-through Program," Washington, D.C., U.S. Government Printing Office, 1970, 20 pp.

"Report by David Ahenakew, Chief of the Federation of Saskatchewan Indians and Mr. Rodney Soonias, President of the Canadian Association for Indian-Eskimo Education," Ottawa, Standing Committee on Indian Affairs and Northern Development, Minutes of Proceedings and Evidence, No. 6, February 24, 1970.

"Press Release: Bilingual Education," Washington, D.C., U.S. Department of Health, Education and Welfare, April 20, 1970, 4 pp.

Fluency First, Prince Albert, Saskatchewan New Start, June, 1970, 38 pp.

Votes and Proceedings of the House of Commons of Canada, Ottawa, Wednesday, June 30, 1971.

"Frog Lake Indians ... hopping mad, school boycott," The Native People, (Edmonton), September, 1970, 3(5).

"Education Report by House of Commons Committee," House of Commons, 1971, 28 pp.

"Report of the library and learning resource seminar," Indian-Eskimo Association of Canada, Toronto, January 6-7, 1971.

"Objectives of Western Canada Training Committee for Adults of Indian Ancestry," unpublished manuscript, June 14, 1971, 4 pp.

"Press release: President's (George Manuel) response to Educational Report, Commons Committee on Indian Affairs," Ottawa, National Indian Brotherhood, July 2, 1971, 3 pp.

"Brief presented to the Royal Commission on Education, Public Services and Provincial -- Municipal Relations," Union of Nova Scotia Indians, October 8, 1971, 43 pp.

"Reserve School Deplorable, Jury Reports," The Globe and Mail, (Toronto), October 25, 1971.

Proposals for the future education of Treaty Indians in Alberta, Brief, Educational Planning Commission, Indian Association of Alberta, January 1971, 200 pp.

Minutes of Proceedings and Evidence of the Standing Committee on Indian Affairs and Northern Development, Ottawa, Issue Nos. 35 and 36, November 25, 26, 1971.

"50 per cent of Indian and Metis students quit within six months: the lonely, bored, disinterested high school dropouts in Winnipeg," The Globe and Mail, (Toronto), April 6, 1972.

"Indian Affairs: From the Archives, The Government Made Promises; But Our Little Children are Being Torn from Their Mothers' Arms', Starblanket," Akwesasne Notes, (Rooseveltown, N.Y.), Summer, 1972.

"Education," in Native Youth News, (Native Youth Association, Ottawa), July 1, 1972.

Indian Control of Indian Education, Policy paper presented to the Minister of Indian Affairs by the National Indian Brotherhood, December 22, 1972, 38 pp.

B -- Special Cultural/Educational Programs and Workshops

Atimoyoo, Smith, "An Indian way of looking at life, (Indian Cultural Centre of Saskatchewan), Involvement, (Newmarket, Ont.), Fall, 1971, 4:21-25.

Berry, John W., "A proposal for native studies, service and research at Queen's University," Kingston, Ontario, unpublished proposal, October, 1972, 4 pp.

Conklin, Paul "Good day at Rough Rock," (reprinted by the Indian-Eskimo Association of Canada, May 1969), 12 pp.

Craig, G. William, "Progress Report by the Director, Fiscal Year, June 17, 1971, to April 15, 1972," Montreal, Native North American Studies Institute, 18 pp.

Gambill, Jerry T., "The North American Indian Travelling College," Ottawa, unpublished Proposal to the Company of Young Canadians, May 29, 1967, 14 pp.

Geddie, Nancy, "Letter to the National Indian Brotherhood from the Association of Universities and Colleges of Canada: re: courses offered at Canadian Universities on aspects of Canadian Indian Life," Ottawa, January 11, 1972, 8 pp.

Ikidluak, Evie, et al., "A Proposal for the Creation of a Native North American Studies Institute and Programme," McGill University, Montreal, P.Q., January 5, 1971, 28 pp.

Lotz, James R., "An Indian Community College in Canada: A Proposal," Ottawa, unpublished manuscript, Canadian Research

Centre for Anthropology, St. Paul University, June, 1969, 21 pp.

McCue, Harvey A., "Brief Summary of the Efforts of the Native Committee on Indian Studies," Peterborough, Ontario, unpublished report, Trent University, December 22, 1970, 9 pp.

Tschirky, Joseph A., Widjiitwin: A Social, Educational and Economic Corporation, Toronto, Indian Development Branch, Ontario, Department of Social and Family Services, September, 1967, 29 pp.

Wabegijig, Carol, ed., "Nish Nawh Be," Canadian Indian Workshop Newsletter, Winnipeg, University of Manitoba, 1966, 24 pp.

Wax, Rosalie H., "A Brief History and Analysis of the Workshops on American Indian Affairs Conducted for American Indian College Students, 1956-1960, Together with a Study of Current Attitudes and Activities of Those Students," Coral Gables, Florida, unpublished manuscript, Department of Anthropology, University of Miami, October, 1961, 40 pp.

Whiteside, Don, "Survey of Amerindia Ethnic Study Programs in North American," Edmonton, unpublished manuscript, University of Alberta, August 31, 1970.

Wien, Fred, "The Final Report on the Canadian Indian Youth Workshop Project," unpublished report, Department of Secretary of State, September, 1968.

Willier, Marvin et. al., "Indian Communication Group Presently known as the Tee-Kah-Mat-Chee Pike-Keche Micu-Tau Win (Roots of Great Peace), Faust, Alta., unpublished proposal submitted to the Department of the Secretary of State, November 16, 1971, 5 pp.

Miscellaneous Reports (by date of Publication)

"Workshops on American Indian Affairs," Boulder, Colorado, 1964, Report, American Indian Development, Inc., 15 pp.

"Workshop on American Indian Affairs, Boulder, Colorado, 1966, Report, American Indian Development, Inc., 25 pp.

"Canadian Indian Youth Council: Report on the Canadian Indian Workshop Held at the University of Manitoba, Winnipeg, Between July-August, 1966," Ottawa, Canadian Indian Youth Council, 13 pp.

"Report of the First Canadian Indian Workshop," Winnipeg, University of Manitoba, January, 1967, 12 pp.

Alberta Indian Education Centre, Edmonton, Indian Association of Alberta, 1969, 132 pp.

"A Proposal for a Department of Indian Studies," unpublished manuscript, Ad Hoc Committee on American Indian Studies, University of Minnesota, May 21, 1969, 8 pp.

"Proposal to do Phase 2: Detailed Planning for the Proposed Indian Heritage Center," unpublished manuscript, Union of New Brunswick Indians, 1970, 22 pp.

"Industrial Environmental Training Centre, and Addendum," (Rivers Air Force Base, Manitoba), Winnipeg, unpublished proposal to the Government of Canada, Manitoba Indian Brotherhood, September, 1970, 71 pp.

"A Working Paper on the Alberta Indian Education Centre Proposal," unpublished report prepared by the Task Force Committee, Government of Canada, September 11, 1970, 19 pp.

"Saskatchewan Indian College and Cultural College: A Proposal for Programs to be Offered Using the Existing Facilities of Emmanuel College, University of Saskatchewan, Saskatoon," Regina, Proposal submitted to the Secretary of State by the Federation of Saskatchewan Indians, ca 1971, 33 pp.

"Proposal for a Learning Centre at the Old Sun School, Blackfoot Reservation, Gleichen, Alta.," Calgary, Mount Royal Community College, 1971, 56 pp.

"Program Proposal for the St. Paul Educational Centre on Blood Reserve, Alberta," Lethbridge Community College, February 2, 1971, 108 pp.

"Institute of American Indian Arts; an outline of the Institute program," Cerrilos Road, Sante Fe, New Mexico, (reprinted by the Indian-Eskimo Association of Canada, November 1971, 11 pp.).

"A proposal for the utilization of the Fish Lake Centre (Chilcotin Forest Indian Training Centre)," Williams Lake (B.C.), District Council, March 30, 1973, 19 pp.

"Coqualeetza Indian Centre of British Columbia: to demonstrate the advisability and feasibility of utilizing the Coqueleetza complex as a cultural education training centre for the Indian People of British Columbia," Brief submitted to the Minister of National Health and Welfare, by the Union of B.C. Indian Chiefs, March 1973.

"Newsletter," Edmonton, The Alberta Education Centre, April 1973, 14 pp.

Adams, Howard J., "Brief to the Senate Committee on Poverty, Metis Society of Saskatchewan," June 14, 1969, 12 pp.

Andras, Robert K., "Notes for a Philosophy of Social Change," Excerpts from a Statement, House of Commons, December 8, 1969.

Armstrong, O.K., "Let's Give the Indians Back the Country," Readers Digest, April, 1948.

Baich, Ben V. and James Whitford, "Re: Hand Clearing Operation at Grand Rapids," (Manitoba), Winnipeg, unpublished manuscript, January 11, 1961, 9 pp.

Balsam, Louis, "Some Economic Problems of the Indian in the United States," in Charles T. Loram and Thomas F. McIlwraith eds., The North American Indian Today, University of Toronto Press, 1943, pp. 207-219.

Bird, Florence, et. al., eds., "Native Women in the North," Report of the Royal Commission on the Status of Women in Canada, Ottawa, September 28, 1970, pp. 210-217.

Booz, Allen, Study of Health Services for Canadian Indians, Ottawa, Department of National Health and Welfare, September, 1969, 50 pp.

Borovoy, A. Alan, "Indian Poverty in Canada," Canadian Labour, (Ottawa), December, 1966, 3 pp.

Bradshaw, Thecla, "Why did Rita kill her sister? Despite treaty promises 88 years ago, Manitoba's Indians still live in poverty, without help or education. On that fatal winter night in a miserable log hut came one result," The Star Weekly Magazine, January 17, 1959.

Brant, Marlene J., Parental Neglect in Indian Families, Master of Social Work Thesis, University of Toronto, 1959, 120 pp.

Briggs, Jean L., Utkuhikhalingminut Eskimo Emotional Expression, Ottawa, Northern Science Research Group, Department of Indian Affairs and Northern Development, June, 1968, 74 pp.

Brock, Philip K., "Patterns of Illegitimacy on a Canada Indian Reserve, 1860-1960," Journal of Marriage and the Family, 1964, 26:142-148.

Card, Brigham, Young, Gordon, K. Hirabayaski, and Cecil L. French, The Metis in Alberta Society, with Special Reference to Social Economic and Cultural Factors Associated with Persistently High Tuberculois Incidence, Edmonton, University of Alberta, 1963, 414 pp.

Carse, M.R., "Americans: With Reservations," Commonwealth, March 5, 1948, 47.

Casselman, E., "Public Health Nursing Service for Indians," Canadian Journal of Public Health, December, 1967, 58:542-546.

Chance, Norman A. and Dorothy A. Foster, "Symptom Formation and Patterns of Psychopathology in a Rapidly Changing Alaskan Eskimo Society," Anthropological Papers of the University of Alaska, December, 1962, 2:32-42.

Chance, Norman A. and Hsien Rin, "Moderization, Value Identification, and Mental Health: A Cross-Cultural Study," unpublished manuscript, McGill University, ca 1965, 22 pp.

Chrétien, Hon. Jean, "Homemakers and the Indian Community," Address, Annual Conference of the Homemaker's Club of Saskatchewan, North Battleford, October 9, 1968, 10 pp.

Clairmont, Donald Hayden, "Notes on the Drinking Behaviours of the Eskimo and Indians in the Aklavik Area," Ottawa, Department of Indian Affairs and Northern Development, 1962, 13 pp.

Clairmont, Donald Hayden, Deviance Among Indians and Eskimos in Aklavik, N.W.T., Master's Thesis (Sociology), McMaster University, May, 1963, (Ottawa, Northern coordination and Research Centre, Department of Northern Affairs and National Resources, 1963, 84 pp.).

Clemons, Mrs. A., et. al., "Brief to the Status of Women Enquiry," Winnipeg, A Group of Indian and Metis Women, February 22, 1968, 5 pp.

Crawley, M., "A Study of Welfare Needs and Services in Northern Saskatchewan, 1956-1958," Saskatchewan, unpublished manuscript, Department of Welfare and Rehabilitation, 1958.

Dailey, R.C., "The role of alcohol among North American Indian Tribes as reported in the Jesuit relations," Anthropologica, 1968, 10:45-59.

Deiter, Chief Walter and Walter Currie, "Presentation to Senate Committee on Poverty," Brief from the National Indian Brotherhood and the Indian-Eskimo Association of Canada, 1970, 17 pp.

Deprez, Paul and Glenn Sigurdson, The Economic Status of the Canadian Indian: A re-examination, Winnipeg, Centre for Settlement Studies, University of Manitoba, December, 1969, 103 pp.

Dozier, Edward P., "Problem Drinking Among American Indians: The Role of Sociocultural Deprivation," Quarterly Journal of Studies of Alcohol, 1966, 27:72-87.

Dunning, Robert William, "Problems of Reserve Indians with Subsidy Economy," Paper presented at the Indian-Eskimo Association Meeting, Kingston, June, 1960, 42 pp.

Eames, Edwin and Judith Goode, "On Lewis' Culture of Poverty Concept," Current Anthropology, October, 1970, 11:479-482.

Eddy, D.H., "How We Scalp the Indians," <u>American</u> <u>Magazine</u>, January, 1950, 149:

Erickson, Gerald, "Mental Health Needs and Resources in a Northern Community," Winnipeg, unpublished report, School of Social Work, Psychological Service Centre, University of Manitoba, 1971, 29 pp.

Ferguson, Frances Northend, "Navaho Drinking: Some Tentative Hypothese," <u>Human Organization</u>, Summer, 1968, 27:159-167.

Ferguson, Frances Northend, "A Treatment Program for Navaho Alcoholics," <u>Quarterly Journal of Studies on Alcohol</u>, December, 1970, 31:898-919.

Forest, Deborah, A., "Analysis of data compiled for 73 female Metis prostitutes of the Edmonton Boyle St. area," Edmonton, unpublished manuscript, 1968, 83 p.

Freestone, A., "Environmental Sanitation on Indian Reserves," <u>Canadian Journal of Public Health</u>, January, 1968, 59:25-27.

Fry, Alan, <u>How a People Die</u>, Double Day, 1970.

Gooderham, Kent, <u>Notice: This is Indian Land</u>, Toronto, Griffin House, 1972, 84 pp.

Graham-Cumming, G., <u>The Influence of Canadian Indians on Vital Statistics</u>, Ottawa, Department of National Health and Welfare, 1966, 17 pp.

Graham-Cumming, G., "Infant care in Canadian Indian Homes," <u>Canadian Journal of Public Health</u>, September, 1967, 58:391-394.

Hallowell, Alfred Irving, "Sin, Sex and Sickness in Saulteaux Beliefs," <u>British Journal of Medical Psychology</u>, 1939, 19:191-197.

Hallowell, Alfred Irving, "Ojibwa world view and disease," in I. Galdston, ed., <u>Man's Image in Medicine and Anthropology</u>, New York, 1973, pp. 258-315.

Hoey, R.R., "Economic Problems of the Canadian Indian," in Charles T. Loram and Thomas F. McIlwraith, eds., <u>The North American Indian Today</u>, University of Toronto Press, 1943, pp. 199-206.

Honigmann, John Joseph, "Drinking in an Indian-White community," <u>Quarterly Journal of Studies on Alcohol</u>, March, 1945, 5:575-619.

Honigmann, John Joseph, <u>Foodways in a Muskeg Community</u>, (Anthropological Report on the Attawapiskat Indians in 1948), Department of Northern Affairs and National Resources, Ottawa, 1961, 215 pp.

Honigmann, John Joseph, and Irma Honigmann, "Alcohol in a Canadian Northern Town," Paper presented at the 1968 annual meeting of the Canadian Sociology and Anthropology Association, 81 pp.

Horton, Donald, "The Functions of Alcohol in Primitive Societies," in Clyde Kluckhohn, and Henry A. Murray, eds., Personality in Nature, Society and Culture, 2nd ed. New York, Knopf, 1953, pp. 680-690.

Hume, Steve (reporter), "N.W.T. booze -- profit and death," The Windsor Star, (Ont.), February 21, 1972.

Hume, Steve (reporter), "Infant mortality in North 3 times that of average," The Ottawa Citizen, July 3, 1972.

Hurt, Wesley R., Jr., and R.M. Brown, "Social Drinking Patterns of the Yankton Sioux," Human Organization, 1955, 24:222-230.

Irwin, A.C., "The Nutrition Survey in Northern Saskatchewan," Prince Albert, unpublished manuscript, Saskatchewan Department of Health and Welfare, 1956.

James, Bernard J., "Continuity and Emergence in Indian Poverty Culture," Current Anthropology, October-December 1970, 2:435-452, (reprinted in Mark Nagler ed., Perspectives in the North American Indian, Toronto, McClelland and Stewart, 1972, pp. 227-240).

Jobe, Paul and Kenneth R. Davidson, Community Development Case Studies, (Sidney Reserve, Pictou Reserve, Hyanan Reserve), Antigonish, N.S., Extension Department, St. Francis Xavier University, 1968, 47 pp.

Kew, J.E. Michael, "Metis-Indian Housing in Northern Saskatchewan," Research Review, (Centre for Community Studies, Saskatoon), 1963.

Knirck, Carola, "Observations and Figures Pertaining to Life Expectancy of Canadian Indians and Eskimos as compared with other Nationalities Throughout the World," Ottawa, unpublished manuscript, March, 1968, 6 pp.

Kupferer, Harriet J., "Health Practices and Educational Aspirations as Indicators of Acculturation and Social Class Among the Eastern Cherokee," Social Forces, 154-163.

Lavallee, Mrs. Mary Ann, "Problems that Concern Indian Women," Address, Saskatchewan Indian Women's Conference, Valley Centre, Fort Qu'Appelle, Saskatchewan, November 6-10, 1967, pp. 10-15.

Lavallee, Mrs. Mary Ann, "Address," Regional Conference on Health Services, n.d., 4 pp.

Lemert, Edwin M., Alcohol and the Northwest Coast Indians, Los Angeles, University of California Press, 1954.

Louttit, Neil (reporter), "The Metis: 'Is there any reason people have to live like that'," The Globe and Mail, (Toronto), March 22, 1972.

Louttit, Neil (reporter), "Home for 8 Metis is 14-foot square shack," The Globe and Mail, (Toronto), March 23, 1972.

Louttit, Neil (reporter), "For Metis, welfare is a way of life," The Globe and Mail, (Toronto), March 24, 1972.

Lubart, Joseph, M., Psychodynamic Problems of Adaptation -- Mackenzie Delta Eskimos, Ottawa, Northern Science Research Group, Department of Indian Affairs and Northern Development, December, 1969, 49 pp.

M., E.K., "Red Lake," Ontario Housing, February, 1964, 12-15.

MacDonald, Alex and Steve Hume (reporters), "Officials deny native women sterilized against will," Ottawa Citizen, April 5, 1973.

Massy, Mrs. Patricia, Foster Home Planning for the Indian Child, Vancouver, Master of Social Work Thesis, University of British Columbia, 1959-61.

McEwen, Ernest Roy, "Report: visit with Native Associations in Western Canada concerning housing and land claims," Ottawa, unpublished manuscript, Native Council of Canada, September, 1972.

McNelly, Peter (reporter), "Mungo: Descended from the Kolus to lead his people: First totem pole raising in 40 years honors a great Chief among Kwakiutl," Victoria Times, (B.C.), September 22, 1970.

Mirrieless, E.R., "Cloud of Mistrust," Atlantic Monthly, February, 1957, 199:

Moore, P., et. al., "Medical Survey of Nutrition among Northern Metis and Indians," Canadian Medical Association Journal, March, 1946, 54:223-233.

Morris, William (reporter), "How Canada Keeps the Indian Poor," Toronto Daily Star, February 9, 1963.

Nagler, Mark, "Minority Values and Economic Achievement: The case of the North American Indian," in John Harp and John R. Hofley, eds., Poverty in Canada, Prentice Hall, 1970, (reprinted in Mark Nagler, ed., Perspectives on the North American Indian, Toronto, McClelland and Stewart, 1972, pp. 131-141).

O'Connell, Martin P., "Canadian Standard of Housing in Indian Reserve Communities," Toronto, Indian-Eskimo Association of Canada, May, 1965, 46 pp.

O'Connell, Martin P., "Breaking the Cycle of Poverty in Indian Reserve Communities," Paper presented at the Ontario Conference on Indian Affairs, sponsored by the Ontario Division of the Indian, Eskimo Association of Canada, London, Ont., 1965, 7 pp.

Parayko, Orest, "A Sociological Survey of Non-White Alcoholic Patients," Edmonton, unpublished manuscript, Alcoholism Foundation of Alberta, n.d.

Parker, Arthur C., "The Social Elements of the Indian Problem," American Journal of Sociology, 22:252-267.

Payne, M.S., "Social Services for Indians," Social Worker, April-May, 1956.

Piepenburg, Roy L., "Rising Death Rates -- An Open Letter," The Native People, (Edmonton), December, 1969, 2(7):8-10.

Platiel, Rudy (reporter), "Jury urges 5 steps to improve health care in northwest Ontario Indian settlement," The Globe and Mail, (Toronto), February 28, 1972.

Platiel, Rudy (reporter), "Alcohol problem among Indians distorted because it's so visible, addiction workers say," The Globe and Mail, (Toronto), April 16, 1972.

Robertson, Heather (reporter), "On the road to nowhere," Saturday Night, (Toronto), August, 1971.

Rudnicki, Walter, "A Sampling from Northern Canada," Northern Welfare 62 -- A Symposium on Northern Social Work, Ottawa, Department of Northern Affairs and National Resources, c 1962.

Rudnicki, Walter, "Indians and Poverty," Ottawa, Indian Affairs Branch of the Department of Citizenship and Immigration for the Federal-Provincial Conference on Poverty, December, 1965, 19 pp.

Schmitt, N. and W.S. Barclay, "Accidental Deaths Among West Coast Indians," Canadian Journal of Public Health, 1962, 53:

Schmitt, N., et. al., "Accidental Deaths Among British Columbia Indians," Canadian Medical Association Journal, 1966, 94:228-234.

Shepard, Gloria, "Can't separate psychology from social and political realities," Involvement, (Newmarket, Ont.) Fall, 1971, 4:42-46.

Slobodin, Richard, "The Indians of Canada Today: Questions on Identity," in W.E. Mann, ed., Canada: A Sociological Profile, Copp Clark Pub. Co., (Canada), 1971, pp. 286-292.

Spence, Ahab, "Challenges to Today's Indian Women," Address, Saskatchewan Indian Women's Conference, Valley Centre, Fort Qu'Appelle, Saskatchewan, November 6-10, 1967, pp. 4-8.

Steele, Elizabeth and Calvin Zacharias, "The Sugar Beet Fields of Southern Alberta, May-September, 1971," Ottawa, Planning Services, Information Canada, 1972, 47 pp.

Stone, Dr. E.L., "A Specific Problem of Health Among the Indians of Canada," in Charles T. Loram and Thomas F. McIlwraith, eds., The North American Indian Today, University of Toronto Press, 1943, pp. 240-246.

Stotesbury, Rev. Earl F., "Placement Program for Indian Children of Public School Age in Private Homes in Cases of Special Need Under the Good Samaritan Plan," Saskatchewan, unpublished manuscript, October, 1959, 14 pp.

Stotesbury, Rev. Earl F., "Purpose and Outline of the Good Samaritan Plan in the Interest of Befriending and Assisting Canadian Indians, Metis, and Eskimos," Saskatchewan, unpublished manuscript, ca 1960, 2 pp.

Stotesbury, Rev. Earl F., "The Good Samaritan Plan of the Saskatchewan Conference of the United Church of Canada," Submission to the Joint Committee of the Senate and the House of Commons on Indian Affairs, Ottawa, February, 1960, 17 pp.

Thomas, W.D., "Maternal Mortality in Native British Columbia Indians," Canadian Medical Association Journal, July, 1968, 99:64-67.

Tinker, Frank, "Poor McDermitt," The Kiwanis Magazine, October, 1965, 50:

Townsend, Dr. J.G., "Problems of Health Among the Indians of the United States," in Charles T. Loram and Thomas F. McIlwraith, eds., The North American Indian Today, University of Toronto Press, 1943, pp. 223-239.

Vallee, Frank G., "Eskimo Theories of Mental Illness in the Hudson Bay Region," Anthropologica, 1966, 8:53-83.

Wallace, Anthony F.C., "Mental illness, biology, and culture," in Anthropology, Homewood, Ill., The Dorsey Press, 1971, pp. 255-295.

Wagner, Carruth J. and Erwin S. Rabeau, "Indian Poverty and Indian Health," Health Education and Welfare Indicators, U.S.D.H.E.W., March, 1964, pp. 24-44.

Wittkower, E.D., and R. Wintrob, "Developments in Canadian Transcultural Psychiatry," Canadian Mental Health, May-August, 1969, 17:21-27.

Zentner, Henry, "Factors in the Social Pathology of North American Indian Society," Anthropologica, 1963, 5:119-130.

Miscellaneous Reports by date of publication

"Developing Resources to Meet Social Needs of Indians: Proceedings of Third Social Workers' Conference," Ottawa, Indian Affairs Branch, Department of Citizenship and Immigration, 1958, 21 pp.

Northern Welfare 62: A Symposium on Northern Social Work, Ottawa, Department of Northern Affairs and National Resources, 1962, 71 pp.

"Community Health Worker Training Programs," Ottawa, Department of National Health and Welfare, April, 1962, 4 pp.

"Indian Resettlement at MacGregor," Ontario Housing, February, 1963, 9:6-8.

"Extracts from Debate on Department of Welfare Estimates Relating to Indian and Metis and Community Development," Debates and Proceedings, Legislative Assembly of Manitoba, April 8-10, 1964, pp. 1670-1773.

"The Introduction of Alcohol into Iroquois Society," Toronto, unpublished manuscript, Alcohol and Drug Research Foundation, 1965, 37 pp.

"Round Table on Indian Housing in Reserve Communities," Toronto, Indian-Eskimo Association of Canada, May 31, 1965.

"Indian Welfare Services," Ottawa, Selections from Speeches by Ministers of Indian Affairs and Senior Departmental Officials, ca 1968, 1 p.

"Alcohol and Indian People," Ottawa, Selections from Speeches by Ministers of Indian Affairs and Senior departmental officials, ca 1968.

"Indian Health," Ottawa, Selections from Speeches by Ministers of Indian Affairs and Senior Departmental Officials, ca 1968, 1 p.

"Welfare Programs in the North," Ottawa, Department of Indian Affairs and Northern Development, February, 1968, 4 pp.

"Hospitals for the North," Canadian Nurse, March, 1968, 64:37-39.

"Indian Off-Reserve and Eskimo Re-Establishment Housing Regulations, amended," The Canada Gazette, Part II, October 23, 1968.

"The Challenge ... health-care for our native people," Canadian Hospitals, June, 1969, 46:23-27.

"Brief on Poverty," Edmonton, Brief to the Senate Committee on Poverty, Metis Association of Alberta, June 13, 1969, 13 pp.

"The Other Indian," Winnipeg, Brief to the Senate Committee on Poverty, Manitoba Metis Federation, June 26, 1969, 8 pp.

"Indians: squalor amid splendor," Time, July 11, 1969.

Rural Indian Americans in Poverty, Washington, D.C., Economic Report no. 167, Economic Research Service, U.S. Department of Agriculture, September, 1969, 27 pp.

"Child dies shortly after discharge from Hospital," The Native People, (Edmonton), October, 1969, 2(5):1.

"Report on Eskimo housing," Ottawa, Department of Indian Affairs and Northern Development, January 26, 1970, 6 pp.

Homes For Our People, Regina, The Metis Nation of Saskatchewan, October, 1970, 23 pp.

Proceedings of the Special Senate Committee on Poverty, Second Session, Twenty-eighth Parliament, 1969-1970, no. 14, January

20, 1970, (witnesses: Department of Indian Affairs and Northern Development), 190 pp.

"Submission of the Native Council of Canada on The White Paper on Income Security," Ottawa, Native Council of Canada, April 5, 1971, 6 pp.

"70% of Indians on Welfare rolls," The Edmonton Journal, May 7, 1970.

"Welfare Conference," Union of Nova Scotia Indians, Truro, N.S., September 1-3, 1970, 36 pp.

"Mental health in north grim picture, expert says," The Toronto Daily Star, December 15, 1971.

"Slum Landlord Exploit Impoverished," The Native People, (Edmonton), February, 1972, 4(7):1-4.

"Adoption Law," Tapwe (Hay River, N.W.T.), February 2, 1972.

"Frobisher's Eskimos: Sad victims of white man's bad habits," Montreal Gazette, February 12, 1972.

"Editorial: Frightening plight of our Eskimos," Windsor Star, (Ont.), February 22, 1972.

"Indian housing in New Brunswick," Union of Nova Scotia Indians, June, 1972, 57 pp.

"Alberta's fly-in medical care to reserve a waste: doctor," The Globe and Mail, (Toronto), August 19, 1972.

"Fish-eating Ojibwa Indians have high mercury levels," Ottawa Citizen, March 8, 1972.

PART XVIII

CRIME AND OTHER LEGAL MATTERS (EXCEPTING TREATIES)
(See also Prejudice and Discrimination)

Adams, Ian (reporter), "Out of jail and into another kind of prison: for an Indian with a record there's not much to do on the outside except hand on," Weekend Magazine, (Montreal), January 6, 1973.

Barbarash, John, and John Yesno, "Legal Rights of Indians," Indian Magazine, as broadcast March 15, 1969, (Canadian Broadcasting Corporation).

Campbell, Joseph, "Indians, Eskimos and the Law: An Interview with Dr. Doug Schmeiser," Our Family, November, 1967, pp. 21, 22 and 27.

Daniels, Christine, and Ron Christiansen, Many Laws: Edmonton, Commercial Printers Ltd., 1970.

Dubienski, Ian V. and Stephen Skelly, "Analysis of arrest for the year 1969 in the city of Winnipeg with particular reference to arrests of persons of Indian descent," Winnipeg, unpublished manuscript, September, 1970, 29 pp.

Dunn, Willie, "Northern 'Justice'," The Western Canadian Journal of Anthropology, 1969, 1:119-120.

Fisher, C.A., A Survey of Vandalism and Its Cultural Antecedents on Four New York State Indian Reservations, D.S.S. Thesis, Syracuse University, 1959.

Flynn, Mike (reporter), "Justice on Northern Reserves," Winnipeg Tribune, April 8, 1972.

Golden, Aubrey E., James A. O'Reilly, Andrew Delisle, Paul V. Walsh, and Len Marchand, "The Law and Native Populations," Panel Discussion, 51st Annual Meeting Canadian Bar Association, Ottawa, 1969.

Hart, C.W.M., "The Problem of Laws," in Charles T. Loram and Thomas F. McIlwraith, eds., The North American Indian Today, University of Toronto Press, 1943, pp. 247-254.

Hillinger, Charles, "Two kinds of justice dispensed in north," Windsor Star, (Ont.), May 11, 1972.

Johnstone, Ken, "Reserves of injustice: Indians and Eskimos in Prison," The Montreal Star, August 7, 1971.

Jubinville, Real, "Correctional services in the Northwest Territories, report of the study committee," Ottawa, Department of Social Development, Northwest Territories and Department of the Solicitor General of Canada, 1971, 123 pp.

Katz, Sidney (reporter), "Sociologist says bloodshed could come to Canadian prisons," (Howard Adams) <u>Toronto</u> <u>Daily</u> <u>Star</u>, September 18, 1971.

Levy, Jerrold E., et al., "Navajo Criminal Homicide," <u>Southwestern</u> <u>Journal</u> <u>of</u> <u>Anthropology</u>, 1969, 25:124-152.

Luebben, Ralph A., "Anglo Law and Navaho Behaviour," <u>The</u> <u>Kiva</u> (Journal of the Arizona Archaelogical and Historical Society), February, 1964, 29:60-75.

McCaskill, J.C., "Problems of Administration of Law and Order among Indians of the United States," in Charles T. Loram and Thomas F. McIlwraith, eds., <u>The</u> <u>North</u> <u>American</u> <u>Indian</u> <u>Today</u>, University of Toronto Press, 1943, pp. 255-264.

McGrath, W.T., "The Offender of Indian Ancestry," in <u>Report</u> <u>of</u> <u>the</u> <u>Alberta</u> <u>Penology</u> <u>Study</u>, Edmonton, Province of Alberta, 1968, pp. 93-98.

Newell, William B., "Crime and Justice Among the Iroquois Nations," <u>Caughnawaga</u> <u>Historical</u> <u>Society</u>, (Montreal), 1965.

Pepin, John, The Incidence of Indian Crime in Canada, unpublished term paper, March, 1970.

Platiel, Rudy (reporter), "Prison Better than Reserve," <u>The</u> <u>Globe</u> <u>and</u> <u>Mail</u>, (Toronto), November 25, 1970.

Price, Monroe E., "Lawyers on the Reservation: Some Implications for the Legal Profession," <u>Law</u> <u>and</u> <u>the</u> <u>Social</u> <u>Order</u>, (Arizona State Legal Journal), 1969, 161-203.

Reid, D.C.S., "Norm-Setting and Norm Violating Behaviour in the Indian or his Descendant," Paper presented at the Staff Conference of the John Howard Society, of After-Care Service to the Indian Offender, Edmonton, May 29, 1962.

Sanders, Douglas Esmond, "A Legal Services Program for Indian Communities in Canada," Paper presented at the Law and Poverty Conference, Ottawa, October, 1971, 23 pp.

Schmeiser, Douglas A., "Indians, Eskimos and the Law," <u>Saskatchewan</u> <u>Law</u> <u>Review</u>, 33:19-40.

Scow, Alfred, "Indians and the Law," Address Annual Meeting of the Indian-Eskimo Association of Canada, Vancouver, December, 1966, 6 pp.

Shepardson, Mary, "Problems of the Navajo Tribal Courts in Translation," <u>Human</u> <u>Organization</u>, 1965, 24:250-253.

Stewart, Omer, "Questions Regarding American Indian Criminality," <u>Human</u> <u>Organization</u>, 1964, 23:61-66.

Swan, "Indian Legal Services Programs: The Key to Red Power?," <u>Arizona</u> <u>Law</u> <u>Review</u>, 1970, 12:594-606.

Ward, William P., The Administration of Justice in the North-West Territories, 1870-1887, Edmonton, Master's Thesis (Arts), University of Alberta, 1966.

Miscellaneous Reports by date of publication

Indians and the Law, Ottawa, The Canadian Corrections Associations, and The Canadian Welfare Council, 1967, 67 pp.

"Law Seen as 'Hoax on Indians'," Toronto Daily Star, November 21, 1967.

"Institutions, Runaways, etc.", in Report of First Alberta Native Women's Conference, Edmonton, Alberta, March, 1968, pp. 11-12.

"Indians and the Law," Training Conference for Law Enforcement Officers and Dealing with their Contact with Indians, Wendigo, 1969.

"Move Ahead on Legal Rights Project," Bulletin (Indian-Eskimo Association of Canada), July, 1969.

"Reasons for Judgement by the Honourable Mr. Justice J.H. Sissons, in the Territorial Court of the Northwest Territories in the matter of Her Majesty the Queen, Complainant, and Jimmy Koglgolak Defendant," April 20, 1969.

"Brief presented by the Union of Nova Scotia Indians to the Committee for the Study of legal aid in Nova Scotia," September 30, 1970, 5 pp.

Toward Equality: The British Columbia Indian Law Programme, Vancouver, Union of British Columbia Indian Chiefs, 1971.

"Proposal to Secretary of State Citizens' Rights and Freedom Programs," (Rights and Freedom Workers), Union of Nova Scotia Indians, Truro, N.S., October, 1971, 13 pp.

"Report of the Special Committee on Legal Education," Toronto, The Law Society of Upper Canada, Osgoode Hall, 1972.

"For minor offences 'Too many native people jailed'," Winnipeg Free Press, February 2, 1972.

"Why are so many Indians in jail? Senator asks," (Guy Williams), The Globe and Mail, (Toronto), March 2, 1972.

PART XIX

BIBLIOGRAPHIES NOT PREVIOUSLY LISTED UNDER
SPECIFIC TOPIC HEADINGS

Beveridge, Louise B., Projects and People: Ontario Indian Research and Related Projects, Toronto, Ontario Economic Council, 1970.

Boudreault, Mireille, et al., "Bibliographie Sommaire sur la Radissonie," in Problèmes voriques des façades la baie James, Quebec City, University of Laval, 1967, pp. 120-155.

Bouknight, Marie, et al., ed., Guide to Records in the Military Archives Division Pertaining to Indian-White Relations, Washington, D.C., The National Archives and Records Service, General Services Administration, 1972, 227 pp.

Brigden, Beatrice, "Bibliography of Non-Fiction Books, Pamphlets, Reports and Acts Concerning the Indians of North America," Presented at the 12th Annual Indian and Metis Conference, Winnipeg, February, 1966.

Cooper, Ardyth, "List of Theses that deal with Indian People, University of Victoria, (McPherson Library)," for the Union of British Columbia Chiefs, August 10, 1972, 16 pp.

Crawford, Richard C., and Charles E. South, eds., Guide to Records in the Civil Archives Pertaining to Indian-White Relations, Washington, D.C., Preliminary Draft prepared for the National Archives Conference on Research in the History of Indian-White Relations, 1972, 37 pp.

DeLaguna, Frederica, ed., Selected Papers from the American Anthropologist, 1888-1820, Evanston, Illinois, Row Peterson, 1960.

Dockstader, Frederick J., ed., The American Indian in Graduate Studies: A Bibliography of Theses and Dissertations, New York, Museum of the American Indian, Heye Foundation, Vol. 15, 1957, 399 pp.

Dore, Madeleine, "Bibliographie Americaniste," Journal de la Société des Americanistes, 1957, 46:239-382.

Dorion, Henri, "Documentation," in Rapport de la Commission d'étude sur l'integrité du territoire du Québec, February, 1971, 264 pp.

Edwards, Everett Eugene, and Wayne D. Rasmussen, A Bibliography on the Agriculture of the American Indians, Washington, D.C., United States Department of Agriculture, Miscellaneous Publications, No. 447, January, 1942, 107 pp.

Erickson, Vincent et. al., "Malecite Teaching Materials Project, Phase I, 'Annotated Malecite Bibliography'," Fredericton, N.B., May, 1969, 21 pp.

Evans, Adye, Bel, et. al., Bibliography: Resource Frontier Communities, Center for Settlement Studies, University of Manitoba, August, 1969, Vol. 2, 164 pp.

Gambill, Jerry T., "Paperback Bibliography on North American Indians," unpublished manuscript, Putney, Vt., 1967, 2 pp.

Geldart, Mrs. Penny, "Accession List," Ottawa, Research and Documentation Library, Citizenship Branch, Department of the Secretary of State, November, 1970 (periodic additions), 201 pp.

Gibson, Gayll, "Bibliography: Metis and Non-Status Indians," Ottawa, Native Council of Canada, March, 1973, 94 pp.

Girouard, Laurent, ed., "Bulletin d'information," recherches amérindiennes au Québec, Janvier, 1971, Vol. I.

Harvey, Bryon III, "The Fred Harvey Collection, 1899-1963," Plateau (Quarterly of the Museum of Northern Arizona), Fall, 1963, 36:33-53.

Helm, June, ed., "Subarctic anthropology: roster of scholars," Iowa City, Iowa, unpublished manuscript, January, 1972, 12 pp.

Hill, Edward E., ed., Preliminary Inventories: No. 163, Records of the Bureau of Indian Affairs, Washington, D.C., The National Archives, National Archives and Records Service, General Services Administration, 1965, 2 Vols.

Hill, Edward E., ed., "Records in the General Archives Division Relating to American Indians," Washington, D.C., Preliminary Draft prepared for the National Archives Conference on Research in the History of Indian-White Relations, 1972, 11 pp.

Hill, Edward E., "The Tucson Agency: The Use of Indian records in the National Archives," Prologue, (Washington, D.C.) Summer, 1972, 4:77-82.

Honigmann, John Joseph, and June Helm, "Bibliography of Northern North America and Greenland," unpublished manuscript, University of Iowa, ca 1968, 23 pp.

Jones, Mary Jane, ed., Mackenzie Delta Bibliography, Ottawa, Northern Science Research Group, Department of Indian Affairs and Northern Development, March, 1969, 119 pp.

Josephy, Alvin M. Jr., "Bibliography," in The Indian Heritage of America, New York, Alfred A. Knoph, 1968, pp. 368-384.

Kelsay, Laura E., ed., Special Lists, Number 13: List of Cartographic Records of the Bureau of Indian Affairs, Washington, D.C., The National Archives, National Archives and Records Service, General Services Administration, 1954, 127 pp.

Kerri, James, N., ed., American Indians (U.S. and Canada): A Bibliography of Contemporary Studies and Urban Research, Winnipeg, Citizenship Branch, Department of the Secretary of State, July, 1972, 193 pp.

Lotz, James R., ed., Government Research and Surveys in the Canadian North, 1956-1961, Ottawa, Northern Co-ordination and Research Centre, Department of Northern Affairs and National Resources, January, 1961, 90 pp.

Lotz, James R., Yukon bibliography, Ottawa, Department of Northern Affairs and National Resources, Northern Co-ordination and Research Centre, 1964, 155 pp.

Lotz, James R., "List of Contributors to the Special Volume of Essays in Memory of Dr. Diamond Jenness," unpublished letter, February 24, 1971, Ottawa.

Lumsden, Paul, "Film Reviews: National Film Board," Prepared for Norcap Management Committee, August, 1966, 6 pp.

MacDonald, Nancy L., "A Bibliography on Attitudes of Native Indian People Toward Non-Indian Society in Canada," Ottawa, unpublished manuscript, Social Research and Documentation Service, Department of the Secretary of State, August 19, 1967, 3 pp.

MacDonald, Nancy L., "Some Sources of Information: Indian Integration," Ottawa, unpublished manuscript, Social Research and Documentation Service, Department of the Secretary of State, August 21, 1967.

Martin, Charles A., "Part C, James Bay Region (Quebec): Prehistory Bibliography (annotated)," recherches amérindiennes au quebec, Juin 1972, 2:51-62.

McDiarmid, Garnet L. and Larry J. Orton, eds., Culture contact, with special reference to the Indians of North America: an annotated bibliography, Toronto, Ontario, Institute for Studies in Education, 1967, 214 pp.

McIlwraith, Thomas F., "Bibliography of Canadian Anthropology for 1961," Ottawa, National Museum of Canada, Bulletin No. 194, 1964, pp. 1-28.

Murdock, George Peter, Ethnographic bibliography of North America, New Haven, Human Relations Area Files, 3rd ed., 1972, 393 pp.

Naumer, Janet Noll, "American Indians: a bibliography of sources," American Libraries Bulletin (American Library Association), October, 1970, 1: 4 pp.

Price, John A., "Resources for the Study of the Contemporary Indian, Metis, and Inuit of Canada," Toronto, unpublished manuscript, Department of Sociology and Anthropology, York University, February, 1972, 13 pp.

Savoie, Donat, "Bibliographie par village population Esquimaude du Nouveau Québec," Ottawa, Bureau de recherches scientifiques sur le Nord, Ministère des Affaires indiennes et du Nord canadien, April 1973.

Stanley, Samuel, and William C. Sturtevant, "Selected References on Present-Day Conditions Among U.S. Indians," Washington,

D.C., Center for the Study of Man, Smithsonian Institution,
December, 1969.

Stevenson, A., "Northern Bibliography," Ottawa, unpublished
manuscript, June 3, 1968, 5 pp.

Suttles, Wayne, P., "Reading list: Indians of British Columbia,"
Department of Anthropology, University of British Columbia,
1962-1963, 36 pp.

Symington, Fraser, "Bibliography," in The Canadian Indian,
Toronto, McClelland and Stewart, 1969, pp. 262-263.

Taylor, James, Bibliography -- Resource Frontier Communities,
Center for Settlement Studies, University of Manitoba,
Vol. 3, September, 1970, 139 pp.

Thomas, Joe Doan, ed., "Audiovisual Records Relating to Indians in
the United States," Washington, D.C., Preliminary Draft
prepared for the National Archives Conference on Research in
the History of the Indian-White Relations, 1972, 21 pp.

Tremaine, Marie, ed., Arctic Bibliography, (Arctic Institute of
North America, Volume 14), Queen's University Press, 1969.

Useem, Ruth Hill, and Ethel Nurge, "Bibliography," in The Modern
Sioux, pp. 291-297.

Vallee, Frank, "Selected Annotated Bibliography," in Indians and
Eskimos in Canada, Vol. II, prepared for the Royal Commission
on Bilingualism and Biculturalism, 1966.

Weaver, Sally Mae, "Anthropology 235, Selected References,"
London, unpublished manuscript, University of Western Ontario,
September, 1971, 15 pp.

Weaver, Sally Mae, Annotated Bibliography 1960-1970, London,
University of Western Ontario, (forthcoming).

Wehmann, Howard H., ed., "Records Pertaining to Indians in Records
of the Contenental and Confederation Congresses and the
Constitutional Convention (Record Group 360), A Preliminary
Guide," Washington, D.C., prepared for the National Archives
Conference on Research in the History of Indian-White
Relations, April, 1972, 35 pp.

White, Hilary, J., Bibliography -- Resource Frontier Communities,
Center for Settlement Studies, University of Manitoba, Vol. 1,
April, 1969, 145 pp.

Miscellaneous Reports by date of publication

"Press clippings," Ottawa, Department of Indian Affairs and
Northern Development, 4 volumes, 1884-1963, 799 pp. (also on

deposit in the National Indian Brotherhood Library, Ottawa, and the Native Council of Canada Library, Ottawa).

Catalog of the Edward E. Ayer Collection of American Indians, Chicago, The Newberry Library, 16 vols.

"Indian Claims Commission Library Lists," Ottawa, periodic.

"Indian-Eskimo Association of Canada, Library Acquisition List," Toronto, periodic.

"Guide to manuscript material: selections related to Indians in the Atlantic Provinces from the Union List," n.d. 17 pp.

"Library lists prepared by the Department of Citizenship and Immigration Library,"
1. Haida Indians, November, 1962, 2 pp.
2. Cree Indians, n.d., 2 pp.
3. Indians of the MacKenzie District, November, 1962, 2 pp.
4. Iroquois Indians, March, 1963, 6 pp.
5. Kutchin Indians, April, 1963, 1 p.
6. Arts and Crafts of the Canadian Indian, September, 1965, 5 pp.
7. Mohawk Indians, March, 1966, 2 pp.
8. Government relations, March, 1966, 11 pp.

"Library lists prepared by the Department of Indian Affairs and Northern Development Library,"
1. Studies of Northern peoples, March, 1967, 7 pp.
2. Nutrition and socio-economic studies, August, 1967, 2 pp.
3. Community development, February, 1968, 4 pp.
4. Indians of Canada, July, 1968, 2 pp.
5. Huron Indians, July 1968, 4 pp.
6. Reserves, 1969, 1 p.
7. Indians of North America, February, 1969, 2 pp.
8. Tecumseh, Shawnee Chief, January, 1969, 1 p.
9. Indians Arts and Crafts, May, 1969, 6 pp.
10. Athapaskan Indians, May, 1969, 3 pp.
11. Abenaki Indians, May, 1969, 2 pp.
12. Point Pelee National Park, May, 1969, 3 pp.
13. Chippeway Indians, May, 1969, 2 pp.
14. Lower Fort Garry, May, 1969, 4 pp.
15. Fort Langley National Park, May, 1969, 1 p.
16. The Montagnais-Naskapi, May, 1969, 2 pp.
17. Indians of the Fraser District, May, 1969, 14 pp.
18. The Northwest Territories, October, 1970, 2 pp.
19. The Yukon Territory, October, 1970, 2 pp.
20. Indians of Ontario, June, 1970, 4 pp.
21. The role of Indian Women, December, 1970, 1 p.
22. Ojibwa Indians, January, 1971, 4 pp.
23. Urbanization, January, 1971, 1 p.
24. Louis Riel and the Metis uprising, January, 1971, 1 p.
25. Manitoba, February, 1971, 8 pp.
27. Intertribal trade--Pacific Coast Indians, March, 1971, 1 p.
28. Eskimo arts and crafts, April, 1971, 7 pp.
29. Nahanni River, March, 1971, 1 p.
30. Publications by Canadian Indian and Eskimo Authors, April, 1971, 2 pp.
31. Arctic Sovereignty, July, 1971, 3 pp.

32. Cree-English publication, n.d., 1 p.
33. Spanish-Indian relations, n.d., 1 p.

The Arctic Bibliography, Arctic Institute of North America, McGill--Queen's University Press, 1953-1972, (annual).

"Indian History: Background Blocks Helpful for Teachers," Madison, Wisconsin, State Historical Society, November, 1951.

"Index," The Annals of the American Academy of Political and Social Science, May, 1957, Vol. 311.

"Canadian Index to Periodicals and Documentary Films, 1948-1959," Ottawa, Library of Parliament, 1959.

Biographical and Historical Index of American Indians, Washington, D.C., United States Department of the Interior, 1960, 8 Vols.

Citizenship, Immigration and Ethnic Groups in Canada: A Bibliography of Research, 1920-1958, Ottawa, Department of Citizenship and Immigration, 1960.

Citizenship, Immigration and Ethnic Groups in Canada: A Bibliography of Research, 1959-1961, Ottawa, Department of Citizenship and Immigration, February, 1962, 54 pp.

"Bibliography," in Sol Tax, ed., Indian Tribes of Aboriginal America: Selected Papers of the 29th International Congress of Americanists, New York, Cooper Square 1967, pp. 386-410.

Citizenship, Immigration and Ethnic Groups in Canada: A Bibliography of Research, 1962-1964, Ottawa, Department of Citizenship and Immigration, July, 1964.

"The Indians of Canada: A Selected Bibliography," Ottawa, Department of Citizenship and Immigration, December, 1965, 6 pp.

"Publications of Indian Interest," Thunderbird, (Toronto), 1966.

"To Read About Eskimos," University of Saskatchewan, July, 1967, 1 p.

A Bibliography on the Canadian Arctic, Ottawa, Northern Co-ordination and Research Centre of the Department of Indian Affairs and Northern Development, 1967.

"Sociological, Economical, Anthropological, Psychological Studies of Northern People; A Select Bibliography," Department of Indian Affairs and Northern Development Library, Ottawa, March, 1967, 7 pp.

"Periodicals--Newspapers--Newsletters," Saskatoon, Indian and Northern Curriculum Resources Centre, University of Saskatchewan, July, 1967.

"Reference List, Education 357-457, University of Saskatchewan," July, 1967.

"Library Accession List," Ottawa, Department of Indian Affairs and Northern Development, 1968, (periodic).

"Indians of Canada: A Reading List for Junior High School Students," Ottawa, Department of Indian Affairs and Northern Development, July, 1968.

"Aire Culturelle I: Nord (Section Eskimo) bibliographie," unpublished manuscript, Ottawa, Department of Indian Affairs and Northern Development, 1967-1968, 8 pp.

"Other Research and Surveys sponsored by the Department," Ottawa, unpublished manuscript, Department of Indian Affairs and Northern Development, ca 1969, 5 pp.

Cree Studies, (Special Issues), Western Canadian Journal of Anthropology, 1969, Vol. I.

"All National Film Board Material on the Subject of the Canadian Indian and Eskimo," Ottawa, unpublished manuscript, Citizenship Branch, Department of the Secretary of State, 1969.

Bibliographical Material Indian Studies, Saskatoon, Indian and Northern Curriculum Resources Centre, College of Education, University of Saskatchewan, 1969.

Teacher's Guide to Resource Materials in Cross-Cultural Education, Part One: Indians, Eskimos and Early Explorers, Saskatoon, Indian and Northern Curriculum Resources Centre, University of Saskatchewan, 1970.

"A bibliography of materials for and about Native People," Edmonton, Department of Education, Government of Alberta, 1970, 53 pp.

"Memorandum: Guide to Indian Affairs Finding Aids," Ottawa, Public Archives of Canada, April 15, 1970.

"Suggested Literature for 'N'Amerind'," 1970, 5 pp.

"Cultures Amerindiennes: Bibliographie," unpublished manuscript, Department of Anthropology, University of Montreal, 1970, 3 pp.

"Selective Bibliography of Works by Authors of Canadian Indian and Eskimo Ancestry," Ottawa, Department of Indian Affairs and Northern Development, May, 1970, 2 pp.

Appraisal of Parliamentary Information on Indian Rights and Treaties, 1867-1961, Ottawa, unpublished manuscript, Research Branch, Library of Parliament, September 30, 1971, 116 pp.

"List of Reports by Northern Science Research Group," Ottawa, Department of Indian Affairs and Northern Development, ca 1971, 5 pp.

"Bibliography of Books, Pamphlets with Reference to the North American People," London, Ontario, Indian Information Centre, 1971, 38 pp.

<u>Select</u> <u>Picture</u> <u>List</u>, Washington, D.C., National Archives and Records Service, General Services Administration, Leaflet No. 21, 1971, 18 pp.

"Sessional Papers Index, 1867-1925," Ottawa, National Indian Brotherhood, 1972.

"Guide to material about Indians in Western Canada, (Black series)," (alphabetically by subject), Ottawa, Public Archives of Canada, c 1972, 180 pp.

"Guide to material about Indians in the East (Red Series)," Ottawa, Public Archives of Canada, 1972, 63 pp. (Series 706 pp.).

"Index, Hansard, 1875-1945," Regina, unpublished manuscript, Federation of Saskatchewan Indians, 1972.

"Guide to Records of the Bureau of Indian Affairs in the Archives Branches of the Federal Records Centers," Washington, D.C., Preliminary Draft prepared for the National Archives Conference on Research in the History of Indian-White Relations, 1972.

<u>The</u> <u>American</u> <u>Indian</u>: <u>Select</u> <u>Catalog</u> <u>of</u> <u>National</u> <u>Archives</u> <u>Microfilm</u> <u>Publications</u>, Washington, D.C., National Archives and Records Service, General Services Administration, 1972, 50 pp.

<u>A</u> <u>Catalogue</u> <u>of</u> <u>Data</u> <u>in</u> <u>the</u> <u>Statistical</u> <u>Information</u> <u>Centre</u>, Ottawa, Department of Indian Affairs and Northern Development, March, 1972, 34 pp.

"List of Acceptances," National Archives Conference on Research in the History of Indian-White Relations," June 15, 16, 1972, Washington, D.C.

"Agenda," National Archives Conference on Research in the History of Indian-White Relations, June 15, 16, 1972, Washington, D.C.

<u>Bibliography</u> <u>for</u> <u>professional</u> <u>development</u>, Saskatoon, Indian and Northern Education, University of Saskatchewan, ca 1972, 63 pp.

PART XX

ABORIGINAL PEOPLE IN OTHER THAN NORTH AMERICAN COUNTRIES

Adams, Richard N., "Ethnohistoric Research Methods: Some Latin American Features," Ethnohistory, Spring, 1962, 9:179-205.

Arcand, Bernard, The urgent situation of the Cuiva Indians of Columbia, Copenhagen, International Work Group for Indigenous People, July, 1972, 28 pp.

Armstrong, Terence, "The Administration of Northern Peoples: The U.S.S.R.," in St. J. Macdonald, ed., The Arctic Frontier, University of Toronto Press, 1966, pp. 57-88.

Bandeira de Mello, General Oscar Jeponimo, "The Indian Policy of Brazil," A paper from the National Foundation for Assistance to Indians (FUNAI) to the VII Congress of the Inter-American Indian Institute, Brazilia, August 7-12, 1972, 14 pp.

Barolome, Miguel Alberto, et. al., Declaration of Barbados, (Barbados Symposium) International Work Group for Indigenous Affairs, Copenhagen, January, 1971, 6 pp.

Bennett, Wendell C., and Robert M. Zingg, The Tarahumara, University of Chicago Press, 1935.

Blom, Frans, and Oliver La Farge, Tribes and Temples, ("Middle American Research Series Publications," No. 1), New Orleans: Tulane University, 1926, 2 Vols.

Boas, Franz, Handbook of American Indian Languages, (Bulletin of the United States Bureau of American Ethnology; No. 40), Washington, D.C., 1911, Part I, pp. 559-768.

Bodard, Lucien, Green hell; massacre of the Brazilian Indians, trans. by Jennifer Monaghan, New York, Outerbridge and Dienstfrey, 1971, 291 pp.

Bodley, John H., Tribal survival in the Amazon: The Campa Case, Copenhagen, International Work Group for Indigenous People, May, 1972, 15 pp.

Castillo-Cardenas, Gonsalos, "The Indian struggle for freedom in Columbia," in Walter Dostal, ed., The Situation of the Indian in South America, Geneva, World Council of Churches, 1972, pp. 76-104.

Cooper, J.M., "Area and Temporal Aspects of Aboriginal South American Culture," Washington, D.C., Smithsonian Report for 1943 , 1944, pp. 429-462.

Coppens, Walter, The anatomy of a land invasion scheme in Yekuana Territory, Venezuela, Copenhagen, International Work Group for Indigenous Affairs, October, 1972, 23 pp.

Davis, Shelton, "Custer is alive and he lives in Brazil," The Indian Historian, Winter 1973, 6:11-18.

De Goeje, C.H., "The Physical World, The World of Magic, and the Moral World of Guiana Indians," in Sol Tax, ed., Indian Tribes of Aboriginal America: Selected Papers of the 29th International Congress of Americanists, New York, Cooper Square 1967, pp. 266-270.

De Wolf, Charles, The Indian Races of North and South America, Brownell, Hurlbur, Kellor and Co., 1861.

Dostal, Walter, ed., The situation of the Indian in South America, (Report of a symposium held in Bridgetown, Barbados January, 1971), Geneva, World Council of Churches, 1972, 453 pp.

Fuerst, René, Bibliography of the Indigenous Problem and Policy of the Brazilian Amazon Region, (1957-1972), Copenhagen, International Work Group for Indigenous People, 1972, 44 pp.

Fuller, O. Torie, "Proposal for a Comparative Study of American and Canadian Indian Policies," Ottawa, unpublished manuscript, Department of Indian Affairs and Northern Development, November 21, 1969.

Fuller, O. Torie, "Indigenous Populations," Ottawa, unpublished manuscript, Department of Indian Affairs and Northern Development, July, 1972, 22 pp.

Goldstein, M.S., Demographic and Bodily Changes in Descendants of Mexican Immigrants with Comparable Data on Parents and Children in Mexico, Austin, Texas: Institution of Latin-American Studies, 1943.

Handler, Bruce (reporter), "Brazil's Indians reported heading toward extinction: Victims of economic expansion," The Ottawa Journal, March 17, 1972.

Handler, Bruce (reporter), "Assimilation of Indians fails to work in Brazil, Vancouver Sun, February 23, 1972.

Harrison, Mrs. Barbara, Aboriginal issues, racism in Australia, Geneva, World Council of Churches, 1971, 29 pp.

Holland, Gordon (reporter), "From Melbourne: No Land Rights for Aborigines," Daily Times,(Victoria, B.C.), May 14, 1971.

Holmberg, Allan R., Nomads of the Long Bow, Washington, D.C., Smithsonian Institution, Institute of Social Anthropology, Publication No. 10, 1950.

Hrdlicka, Ales, W.H. Holmes, B. Willis and C.N. Fenner, Early Man in South America, Washington, D.C., Bulletin of the United States Bureau of American Ethnology, No. 52, 1912.

Hrdlicka, Ales, "Early Man in South America," Proceedings of the 18th International Congress of Americanists, London, 1913, pp. 1-23.

Jacobs, Wilbur R., "The Fatal Confrontation: Early Native-White Relations on the Frontiers of Australia, New Guinea, and America -- A Comparative Study," Pacific Historical Review, August, 1971, pp. 283-309.

Jochelson, W., Peoples of Asiatic Russia, New York: American Museum of Natural History, 1928.

Johnson, Frederick, "Central American Cultures, an Introduction," in Julian H. Steward, ed., Handbook of South American Indians, Washington, D.C., (Bulletin of the United States Bureau of American Ethnology, No. 143), 1948, VI, 51-68.

Kirchhoff, Paul, "Food-gathering Tribes of the Venezuelan Llanos," in Julian H. Steward, ed., Handbook of South American Indians, Washington, D.C., (Bulletin of the United States Bureau of American Ethnology, No. 143), 1948, IV, 445-468.

Krieger, Alex D., "Importance of the 'Gilmore Corridor' in Culture Contacts Between Middle America and the Eastern United States," Bulletin, of the Texas Archaeological and Palaeontological Society, Abilene, Texas, 1948, 19:155-178.

Kupferer, Harriet J., "Impotency and Power: A Cross-Cultural Comparison of the Effect of Alien Rule," in Marc J. Swarts, et. al. eds., Political Anthropology, Chicago, Aldine, 1966, pp. 61-71.

Lagassé, Jean-Henry, "Proceedings of the VII Congress of the Inter-American Indian Institute held in Brazilia, August 7th to 12th, 1972," Ottawa, unpublished manuscript, August, 1972, 42 pp.

Landes, Ruth, "Techniques of Dealing with Cross-Cultural Problems," Address to Resolving Conflicts -- a Cross-Cultural Approach, May 13, 1967, Kenora, Ontario, pp. 148-156.

Laraque, Marie-Helene, "Indigena: a center for information on the Native Peoples of the Americas," Berkeley, California, unpublished manuscript, ca 1973, 11 pp.

Lescaze, Lee (reporter), "Philippines re-enact U.S. West," Ottawa Citizen, August 29, 1972.

Levi-Strauss, Claude, "On Dual Organization in South American," American Indigena, 1944, 4:37-47.

Loehr, Max, "Das Rolltier in China," Ostrasiatische Zeitschrift, (Berlin), 1938, 24:137-42.

Lowie, Robert H., "The Heterogeneity of Marginal Cultures," in Sol Tax ed., Indian Tribes of Aboriginal America: Selected Papers of the 19th International Congress of Americanists, New York, Cooper Square 1967, pp. 1-7.

Lumholtz, Carl, Unknown Mexico, New York: Charles Scribner's Sons, 1902, 2 Vols.

Maidenberge, H.J. (reporter), "Peru to Teach Indians in Own Tongues," The New York Times, March 25, 1972.

Manuel, Chief George, "Report on the National Brotherhood President's Tour of New Zealand and Australia," Annual General Assembly, Regina, July, 1971.

Martens, Ethel G., Mexico and Canada: A Comparison of Two Programs where Indians are Trained in Community Development, Ottawa, Department of National Health and Welfare, November, 1966, 48 pp.

Métraux, A., The Native Tribes of Eastern Bolivia and Western Matto Grosso, Washington, D.C., (Bulletin of the United States Bureau of American Ethnology, No. 134), 1942.

Moorehead, Alan, The Fatal Impact: An Account of the Invasion of the South Pacific, 1767-1840, Hamish Hamilton, England, 1966, (Penguin Books, 1968), 283 pp.

Moser, Rupert R., The situation of the Adivasis of Chotanagpur and Santal Parganas, Bihar, India, Copenhagen, International Work Group for Indigenous People, April, 1972, 11 pp.

Muller, Michael, More facts and figures, aboriginal issues, Geneva, World Council of Churches, 1972, 37 pp.

Munzel, Mark, The Ache Indians: genocide in Paraguay, Copenhagen, International Work Group for Indigenous Affairs, 1973, 82 pp.

Murphy, Hammett, "Internview with Thomas Cramer, Lapps ombudsman," unpublished, Akwesasne Notes, January 10, 1973, 12 pp.

Nordenskiold, Erland, Comparative Ethnographical Studies, Goteborg: Elanders Boktryckerei Aktiebolag, 1924, Vol. 3.

Oosterwal, Gottfried, "A Cargo Cult in the Mamberamo Area," Ethnology, January, 1963, 2:1-14.

Parabirsing, B.J., "The situation of the Indian Communities in Surinam," Paper presented to the VII Conference of the Inter-American Indian Institute, Brazilia, August 7-12, 1972, 7 pp.

Persson, Lars, "What odds survival?," Weekend Magazine, (Montreal), May 31, 1969.

Pittock, A. Barrie, Aboriginal land rights, Copenhagen, International Work Group for Indigenous People, March, 1972, 24 pp.

Pittock, A. Barrie, "Aboriginal Land Rights," in Frank Stevens, ed., Racism: The Australian Experience: a Study of race prejudice in Australia, Artarmon, N.S.W., New Zealand Book Co., 1971-1972. Volume 2.

Price, A. Grenfell, White Settlers and Native People: An Historical Study of Racial Contacts between English-Speaking Whites and Aboriginal Peoples in the United States, Canada,

Australia, and New Zealand, Melbourne, Australia, Georgian House Pty, Ltd., 1950, 232 pp.

Raby, Stewart, "Native Peoples, Europeans and the land in Canada: comparative enthographic historical and political geography," Ottawa, unpublished manuscript, October, 1972, 21 pp.

Radin, Paul, Indians of South America, New York, Doubleday, Doran and Co., Inc., 1942.

Reeves, Christopher (reporter), "Aborigines won't waltz for Aussies," Vancouver Province, March 24, 1972.

Ross, Timothy (reporter), "South America's Indians in peril," Ottawa Citizen, July 26, 1972.

Seeman, Berthold, The Aborigines of the Isthmus of Panama, New York, Transactions of the American Ethnological Society, 1953, Vol. III.

Siverts, Henning, Tribal survival in the Alto Maranon: the Aguaruna Case, Copenhagen, International Work Group for Indigenous Affairs, December, 1972, 81 pp.

Spencer, B., and F. Gillen, The Native Tribes of Central Australia, London and New York, Macmillan Co., 1899.

Spier, Leslie, "The Population of Ancient America," Geographical Review, (New York), 1928, 68:641-60.

Spier, Leslie, Ancient Civilizations of Mexico and Central America, New York, (Handbook Series of the American Museum, No. 3), American Museum Press, 1928.

Tatz, Colin, "Aborigines: law and political development," The Australian Quarterly, December, 1970, 42:33-46.

Trumbull, Robert (reporter), "Court ruling against aborigines (Australia) causes gloom, anger among tribe," The Globe and Mail, (Toronto), July 21, 1971.

Varese, Stefano, The Forest Indians in the present political situation of Peru, Copenhagen, International Work Group for Indigenous People, August, 1972, 28 pp.

Webster, Paul (reporter), "Controversy in Australia: an explosive issue for aborigines," The Globe and Mail, (Toronto), February 5, 1972.

Whiteside, Don, "Native People: Comparative study of social development problems," Ottawa, unpublished proposal, Department of Secretary of State, July 24, 1972, 9 pp.

Whiteside, Don, "International aboriginal peoples' conference," Ottawa, National Indian Brotherhood, October 13, 1972, 17 pp.

Worsley, Peter, The Trumpet Shall Sound: A Study of 'Cargo' Cults in Melanesia, Great Britain, MacGibbon and Kee Ltd., 1957, (reprinted Paladin Press, 1970, 389 pp.).

Miscellaneous Reports by date of publication

Indigenous Peoples: Living and Working Conditions of Aboriginal Populations in Independent Countries, Geneva, International Labour Office, 1953, 628 pp.

Protection and Integration of Indigenous and Other Tribal and Semi-Tribal Populations in Independent Countries, Geneva, International Labour Office, 1956, 58 pp.

Living and Working Conditions of Indigenous Populations in Independent Countries, Geneva, International Labour Office, 1956, Report 8(2), 174 pp.

Protection and Integration of Indigenous and Other Tribal and Semi-Tribal Populations in Independent Countries, International Labour Office, 1957, Report 6(2), 82 pp.

"Some Notes on the National Indian Institute of Mexico," (translated from Realidades Y Proyectos 16 Anos De Trabajo), Achievements and Projects, 16 Years of Work, National Indian Institute, Mexico, 1964, 19 pp.

"Final Act of the Fifth Inter-American Indian Conference," Quito, Ecuador, Inter-American Indian Institute, Mexico, 1965, 49 pp.

"Brazil's Death Indians: The Killing of an Unwanted Race," The Warpath, (San Francisco), 1970, Vol. 2, No. 2, pp. 6-7.

"Chrétien says Maori example for Indians," The Globe and Mail, (Toronto), April 11, 1971.

"Aboriginal Issues: Racism in Australia," Geneva, World Council of Churches, 1971, 29 pp.

"Black power movement appears among Australia's aborigines," The Globe and Mail, (Toronto), January 31, 1972.

"N.Z. Ahead of Canada in race ties," Ottawa Citizen, March 9, 1972.

"An Indian sees Africa and returns in despair," (George Manuel), Ottawa Citizen, March 11, 1972.

"Aboriginal, Indian beefs similar?," (Australia), Montreal Star, April 3, 1972.

"New Action on aborigines, says Tory series lecturer," (Australia), Edmonton Journal, May 4, 1972.

"South America: Columbia Trial Reveals Life 'Everyone Kills Indians' on Plains," Akwesasne Notes, (Rooseveltown, N.Y.), Summer, 1972.

"White Australians fret at link-up of aborigines with Chinese," Akwesasne Notes, (Rooseveltown, N.Y.), Summer, 1972, p. 27.

"What is happening to Brazil's Indians?," _Awake_ (Jehovah's Witnesses), June 8, 1972, pp. 21-23.

"Australia Senate Gets an Aborigine: He will be first of race in country's parliament," _The New York Times_, June 13, 1971.

"Indian girl, baby killed by 7 hunters in Brazil," _The Globe and Mail_, (Toronto), June 28, 1972.

"Massacre of Indians uncovered in Brazil," _The Toronto Star_, June 28, 1972.

"Told not wrong to kill Indians, 7 are acquitted," _The Globe and Mail_, (Toronto), June 29, 1972.

"Police clash with aborigines in Canberra," _The Globe and Mail_, (Toronto), July 24, 1972.

"Indian giants flee whites in Brazil," _Toronto Daily Star_, July 26, 1972.

"Shy giants: Brazil Indians like coloured ribbons but steer clear of white man," _The Globe and Mail_, (Toronto), August 5, 1972.

"Agenda," International Congress of Americanists, Rome, September 3-10, 1972.

"Indians of Brazil," _Our Native Land_, (Canadian Broadcasting Corporation), November, 1972.

"More Facts and Figures, Aboriginal Issues: Racism in Australia," Geneva, World Council of Churches, 1972, 37 pp.

PRINCIPLE AUTHOR INDEX

Alphabetically and by date of Article
(* denotes author of aboriginal descent)

Aalborg, Gordon (reporter)
52-Metis get 4,150 acres in aboriginal claims

Abbott, Frederick H.
83-The administration of Indian affairs in Canada

Abel, Annie Heloise
141-The American Indian as slaveholder and secessionist
141-The American Indian as participant in the Civil War

Aberle, David F.
42-The peyote religion among the Navaho

Ablon, Joan
179-Relocated American Indians in San Francisco
179-Relocated American Indians in San Francisco

Abrahamson, G.
156-Tuktoyaktuk-Cape Parry: an area economic survey.

Abu-Laban, Baha
188-In-group orientation and self-conceptions
188-The impact of ethnicity and occupational background

Adair, John and Evon Z. Vogt
168-Navaho and Zuni veterans, culture change

*Adams, Howard J.
188-The education of Canadians, 1800-1867
125-A better deal for the Indians
188-Opening remarks and comments, education conference
125-The Cree as a colonial people
208-Brief to the Senate Committee on Poverty
125-Three views of Canada's third world people
125-Red power: an interview with Howard Adams
125-Its inevitable: Indians and Metis will use violence
188-The outsiders: an educational survey

Adams, Ian
100-The Indians: an abandoned and dispossessed people
188-Why did Charlie Wenjack die?
217-Out of jail and into another sort of problem

Adams, Richard N.
228-Ethnohistoric research methods

Aginsky, Burt W.
16-Central Sierra
100-The interaction of ethnic groups

*Ahenakew, Chief David and Rodney Soonias
204-Report to Standing Committee of Indian Affairs and
Northern Development

*Ahenakew, Edward
141-An opinion of the Frog Lake massacre

*Akweks, Aren (Ray Fadden)
141-Six Nation Iroquois Confederacy Record (World Ward II)

Alexander, Hartley Burr
    35-The world's rim

Allan, D. J.
    156-Indian land problems in Canada

Allan, Iris
    1-White Sioux, Major Walsh of the Mounted Police

Allan, Victor
    1-The Eskimo and the Indian today

Alvord, Clarence Walworth
    52-The genesis of the Proclamation of 1763

Ames, David W. and Burton R. Fisher
    64-The Menominee termination crisis

*Anderson, Anne (Namoya Ayiman)
    188-Let's learn Cree

Anderson, Francis Garfield
    100-Personal contact affecting city children's attitudes

Anderson, James G. and Dwight Safar
    188-Community perceptions of equal opportunities

Andras, Robert K.
    1-Address, Citizenship Seminar
    208-Notes for a philosophy of social change

Andres, G. and J. Morissett
    156-Rae-Lac La Marte: an area economic survey

Andrews, J. Eldon
    1-Toward a better understanding of the Canadian Indian

Angers, Jean-Claude
    53-Federal, provincial statutes, treaty rights, hunting,
       fishing

Angle, Jerry
    93-Federal, state and tribal jurisdiction in Arizona

Anglin, Perry (reporter)
    125-They organized the march that killed Kenora's apathy

Angule, Jaime De
    47-Religious feeling in a primitive tribe

Annett, William S.
    141-Massacre, Frog Lake

Arbess, Saul E.
    168-Eskimo co-operative at George River, Quebec

Arcand, Bernard
    228-Urgent situation, Cuiva Indians of Columbia

Armillas, Pedro
    1-Program of the history of American Indians

Armstrong, O. K.
    208-Lets give the Indians back the country

Armstrong, Terence
    228-Administration of northern peoples: the U.S.S.R.

Armstrong, Virginia Irving
    125-American history through voices of the Indians

Arnold, A. J.
    100-Human rights and social welfare experience

Arnold, Ross R.
    141-Indian Wars of Idaho

Asimi, A. D.
    179-The urban setting

Assheton-Smith, Marilyn I., and W. Bruce Handley
    125-The Lac La Biche native sit-in

*Atimoyoo, Smith
    205-An Indian way of looking at life

Atwell, Phyllis Harryette
    179-Kinship, migration among Calgarians of Indian origin

Austin, Mary
    35-One Smoke stories

Avali-Oliver, Philip B.
    53-Rights of minorities within Canada

Axtell, James
    93-The white Indians of colonial America

Bachop, Bill (reporter)
    125-Japanese support Indians

Bachrach, William B.
    125-An assault on the sixties

*Bacon, Georges
    129-Presentation

Baetz, Reuben
    1-We must avoid mere tokenism

Baich, Ben V. and James Whitford
    208-Hand-clearing operations at Grand Rapids, Manitoba

Bailey, Alfred Goldsworthy
    83-Indian problem in early Canada
    16-Conflict, european and eastern Algonkian cultures

Bailey, L. R.
141-Indian slave trade in the southwest

Baillie, Pierre
1-Etude Indiens et des Esquimaux au Canada

Baird, Irene
1-The Eskimos in Canada

Baker, Marie
188-School program and native children

Baker, W. B.
144-Application, community development, northern Saskatchewan

Baldwin, Gordon C.
32-Games of the American Indian

Balikci, Asen
168-Acculturative trends, the eastern Canadian Eskimos
168-Vunta Kutchin social change, Old Crow, Yukon Territory
32-Bad friends

Ball, Nelson E.
144-Profile of Indian community, Burnt Church
144-Burnt Church, a Canadian Indian community

Balsam, Louis
208-Economic problems of the Indians in the United States

Bandeira de Mello, General Oscar Jeponimo
228-Indian policy of Brazil

Baptie, Sue
83-Edgar Dewdney

Baraca, Bishop
1-Customs and manners of the Indians

Barbarash, John and Johnny Yesno
119-Federation of Saskatchewan Indians
217-Legal rights of Indians

Barbeau, Charles Marius
42-Huron-Wyandot mythology
16-Iroquoian clans and phratries
168-Our Indians-their disappearance
42-The Hydra reborn in the new world
36-Totem poles
46-Indian days on the western prarie
42-Medicine-men on the north Pacific coast

Barber, Bernard
47-Acculturation and messianic movements

Barber, Lloyd
188-University of Saskatchewan

Barnes, Peter
    156-Rational land use, unfreezing Alaska

Barnett, Homer G.
    16-Gulf of Georgia Salish
    16-The coast Salish of Canada
    16-Oregon coast Indians

Barnett, M. L. and D. A. Baerreis
    168-Problems in the changing status of American Indians

Barney, Ralph, A.
    64-Legal problems under Indian Claims Commission Act

Barnouw, Victor
    168-Acculturation, personality among the Wisconsin Chippewa

Barrett, S. M. ed.
    38-Geronimo: his own story

Bartolome, Miguel Alberto et. al.
    228-Declaration of Barbados

Basso, Keith H.
    16-The Cibecue Apache
    16-Fort Norman Slave, folk taxonomies and cultural rules

Batan, Jorge
    179-Migrant socio-economic difference, Latin America cities

Battle, Robert F.
    83-Review of Indian affairs policies and new directions
    53-Address, legal rights of Indians

Bauer, George W. (reporter)
    156-James Bay: last massacre of Indian rights

Bauman, Gwelda, et.al.
    16-Metis of Saskatchewan

Bayard, Charles Judah
    93-Development of public land policy, 1783-1820

*Bear Robe, Andrew
    179-Indian urbanization
    184-Tour of Canadian Native Friendship Centres
    185-Friendship Centres in Canada

Beattie, Jessie Louis
    53-The split in the sky: chronicle of the Six Nations

Beatty, Willard W.
    188-Indian education in the United States
    168-The goal of Indian assimilation

Beaty, Robert E.
    93-Study of B.I.A. timber management, Quinault Reservation

*Beaulieu, Isaac
    179-Urbanizing the Indian
    118-Organizational aspects of the Manitoba Indians

Bedford, C. M.
    100-The rights of Indian people

Bee, Robert L.
    168-Changes in Yuma social organization

*Belcourt, A. (Tony) E.
    100-Address, Canadian Conference on Social Welfare

Bell, Dennis (reporter)
    39-William Wuttunee, friend or foe of the Indians
    39-Harold Cardinal, wild radical or new messiah
    168-Same class, equal chance?
    129-Spirit of red power in Canada (NARP)

Bell, G. E.
    83-Notes, presentation of Red Paper to the Prime Minister

*Benedict, Ernest
    125-Information, the Jay Treaty and Customs
    125-Indians and a treaty
    53-Brief, Joint Committee on the Constitution

Benedict, Ruth Fulton
    42-The concept of the guardian spirit in North America

Bennett, John W. and Niels Braroe
    168-Northern plainsmen

Bennett, Lerone Jr.
    126-Red and black, Indians and Africans

Bennett, Peter H.
    83-Unacceptable words, phrases, in the Indian context

Bennett, Robert L.
    156-Building Indian economies, land settlement funds
    156-Problems, prospects, developing Indian communities

Bennett, Wendell C. and Robert M. Zingg
    228-The Tarahumara

Berger, Edward B.
    156-Mineral interest-potential, economic advancement

Bergeron, Léandre
    83-The history of Quebec, a patriot's handbook

Berkhofer, Robert F. Jr.
    48-Protestant missions, American Indian response 1787-1862
    48-Protestants, pagans and sequences
    93-Comments

Berlin, Heinrich
    29-El Indigena frente al estado

Bongartz, Roy (Reporter)
    126-The new Indian

Bonnycastle, R. H. G.
    156-The role of the trader in Indian Affairs

Booz, Allen
    208-Study of health services for Canadian Indians

Borovoy, A. Alan
    208-Indian poverty in Canada

Boswell, Marion Joan
    42-State, church, and the Canadian Indian (in process)

Botelho de Magalhaes, Amilcar A.
    29-Indios Do Brazil

Boudreault, Mireille et.al.
    220-Bibliographie sommaire sur la radissonie

Bouknight, Marie et.al.
    220-Guide to records in the Military Archives

Bourne, L. S.
    156-Yellowknife, N.W.T., a study of its economy

Bowker, Mabel Edna
    93-The Indian policy of the United States, 1789-1841

Bowker, W. F.
    76-The Canadian Bill of Rights, irreconsiable conflict

Bowman, Norman
    189-Progress in Navajo education

Bowsfield, Hartwell, ed.
    100-Louis Riel, rebel or victim of politics and prejudice

Boyd, Eric E.
    1-Indian people and the next one hundred years

Braddock, John
    53-Indian reserves, how long will they last

Bradshaw, Thecla
    208-Why did Rita kill her sister?
    189-Here we are...where do we go? Indian child and education

Brand, Donald D.
    29-The present Indian population of the Americas

Brant, C. S.
    141-History of the great massacre of the Sioux

Brant, Charles Sanford
    189-Conditions, consequences, native education in the Arctic
    17-Life of a Kiowa Apache Indian

*Brant, Marlene J.
   208-Parental neglect in Indian families

Braroe, Niels Winther
   100-Reciprocal exploitation, Indian-White community

Brasser, T.
   144-Leadership, northeastern Algonkians of Canada

Braun, Gordon A.
   179-Determinants of labour mobility, Indians and Metis

Brennan, L. A.
   1-An almanac of North American prehistory

Brigden, Beatrice
   220-Bibliography of non-fiction books

Briggs, Jean L.
   208-Utkuhikhalingmiut Eskimo emotional expression
   168-Kapluna daughter: living with Eskimos

Bright, David
   1-Canada remiss in duty to these Indians

Brimlow, George Francis
   141-The Bannock Indian War of 1878

Brock, Philip K.
   208-Patterns of illegitimacy, Indian reserve 1860-1960

Brody, Hugh
   179-Indians on skid row

Brohough, Gustave O.
   94-Sioux and Chippewa half-breed script, Minnesota

Brookbank, C. Roy
   100-The search for justice

Brophy, William A. et.al.
   94-Policies which impede Indian assimilation

Brouillard, Claude F.
   185-Friendship Centres

Brown, Dee Alexander
   141-Showdown at Little Big Horn
   141-Bury my heart at Wounded Knee

Brown, Jennifer
   42-Cure and feeding of Windigos, a critique

Brown, Joseph Epes
   42-Spiritual legacy of the American Indian

Brownie, P. W.
   17-Story of Labrador, the Montagnais Indians

246

*Cardinal, Harold
    126-The Unjust society
    126-Canadian Indians and the federal government
    101-Address, Indian-Eskimo Association of Canada
    120-Address, Alberta All Chiefs' Conference

Carney, R. J. and W. O. Ferguson
    189-Annotated bibliography, sociology of Eskimo education

Carpenter, E. S.
    32-Timeless present in mythology of Akvalik Eskimos

Carpenter, Mary
    189-Address, conference on Indian education

Carr, D. William and Associates
    157-The Yukon economy, its potential for growth

Carse, M. R.
    208-Americans, with reservations

Carter, E. Russell
    179-Rapid City, South Dakota

Caso, Alfonso
    29-Definicion del Indio y lo Indio

Casselman, E.
    209-Public health nursing service for Indians

Castaneda, Carlo
    42-Teachings of Don Juan, a Yaqui way of knowledge
    42-Further conversations with Don Juan
    42-A separate reality, further conversations with Don Juan

*Castellano, Marlene
    126-Vocation or identity, the dilemma of Indian youth
    144-Out of paternalism and into partnership

Castillo-Cardenas, Gonzalos
    228-Indian struggle for freedom in Columbia

Catlin, George
    35-Manners, customs, conditions of North American Indian
    2-North American Indians

Cawley, Janet (reporter)
    126-Kahn-Tineta Horn, she's a racist and proud of it

Chafe, Wallace L
    29-Estimates regarding speakers of Indian languages
    29-Estimates regarding speakers of Indian languages

Chalmers, J. W.
    189-A new deal in Indian education

Chance, Norman A.
    169-Culture change and integration, an Eskimo example
    209-Patterns of pyschopathology, Alaskan Eskimo society
    169-Integration, Eskimo and the Cree
    83-Changing role, government, North Alaskan Eskimo
    209-Modernization and mental health
    169-Acculturation, self-identification personality adjustment
    17-The Eskimo of north Alaska
    169-Conflict in culture, developmental change, the Cree
    169-Developmental change among the Cree of Quebec

Chapin, Miriam
    101-Our changing Indians

Chapman, Harold H.
    76-Band membership

Chapman, Laura A.
    76-Some social implications of the Lavell case

*Charley, Robert
    157-Response of native people to Mr. Chretien's address

Chatain, Dennis
    157-Total community approach, socio-economic development

Cheechoo, Margaret
    101-White squaw

Childerhose, R. J. and Peter Ferguson (reporters)
    101-For the first Canadians, second-class citizenship

Chretien, Hon. Jean
    209-Homemakers and the Indian community
    84-Indian policy, statement of the Government of Canada
    84-Statement, government of Canada on Indian policy
    84-Why an old Indian pattern was broken
    84-Address at Regina
    84-Indian policy, where does it stand?
    84-From the Minister of Indian Affairs
    84-Address, Canadian Institute of Forestry
    84-Address, Native Women's Society of British Columbia
    84-Opening statement, Standing Committee on Indian Affairs
    53-Brief, Joint Committee on the Constitution
    157-Pipeline guidelines
    157-Northern development for northerners

Clairmont, Donald Hayden
    209-Drinking behaviour, Eskimos and Indians, Aklavik area
    209-Deviance, Indians and Eskimos Aklavik, N.W.T.

Clark, Ella Elizabeth
    35-Indian legends of Canada

Clark, George Frederick
    17-Someone before us, our Maritime Indians

Clarkin, P. C.
    189-The teacher of Indian pupils (some points to consider)

Clemons, Mrs. A. et.al.
    209-Brief to the status of women inquiry

Clifton, James A.
    17-The Kansas Prairie Potawatomi
    169-Factional conflict and the Indian community

Clipsman, Muriel
    118-The Native Brotherhood Society, Regina

*Clutesi, George
    328-Potlach

Cobb, John C.
    189-Emotional performance of Indian students

Codere, Helen
    42-Swaixwe myth of the middle Fraser River
    17-Harrison Lake physical type

Coelho, G. V.
    189-Study of Indian students' perceptions

Cohen, Felix S.
    94-Indian rights and the federal courts
    64-Handbook of federal Indian law
    94-Spanish origin of Indian rights
    94-Indian claims
    94-Indians are citizens
    94-Original Indian title
    94-Erosion of Indian rights
    126-Americanizing the White man

Cohen, Joan (reporter)
    101-Why our Indians are frustrated

Cohen, R.
    144-Communities, MacKenzie-Slave Lake region, Canada

Cohen, Warren, H. and Philip J. Mause
    2-The Indian: the forgotten American

Colley, Louise
    144-Community recreation on Christian Island, Ontario

Collier, Donald
    43-Conjuring among the Kiowa

Collier, John
    126-Indians come alive, new hope for Native Americans
    94-Policies and problems in the United States
    2-Indians of the Americas: the long hope
    95-The Indian Bureau and self-government
    127-Indian takeaway
    169-Comments on pluralism, American Indian
    95-Divergent views on pluralism, American Indian
    127-Back to dishonour

Collier, Peter (reporter)
    127-The red man's burden
    127-Salmon fishing, Indians vs. State of Washington

Collins, Douglas (reporter)
    101-A win for the Indians

Commes, Madison, L.
    190-Doorway toward light; Navajo education program
    189-Implications of achievement level, Indian students

Con, Ronald J.
    84-Canadian immigrants, Indians and government policy

Conde, Le Roy
    190-An experiment in second-language instruction

*Conklin, Paul
    205-Good day at Rough Rock

Conn, Hugh R.
    53-Treaties related to wildlife and fishery resources
    53-Treaties and the game and fishery laws: a summary
    53-Hunting, fishing rights - application of Royal Proclamation
    54-Integrity, territory the Province of Quebec

Connelly, Bob
    190-What's lacking in the integration kit

Connor, Desmond
    144-Workshop for Manitoba Metis Federation

Cooke, Katherine B.
    2-Contemporary Indians of Canada: notes on Vol.2.

Cooper, Ardyth
    220-List of theses that deal with Indian people

Cooper, J. M.
    43-Shaking Tent Rite, plains and forest Algonquins
    228-Area, temporal aspects, aboriginal South American culture

Cooper, John M.
    2-Land tenure, Indians of eastern and northern North America

Cooper, P. F. Jr.
    157-The Mackenzie Delta-technology

Coppens, Walter
    228-Anatomy of a land invasion scheme, Venezuela

*Corbiere, Jeanette and *Wilfred Pelletier
    144-Canada's Indians, the Company of Young Canadians

Cork, Ella
    54-Dilemmas inherited, Iroquois of Grand River Reserve

Corkran, David H.
    18-Cherokee frontier; conflict, survival 1740-1762
    18-Creek frontier, 1540-1783

Corrigan Samuel W.
    46-Plains Indian powow: cultural integration

Costo, Rupert ed.
    101-Textbooks and the American Indian

Cote, Francois (reporter)
    101-Les griefs des Indiens de la region de Sept-Iles

Coulter, E. J.
    185-Indians on the move - friendship centres

Coulter, John
    141-Trial of Louis Riel

Coulter, Robert T.
    95-Federal law, Indian tribal law: rights to civil counsel

*Courchene, Chief Dave
    127-Address of welcome to H.M. Queen Elizabeth II
    145-It takes an Indian to help an Indian
    54-Address, Treaty Centennial Commemorations,
    54-Address, St. James Collegiate
    84-Remarks at the presentation of 'Citizens Plus'

Covarrubias, M.
    36-Eagle, jaguar, serpent, Indian art of the Americas

Cowan, Edward (reporter)
    157-Good-doing won't replace traplines

Cowell, Mrs. V.
    190-Kindergarten in Moosonee

Cox, Bruce
    157-Environmental disturbrances, northern peoples' land

Craig, Barrie (reporter)
    127-Indian protest of housing, schools, may spread

*Craig, G. William
    205-Progress Report, Native North American Studies

Crawford, Richard C. and Charles E. South
    220-Guide, records, Indian-white relations

Crawley, M.
    209-Welfare Needs, Services, in Northern Saskatchewan

Crerar, Hon. Thomas Alexander
    2-Rehabilitation of our Indian wards
    2-Indians of Canada

Creswell, Dean (reporter)
    101-Frustration: trial in a foreign language

Dallyn, Frederick John Gallinger and Frazer George Earle
    102-Study of attitudes towards Indians, Selkirk, Manitoba
    102-Attitudes towards Indians, Portage La Prairie, Manitoba
    102-Attitudes towards Indians, The Pas, Manitoba

Daly, D.
    2-Report on the affairs of the Indians in Canada

Damas, David
    145-Diversity in White-Eskimo leadership interaction

*Daniels, Christine and Ron Christiansen
    217-Many laws

Davis, Arthur Kent, eds.
    2-A Northern dilemma: reference papers, Volume I
    2-A Northern dilemma: reference papers, Volume II
    2-Canadian Confrontations (selected speeches and papers)
    2-Toward mainstream
    180-Edging into mainstream: urban Indians in Saskatchewan
    180-Urban Indians in western Canada

Davis, E. N. (reporter)
    102-Neglect charged on Indian reserve

Davis, Shelton
    229-Custer is alive and he lives in Brazil

Dawber, Mark A.
    48-Protestant missions, Indians in United States

Debo, Angie Elbertha
    18-Rise and fall of the Choctaw Republic
    127-The road to disappearance

De Cocq, Gustave
    145-Northeast Edmonton youth survey

De Goeje, C. H.
    229-Physical, magic and moral worlds of Guiana Indians

*Deiter, Chief Walter, and *Walter Currie
    209-Presentation, Senate Committee on Poverty

DeLaguna, Frederica, ed.
    220-Selected papers, The American Anthropologist, 1888-1920

*Delisle, Chief Andrew Tanahokate
    102-Human rights and the Indian
    3-The Canadian Indian - 1968
    115-Letter to Harold Cardinal
    54-Brief on Indians of Quebec territorial rights

*Deloria, Vine Jr.
    127-Custer died for your sins: an Indian manifesto
    127-Custer died for your sins.
    127-We talk you listen: new tribes, new turf
    127-This country was a lot better off when Indians ran it
    52-Of utmost good faith: American Indian vs. Gov't of U.S.A.

Dorion, Henri
   220-Documentation

Dorner, Peter P.
   158-Economic position of the American Indians

Dorsey, George Amos
   43-Dwamish Indian spirit boat and its use

Dosman, Edgar Joseph
   180-Urban dimension of the Indian problem in Canada

Dostal, Walter, ed.
   229-Situation of the Indians in South America

*Doucette, Noel
   54-Brief,Joint Committee on the Constitution

Douglas, Hon. Thomas C
   119-Record, establishment of Indian unity, Saskatchewan

Dowling, John H.
   180-A rural Indian community in an urban setting
   169-Evolution of funerary customs in Oneida society

Downey, Fairfax
   142-Indian fighting army
   142-General Crook, Indian fighter
   142-Indian wars of the U.S. Army

*Dozier, Edward P.
   127-Resistance, acculturation, assimilation, Indian Pueblo
   170-Integration of Americans of Indian descent
   95-Address, American Indian Chicago Conference,
   209-Problem drinking among American Indians

Drapeau, Claude and Victor Piche
   29-Internal migration, Indian population of James Bay

Drimmer, Frederick, ed.
   142-Scalps and tomahawks, narratives of Indian captivity

Driver, Harold Edson
   18-Culture element distributions, Southern California
   32-Comparative studies of North American Indians
   3-Indians of North America

Drucker, Philip
   145-Rank, wealth, kinship in northwest Coast Society
   114-Native Brotherhoods: modern organizations

Dubienski, Ian V. and Stephen Skelly
   217-Analysis of arrests, 1969, Winnipeg

Du Bois, Cora
   43-The 1870 ghost dance

Ducheneaux, Franklyn
   95-Indian legislation

257

Duesenberry, Verne
    43-Montana Cree: a study in religious persistence

Duff, Wilson
    18-Histories, territories, laws of the Kitwancool
    170-Indian history of British Columbia, Vol. 1

Dufour, Joseph (reporter)
    127-The Ontario Indian - low man on totem pole

Du Mars, Charles T.
    64-Indictment under the major crimes act

Dumond, D. E.
    18-Prehistory of Na-Dene, movements among nomadic hunters

Dumont, Robert V. Jr. and Murray L. Wax
    190-Cherokee school society, the intercultural classroom

Dundes, Alan
    35-Washington Irving's version, Seminole origin of races

Dunn, Marty
    39-Red on White, the biography of Duke Redbird

*Dunn, Willie
    217-Northern justice

Dunne, Mrs. N. R.
    158-Economic possibilities for native communities

Dunning, Robert William
    158-Some implications of economic change in Ojibwa
    170-Social - economic change among northern Ojibwa
    102-Ethnic relations the marginal man in Canada
    209-Problems, reserve Indians, subsidy economy
    84-Aspects, governmental Indian policy, administration
    145-Problems, reserve Indian Communities:
    95-Indian Affairs, book reviews

Dunphy, Pat
    145-Devlopments, Roseau River, Buffalo Point Reserves

Dunstun, William
    3-Canadian Indians today

Duran, James A. Jr.
    55-Canisius Professor, St. Regis Indians are right
    127-Why Canadian Indians demonstrate
    85-Indian policy: a reply to the Minister

Duran, James A. Jr., *Walter Currie, *Walter P. Deiter, Douglas
Sanders, Nancy O. Lurie and William Fox
    55-Panel discussion, Canadian Indian treaties, aboriginal
        rights and U.S. Indian land settlements

Dyck, Noel Evan
    85-Administration of Indian aid in the N.W.T.

Dyk, Walter
    38-Son of Old Man Hat

Eames, Edwin and Judith Goode
    209-On Lewis' Culture of Poverty concept

Earle, Fraser George
    3-You are an Indian

*Early, Mary Two Axe
    77-Injustices, Indian women married to non-Indians

Easton, Robert
    32-Humor of the American Indian

Ebihara, May M. and Gail Margaret Kelly
    180-Survey of the Indian population of Portland, Oregon

Eddy, D. H.
    210-How we scalp the Indians

Edgerton, R. B.
    64-Menominee termination, observations, end of a tribe

Edmonds, J. K. (reporter)
    102-Our fast-growing Indian problem

Edmonson, Munro S.
    85-Status terminology, social structure, North American
        Indians

Edwards, Everett Eugene and Wayne D. Rasmussen
    220-Bibliography, agriculture of the American Indians

Edwards, Newton
    158-Economic development of Indian Reserves

Eggan, Dorothy
    190-Instruction, affect, Hopi cultural continuity

Eggan, Fred
    3-Social anthropology of North American tribes
    170-American Indian: perspectives for study of social change

Eicher, Carl K
    158-Approach, income improvement, Rosebud Reservation

Eiseley, Loren C
    3-Review: land tenure in the Northeast
    170-Paleo Indians, survival and diffusion

Elkin, Frederick
    102-Employment of visible minority groups in mass media

Elliott, Jean Leonard ed.
    3-Minority Canadians: native peoples

Elliott, John G.
    190-Comparative study, Indian, non-Indian youth, education

Embree, Edwin R.
    3-Indians of the Americas

Embree, John F.
    95-The Indian Bureau and self-government.
    95-Rejoiner to Dr. Collier's remarks.

Embry, Carlos, B.
    128-America's Concentration Camps.

Emmitt, Robert
    142-The last war trial

Erickson, Gerald
    210-Mental health needs, resources northern community.

Erickson, Vincent et.al.
    220-Malecite teaching materials project

Ericson, Robert and D. Rebecca Snow
    3-The Indian battle for self-determination

Erikson, Erik H.
    145-Observations on Sioux education
    145-Fisherman along a salmon river
    145-Hunters across the prairie.

Erskine, J. S.
    3-The Indian dilemma

Ervin, Alexander M
    170-New northern townsmen in Inuvik

Esche, Sandra
    190-Teaching in an elemental land - northern Labrador

Essene, Frank
    18-Culture element distributions, Round Valley

Euler, Robert C. and Henry F. Dobyns
    158-Ethnic group land rights in the modern state

Evans, Adye Bel et.al.
    221-Resource frontier communities, bibliography

Evans, Enos
    18-The Cree Indians

Evans, Jon
    158-Ungava Bay: an area economic survey

Ewans, Marjorie
    185-Fellowship centres for urban Canadian Indian

Ewers, John Canfield
    170-The horse in Blackfoot culture
    37-Plains Indian painting
    18-The Blackfeet, raiders on the northwestern plains
    37-Folk art in the fur trade of the upper Missouri

Ewing, A. F., J. M. Douglas and E. G. Braithwaite
   55-Commission, conditions of half-breed population

Fairclough, Hon. Ellen L.
   85-A review of Indian Affairs

Fairfield, Roy P.
   102-Indignation keeps us warm

Fairholm, Cy I.
   95-U.S. termination policy, reports and documents

Fall, Thomas
   170-The ordeal of Running Standing.

Fannin, Hon. Paul J.
   190-Indian education - test case for democracy

Fantini, Mario D. and Gerald Weinstein
   190-Taking advantage of the disadvantaged

Farb, Peter
   128-The American Indian: a portrait in limbo
   3-Man's rise to civilization, Indians of North America

*Favel, Fred
   128-Wabasca--a lesson in politics.

Favreau, Hon. Guy
   85-Address, Third Annual Conference of National Indian Council

Feit, Harvey and José Mailhot
   18-James Bay Region (Quebec) bibliography

Fenton, William N.
   46-Masked Medicine Societies of the Iroquois
   47-Museum and field studies of Iroquois masks
   47-Towanda Longhouse ceremonies
   18-Symposium on local diversity in Iroquois culture
   18-Development of Iroquois social structure
   47-The Iroquois eagle dance
   3-American Indian and white relations to 1830

Ferguson, Frances Northend
   210-Navaho drinking: some tentative hypotheses
   210-A treatment program for Navaho alcoholics

Ferguson, Hattie Mrs.
   190-Problems and its phases, education

Ferguson, Jack D.
   158-Human ecology, a social-economic change, Tuktoyaktuk

Ferguson, John
   102-Exploitation, discrimination, Alberta beet fields

Fey, Harold Edward and *D'Arcy McNickle
   3-Indians, other Americans, two ways of life meet

Forer, Mort
    19-The Humback

Forest, Deborah A
    210-Analysis, 73 female Metis prostitutes

Forget, A. E.
    85-Circular re: marriage of girls from residential schools

Forsyth, Thomas
    4-French, British and Spanish methods of treating Indians

Foster, Ashley
    191-Predispositions, academic success, Alaska native people

Foster, Douglas R.
    191-Canadian Indian, a study of education

Foster, Laurence
    128-Indian-Negro relationships in the southwest

Fotheringham, Allan
    40-Dan George's last stand.

Fowler, W. S.
    4-Ten Thousand Years in America

*Francis, Chief Anthony
    55-Brief Joint Committee on the Constitution

Fransen, Jack Jacob
    158-Employment, economic position, Indians in Toronto

Frantz, Charles
    180-Urban migration and adjustment American Indians, since
        1940

Fraser, William Bernard
    19-The Alberta Indian

Frazer, Robin
    32-Indian Culture

Freeborn, Elizabeth D.
    19-The Kutenai

Freedman, Jan
    170-Review of Changes, Indians Metis, Northern Saskatchewan
    180-Examination of services, native people, Toronto, Vancouver

Freeman, John Leiper, Jr.
    95-New deal for Indians, study of bureau-committee relations

Freeman, Milton R.
    29-Female infanticide among the Netsilik Eskimo

Freestone, A.
    210-Environmental sanitation, Indian reserves

Freilich, Morris
    128-Cultural persistence among the modern Iroquois
    19-Scientific possibilities in Iroquoian studies

French, Cecil L.
    32-Social Class, motivation, Metis, Indians, whites, Alberta
    191-Social Class and motivation

Fried, Jacob
    145-White-dominant settlements, Northwest Territories

Friedl, Ernestine M.
    128-Attempt at directed culture change, Chippewa leadership

Frisch, Jack A.
    170-Conflict, confrontation, social change, St. Regis Reserve

Frum, Barbara
    103-Nos Indiens depossedes
    180-Canadian Indians, 1968. how Ottawa (and we) slept.

Fry, Alan
    210-How a people die

Fuerst, René
    229-Problems and policy, Brazilian Amazon Region

Fuller, O. Torie
    229-Proposal, study American and Canadian Indian policies
    229-Indigenous populations

Fulton, E. David
    85-White paper policy, Indian Claims Commission

Gaddes, W. H., Audrey McKenzie, and Roger Barnsley
    191-Psychometric intelligence and spatial imagery

Gagne, Raymond C.
    32-Spatial concepts in the Eskimo language
    128-Amerindian cultural survival: a dilemma

Gaillard, Frye
    128-North Carolina's Lumbees, Haliwas, possible coalition

Gallaher, Ruth A.
    95-Indian agent in the U.S. before 1850

Gambill, Jerry T.
    221-Paperback bibliography, North American Indians
    205-North American Indian Travelling College
    145-Company of Young Canadians and Indians of Canada
    128-Indians, white men and I.
    129-How democracy came to St. Regis
    103-How students meet the North American Indians
    128-The Thunder Water Movement
    55-Controversy: hunting, fishing rights, Indians, of Ontario
    103-On the art of stealing human rights
    85-Sitting Bull: Canada's Indian hero

Garber, Malcolm
    191-Ethnicity, measures of educability differences

*Garner, Bea Medicine
    43-Use of magic Among the Stoney Indians

Garthson, Robert J. W.
    43-Attempted de-Indianization, Protestant missionary
        cooperation

Gazan, Albert
    103-Social conflict and problems of acculturation

Gearing, Fred
    145-Today's Mesquakies

Geddie, Nancy
    205-Letter to National Indian Brotherhood

Geldart, Mrs. Penny
    221-Accession list, Research and Documentation Library

*George, Chief Dan
    129-Confederation lament
    129-My very dear friends
    103-Thoughts by Chief Dan George
    129-Our sad winter has passed

Gerin, D.
    19-The Hurons of Lorette

Getty, Harry Thomas
    103-Interethnic relationships in Tuscon
    158-San Carlos Apache cattle industry

Ghobashy, Omar Z.
    55-Caughnawaga Indians and the St. Lawrence Seaway

Gibson, Gayll and *Don Whiteside
    145-Linkages between action groups in the community
    221-Bibliography: Metis and Non-Status Indians

Giddings, James Louis
    19-Ancient men of the Arctic

Gifford, E. W.
    19-Cultural element distributions - Apache-Pueblo

Gilbert, William H. Jr.
    129-The Cherokees of North Carolina

*Gill, Dennis
    129-Change

Gimmer, David
    158-Milady's fur: the trapper

Girauad, Marcel
    19-Le Metis Canadien

Girouard, Laurent
    221-Bulletin d'information

Gladwin, Thomas
    170-Personality structure in the plains

Glooschenko, Valanne
    158-James Bay power proposal

Glynn-Ward, H.
    4-Canada's Indian problem

Goddard, Pliny Earle
    38-Slender-Maiden of the Apache
    19-Tlingit, a genetic relation to Athapascan?

Godsell, Philip H.
    85-Indians and Indian Affairs in Canada
    85-Red hunters of the snows
    103-Tragic economic story of northern Indians

Godt, P.
    158-Co-operatives among Indian people in Canada

Goedhart, Bernie (reporter)
    129-Chief Smallboy plans to lead band to public land

Gold, Dolores
    170-Psychological changes, acculturation, Saskatchewan Indians

Golden, Aubrey E., James A. O'Reilly, *Andrew Delisle,
Paul V. Walsh, and *Len Marchand
    217-The law and native populations

Goldenweiser, Alexander A
    38-Hanging-Flower, The Iroquois

Goldfrank, E. S.
    170-Historic change and social character - Teton Dakota
    170-Changing configurations, social organization, Blackfoot
    170-Different patterns, Blackfoot, Pueblo, white authority

Goldstein, M.S.
    229-Demographic, bodily changes, descendants, Mexican
        immigrants

Gooderham, Kent ed.
    210-Notice: This is Indian Land
    35-I am an Indian
    4-Nestum Asa (this is the way it was in the beginning)

Goodfellow, W. A. et.al.
    103-Civil liberties and rights of Indians in Ontario

*Goodleaf, Chief Frank
    55-Letter to Members of Parliament

Hallowell, Alfred Irving
    210-Sin, sex and sickness in Saulteaux beliefs
    4-The impact of American Indian on American culture
    20-Ojibwa ontology, behavior, and world view
    171-American Indians, white and black, transculturalization
    210-Ojibwa world view and disease

Halpin, Lester A.
    129-Massacres not new to U.S.

Hamilton, C. Everett
    4-Cry of the thunderbird - American Indian's own story

Hammershmith, Jerry
    129-Interview with Dr. Howard Adams

Handler, Bruce (reporter)
    229-Brazil's Indians reported heading toward extinction
    229-Asimilation of Indians fails to work in Brazil

Handley, Bruce
    191-A study of the academic program in Alberta New Start

Hanks, Lucien Mason Jr. and Jane Richardson Hanks
    20-Tribe under trust; the Blackfoot reserve in Alberta

Hanley, David W.
    191-School integration in The Pas, Manitoba
    146-Report to Bosco Centre Study Committee

Hannula, Don (reporter)
    129-Indians storm Ft. Lawton for 3rd time

Hanson, Marshall Roy
    181-Plains Indians and urbanisation

Harding, James
    104-Canada's Indians: a powerless minority
    129-Two padlocks on the doors: Council House locked again

Harkins, Arthur M.
    33-Attitudes, characteristics of selected Wisconsin Indians

Harmsworth, Harry C.
    146-Family structure, Front Hall Indian Reservation

Harper, Allan G.
    159-Indian land problems, United States
    85-Canada's Indian Administration: basic concepts, objectives
    77-Canada's Indian Administration: the Indian Act
    55-Canada's Indian Administration: the treaty system

Harrington, John P.
    20-Culture element distributions, Central California Coast

Harrington, M. R.
    38-Thunder power of Rumbling-Wings

Harris, Marianne
    20-Bella Coola Indians of the north Pacific coast

Harris, Michael
    181-American cities: the new reservations

Harrison, Mrs. Barbara
    229-Racism in Australia

Harrison, Fred (reporter)
    191-Metis Society report on education study

Hart, C. W. M.
    217-The problems of laws

Hart, George
    142-Geronimo's last fight

Harvey, Bryon III
    221-The Fred Harvey Collection, 1889-1963

Harvey, Ian, Harold Huston, and James R. Whitford, et.al.
    146-Steps in problem solving

Hatt, Fred, Kenneth
    146-Appendix A. Metis of the Lac Biche area
    171-Response to directed social change on Alberta metis colony
    20-Social science and the metis: recent perspectives

Hatt, Judy Lynn Keever
    146-Social structure, life cycle, Beaver Metis Colony

Havighurst, Robert James
    191-The intelligence of Indian children
    191-American Indian and white Children
    191-Education among American Indians
    192-The national study of American Indian education
    192-National study of American Indian education
    192-National study of American Indian education
    192-The national study of American Indian education, summary

Hawthorn, Harry Bertram
    171-The Maori: a study in acculturation
    171-Enter the european, among the Indians of Canada
    171-Indians of British Columbia; study social adjustment
    4-Research and the Indians of Canada
    104-Relations between whites and Indians
    171-Problems of cultural adjustment
    4-Research on the Indian,
    146-Epilogue: the Indian decides
    4-A survey of the contemporary Indians of Canada 2 Volumes
    171-The survival of small societies
    159-Paper, guidelines for scientific activities

Hay, Thomas H.
    43-Windigo psychosis

Hazeltine, A. I.
    35-Red man, white man: legends, tales, of American Indians

Hellaby, Hilda Alice
    171-The Indian in social adjustment

Helm, June
    159-Subsistence economy Dogrib Indians, Lac La Martre
    171-Contact-tradition native community of Canadian north
    221-Subartic anthropology: roster of scholars

Henderson, Norman B.
    4-Cross-cultural action research, advantages and problems

Hendry, Charles E.
    48-Traplines and beyond, does the church really care?

Henry, Hill
    96-From where the sun now stands

Herron, Shawn
    85-Time to bury the hatchet

Hertzberg, Hazel W.
    146-The search for an American Indian identity

Heshidahl, Gladys, et.al.
    192-How well do we teach Indian children?

*Hewitt, J. N. B.
    4-Constitutional league of peace in stone age America

Hibben, F. C.
    4-Treasure in the dust - exploring ancient North America
    4-L'homme primitif américain des origines préhistoriques

Hickerson, Harold
    20-Algonkians of the upper Great Lakes
    43-Notes on the post-contact origin of the Midewiwin
    47-Socio-historical significance, two Chippewa ceremonials

Higgins, G. M.
    159-South coast-Baffin Island: an area economic survey

Hill, Bernard and Wilma J. Hill
    146-The Buffalo Narrows project

Hill, Edward E. ed.
    221-Preliminary inventories: records of Bureau Indian Affairs
    221-Records in the General Archives Division
    221-Tucson Agency: use of Indian records in National Archives

Hill, Willard Williams
    171-Some Navaho culture changes during two centuries
    43-The Navaho Indians and the Ghost Dance of 1890
    33-Navaho trading and trading ritual

Hillery, George A.
    181-Navajos, eastern Kentuckians, demographic transition

Hilliard, Sam B.
    96-Indian land cessions, map

Hillinger, Charles
217-Two kinds of justice dispensed in north

Hinckley, Edward C.
146-Indian participation in community development programs

Hirabayashi, Gordon K.
185-Challenges assisting Canadian aboriginal people
171-Apathy as a mode of adjustment
104-Social distance and the modernizing Metis

Hiroko, Sue
146-Pre-school children of the Hare Indians

Hlady, Walter, M.
159-Sandy Bay, Saskatchewan: social and economic study
104-Power structure in a Metis community
171-Directed social change and the agencies involved
30-Indian migration in Manitoba and the west
146-Community development project Churchill Band
5-Sociology of native Canadians
173-Path to Indian acceptance in Canadian society
159-Sociological study, Cumberland House
159-Cumberland House fur project, first two years

Hobart, Charles W. and Charles Sanford Brant
192-Eskimo education, Danish, Canadian comparison

Hodge, Frederick Webb
20-Narrative of Alvar Nunez Cabeca de Vaca
40-Handbook, American Indians north of Mexico
5-Handbook of Indians of Canada

Hodge, William H.
43-Navaho pentecostalism
181-Navaho urban silversmiths
181-Urban Indian bibliography, Canada, United States

Hodges, Percy G. and F. D. Noonan
55-Saskatchewan Metis, legal, moral claims to Indian title

Hodgson, Stuart M.
114-Letter re: native organizations

Hoebel, Adamson E.
20-The Cheyennes

Hoey, R. R.
210-Economic problems of the Canadian Indian

Hoffmann, Hans
171-Culture, personality modification, James Bay Cree

Hogg, Carol (reporter)
129-Aboriginal unity proposed
130-More Indians joining back-to-wilds movement
181-Cities can be cruel

Holden, David E. W.
    171-Modernization among town and bush Cree in Quebec

Holland, Gordon (reporter)
    229-From Melbourne: no land rights for aborigines

Holland, N. Huntley
    65-Inquiry into proposed Colville termination

Holmberg, Allan R.
    229-Nomands of the long bow

Holmes, Alvin
    77-Implications, the Indian Act, social welfare aspects

Homewood, E. L.
    192-Indian education, the plight of Canada's Indians

Hongimann, John Joseph
    146-Frobisher Bay Eskimo childhood
    210-Drinking in an Indian-White community
    210-Foodways in a muskeg community
    146-Social networks in Great Whale River
    172-Community organization patterns of change, Indians,
        Eskimos
    20-Eskimo townsmen
    172-Arctic town life, stimulus to Eskimo culture change
    172-Social disintegration, five northern communities
    221-Bibliography, northern North America and Greenland
    210-Alcohol in a Canadian northern town
    172-Deculturation, protelarization, Canada's north
    172-Arctic townsmen, ethnic backgrounds, modernization
    20-Formation of Mackenzie Delta frontier

Hook, H. M.
    35-Thunder in the mountain, legends of Canada

Hooper, Anthony
    55-Aboriginal title, has it been extinguished?

*Hope, Adrian
    146-Brief history of Kikino settlement, Alberta

Hopkins, Thomas R.
    192-Secondary education of native North Americans

*Horn, Audrey (Kahn-Tineta)
    130-Indians seek to regain their rightful status
    192-Indian education crisis
    192-Role of church and school
    77-Indian status for Metis?
    77-The Canadian Bill of Rights
    159-James Bay

Hornaday, William T.
    5-Extermination of the American bison

Horton, Donald
    211-Functions of alcohol in primitive societies

Horwood, Harold (reporter)
    20-People who were murdered for fun, Beothuk Indians

*Houle, Robert
    47-False face society

Houston, James A.
    37-Eskimo carvings

Howard, Frank
    5-We made the Indian poor and irresponsible

Howard, James H.
    130-Pan-Indian culture of Oklahoma
    20-Plains Ojibway or Bungi,
    5-True partnership here in our land
    33-Indian cultures, their history and contributions

Howard, Joseph Kinsey
    142-The strange empire of Louis Riel

Howard, S. H.
    159-New day on James Bay dawning for Indians

Howe, Joseph
    85-Report on Indian Affairs (1844)

Howley, James Patrick
    20-Beothuks or Red Indian, inhabitants of Newfoundland

Hrdlicka, Ales
    229-Early man in South America
    229-Early man in South America
    5-Genesis of the American Indian

Hryniuk, Morris D. ed.
    33-Stories of Wesakachak

Hudson, Charles M. ed.
    130-Red, White, and Black, Indians in old south

Huel, Raymond
    43-Adrien-Gabriel Morice, O.M.I. brief sojourn in Saskatchewan

Hughes, Barry Conn (reporter)
    104-Town on a powder keg, Kenora, Ontario

Hughes, Charles C.
    172-Observation on community change in the north

Hughes, Daniel T.
    147-Democracy in a traditional society

Hulbert, Janice
    147-Age, factor in social organization, Ft. Good Hope

Hume, Steve (reporter)
    211-N.W.T. booze - profit and death
    211-Infant mortality in north 3 times that of average

Jenness, Diamond
    5-The Indian background of Canadian history
    5-Canada's Indian problems
    6-Canada's Indians yesterday - what of today?
    172-Enter the european - among the Eskimos
    35-The corn goddess and other tales from Indian Canada
    6-Canada's debt to the Indians
    6-The Indians of Canada
    86-Eskimo administration: I, Alaska
    86-Eskimo administration: II, Canada
    86-Eskimo administration: III, Labrador
    86-Eskimo administration: IV, Greenland
    86-Eskimo administration: V, Analysis and Reflections

Jobe, Paul, and Kenneth R. Davidson
    211-Community development case studies

Joblin, Elgie Ellingham Miller
    192-The education of the Indians of western Ontario

Jochelson, W.
    230-Peoples of asiatic Russia

*Johnson, E. Pauline (Tekahionwake)
    33-Flint and feather: complete poems of P.E. Johnson

Johnson, Frederick
    230-Central American cultures: an introduction

*Johnson, Greg
    21-Indians in the Maritimes
    130-Micmac soveignty vs Indian Affairs

Johnson, Guy B.
    172-Personality in a White-Indian-Negro Community

Johnson, President Lyndon Baines
    96-The American Indian

Johnson, Peter A. (reporter)
    6-The Canadian Indian and the just society

Johnson, William A. et. al.
    181-Adjustment factors, moving to urban community

Johnson, William D.
    104-Exploratory study, ethnic relations-Great Whale River

Johnston, A.
    142-Battle at Belly River: stories, last great Indian battle

Johnston, Alexander
    44-Uses of native plants by the Blackfoot Indians

*Johnston, Basil
    104-Address general meaning of human rights
    130-Bread before books or books before bread

Johnston, Charles M.
    56-Joseph Brant, Grand River Land and the northwest crisis
    56-Valley of the Six Nations

Johnstone, Ken
    217-Reserves of injustice: Indians and Eskimos in prison

Jones, Dorothy V.
    21-John Dougherty the Pawnee rite, human sacrifice
    172-A Potawatomi faces the problem cultural change

Jones, James (reporter)
    181-Woes in city worse than on reservations

Jones, Mary Jane, ed.
    221-Mackenzie Delta bibliography

Jones, Peter
    21-History of the Ojibway Indians

Jones, Thomas Jesse
    192-Essentials of education for American Indians

Josephy, Alvin M. Jr.,
    38-The patriot chiefs
    6-The Indian heritage of America
    221-Bibliography
    96-American Indian, the Bureau of Indian Affairs
    130-Indians in history
    130-Red power: American Indians fight for freedom
    160-Here in Nevada a terrible crime: Pyramid Lake

Jubinville, Real
    217-Correctional services in the northwest

Judson, Hon. Mr. Justice
    56-Frank Calder v Attorney-General of B.C.

Kaegi, Gerda and *Terry Bigwin
    193-Comprehensive view of Indian education

Kaplan, Robert B
    193-Present failure to educate the American Indian

Kappler, Charles J.
    96-Indian affairs: laws and treaties

Kassirer, Eve
    86-Programs of interest to Indians and Metis

Katz, Sidney (reporter)
    193-The lost children of British Columbia
    218-Sociologist, bloodshed could come to Canadian prisons

Kawakami, K. K.
    104-Canada as a white man's country

Keeler, W. W. et. al.
    96-The Secretary's task force on Indian affairs

Keen, Ralph
    130-The question what is an Indian?

Keenleyside, David
    193-Fallacy of freedom: education for the adult Eskimo

*Keeper, Cyril George
    56-A survey of commissions of inquiry and investigations

*Keeper, Joseph Irwin
    147-Community development methods
    185-Friendship Centres

Kehoe, Alice B
    44-Saskatchewan Indian religious beliefs
    21-The Dakotas in Saskatchewan

Keirstead, Charles Wesley
    44-The church history of the Canadian northwest

Keiser, Albert
    104-The Indian in American literature

Kellar, H. Phyllis
    47-Indian dance interpretations

*Kelly, Fred
    130-The fresh assertiveness - red power

Kelly, William H.
    172-The changing role of the Indian in Arizona
    160-The economic basis of Indian life
    30-Methods and resources for Navajo population register
    96-Indian Adjustment and the history of Indian affairs

Kelsay, Laura E. ed.
    221-Cartographic records

Kemp, Herbert Douglas
    86-Department of the Interior 1873-1883

Kemp William B.
    160-The flow of energy in a hunting society

Kennard, Edward A.
    160-Post-war economic changes among the Hopi

*Kennedey, Alex
    160-Agricultural development on Indian reserves

Kennedy, Fred
    131-The Indian ride to nowhere

Kennedy, Jacqueline Judith
    193-Qu'Appelle Industrial School

Kennedy, President John Fitzgerald
    96-To all American Indians: declaration of Indian purpose

Kerr, A. J.
    147-Subsistence, social organization, a fur trade community

Kerr, Wendie (reporter)
    122-A white man fights for the Indian: Martin O'Connell

Kerri, James N.
    114-Utilization of native peoples' voluntary association
    147-Inuvik Town: Structural-functional analysis
    181-Adjustment of people of Indian ancestry in urban centers
        a bibliography
    221-American Indians (U.S. and Canada), a bibliography

Kerwin, Patrick
    86-The plight of Canadian Indians

Ketchum, W. Q. (reporter)
    123-Ernie McEwen

Kew, J. E. Michael
    221-Metis-Indian housing in northern Saskatchewan

Kieran, Shiela H.
    6-Indians

Kim, Yong C.
    193-Social origins of school retardation, Indian pupils

King, Alfred Richard
    193-A case study of an Indian residential school
    193-The school of Mopass

*King, Hector
    181-Brief presented to Honorable Jean Chrétien

King, Wain (reporter)
    86-The Mounties - their first 100 years (3)

Kinsella, Noel A.
    193-Dimensions of ego-identity, Acadians, Blacks, Indians,
        etc.

Kirchhoff, Paul
    230-Food-gathering tribes of the Venezuelan Llanos

Kitpou, Shaman Chief (pseudonym)
    33-Tribal laws of the children of light

Kluckhohn, Clyde and Dorothea Leighton
    21-The Navaho

Klyn, Doyle (reporter)
    40-Girl with the best of two worlds, Kahn-Tineta Horn

Knight, R.
    172-Changing social, economic organization-Rupert House Cree

Knight, Rolf
    147-Big Beaverhouse and Wunnumen Lake Project

Knill, William D. and Arthur Kent Davis
193-Provincial education-northern Saskatchewan-1944-1962

Knirck, Carola
131-The story of 'Set-OK'-son of Polish immigrant......
21-The Assiniboine Indians of Canada
211-Observations and figures-life expectancy, Canadian Indians
21-The Beothuks of Newfoundland
30-Remarks on Indian and Metis population, Canada

Koolage, William W. Jr.
172-Relocation and culture change

Kopas, Clifford Leslie
147-Political action of Indians of British Columbia

Kopit, Arthur
6-Indians

Korchinski, Emil
181-Social detriments of rural urban mobility, Indians

Kraenzel, Carl F.
173-The Great Plains in transition

Krieger, Alex D.
230-'Gilmore Corridor' in culture contacts

Kroeber, Alfred Louis
38-Earth-Tongue, Mohave
21-Cultural and natural areas of native North America

Kronin, Kay
193-Address, Conference, Principles of Roman Catholic
    Residential Schools

Krush, Thaddeus P. John W. Bjork, Peter Sindell, and Noanna Nelle
193-Thoughts on the formation of personality disorder

Kuh, Katherine
37-The first Americans as artists

Kupferer, Harriet J.
173-Cherokee change: a departure from lineal models
230-Impotency and power: cross-cultural comparison
211-Health practices and educational aspirations
21-The isolated eastern Cherokee

Kurath, Gertrude Prokosch
47-Dance and Song Rituals of Six Nations Reserve, Ontario

*Kurtness, Jacques
6-From nomadism to sedentarisme

Kurtz, Ronald J.
173-Role change and culture change: the Canyoncito case

La Barre, Weston
    44-The peyote cult
    44-Statment on peyote
    44-Twenty years of peyote studies
    44-The Ghost Dance: origins of religion

LaClair, Leo
    65-Muckleshoot fishing rights question

LaCoste, Sir Alexander
    56-The Seminary of Montreal: their rights and title

LaCourse, Richard
    96-Who runs Indian Affairs?

LaCroix Marc
    104-Integration or disintegration?

Lafarge, Oliver
    173-The changing Indian
    6-Laughing boy
    65-Termination of federal supervision
    6-Pictorial history of the American Indian

Laflesche, Francis
    193-The middle five: Indian school boys of Omaha Tribe

LaForest, Gerard. V.
    86-Property in Indian Lands

*Lagassé, Jean-Henry
    21-People of Indian ancestry in Manitoba: Main report
    21-People of Indian ancestry in Manitoba: Appendix I
    21-People of Indian ancestry in Manitoba: AppendixII
    147-Community development in Manitoba
    147-A community development program for Manitoba
    86-Notes for an address
    6-The poeple and Indian ancestry in Canada
    6-Indians of Canada
    147-Indians and social cultural development
    86-Social factors affecting native development
    230-Proceedings of VII Congress-Inter-American Indian

Lahr, John
    131-Arthur Kopit's 'Indians'; dramatizing national amnesia

Laing, Hon. Arthur
    77-The Indian people and the Indian act
    147-Program for physical development of Indian communities
    86-Cultural identity of Indian and Eskimo people
    147-Role of other citizens in Indian Affairs
    87-Tripod; Indian people, government, community
    193-Educating young Canadian Indians
    194-Address, Canadian Assoc. for Indian and Eskimo Education

Laird, Hon. David
    56-North-west Indian treaties

Lake, Stuart (reporter)
    131-Nellie (Cournoyea): many whys, much bitterness

Lal, Ravindra
    181-From Duck Lake to Camp 10: old fashioned relocation
    147-Observations on social life of Chipewyans of Camp 10

Landes, Ruth
    230-Techniques of dealing with cross-cultural problems

Lang, Gottfried O.
    160-Economic development, self-determination, Ute case

Langevin, Hector L.
    87-Letter re: appointment of Indian Agents

Lanternari, Vittorio
    48-The religions of the oppressed

*Lapierre-Assiniwi, Bernard
    37-Talent among Canadian Indians

*Laraque, Marie-Helene
    230-Center for information, native peoples of the Americas

Larner, Jack and James O'Reilly
    56-Aboriginal people of Canada and their environment

*LaRoche, Emma
    131-Indian in society today- an opinion: Part I
    131-Indian in society today- an opinion: Part II

Laronde, Louis
    194-Education of the Indian in Canada

Larsen, Helge
    21-Ipiutak Culture

La Rusic, Ignatius E.
    173-New Auchimau: study of patron-client relations
    173-From hunter to proletarian, involvement of Cree Indians
    173-Indian power Waswanipi, political process, social change
    117-Influence of Indians of Quebec Association in Waswanipi

*Latham, Carl H.
    181-The Indian in the city

Laurie, John
    119-General Meeting 1950, Indian Association of Alberta
    119-General Meeting 1951, Indian Association of Alberta
    120-General Meeting 1952, Indian Association of Alberta
    120-Indian Association to hold 10th Annual Meeting
    120-The Indians organize
    120-General Meeting, Indian Association of Alberta
    120-Eleventh Annual Convention, Indian Association of Alberta

*Lavallée, Ed
    194-School drops-out

283

*Lavallée, Mrs. Mary Ann
211-Address, Regional Conference on Health Services
211-Problems that conern Indian Women
194-School integration
148-Problems that concern Indian women

Lavender, David
6-The American Heritage History of the great west

LaViolette, Forrest Emmanuel
173-Struggle for survival, Indian cultures, protestant ethnic

LaViolette, G.
22-The Sioux Indians in Canada

Leacock, Eleanor Burke
173-Montagnais hunting territory and fur trade

LeBlance, Dudley J.
87-Unbelievable cruelty to Acadians and Indians by the English

Leboeuf, Robert
6-Les Indiens, le plus grave problème social au Canada

Le Clerco, Father Chrestien
23-New relation of Gaspesia: customs and religion

Leechman, John Douglas
22-Vanta Kutchin
7-Native tribes of Canada

Lefebvre, Madeleine
6-Quand un récit m'était livré

Leigh, L. H.
77-Indian Act, supremacy of Parliament and equal protection

Lemay, Guy (reporter)
104-Les Indiens sont bien décidés à faire respecter- autonomie

Lemert, Edwin M.
211-Alcohol and northwest coast Indians
131-The life and death of an Indian State

Leon, Robert L.
104-Maladaptive interaction, Bureau Indian Affairs and Indian
    clients

Lescaze, Lee (reporter)
230-Philippines re-enacts U.S. west

Leslie, A. G.
77-Remarks on reserve trusts

Lesser, Alexander
44-Cultural significance of the ghost dance
194-Education and future of tribalism in U.S.

Linton, Ralph ed.
    173-Acculturation in Seven American Indian Tribes

List, Wilfred (reporter)
    105-Social worker who's become Ombudsman to Indians (Pat
       Kerwin)

Lloyd, Anthony John
    7-Indians of Canada
    148-Community development in Canada

Locke, Jeannine (reporter)
    7-The Canadian Indians
    105-Outcasts in their own land (Part II)
    7-What our Indians really want and need (Part IV)

Locklin, G. R.
    194-Study, secondary school pupils, Indian reservation

Lockwood, Thomas J.
    7-A history of Royal Commissions

Loehr, Max
    230-Das Rolltier in China

Long, J.
    7-Voyages and travels, an Indian interpreter and trader

*Long Lance, Chief Buffalo Child
    30-When the Crees moved west

Loram, Charles T.
    7-Fundamentals of Indian-White contact, U.S., Canada
    194-Church and state, Indian education, U.S., Canada
    7-North American Indian today

Loree, Don
    173-Marginal situation of Dogrib Tribe of N.W.T.

Lotz, James R.
    222-Government research, surveys, Canadian north 1956-61
    222-Yukon bibliography
    160-Chilkoot Trail to-day, Dyea to Bennett-guide to trail
    105-Human rights of Indians and Eskimos
    160-The squatters of Whitehorese: an area economic survey
    148-The community developer: outsider in the middle
    205-An Indian community college in Canada: a proposal
    194-Eskimos as educators
    222-List of contributors, special volume, essays, Dr. D.
      Jenness
    22-Future of the Eskimo

Louttit, Neil (reporter)
    40-David Courchene: tough, fair, and never on tiptoe
    211-Metis: is there any reason people have to live like that
    211-Home for 8 Metis is 14-foot square shack
    212-For Metis, welfare is a way of life
    105-For Metis, discrimination is everyday occurence
    131-Red power not militant say Indians

MacArthur, R. S.
194-Cognitive abilities, Eskimo, White, Indian, Metis pupils

MacDonald, A.A.
174-Community resources and dimensions of alienation

MacDonald, A. H.
160-Co-operatives and people of Indian ancestry

MacDonald, Alex and Steve Hume (reporters)
212-Officials deny sterilization against will

MacDonald, John A.
77-Canadian Bill of Rights, Indians and the courts

MacDonald, Nancy L.
124-List of Indian publications, newspapers and bulletins
124-List of Indian associations
222-Bibliography, attitudes Indians toward non-Indian society
222-Sources of information, Indian integration

MacGregor, Gordon
148-Warrior without weapons, Pine Ridge Sioux
148-Community development and social adaptation

MacInnes, T. R. L.
87-History of Indian administration in Canada
87-History and policies of Indian administration in Canada
87-History of Indian administration in Canada

MacKenzie, N. A. M.
56-Indians and treaties in law

MacLean, Hope
194-Review of Indian education in North America

MacLean, John
7-Native tribes of Canada

MacLean, Robinson (reporter)
7-Indians go hungry under treaty, Queen Victoria's word broke

MacLeod, John
195-Indian education in Canada

MacLeod, William C.
160-Big business and the North American Indian

MacNeish, June Helm
148-Leadership among the northeastern Athabascans

MacPherson, Norm
195-Devlopments in teacher training, intercultural education

Madigan, LaVerne
182-American Indian relocation program

Magoon, M. A.
22-Ojibway drums

*Magowan, N. (Littlefoot)
    131-Indians attack army

Maidenberge, H. J. (reporter)
    231-Peru to teach Indians in own tougues

Mailhot, Jose
    148-Inuvik community structure - Summer 1965

Majowicz, Mrs. Tricia
    148-Native people and the media

Malan, Vernon D.
    22-Social system of the Dakota Indians
    174-Acculturation of the Dakota Indians

Malling, Eric
    131-Regina's Indians, the hate is rising in whitey's town

*Mandamin, Tony
    131-On education

Mandelbaum, David G.
    22-The plains Cree
    22-The world of the plains Cree

*Manitowabi, Edna
    182-An Ojibwa girl in the city

Manners, Robert A.
    96-Pluralism and the American Indian

Manning, Ernest C.
    148-White paper on human resources deveopment

Mansell, R. L.
    148-Socio-economic study, isolated communities, northern
        Alberta

*Manuel, Chief George
    57-Brief, Joint Committee on the Constitution
    87-Daily press serve as agents of Indian Affairs
    87-Address, B.C. Association, Non-Status Indians
    87-Address, Progressive Conservative Youth
    231-Report, tour of New Zealand and Australia
    132-Discussion paper on the Cold Lake issue
    174-Canadian Indians and Maoris share common problems
    7-Indians not against idea of integration
    7-Justice in the world as it applies to Indians of Canada
    132-The fourth world
    57-Original rights and the native people
    204-Press release: response to education (fifth) report

*Markoosie,
    22-Harpoon of the hunter

Marriott, Alice Lee
    7-Experiences among the American Indians

Marshall, Brian David
    87-Problems in Indian Affairs field administration

Marshall, John (reporter)
    182-Ontario's ghettos
    105-Plight of James Bay Crees, Ottawa's impractical rules
    182-Migration the solution for our Indians
    22-Northern Ontario's Indians, tough people, tough land
    7-Let Indians tell story, even if its embarrassing

Martens, Ethel G.
    231-Mexico and Canada, comparison of community development

Martin, Charles A.
    222-James Bay Region (Quebec) pre-history bibliography

Martin, Harry W.
    182-Adjustment among American Indians in an urban environment
    160-Report, Alaskan consultation with employment assistance

Martin, P. S.
    7-Indians before Columbus

Mason, Evelyn P.
    195-Personality characteristics, Indians, Mexicans, Caucasians

Mason, John Alden
    22-Indians of the Great Slave Lake area

Masson, Leonard
    174-Swampy Cree, a study in acculturation

Massy, Mrs. Patricia
    212-Foster home planning for the Indian child

Matheson, G. M.
    87-Historical sketch of administrators of Indian Affairs
    87-Directory of Indian agents in Canada

Matthiasson, John S.
    174-Forced relocation, a case study (Easterville, Man.)
    160-Cree communities, South Indian Lake hydro electric
        controversy

McCaskill, Donald N.
    182-Migration adjustment, integration, in the urban
        environment

McCaskill, J. C.
    218-Administration of law and order, Indians, United States

McClelland, Joseph (reporter)
    174-The Indian: challenge of 70s

McCloud, Mrs. Janet
    105-The continuing 'last Indian war'

*McCue, Harvey A. (Wasubageshig) see also Waubageshig
    206-Brief, efforts of native committee on Indian studies

McDiarmid, Garnet L.
    105-Teaching prejudice, analysis of textbooks
    195-Challenge of differential curriculum, Ontario's Indians
    222-Culture contact, an annotated bibliography

McDowell, Stanley (reporter)
    105-Alberta Indians admit defeat, will drop Federal programs

McElroy, Ann P.
    182-Effects urbanization, Eskimo child life, personality
    117-Origins and development of Inuit alliance movements

McEwen, Ernest Roy
    182-Action research project, migrating native people
    105-Voluntary sponsorship of self-help among Indians, Eskimos
    105-Rights of Canada's first citizens, Indian, and Eskimo
    148-Community development services for Indian and Metis
    87-Reflections upon the needs for a comprehensive govt. policy
    212-Report, concerning housing and land claims

McFeat, Thomas
    160-Two Malecite family industries, a case study

McFee, Malcolum
    174-Modern Blackfeet, differential acculturation

McGann, David
    195-Social action and the Indian boarding home program

McGee, John T.
    174-Stability and change, Lake Melville Region, Labrador

McGill, Dr. H. W.
    88-Policies and problems in Canada

McGilp, John G.
    88-Relations of Canadian Indians and Canadian government

McGimpsey, Earl R.
    65-Indian tribal sovereignty

McGrath, G. D., Robert Roessel, et. al.
    195-Higher education, southwestern Indians, success, failure

McGrath, W. T.
    218-The offender of Indian ancestry

McIlwraith, Thomas F.
    8-Basic cultures of the Indians in Canada
    8-Indians of Canada
    222-Bibliography of Canadian anthropology for 1961

McInnes, R. W.
    56-Indian treaties and related disputes

McInnes, T. R. E.
    56-Report, Indian title, especially in British Columbia

McKay, Fortescue
    35-Indian tale of birch bark, musk-rat tails, rabbit ears

McKay, Sandy, et. al.
    106-Attitudes of Toronto students towards Indians

McKee, Sandra Lynn ed.
    38-Gabriel Dumont, Indian fighter

McKenzie, Fayette A.
    174-Assimilation of the American Indian

McKern, Sharon S. and W. Thomas
    44-The peace messiah

McKernin, Harold J.
    106-Indian integration, the Perth, N.B. situation

McLelland, Helen
    185-Our Indian and Metis committee

McLoone, John J.
    65-Indian hunting and fishing rights

McLuhan, Teri C.
    8-Touch the earth

McNab, Frances (reporter)
    8-The forgotten Canadians

McNeil, Garry (reporter)
    106-Humble Indian maid may become a saint

McNeil, J. D.
    106-Changes in ethnic reaction tendencies during high school

McNelly, Peter (reporter)
    57-Douglas chiselled Indians with legal treaties
    212-Totem pole raising honors a great chief, Kwakiutl

*McNickle, D'Arcy
    8-Indian-White relations to 1887
    114-Private intervention
    8-Indian tribes of the United States, cultural survival
    132-Definition of a problem

McNutt, C. S.
    8-Life on an Indian reservation

Mead, Margaret
    174-Changing culture of an Indian tribe
    44-Mountain Arapesh, supernaturalism

Means, John E.
    106-Human rights and Canadian federalism

Melling, John
    148-Canadian Indian Affairs and 'derogated' authority
    88-Recent Indian affairs in Canada
    88-Recent development, policy towards Indians and Eskimos
    8-Right to a future, native people of Canada

Memorian, Brother
    48-Roman Catholic missions in Canada

*Menarik, Elijah
    195-Education

Meriam, Lewis
    96-Problem of Indian administration

Merrit, General Wesley
    142-Three Indian campaigns

Metcalfe, Robert (reporter)
    106-Dorothy Betz knows the pain of being an Indian

Métraux, A.
    231-Native tribes of eastern Bolivia

Metzler, William
    161-Relocation of the displaced worker

*Meyer, William (yonv ut sisla)
    132-The new Indian resistance

Michelson, Truman
    148-How Meskwaki children should be brought up

Mickenberg, Neil H.
    57-Aboriginal rights in Canada and the United States

Mierzwinki, Alexandre, et. al.
    106-Administration of justice beyond the 50th parallel

Miller, Frank C. and D. D. Caulkins
    148-Chippewa adolescents, a changing generation

*Miller, George William
    38-Handsome Lake movement

Milloy, John S.
    22-Plains Cree, trade and military chronology 1670-1870

Mills, Mrs. R. S.
    148-Family life in Indian communities in Ontario

Milord, James E.
    132-Genocide in Canada, we call it integration

Minor, Nono
    38-Famous Indian women in early America

Mirrieless, E. R.
    212-Cloud of mistrust

Mishkin, B.
142-Rank and warfare among plains Indians

Mitchell, J.
182-Mohawks in high steel

Mitchell, Lonnie and Leroy Jones
195-Training and education for career development

*Molohon, Kathryn T.
195-Abstracts, literature on psychological testing, Indians

Monahan, Gene Ritchie
37-Report, experiment in art exposure among Indians

*Montgomery, Malcom
57-Legal status of the Six Nations Indians in Canada
57-Historiography of the Iroquois Indians 1925-1963
57-Six Nations Indians and the MacDonald Franchise

*Monture, Ethel Brant
38-Brant, Crowfoot, Oronhyatehka, famous Indians

*Monture, Gilbert C.
22-The Indians of the north

Mooney, James
44-Sacred formulas of the Cherokee
44-Ghost Dance religion and the Sioux outbreak of 1890
30-Aboriginal population of America north of Mexico

Moore, P. et. al.
212-Medical survey of nutrition, northern Metis and Indians

Moorehead, Alan
231-Account of the invasion of the South Pacific 1767-1840

Morey, S.
8-Can the red man help the white man?

Morgan, Lewis Henry
22-League of the Ho-De-No-Sau-Nee or Iroquois

Morin, Francoise, and Jacques Rousseau
88-La'paix blanch' conversation with Robert Jaulin

*Morning Runner
96-New directions in native affairs

Morris, Alexander
52-Treaties of Canada

Morris, James Lewis
57-Indians of Ontario

Morris, Lillian and Philip Procter
96-Trail of tears

Morris, William (reporter)
88-Let's liberate Canada's Indians from paternalism
212-How Canada keeps the Indian poor
106-His choice, is it integration or cultural suicide?

Morris, William J.
8-Plight of the Indian in Canada
149-Indian integration into the community
149-Policies of integration of agencies, for Indians

*Morriseau, Norval
35-Legends of my people

Morrison, Walter M. (reporter)
132-Old Coast guard station occupied by militants

Morrison, William A. et. al
182-Urbanizing Indian adjustment project

Morrow, Justice William George
106-Inquiry, re administration of justice, Hay River, N.W.T.
106-Administration of justice and native people

Mortimore, George E.
8-Indians of Canada
106-Indians were here first, treat them as citizens plus
161-Indian in industry, roads to independence
174-Caught between cultures

Morton, Desmond
142-The last drum, the North-West campaign of 1885

Morton, Rogers B.
65-Letter, re draft bill, provision of Alaskan land claims

Morton, W. L.
8-The west and confederation 1857-1871

Moser, Rupert R.
231-Situation of the Adivasis of Bihar, India

Motyl, John
33-Insights into cultural differences

Mouat, W. Ivan
195-Education in the arctic districts

Mowat, Farley G.
23-The desperate people

Muller, Michael
231-Facts and figures, aboriginal issues

Nash, Philleo
    106-Introduction to the problem of race tension
    9-Programmes of action in areas other than Kenora

Naumer, Janet Noll
    222-American Indians, a bibliography of sources

Naysmith, John K.
    161-Management of polar lands

Neihardt, John G.
    44-Black Elk speaks

Nelson, John C.
    57-Description of Indian reserves, Manitoba and N.W.T.

Nelson, N. C.
    47-Wixi of the Shellmound people

Newcomb, W. W.
    174-Culture, acculturation of the Delware Indians

Newell, William B.
    218-Crime and justice among the Iroquois Nations

Newman, Nicholas C.
    97-Jurisdiction over Indians and Indian lands in Washington

*Nicholas, Chief Andrew
    132-New Brunswick Indians, conservative militants

Nicholas, D. J.
    196-Dispute at Assumption

Nicholson, Patrick
    106-Look at Canada's Indian ghettos

Nickols, Peters
    175-Since the days of barter

Nixon, President Richard Milhouse
    97-To the Congress of the United States, Indian Affairs

*Nolet, Jean-Paul
    161-James Bay development project

Nordenskiold, Erland
    231-Comparative ethnographical studies

Novack, George
    132-Genocide against Indians, role in the rise of capitalism

*Nujoweket
    132-Indians plan research on whites

Nyerere, Julius K.
    132-Press statement

Osborn, Ralph ed.
    9-Who is chairman of this meeting? collection of essays

Oschinsky, L.
    23-The most ancient Eskimos

Oswalt, Wendall and James Van Stone
    175-Future of the Caribou Eskimo
    175-Canadian Athabaskan and west Alaska Eskimos, acculturated

Owen, Roger C., James J. F. Deetz and Anthony Dwight Fisher
    9-The North American Indian, a sourcebook

*Owl, Frell M.
    30-Who and what is an American Indian?

Paget, Amelia M.
    23-People of the plains

Palmer, C. A. G.
    57-Unilateral abrogation of Indian, Eskimo treaty rights

Parabirsing, B. J.
    231-Situation of the Indian communities in Surinam

Parayko, Orest
    212-Survey of non-white alcoholic patients

Park, W. Z.
    44-Shamanism in western North America

*Parker, Arthur C.
    212-Social elements of the Indian problem

Parker, Seymour
    44-Motives in Eskimo and Ojibwa mythology
    23-Kwakiutl Indians, 'amiable' and 'atrocious'

Parkhill, Forbes
    142-Last of the Indian wars

Parman, Donald L.
    175-J. C. Morgan, Navajo apostle of assimilation

Parmee, Edward A.
    196-Modern Apache community, government education programs
    196-Social factors affecting education, San Carlos Apaches

Parson, Elsie Clews
    9-American Indian life
    47-Sacred clowns of the Pueblo and Mayo-Yanqui Indians
    39-Waiyautitsa of Zuni, New Mexico

Parsons, George F.
    106-Arctic suburb, a look at the north's newcomers
    175-Retreatists, innovators in an Indian community

Platiel, Rudy (reporter)
    133-All is quiet on occupied Stanley Island
    218-Prison better than reserve
    132-Breaking the chain
    107-Will white backlash against Indian spread from
        Yellowknife?
    107-Has Ottawa imposed reverse discrimination in N.W.T.?
    213-Alchohol problem among Indians distorted
    213-Jury urges 5 steps to improve health care, northern
        Ontario
    9-1970 in retrospect, Indian-Eskimo Association of Canada

Podolinsky, Alika
    107-Bitter plight of Labrador's Indians

Pohorecky, Zenon
    10-Saskatchewan Indian heritage

Poole, D. G.
    10-Discussion of Indian objectives
    107-Integration

Poole, Ted
    133-Conversations with North American Indians
    33-A modern legend

Porter, C. Fayne
    142-Battle of the 1,000 slain

Porter, Kenneth W.
    133-Negroes and the Seminole War, 1835-1842

Posluns, Michael
    133-Conflict at Akwesasne

Pothier, Roger
    149-Report, Seminar on Indian community government
    175-Community complexity and Indian isolation

Powell, John Wesley
    10-English policy toward the Indians
    10-French policy toward the Indians

Presant, Joan Elizabeth
    88-Indian Affairs Branch of Canada, aspect of acculturation

Pressly, Thomas J.
    48-Freedom of religion for the American Indian

Price, A. Grenfell
    231-White settlers, native people, U.S., Canada, Australia

Price, John A.
    182-Migration and adaptation of Indians to Los Angeles
    124-U.S. and Canadian Indian periodicals
    222-Resources for the study of Indians, Metis and Inuit

Price, Monroe, E.
    218-Lawyers on the reservation

Pritchett, John P.
    24-Historical aspects of the Canadian Metis

Provinse, John et. al.
    175-The American Indian in transition

Prufer, O. H.
    45-The Hopewill cult

Purdie, James (reporter)
    40-Rhythms and contours of prairie hills flow through designs
        of Douglas Cardinal

Quig, James (reporter)
    133-Trouble in the land where the partridge drums

Quimby, George I.
    24-A year with a Chippewa family, 1763-64
    24-Indian life, upper Great Lakes, 11,000 BC to 1800 AD

Raby, Stewart
    57-Indian Treaty # 5, The Pas Agency, Saskatchewan, N.W.T.
    232-Comparative geography, native people, europeans and land
    57-Indian land surrenders in southern Saskatchewan

Rachlin, Carol K.
    24-Tight Shoe Night, Oklahoma Indians today

Radin, Paul
    39-Thunder-Cloud, a Winnebago Shaman relates and prays
    10-Story of the American Indian
    24-Culture element distributions: Plateau
    232-Indians of South America
    10-Road of life, death, ritual drama of the American Indian

Radojic, D. and G. Anders eds.
    161-Great Slave lake, South shore: an economic study

Rancier, G. J.
    197-Curriculum programs for pupils of Indian ancestry

Randle, M. C.
    77-New (Canadian) Indian Act
    197-Educational problems of Canadian Indians

Rapoport, Robert N.
    45-Changing Navaho religious values

Rasky, Frank (reporter)
    182-Trapped in the ghetto, (Winnipeg)

Ray, Charles K.
    197-Program of education for Alaskan natives
    197-Alaskan native secondary school dropouts

Read, Margaret
    149-Tribal areas in India and community development program

Reading, R. S.
    10-Indian civilizations

Reaman, G. Elmore
    24-Trail of the Iroquois Indians

*Redbird, Duke
    34-Living and learning the Indian way

Reed, T. B. and Elsie Clews Parsons
    39-Cries-For-Salmon, A Ten'a woman

Reeves, Christopher (reporter)
    232-Aboriginies won't waltz for Aussies

Regan, Timothy F. and Jules Pagano
    197-Place of Indian culture in adult education

Regeher, Theodore D.
    10-Land ownership in Upper Canada 1783-1796

Reguly, Robert (reporter)
    133-Angry Indians threaten to fight like U.S. Negro

Reiblich, G. Kenneth
    66-Indian rights under the Civil Rights Act of 1968

Reid, D. C. S.
    218-Norm-setting and norm-violating behavior in the Indian

Reifel, Benjamine
    175-To die or to become? Cultural factors in adjustment

Renaud, André
    10-Les Canadiens de descenance Indienne
    197-Psychometric study, Indian residential school students
    197-Indian education today
    10-Twentieth century Indian at home, on the reserve
    149-Study, fostering native community development
    10-The Indian Canadians
    10-From oldest to newest, our Indian citizen
    10-Indians of Canada as an ethnic minority
    10-Indian and Metis, possible development as ethnic groups
    197-Curriculum programs for pupils of Indian ancestry
    197-In-service and pre-service training of teachers
    197-Education from within, experiment in curriculum
        development
    197-National conference, Indian and northern education
    10-Possible development, ethnic groups, Indians and Metis

Ressler, T. W.
    36-Treasury of American Indian tales

Reynolds, E. E. ed.
    34-A book of Grey Owl

Ricciardelli, Alex Frank
    149-Factionalism at Oneida, an Iroquois Indian community
    175-Adoption of white agriculture by the Oneida Indians

Richards, C. A.
    175-Role of Iroquois women, study of the Onondaga Reservation

Richardson, Boyce (reporter)
    107-Indians, non-Indians live in two separate worlds
    11-Indian lives could make good novels
    10-The emergent Indian
    107-White structure unhappy, Native power becoming fact,
    133-Struggle for equality
    175-James Bay, the plan to drown the north woods
    133-Angry Crees burn hundreds of James Bay ecology reports
    133-Metis showing leadership in fight for Native rights
    133-Natives start to fight back, oppose development schemes
    161-Canadian racism in full flower (James Bay)

Richardson, Robert Alan
    175-Acculturation among the Seven Island Montagnais

Richmond, Robin
    133-Rediscovery of the redman

Ridington, Robin
    45-Medicine fight, political process, the Beaver Indians
    45-Anthropology of experience
    47-Beaver dreaming and singing

Ridley, Frank
    57-Ontario Iroquion controversay

Ritzenthaler, Robert and Mary Sellers
    183-Indians in an urban setting

Rivers, W. H. R.
    11-Social organization

Robertson, Heather (reporter)
    57-One hundred years after the treaties, conquered celebrate?
    133-Reservations are for Indians
    213-One the road to nowhere

Robertson, R. W. W.
    142-Execution of Thomas Scott

Roe, Frank Gilbert
    161-Hudson's Bay Company and the Indians
    176-North American buffalo
    176-Indian and the horse

Rogers, Edward S.
    24-Individual in Mistassini society from birth to death
    161-Hunting group territory complex among Misstassini
    34-Notes on lodge plans in the Lake Indicator area of Quebec
    176-Changing settlement patterns of the Cree-Ojibwa
    107-Thatown
    34-Ojibwa culture, the traditional culture history
    24-Indians of the north Pacific coast
    24-Algonkians of the eastern woodlands
    24-Indians of the plains
    24-Indians of the subarctic
    150-Indian and Euro-Canadian society
    150-Leadership among the Indians of eastern subarctic
    161-Programme for Ontario Indians

Roger, Maysie
    150-Radio address on the Indian and Metis conference

Rogin,Michael
    11-And then there were none (book reviews)

Roheim, Geza
    34-Culture hero and trickster in North American mythology

Rohner, P. Ronald and C. Evelyn Rohner
    24-The Kwakiutl, Indians of British Columbia

Rohrl, Vivian J.
    45-Nutritional factor in Windigo psychosis

Rosenthal, Elizabeth Clark
    150-Culture and the American Indian community

Rosenthal, Eric
    176-Acculturation without assimilation

Rosenthal, Jack (reporter)
    30-1970-Census finds Indians no longer vanishing American

Rosenthal, Robert and Lenore F. Jacobson
    197-Teacher expectations for the disadvantaged

Ross, Timothy (reporter)
    232-South America's Indians in peril

Rosset, H. M.
    88-Governmental policy with respect to Canadian Indians

Rousseau, Jacques
    11-Les premiere canadiens
    143-Le derneir des peaux-rouges

Rowley, Graham W.
    11-What are Eskimos?
    176-Canadian Eskimo today

Roy. Prodipto
    183-Assimilation of the Spokane Indians
    183-Measurement of assimilation of the Spokane Indians

Royce, Charles ed.
    66-Indian land cessions in the United States

Rubin, Abraham
    57-Brief, Joint Committee on the Constitution

Ruddell, Rosemary
    24-The Kwakiutl

Ruddy, Jon (reporter)
    40-Willie Dunn, song writer trouble maker his own man
    133-This is Harold Cardinal

Rudnicki, Walter
    213-Northern welfare 62, a symposium
    213-Indians and poverty

Russell, Frances (reporter)
    133-Reason wears a steel will
    88-10 Indian officials quit: legislation in uproar

Sagi, Douglas
    198-Should school children leave reserve?

Sahlins, D. Marshall
    11-Tribesmen

*St.-Onge-Andre, Anne-Marie
    134-Where will they move us to next?

St.-Pierre, Paul
    198-Apartheid and the Indian

Salisbury, Lee H.
    198-College orientation program for Alaskan natives
    198-Conceptual approach, speech problems, Alaskan natives

Salisbury, Richard F.
    88-Letter, re: government policy and the Hawthorn report

Sampat-Meta, Ramdeo
    58-The Jay Treaty

Sanders, Douglas Esmond
    58-Native rights in Canada
    58-New Indian policy and Native claims
    58-Native rights
    58-Indian law center proposal
    218-Legal services program Indian communities, Canada
    58-Native hunting and fishing rights
    58-Group rights-the constitutional position, Canadian Indian
    58-Foundations of Indian law after 1867
    77-The Bill of Rights and Indian status
    77-The implications of the Lavell case
    58-Annotated bibliography of Indian case law 1867-1972

Sanderson, James F.
    36-Indian tales of the Canadian prairies

Sapir, Edward
   150-Social organization of the Nass River Indian
   39-Sayach'apies, a Nootka trader

Sasaki, Thomas and Harry W. Basehart
   162-Sources of income, Many farms, Rough Rock, and Jicarilla

Sauer, C. O.
   11-America before the days of the white man

Saulnier, Joseph Maurice
   34-Teamwork at Red Earth

Saum, O. Lewis
   176-The fur trader and the Indian

Sauve, Clayton
   162-Theorectical considerations, socio-economic development

Savard, Remi
   45-Différenciation des activitée sexuelles et alimentaires
   36-L'Hôte maladroit, essai d'analyse d'un conte montagnais
   107-Et les autres Quebecois

Savoie, Donat
   48-Les Amérindiens selon Emile Petitot, les esquimaux Tchiglit
   48-Les Amérindiens selon Emile Petitot, les Indiens Loucheux
   107-Discrimination at The Pas and means to cope with it
   222-Bibliographie, village population, Esquimaude du
      Nouveau-Quebec

Sayres, William C.
   40-Sammy Louis, the life of a young Micmac

Schalm, Philip
   198-Administrators, perceptions, integration of Indian
      children, Saskatchewan

Schlesier, Karl H.
   133-An essay on cultural resistance

Schmeiser, Douglas A.
   218-Indians, Eskimos and the law
   107-Civil liberties in Canada

Schmidt, John T.
   133-Lo, the poor, irresponsible, lazy Indian

Schmitt, N. et. al.
   213-Accidental deaths among west coast Indians
   213-Accidental deaths among British Columbia Indians

Schrader, Alvin
    78-Background of the Indian Act of 1877

Schultz, James Willard
    39-My life as an Indian

Schusky, Ernest L.
    150-Politics and planning in a Dakota Indian community
    183-Contemporary migration, culture change, two reservatioɪ
    134-The right to be Indian

Schwartz, H.T.
    36-Windigo and other tales of the Ojibways

Scott, Duncan Campbell
    88-Administration of Indian affairs in Canada

Scott, John (reporter)
    134-Peaceful invasion, Indians land at second site (Loon
        Island)

Scott, Rev. William
    58-Report, Oka Indians
    58-Letter to editor, the Oka Indian question

*Scow, Alfred
    218-Indians and the law

Secoy, Frank Raymond
    176-Changing military patterns on the great plains

Seeman, Berthold
    232-Aborigines of the Isthmus of Panama

Serl, Vernon C.
    150-Provincial policies and programs, northern Saskatchewan

Seton, Ernest Thompson and Julia M. Seton
    45-The gospel of the redman, an Indian Bible

Shackleton, Doris
    183-The Indian as newcomer
    88-Editorial

Shames, Deborah ed.
    97-Freedom with reservation: the Menominee struggle

Shankel, George Edgar
    89-Development of Indian policy in British Columbia

Shannon, Lyle and Patricia Morgan
    183-Prediction of economic absorbtion, Mexican, Indian,
        Negroes

Sharpe, Fred (reporter)
    11-Our Canadian Indian, who cares?

Sheffe, Norman ed.
    11-Canada's Indians, issues for the seventies

Shepardson, Mary
    176-Change and persistence in an isolated Navajo community
    218-Problems of the Navajo tribal courts in transition

Shephard, Douglas (reporter)
    89-Winds of change rise at Indian Affairs

Shephard, Gloria
    213-Can't separate psychology from social, political realities

Shepherd, Harvey L.
    11-The new doctors of the Indian frontier
    183-Indians in the city, will help be too little too late?

Sherman, Paschal
    97-Indian policy of the United States

Shields, Roy
    143-He set the west aflame, Gabriel Dumont

Shimpo, Mitsuru
    34-Social structure and value system of fringe Saultaux
    176-Socio-cultural disintegration among the fringe Saultaux
    198-Social process, residential school as a total institution

Shipley, Nan
    58-Twilight of the treaties

Showalter, Don
    150-Report, recreation programs at Round Lake

Shulsinger, Stephanie Cooper
    11-Great Indian speeches

Shumiatcher, Morris C.
    24-The plains Indians
    11-Welfare, hidden backlash

Siegel, Bernard J.
    176-Acculturation
    176-Recent developments, studies, social, cultural change
    176-Recent developments, studies, social, cultural change

Silver, A.I.
    11-French Canada and the prairie frontier

Silverman, J.
    45-Shamans and acute schizophrenia

Silverman, Peter G. and Karl E. Francis
    11-Dealing with the government of Canada, political action

Sim, R. Alexander
    11-Radio forum project for the Canadian north
    185-Study of Friendship Centres
    150-Foundation for Indian and Metis people in western Canada
    198-Indian schools for Indian children
    198-Education of Indians in Ontario
    150-Community development training

Simmons, Ellen (reporter)
    108-It's a white man's Canada
    108-Indians problem in microcosm: the lessons of Kenora

Simpson, D. W., and D.K.F. Wattie
    198-Impact of the education program in Eskimo communities

Sinclair, J. Grant
    78-Queen v Drybones, Supreme Court and the Bill of Rights

Sinclair, R.V.
    89-Canadian Indians

Sindell, Peter Samuel
    176-Continuity and change in Micmac values

*Sioui, Eleonore
    198-The right to exist

*Sioui, Georges
    134-Food for thought for whites and other strangers

*Sioui, Jules
    134-War... and peace in Canada

*Sister of Crashing Thunder
    39-Mountain Wolf Women: autobiography, a Winnebago Indian

Siverts, Henning
    232-Tribal survival in the Alto Maranon

Skinner, Alanson
    45-Little-wolf joins the medicine lodge

Slager, William R. and Betty M. Madsen
    198-English for American Indians

Slight, Benjamin
    11-Indian researches of facts, North American Indians

Sloan, Marilyn
    66-The Indian Bill of Rights

Slobodin, Richard
    150-Band organization of the Peel River Kutchin
    150-Metis of the Mackenzie District
    45-Kutchin Indian concept of reincarnation
    213-Indians of Canada today, questions on identity

Slotin, J.S.
    45-The peyote religion

Sluman, Norma
    108-Survey of Canadian history textbooks
    39-Poundmaker

*Smallboy, Robert
    134-Decision to leave Hobbema

Smith, Derek G.
    162-Mackenzie Delta
    198-Occupational aspirations of Mackenzie Delta students
    176-Implications of pluralism for social change programs

Smith, Gordon
    162-Territorial sovereignty in the Canadian north

Smith, June E.
    176-Anomie, acculturation, a case study among the Ojibwa

Smith, Maurice G.
    114-Political organization of the plains Indians

Smith, Michael
    97-Tribal sovereignty and the 1968 Indian Bill of Rights

Smith, Robert J.
    176-Culture change and the small community

*Smitheram, Henry (Butch) Arthur
    176-Culture conflict-general and specific
    24-Native Indians of British Columbia
    121-Organization and future of the B.C. Non-Status Association
    151-Recommendations for self-help programs
    114-Modern Indian organizations and their ideology

Smythe, Marion and *Morris Isaac
    11-Indian summer

Snider, James G.
    198-Intelligence test performance, acculturated Indian
        children
    199-Achievement test performance, acculturated Indian children

Snow, Alpheus Henry
    58-Question of aborigines in the law and practice of nations

Snyderman, George S.
    58-Concepts of land ownership among the Iroquois

Solomon, Arthur
    199-Brief, provincial committee aims and objectives of
        education

*Soonias, Rodney
    199-Federation of Saskatchewan Indians educational task force

Sophia, Elmer
    108-Human rights and the law

Sorokin, Alan L.
    183-Aspects of American Indian migration

Soveran, Mrs. Marilylle
    199-From Cree to English

Sparks, Joseph P.
    177-Indian stronghold and the spread of urban America

Spaulding, Philip
    151-Social integration of a northern community

Speck, Frank Gouldsmith
    177-Cultural problems in northeastern North America
    25-Savage hunters of the Labrador Peninsula, Naskapi
    24-In Montagnais Country
    47-Midwinter rites of the Cayuga Longhouse
    24-Beothuk and Micmac

*Spence, Ahab
    213, 151-Challenges to today's Indian women
    199-Is the contemporary educational programs failing native
        people?

Spence, Ian
    177-Study in facilitating the adjustment to rapid social
    change

Spence, Lewis
    36-Myths and legends of the North American Indian

Spencer, B. and F. Gillen
    232-Native tribes of central Australia

Spicer, Edward Holland, ed.
    177-Perspectives in American Indian culture change

Spier, Leslie
    47-Havasupai days
    45-Ghost Dance of 1870 among the Klamath of Oregon
    232-Population of ancient America
    232-Ancient civilizations of Mexico and Central America
    45-Prophet dance of the northwest, sources

Spinden, Herbert J.
    37-Power animals in American Indian art

Steinbring, Jack
    151-Recent studies among the northern Ojibwa
    34-Ojibwa culture

Steiner, Stan
    134-The new Indians

*Steinhauer, Eugene
    151-Alberta Native Communications Society, role, structure

Stephen, A.M.
    46-When John the Jeweler was sick

Stern, Theodore
    162-Livelihood, tribal government, Klamath Reservation

Stevens, James and Carl Ray
    36-Sacred legends of the Sandy Lake Cree

Stevenson, A.
    223-Northern bibliography

Stevenson, David S.
    162-Problems of Eskimo relocation for industrial employment
    183-Proposals for an Eskimo relocation project

Stewart, James (reporter)
    162-Power project tightens grip on James Bay

Steward, Julien H.
    47-Ceremonial buffons of the American Indians
    12-Limitation of applied anthropology, case of Indian New Deal

Stewart, Omer
    218-Questions regarding American Indian criminality

Stewart, W.D. and Doug Schweitzer
    151-Definition and evaluation of values and goals

Still, Larry (reporter)
    177-Collision of cultures, Eskimo v mechanization

Stipe, Claude E.
    151-Eastern Dakota clans

Stirling, M.W. et. al.
    12-Indians of the Americas

Stockand, Dave (reporter)
    108-Indians tell of Fred's death (Fred Quilt)
    108-Indians just lumped in with coal says Gloria Gabert

Stone, Dr. E.L.
    213-Problem of health among the Indians of Canada

Stotesbury, Rev. Earl F.
    213-Placement program, Indian children, Good Samaritan Plan
    214-Purpose and outline of Good Samaritan Plan
    214-Good Samaritan Plan, United Church of Canada

Tarasoff, Koozma John
162-Broadview rural development area
162-Problems and prospects, development, northern Saskatchewan
183-Experience, geographic, socialization, Canadian prairies
162-Trends, development of Canadian Indian handicrafts
151-Pine Creek, Camperville and Duck Bay area, Manitoba
183-Guidelines, conceptualization, transition centres
162-Garment plant, Fisher River and Peguis communities
163-Evaluation of the opportunity corps program

Tatz, Colin
232-Aborigines, law and political development

Tax, Sol
12-Heritage of conquest
177-Acculturation in the Americas
30-Distribution of descendants, aboriginal population
134-The freedom to make mistakes
12-Importance of preserving Indian culture

Taylor, Benjamine J.
163-Indian manpower resources, five southwestern reservations

Taylor, Christopher James
25-Metis, non-status Indian history of Prairies and B.C.

Taylor, Herbert C., Jr.
151-Parameters of a northern dilemma

Taylor, J. Garth
25-The Canadian Eskimo

Taylor, James
225-Bibliography, resource frontier communities

Taylor, Walter
12-Relevance of the Indian heritage to the survival of man
163-The defense of James Bay

Tebbel, John
143-Compact history of the Indian wars

Tennelly, Rev. J.B.
48-Catholic Indian missions in the United States

Terrell, John Upton
12-American Indian almanac

*Tetso, John
40-Trapping is my life

Thatcher, W. Ross
108-Address

Thévenin, R. and P. Coze
143-Moeurs et histoire des Peaux-Rouges

Thomas, Joseph Doan
25-Indians of the southwest
223-Audiovisual records

Underhill, Ruth Murray
    12-Basic cultures of the Indians of the United States
    47-Ceremonial patterns in greater southwest
    12-History of the Indians in the United States
    25-The Navajos
    46-Religion among American Indians
    42-Red man's religion, beliefs and practices north of Mexico

Unseem, John, J.D. Donogue and Ruth Hill Unseem
    135-Men in the middle of the third culture

Unseem, Ruth Hill and Ethel Nurge
    223-Bibliography

Uppal, Krishan Dev
    152-Community development institute for assistants
    152-Training in community and staff development

Usher, Jean
    177-The evangelical approach to the Tsimshian

Usher, Peter J.
    177-Canadian western arctic, a century of change
    163-The Banklanders, Volume 1
    177-Fur trade posts of the Northwest Territories, 1870-1970
    163-Banks Island
    163-The Banklanders, Volume 2
    163-The Banklanders, Volume 3

Valentine, Victor Fortune
    25-Metis of northern Saskatchewan
    26-Some problems of the Metis of northern Saskatchewan
    26-The forgotten people
    177-Situation of Metis of northern Saskatchewan
    26-Eskimos of the Canadian arctic

Vallee, Brian (reporter)
    89-Native people, angry, frustrated over policies

Vallee, Frank G.
    135-Unrest at Brantford
    178-Kabloona and Eskimo in the central Keewatin
    152-Differentiation among the Eskimo
    214-Eskimo theories of mental illness
    223-Selected annotated bibliography
    12-Indians and Eskimos, studies relevant to the Royal
       Commission

Vallery, H.J.
    199-History of Indian education in Canada

Vance, John
    97-Indian claims, the U.S. experience

Vanderburgh, Mrs.
    108-Canadian Indian in Ontario's school texts

Vandersteen, Roger
    36-Woodland Cree traditions and legends

Van Dusen, Conrad
   37-Labors, losses, sufferings, oppression, an Indian chief

Van Every, Dale
   135-Lost birthright of the American Indian

Van Rijn, Nick (reporter)
   109-Brandon petition described as discriminatory

Van Steen, Marcus
   12-Canadian Indians or just Canadians?

Van Steensel, Maja
   13-The people of light and dark

Van Stone, James W.
   163-Economy of a frontier community
   26-The Snowdrift Chipewyan

Varese, Stefano
   232-Forest Indians in the present situation of Peru

Verdet, Paula
   183-Summary of research on Indians in St. Louis and Chicago

Verrill, A. Hyatt
   13-The real Americans

Vestal, Stanley
   13-New source of Indian history, 1850-1891

Villiers, Desme
   163-Central Mackenzie: an area economic survey
   26-Review of literature on Metis people
   183-Review of literature on migrating Indians
   163-Central Arctic: an area economic survey

Voegelin, Erminie W.
   26-Culture element distrubution: northeast California

Vogel, Bart
   66-Who is an Indian in federal Indian Law

Vogel, Virgil J.
   46-American Indian medicine

Voget, Fred
   163-Introductory comment
   178-Acculturation at Caughnawaga
   26-Kinship at Caughnawaga
   178-The American Indian in transition
   178-The American Indian in transition

Vogt, Evon Z.
   178-The acculturation of American Indians

Vyvyan, C.C.
   26-Arctic adventure

Warren, Roland and Ed Moe
    152-Dimensions of community analysis

Warren, W.W.
    26-History of the Ojibway Nation

*Warrior, Clyde
    135-Poverty, community and power

Washburn, Wilcomb E.
    13-Moral history of Indian-White relations
    97-Red man's land - white man's law

Waterman, T.T.
    135-All is trouble along tha Klamath

Waters, Frank
    46-Book of the Hopi

Watkins, Arthur V.
    66-Removal of restrictions over Indian property and person

Wattie, D.K.F.
    199-Education in the Canadian Arctic

*Waubageshig (Harvey McCue) see also Harvey McCue
    13-The only good Indian, essays by Canadian Indians

Wax, Murray L.
    200-Publications on American Indians and Indian education
    200-American Indian education as a cross-cultural transaction
    200-Cultural deprivation as an educational ideology
    200-Dropout of American Indians at the secondary level
    200-Indian education for what?

Wax, Rosalie H.
    206-History, analysis, workshops on American Indian Affairs
    109-American Indians and white people
    200-The warrior dropouts

Weatherby, H.
    36-Tales the totem tell

Weaver, Sally Mae
    78-Archival research regarding Indian women's status
    135-Study of non-conservative Iroquois Six Nations Reserve
    223-Anthropology 235, selected references
    223-Annotated bibliography

Weaver, Thomas
    178-Social, economic change in Pima-Maricopa history

Webster, Paul (reporter)
    232-Controversy, Australia, explosive issue for aborigines

Wehmann, Howard H. ed.
    223-Records pertaining to Indians

Weitz, Jacqueline
    200-Culture change in two native linguistic families

Weltfish, Gene
    26-The lost universe
    37-Study of American Indian crafts

Wenner, Lambert N.
    200-American Indian and formal education

Wescott, A.E.
    200-Curricula for Indian schools

West, Bruce (reporter)
    109-Indian issue

West, Lloyd W.
    200-Assessing intellectual ability, Metis and Indian children

Western, Maurice (reporter)
    109-Bad way to win Indians confidence
    78-Recognition of rights denied

Westgate, Rev. T.B.R.
    48-History of Protestant missions to Indians in Canada

Whelan, Mary E.
    200-Reading achievement scores of Indian children

Whitaker, Jody
    26-Cowichan Indian tribe of Vancouver Island

White, Hilary J.
    223-Bibliography, resource frontier communities
    152-Study of social adaptation to northern isolation

White, James
    59-Boundary disputes and treaties

White, Jay V.
    97-Taxing those they found here

White, Lynn Carlton
    178-Assimilation of the Spokane Indians

White, Robert
    178-Assimilation of the Dakota Indians

Wood, Kerry
  46-The Medicine man

Woods, Doris
  59-Indian Claims Commission

Woods, Richard G. and Arthur M. Harkins
  164-Indian employment in Minneapolis

Woodsworth, J.F.
  201-Problems of Indian education in Canada

Woolworth, Alan R.
  143-Intrigue in the Red River country in 1864

Worsley, Peter M.
  109-Democracy from on top, problem of the white man
  178-Economic and social survey of north Saskatchewan
  232-Study of 'cargo' cults in Melanesia

Worth, Sol and John Adair
  152-Navajo filmakers

Wray, Robert
  109-Yellowknife

Wrinch, Leonard A.
  89-Land policy, Colony of Vancouver Island, 1849-1866

*Wuttunee, William Ivan Clark
  13-Renaissance of the Indians
  136-Integration the best solution
  89-Conflicts between Indian values, the new Indian policy
  40-Under attack
  13-Ruffled feathers, Indians in Canadian society

Wutzke, Richard and David Tanaka
  201-Education and the native students

Wyant, William K. Jr.
  164-Sharing the wealth of Alaska, the oil rush

Wylie, Elizabeth A.
  27-Malecite Indians of New Brunswick

Yawney, Carole Diane
  201-Indian youth, education for what?
  178-Indian response to change

*Yellowbird, Lydia
  34-You are an Indian

*York, Mrs. Cecilia
  152-Proud to be Indian

Young, John (reporter)
  201-How schools teach Indians to become failures

Young, Scott
    136-New deal smoke signals read clearly

Zakoji, Hiroto
    66-Termination and the Klamath Indian education program

Zakoji, Miles
    13-Indian research study

Zeleny, Carolyn
    89-Government treatment of the Indian problem in Canada

Zentner, Henry
    201-Blackfoot adolescents and their non-Indian peers
    214-Factors social pathology of the North American Indian
    201-Parental behavior, student attitudes, further training
    201-Value congruence among Indian and non-Indian students
    201-Cultural assimilation between Indians and non-Indians
    201-Reference group behavior among high school students
    34-Pre-machine ethic of Athabascan-speaking Indians
    34-Reservation social structure and anomie

Zimmerman, William Jr.
    97-Role of the Bureau of Indian Affairs since 1933

Zionty, Alvin J.
    136-New consciousness: the Indian uprising

N.B. All Miscellaneous Reports <u>are</u> <u>omitted</u> from this Index

A

Abenaki Indians, p. 224

Aborigines
  of Australia, 229-234
  of Brazil, 29,228-230,233,234
  of Bolivia, 231
  of Central America, 230
  of Columbia, 228,233
  of Denmark, 231
  of Guiana, 229
  of Hawaii, 130,140
  of Melanesia, 232
  of Mexico, 229,230-233
  of New Zealand, 231,233
  of Panama, 232
  of Paraguay, 231
  of Peru, 231 ,232
  of the Phillipines, 230
  of South America, 228-230,232
  of Surinam, 231
  of U.S.S.R., 228,230
  of Venezuela, 228,230
  see also Indians, Eskimos

Aborigines Committee, 13

Aborigines Protection Society, 59

aboriginal rights, 52-63,167,231
  see also treaty rights

Ache Indians (Paraguay), 231

acculturation, 45,47,103,127,135,
  168-171,173-179,201,211

Adams, Howard, 41,125,129

adoption, 216

Afton Band, 62

agriculture, 99,157,160,162,168,
  175,220

Aguaruna Indians, 232

Akaitcho Hall; Yellowknife, 203

Akwesasne Indian Reserve
  see St. Regis Indian Reserve

Alberta Indian Education Centre,
  206,207

Alberta Native Communiçation
  Society, 151,155

Alcatraz, 128,138

alcohol, 215
  alcoholism, 212
  as a problem, 209,210,213
  role of, 179,211

Algonquin Indians, 16,19,20,24,
  26,27,144
  plains, 43
  forest, 43

Allied Indian Tribes of British
  Columbia, 60

American Indian Movement, 140

Annette Island Reservation,
  Alaska, 98

Apache Indians, 19,38,158
  and education, 196,203
  Cibecue, 16
  Kiowa, 17
  Slender Maiden, 38

apartheid, 198

A.R.D.A. (Agriculture and Rural
  Development Act), 154,157

art and crafts, 36,37,159,162,
  165,166,224
  eskimo, 224

assimilation, 34,94,127,168,174-
  176,178,181,183,201

Assiniboine Indians, 21

associations, see organizations

Association of Iroquois and
  Allied Indians, 93

Athabaskan Indians, 19,34,148,
  175,224

B

Baffin Island, N.W.T., 156,159

band
    membership, 76
    organization, 91,92,150

Banks Island, N.W.T., 163

Bannock Indian War, see war

Barbados, Declaration of, 228

Beaverhouse Project, Ontario, 147

Beaver Indians, 45,47

Beaver Metis Colony, Alberta, 146

Belcher's Proclamation, 71

Belcourt, Tony, 41

Bella Coola Indians, 20,28

Belly River, 142

Beothuks Indians, Newfoundland,
    20,21,24

Betz, Dorothy, 106

bibliographies, 220-227
    black series, 227
    education, 189,200,202
    legal cases, 58
    red series, 227
    treaties, 54
    urbanization, 181

Big Trout Lake, Ontario, 159

Bill of Rights, Canadian, see
    Canadian Bill of Rights

Bills, (House of Commons)
    #2, 76
    #30, 76
    #79, 79
    II-C-120, 75
    C-7, 75
    C-30, 166
    C-77, 76
    C-84, 76
    C-108, 76

C-123, 75
C-124, 76
C-130, 60,75

biographies, 38-39

bison, see buffalo

Black Elk, 44

Blackfoot Indians, 18,20,22,27,38,
    43,44,52,170,173,174,201
    Smoking Star, 46
    Blackfoot Reservation, 207

Blood Indian Reserve, Alberta, 207

Blue Quills School, Alberta, 138

boarding schools, see residential
    schools

book reviews, 4,94

Brandon, Manitoba,
    Petition on Indians, 109
    Conference, 110

Brandy Trade, 177

Brant, Chief Joseph, 38,56

Brantford, 129,135

British Columbia Association of
    Non-Status Indians, 121

British Columbia Indian Law
    Program, see Law

British Columbia Indian Reserve
    Mineral Resources Act, 74,75

British North America Act, 57,73

Broadview Rural Development,
    Saskatchewan, 162

buffalo, 5,176

Buffalo Narrows Project,
    Saskatchewan, 146

Buffalo Point Indian Reserve,
    Manitoba, 145

Courchene, Chief Dave, 2,40,41

Cournoyea, Nellie, 131,140

Cousins, Mary, 41

Cowichan Indians, 26

crafts   see art and crafts

Cramer, Thomas, 231

Cree Indians, 18,19,30,51,125,160,
    169,171,173,175,224,226
    and education, 200
    and integration, 169
    of James Bay, 105,133,158,171
    Montana Cree, 43
    Plains Cree, 22,44,52
    Rupert House Cree, 172
    of Sandy Lake, 36
    Swampy Cree, 51,174
    Waswanipi Cree, 173
    Woodland Cree, 36,52

Creek Indians, 18,23,25

Cries-for-Salmon, A Ten'a Woman,
    39

crime, 217-219

Crook, General, 142

Crow Indians, 22,23,38
    Takes-the-Pipe, 38

Crowfoot, Chief, 38

Cuiva Indians, Columbia, 228

culture, 1,8,12,16,32-34,150,214,
    222,
    cultural changes, 168-178,183,
    200

cultural-education centres see
    education

Cumberland House
    Area, Manitoba, 159
    Fur Project, 159

D

Dakota Indians, 21,22,174,178,183
    Teton Dakota, 170
    Yankton Dakota, 43

dance, 32,47
    eagle, 47
    ghost, 43-45
    prophet, 45
    sun, 44

death, 46
    rates   see mortality

Deleware Indians, 174
    of Moraviatown, Ontario, 17

Delisle, Chief Andrew T., 41,137

Dene Indians, 23,27

Department of Indian Affairs, 90,
    93,226

Department of Secretary of State,
    90,221

Dewdney, Edgar, 83

discrimination, 100-113
    see also prejudice

Dogrib Indians, 159,173

Dominion Lands Act, 73

Don Juan, 42

Dorion Report, 63

Doucette, Chief Noel, 41

dreams, 46-47

Dumont, Gabriel, 38,143

Dunn, Willie, 40

Dwamish Indians, 43

E

Earth-tongue, 38

economic development, 156-167

of Oregon, 16,45
of the Pacific Coast, 27,178,
224
of the plains, 18,21-24,26,27,
34,37,43,46,114,142,168,170,
173,181
of the prairies, 28,36,46,145,
178
of Prince Edward Island, 28
of Quebec, 28
Queen Charlotte Island, 27
of Regina, 131
of Saskatchewan, 21,44,103,109,
113,119,140,144,179,180,209
of South Dakota, 36,140
of the Southwest, 25
of Toronto, 158
of the U.S.A., 48,98,133,208,
223
of Wisconson, 19,33
of Winnipeg, 21
of the woodlands, 21
of the Yukon, 28

Indians of Quebec Association,
54,117

Indian Sport Olympic (INSPOL),
155

Indian - white relations, 2-5,7,
8,13,25,93,94,100,103,104,107,
110,111,124,126,139,147,171,
173,175,176,199,218,220-222,
231,232
see also Eskimo-white relations

Indian - white - black relations,
136,171,172,183   see also
Indian - black relations

industry, 161,162,164

Institute of American Indian
Arts, 207

integration, 7,102,104,106,107,
110,132,136,149,151,169,170,
182,183,190,222,233
and education, 188-191,194,
195,198,202
in Kenora, 108

Inuit Tapirisat of Canada, 116

Inuvik, N.W.T., 147,148,170

Ipiutak Indians, 21

Iroquois Indians, 13,16,18,19,22,
24-27,37,43,46,47,57,58,131,
135,152,215,224
crime, 218
cultural change, 128,178
Hanging-Flower, 38
of New York, 23
wars, 142
women, 175   see also Mohawk,
Oneida, Seneca Indian

Isaac, Morris, 41

J

James Bay, 18,105,133,156,158,
159,163,222
Hydro-electric Project, 62,
158,161,162,163,167,175
Treaty, 52

Jay Treaty, 51,58,61
and Cornwall Bridge Blockade,
125

Janvier Indian Reserve, Alberta,
83

Jennes, Diamond, 222

Johnson, Pauline, 33,39

justice, 7,100,106,217
administration of, N.W.T., 102,
106,110,219
administration of, Quebec, 73

K

Kainai Industries, Alberta, 161

Keeseekoose Indian Reserve,
Saskatchewan, 18

Kenora, Ontario, 104,108,110,111,
125,135

Key Indian Reserve, Saskatchewan,
18

Kikino Settlement, Alberta, 146

Kiowa Indians, 43

Kispiox Indians, 90

Kitwancool Indians, 18

Klamath Indians, 45

Klamuth Indian Reservation, 135,162
  162
  education program, 66

Koglgolak, 219

Kootenay Indians, 27

Ksan, 37

Kutchin Indians, 16,22,45,224
  Vunta-Kutchin, 168

Kutenai Indians, 19

Kwakiult Indians, 23,24
  education, 200

L

labour force, 31,179

Lac LaBiche, Alberta, 125,146

Lac La Martre, N.W.T., 156

Lake Winnipeg Channel,
  Manitoba, 164
land, 14,72,73,156
  allotment, 66,67,76
  claims, 53,56,58,60,62,63,68,
  75,90,97,212
  claims, Alaska, 64,65,67,94,
  99
  freeze, 167
  flooding, 64
  heirship, 66,67
  North of '60, 157
  in Nova Scotia, 75
  ownership, 10,58
  rights, 63,158,167
  sales, 57,76,81
  sessions, U.S.A., 66,96
  surrenders, 57
  tenure, 2,3,60,94
  tribal land, 66
  see aboriginal and treaty

rights, Indian Act, Natural
Resources Act

language, 29,228
  Cherokee, 129
  Cree, 188,199
  in education, 190
  english, 98
  Eskimo, 32
  Ojibway, 26
  sign language, 34

Laurentian Alliance of Metis and
  Non-Status Indians, 41

Lavell case, 76-78,81,82

law, 58,64-66,113,217-219
  British Columbia Indian Law
  Program, 219

League of Indians of Canada, 115

legal cases, 54-57,61,63-64,67,78,81,82

legal rights, 217,219

Legal Services Program, 218

legends, 35,36

Lennox Island Bank Workshop,
  Prince Edward Island, 166

Lesser Slave Lake, Alberta, 163

life expectancy, 211

liquor, see alcohol

Little Big Horn, South Dakota, 141

Little Wolf, 45

longhouse, 47

Loon Island, Ontario, 134
  see also Stanley Island

Lower Brule Indian Reservation,
  150

Lumbee Indians, North Carolina,
  128

M

MacDonald Franchise, 57

MacKenzie Delta, N.W.T., 157,162, 163,221
Task Force, 166

magic, 43,229

Major Crimes Act, 64

Malecite Indians, 27,160
Teaching Materials Project, 221

Manitoba Act, 73

Manitoba Indian Brotherhood, 62, 93,102,110,119

Manitoba Metis Federation, 111, 119,144

Manuel, Arthur, 139

Manuel, Chief George, 129,140,233

Maori, 171,174,233

maps, 15
of Manitoba, 31
treaty, 62,93

Marchand, Len, 41

Marie, Buffy Saint, 137

Mayo Yaaniqui Indian, 47

McEwen, Ernest Roy, 123

media, 148

medical attention, 67,216

medicare, 138

medicine, 33,45,46
medicine man, 39,42,46
see also Shaman

Meekitjik, Anne, 41

Memramcook Conference of North American Indian Young People, 204

Menomini Indians, 45,64,97,109, 177
and education, 199

mercury pollution, 216

Meskwaki Indians, 145,148

Metis, 10,20,25,26,29,32,40,86, 91,104,105,113,125,127,133,137, 143,146,151,153,184,210-212,221
of Alberta, 28,61,171,208
Betterment Act, 74,75
of British Columbia, 121
economic development, 165
education, 108,188,194,200,203
history, 24
housing, 211
land claims, 52,61-63,75
of Mackenzie District, 150
of Manitoba, 27,28,118,119,140
of Saskatchewan, 16,25,26,55, 108,119,144,170,177
uprising, 143,224
see also non-status Indians

Metis Association of Alberta, 41, 61,63,111,121

Metlakatia Indian Community, 98

Michael, Simone, 41

Micmac Indians, 24,26,50,51,71, 130,176
of Cape Breton, 177
of Restigouche, 17
Sammy Louis, 40

Midwiwin Indians, 43

migration, 29,30,182,183

migrant workers, Alberta, 111

Migratory Birds Convention Act,
61,62
    regulations, 64

minerals, 71,156,157,166
    see also natural resources

mines, 148,152,156

Mississauga Indians, 52,59,90

Misstassini Indians, 24,161

missions, 48
    see also church

Mohawk Indians, 19,28,133,140,224
    and high steel, 179,182
    land disputes see Stanley and
    Loon Islands
    of Tyendinaga, 25

Montagnais Indians
    Labrador-Montagnais, 17
    Montagnais-Naskapi, 224
    of Seven Island, 175

Monture, Dr. Gilbert, 41

Moosonee, Ontario, 101

Moore, Kermit, 41

Mopas School, 193

Morgan, J.C., 175

Morice, Adrien-Gabriel, 43

mortality
    infant, 211
    maternal, 214
    rates, 214

Mungo, 212

myths, 34,36,42
    Eskimo, 32,44
    Ojibway, 44

N

Native Alliance for Red Power
    (N.A.R.P.), 138

Narrows Area, Manitoba, 164

Naskapi Indians, 25, 224

Nass River Indians, 150

National Committee on Indian
    Rights and Treaties, 61,62

National Council on Indian
    Opportunity, 166

National Indian Brotherhood, 51,61
    62,88,89,115,116,123,155,204,
    205,209

National Indian Council, 115

National Indian Institute of
    Mexico, 233

National Indian Movement of
    Canada, 140

National Native Development
    Fund, 164

Native Aboriginals of the
    Americas Unity Conference, 137

Native Brotherhood Society,
    Saskatchewan, 118

Native Council of Canada, 93,111,
    116,117

Native North American Studies
    Institute, 205

natural resources, 76
    Act, 165
    in Alberta, 74
    development, 171
    in Manitoba, 74
    in Saskatchewan, 74
    Transfer Act, 75

Navajo Indians, 21,25,33,43,148,
    151,152,160,168,175,176,180,
    181
    and crime, 218
    and cultural change, 171
    and drinking, 210
    education, 189-191,199
    law, 218
    population, 29,30

and prejudice, 105
religion, 42,44
Rimrock-Navajo, 44

New Brunswick Association of
Non-Status Indians, 117

NewStart of Alberta, 125,138

Nez Perce, 135

Neilson, Jim, 41

non-status, 25,59,76,188,221
(see also Metis)

North American Indian Brotherhood, 115,121

North American Indian Traveling
College, 205

Northern Community Action
Program (Norcap), 153

Northwest Campaign of 1885, 142,
143

Northwest Rebellion, 141

nursing, 209

nutrition, 211,212,224

O

Office of Economic Opportunity
(O.E.O.). 165

Ohsweken, Ontario, 134

oil, 164,167

Ontario Institute of Studies in
Education, (O.I.S.E.) Projects,
134

Ojibway Indians, 20-22,26,34-36,
144,151,158,182,210,216,224
and acculturation, 172,176
history of, 26
of Kenora, 108
Ke-Zig-Ko-e-ne-ne, 39
of Lake Superior, 51
mythology, 44

social change, 170,176

Oka(see also Seminary of Montreal)
Band, 79
Indian Reserve, Quebec, 56, 58, 63.

Old Sun School, Alberta, 207

Omaha Indians, 193

Oneida Indians, 169,175

Onedia Indian Reservation,
Ontario, 149

Onondaga Indian Reservation, 175

Ontario Metis and Non-Status
Association, 118

Opportunities for Youth (O.F.Y.),
139

Ordeal of Running Standing, 170

organizations, 114-124
directories of, 123-124
of Eskimos, 117

Oronhyatehka, 38

P

Padlo, Ann, 41

Paleo Indians, 170

The Pas Indian Reserve, Manitoba,
57,107,152,191

Passamaquoddy Indians, 25,51

Paull, Andrew, 40

Pawnee Indians, 21

Peace River Block Act, 74

Peel River Kutchin, 150

Peguis Community, Manitoba, 162

Petawabano, Buckley, 41

peyote, 42,44,45

in Manitoba, 57
in New Brunswick, 72,75
in the Northwest Territories,
57
in Nova Scotia, 75
on-reserve vs off-reserve
residence, 178
in Saskatchewan, 160
schedules of, 30,31
in the U.S.A., 93,95,98

reserve trusts, 77

residential schools, 189,193,195,
197,198,201

resistance, 125-143

Resolute, N.W.T., 156

Restigouche, Quebec, 138

Riel, Louis, 100,134,136,141,142,
224
Rebellion, 143
see also Northwest Campaign
and Northwest Rebellion

Robinson Treaty, 51,60

Roots of Great Peace, 206

Roseau River Indian Reserve,
Manitoba, 145

Round Lake, Ontario, 150-154

Rough Rock, Arizona, 205

Royal Canadian Mounted Police,
1,86,102,111-113,136,137,139

Royal Commission, 12,91
history of, 7
on Indian Affairs for the
Province of B.C., 60

Royal Proclamation of 1763,
51-53

Ruperts House Indians, 147

Ruperts Land Act, 73

S

Saddle Lake, Alberta, 154

Salish Indians, 28,37
Coast Salish, 16,151
Gulf of Georgia Salish, 16

San Carlos Apache Cattle
Industry, 158

Sandy Bay, Saskatchewan, 159

Sandy Lake Indian Reserve,
Ontario, 37,167

sanitation, 210

Sapp, Allen, 41

Sarcee Indian Reserve, Alberta, 167

Sarnia Indian Reserve, (St. Clair),
Ontario, 190

Saskatchewan Indian and Metis
Department, 76

Sasquatch, 33

Saulteaux Indians, 51,210
Fringe Saulteaux, 34,176

Scott, Thomas, 142

seal hunt, 165

segration, 103,110

self-determination, 3,160,196

self-government, 95,152,154

self-help, 105,151

Seminary of Montreal, 56
see also Oka Reserve

Seminole Indians, 35,133

Seneca Indians, 46,55

Sequoyah, 38

Set O.K., 31

shaking tent rite, 43

Shaman, 39,44-46
  see also medicine man

Sioux Indians, 20,22,94,142
  and education, 145
  outbreak of 1890, 44
  Pine Ridge Sioux, 148
  reserves, 171
  Rosebud-Sioux, 98
  Rosebud-Sioux Indian Reserva-
    tion, 158
  war, 141
  Yankton-Sioux, 181,211

Six Nations
  Indian Reserve, 47,56,57,59,
    90,117,135,136,143
  Iroquois Confederacy, 53,54,141

Sitting Bull, 85

Slave Indians, 16

Slave trade, 141

Slender-Maiden, see Apache
  Indians

Smallboy, Chief Robert, 126,129

Smoking Star see Blackfoot
  Indians

social change, 168-178

Son of Old Man Hat, 38

South Indian Lake, Manitoba, 166

South Tuba, Arizona, 160

Spokane Indians, 178,183

sports, 155

Stanley Island, Ontario, 133, 138
  see also Loon Island

status
  Eskimo, 85
  legal, 55,57,58,77,81,85,97,
    130,178
  Metis, 77
  woman's, 76-78,209

St. Catherine's Milling Case, 53

St. Clair Indian Reserve see
  Sarnia Reserve

sterilization, 212

Stoney Indians, 29,43

St. Mary's Home and School
  Associations, 152

St. Paul Education Centre,
  Alberta, 207

St. Regis (Akwesasne) Indian
  Reserve, Ontario, Quebec and
  New York State, 28,55,64,129,
  170
  and Cornwall Bridge Blockade,
    59,61,125,133

sugar beet industry, 111, 213

Swaixwe Indians, 42

T

Takes-the-Pipe see Crow Indians

Talking Tree (Ts'igonde), 33

Tarahumara Indians, 228

tax, 62,64,97

Teamwork Enterprises of Alberta
  and Mackenzie, 165

Techumseh, 39,130,224

termination, 43,64,65,95,150

textbooks, 101,102,108
  and discrimination, 105,108,
  112

Thomas, William, 41

Thompson, Phil, 138

Thunder Cloud, see Winnibago
  Indians

Thunderwater Movement, 128

Winnebago Indians, 39
    Sister of Crashing Thunder, 39
    Thunder Cloud, 39

witchcraft, 45

women, 38,145,148,149,151,154,177,
    211,213
    Alberta Native Women's
    Conference, 154
    and cultural change, 169,177
    National Native Women's
    Conference, 155
    in the North, 208
    rights of, 76,80,81
    role of, 175,224
    Saskatchewan Indian Women, 154
    status of, 76-78,209

Wounded Knee, South Dakota, 140, 141

Wunnumen Lake Project, Ontario,
    147

Wuttunee, William Ivan Clark, 39

Y

Yaqui Indians, 42

Yellowknife, N.W.T., 109

youth, 117,121,126,144-146,148,
    151,153,178,188,190,204,206

Yukon Association of Non-Status
    Indians, 122

Yukon Native Brotherhood, 63,122

Yuma Indians, 19
    and social organization, 168,179
    179

Z

Zuni Indians, 39,168
    Waiyatitsa, 39